Software Testing Tools

Covering WinRunner, SilkTest, LoadRunner, JMeter, TestDirector and QTP with case studies

Dr. K.V.K.K. Prasad

Published by

dreamTech
PRESS

19-A, Ansari Road, Daryaganj,
New Delhi-110002

Revised Edition : 2005

Printed at : PrintWell Offset, Bhikaji Cama Place. New Delhi-66

Preface

In this era of Information Technology, software has become the lifeline of every human activity. It is not an exaggeration if we say that our lives will come to a standstill if all the computers in the world stop working! When software plays such a crucial role in our lives, it is very important that the software we use should be of very high quality and of high reliability. We don't like it if there is a software bug in the ATM machine from which we withdraw cash, or if there is a bug in one of the embedded systems of the aircraft in which we are traveling. Every software professional has to commit himself/herself to deliver quality software products. To deliver quality products, software testing is the most important phase in development. But then, testing the software is a very challenging and creative task.

Many software engineers have a wrong notion that software testing is a second-rate job; the first-rate job being development! These engineers tend to forget that testing is a part of development. The test engineers play the most important role in delivering high quality products. And to deliver high quality products, the test engineers need to be very systematic, eagle-eyed; and yes, they need to be perfectionists. They also need to use sophisticated tools that are available for testing so that they become very productive.

The aim of this book is to motivate you to take up software testing as a career, to introduce you to the concepts of software quality assurance and testing process, and to make you gain expertise in the most widely used software testing tools.

Who should read this Book

This book is addressed to the young engineering students/graduates who would like to take up software quality assurance and testing as their career. This book gives a comprehensive coverage of software quality assurance, testing process and the various automated test tools that are used widely in the software industry.

Even if you are a software developer, this book will help you in getting an insight into the software testing process so that you can develop high quality software.

Project managers involved in software quality assurance and testing will also be benefited by this book as it gives the details of the testing process and the testing tools under one cover.

As India has become a force to reckon with in the field of software, many organizations throughout the world are looking towards India for getting their software developed through outsourcing. Many organizations in the developed countries are now outsourcing software testing also. Many leading Indian software companies are putting up dedicated testing teams for their clients. In the future, there will be many lucrative opportunities for young engineers who would like to take up software quality assurance and software testing as their career option. This book will lay the foundation for such a career.

Irrespective of your educational background—whether it is engineering, science, commerce or arts—you can take up software quality assurance and testing as your career if you have the commitment to quality of work, attitude to achieve perfection, aptitude to learn the software testing process and expertise in using the testing tools. This book is addressed to these young prospective quality gurus of the Indian software industry.

Organization of the Book

This book has 10 chapters. The first three chapters cover the software quality assurance, software testing, and an overview of software testing tools. The subsequent seven chapters explain how to use the various testing tools. Please note that it is very easy to gain expertise in using the testing tools, however, a thorough understanding of the testing process is a must to become a good test engineer. The first three chapters lay the foundation for the testing process.

Chapter 1 gives an overview of software quality assurance. The importance of software engineering is discussed and the criteria for a successful project are defined. The characteristics of software quality are discussed in detail. The various software development life cycle models are also presented. ISO9000:2000 and CMMI quality management standards are explained.

Chapter 2 focuses on software testing process. The concepts of unit testing, module testing, integration testing and system testing are explained. The various types of testing to be carried out on the software products are presented. How to write a test plan and acceptance test procedure are discussed. As generation of test cases is the most important activity of test engineers, test case generation is discussed in detail with examples.

Chapter 3 gives an overview of software testing tools. The importance of automated testing tools is explained. The various categories of automated testing tools are described. The features of functional/regression testing tools, performance/load testing tools and testing management tools are listed. How to select a tool is also discussed.

Chapter 4 explains how to use Mercury Interactive's WinRunner for functional/regression testing. Using case studies, the various features of WinRunner are explained.

Chapter 5 explains the important features of Segue Software's SilkTest and how to use this tool for functional/regression testing.

Chapter 6 presents the details of IBM Rational SQA Robot. Through case studies, how to use this tool for functional/regression testing is discussed.

Chapter 7 explains the important features of Mercury Interactive's LoadRunner. The details of carrying out performance testing on web sites and database applications are presented through a case study.

Chapter 8 describes the features of Apache JMeter, an open source software for testing Java applications. How to use JMeter for performance testing of database and HTTP connectivity is described through case studies.

Chapter 9 describes the features and usage of Mercury Interactive's TestDirector. How to manage the testing process systematically using TestDirector is illustrated through a case study.

Chapter 10 gives a description of the various utilities available on Unix/Linux systems for source code testing and maintenance. How to measure the time taken to execute portions of the code and how to carry out code optimization are described with illustrative examples. Portability testing utilities and configuration management utilities are also described. The guidelines to be followed while writing C and Java programs are also presented.

Chapter 11 focuses on a sophisticated and powerful functional/regression testing tool, QTP (QuickTest Professional), used for testing application software packages, database applications, web sites, ERP/CRM packages and web services. Discover through case studies how synchronization point and different checkpoints are created; how a test script behaves for multiple data; how the number of links, images, load time, web tables etc. on a web site are tested and, many more.

Appendix A gives a list of acronyms and abbreviations.

Appendix B gives the glossary of terms used in software quality assurance and testing. If you have not done a formal course in software engineering in your college, this is the best place to start reading this book.

Appendix C gives a set of review questions to test your knowledge in software quality assurance, testing process and testing tools. In addition to objective questions, some frequently asked questions in job interviews are also listed. Please ensure that you know the answers to these questions before walking in to an interview boardroom. And, good luck!

Appendix D gives a list of references and Internet resources.

The CDROM that accompanies the book contains the executable files of sample applications that have been used in this book for illustrating the use of various testing tools. It also contains Apache JMeter software. How to install the sample applications in your system is explained in Appendix E. Before working on the case studies presented in Chapters 4 through 9, you need to install the sample applications on your computer.

Credits

The author acknowledges the contributions of Mr. A. Veerraju, Ms. K. Aparna, Ms. Supriya Majumdar, Mr. K. Chandrasekhar Varma, and Mr. Vipul Pawaskar in the preparation of the manuscript.

Contents

1 Software Quality Assurance: An Overview

In this chapter

- Appreciate the need for a systematic approach to software development
- Understand what is software engineering and its importance
- Define software quality and learn about the quality triangle
- Grasp the various phases of software development and the activities to be performed in each phase
- Know about the various software life cycle development models
- Learn about quality management standards

During the first two decades of computing, the software development was being carried out on ad hoc basis without any methodology. This led to a lot of difficulties in maintaining the software. To overcome these difficulties, software engineering emerged as a discipline. Software engineering focuses on systematic development of software. To ensure quality, quality assurance in every phase of development is required. In this chapter, we will discuss software engineering and quality assurance in detail.

1.1 The Software Crisis

During initial days of computing, software was largely developed by small groups of people. When this software was to be maintained by another set of people, it used to be a nightmarish experience. When large commercial projects were to be handled, it used to be an almost impossible task to keep the time and budget under control, projects used to get delayed and many projects were abandoned halfway.

Note that during these years, software development was carried out in assembly languages; and procedural languages such as FORTRAN, COBOL, BASIC and LISP. Programming was mainly an art—confined to a set of highly specialized persons who developed and maintained the software for years. There was no systematic procedure for the software development; everything was done on ad hoc basis. This ad hoc approach led to the 'software crisis'.

1.2 The Birth of Software Engineering

In the year 1968, a conference sponsored by the NATO Science Committee addressed the "software crisis" that was prevailing in those days. The outcome of the discussions in that conference was "software development is not an art, it has to fall in the realm of engineering". The term "software engineering" was introduced in this conference.

It is more than three decades since the birth of software engineering. During this period, lot of research went on in making the software development an engineering discipline. Software engineering defines a disciplined approach to software development.

1.3 What is Software Engineering?

In most of the software development organizations, there is no systematic methodology for the development. Software development is considered as coding, though coding forms a very small percentage of the total development effort. Before starting the coding, one has to systematically approach the problem. One has to understand the requirements (what the software is supposed to do), carry out the design, do the coding, carry out a rigorous testing and if the software is as per the requirements, release the software to the customer. Subsequently, if the customer wants some changes—refinements or enhancements—then the software has to be modified.

Software engineering can be defined as systematic development of software. IEEE Standards [IEEE 1990] define software engineering as "the application of a systematic, disciplined, quantitative approach to the development, operation and maintenance of software i.e., the application of engineering to software".

For developing a software product, the development process is divided into different stages. A convenient way of splitting the whole process is to divide the development into the following five stages:

- Specifications
- Design
- Implementation
- Testing
- Maintenance

In addition, to ensure that the people are effectively utilized, management processes are defined such as planning process, review process, monitoring process, etc. So, software engineering encompasses all activities of managing technology, money, people and time to deliver quality software products.

1.4 Why Software Engineering?

Every organization involved in software development is realizing that utmost importance is to be given to software engineering. Organizations are being assessed and graded based on the software engineering principles being implemented. If an organization has to survive and grow in the competitive environment, software engineering plays the key role. Why? Here are the reasons:

■ To deliver quality product

To ensure that the software meets all the expectations of the customer is the most important goal for any organization, because a satisfied customer can enhance the image of the organization and bring in more growth. Software engineering helps in achieving this goal.

■ Increasing competition in the software industry

As software industry is one of the highest growth industries, the number of players has increased tremendously. To survive in a competitive market, organizations have to show their commitment to quality and also get their software development processes assessed for better visibility and software engineering is the medicine.

■ High manpower attrition

Because of the shortage of highly skilled manpower, every organization is facing the problem of manpower leaving in the middle of the projects. As software development is people-oriented, organizations have to define processes so that even if people leave in the middle of the project, the project will not be adversely affected. Software engineering contributes significantly in achieving this goal.

■ Increasing development costs

Over the years, the cost of hardware is coming down thanks to the developments in semiconductor technology, but the cost of software is growing up drastically because of the rise in establishment charges, manpower charges etc. Software engineering helps in reducing the development costs.

■ Time to market

Because of increased competition, software products have to be delivered as per schedule and one cannot afford to miss the deadline. The "Just in Time" release of the product is of utmost importance. Software engineering defines processes whereby time schedule can be kept under control.

■ Fast changing technology

In software, the technology is changing very fast, so fast that it is becoming very difficult to cope with the pace—for organizations and for people. To manage the change also, processes need to be defined so that the organization is not left behind in adapting new technologies.

■ Sensitivity involved in software products

As society becomes more and more dependent on software, particularly when used in life saving equipment (such as medical equipment), utmost care has to be taken to ensure that the software is highly reliable and meets the safety requirements. Software engineering helps in achieving this goal as well.

■ Increasing complexity of projects

The complexity of software projects is increasing tremendously. The complexity involved in developing software for organizations having global operations, or satellite launching, or telecommunication software, is very high. Managing such projects involving hundreds or thousands of software engineers working for a few years is a gigantic task. Using an ad hoc approach to manage such projects will result in chaos. To develop and test such large-scale software products is a very challenging task and software engineering is a must to manage such projects.

■ Rise of subcontracting of software development and IT services

Many non-IT organizations (such as service industries, hospitality industries, manufacturing industries whose main activity is not IT) are subcontracting their software development and maintenance work to software companies, as it will be cost-effective for them as compared to having their own development staff. Subcontract management is crucial and has to be done in a systematic way. Software engineering helps in achieving this. Because of the complexity involved in testing the software, software testing is nowadays being outsourced.

■ Off-shore development of software

Many developed countries are outsourcing their software development work as the development costs are comparatively lower in developing countries like India, China, Malaysia, Thailand, Indonesia etc. Managing the off-shore development work (when things are not directly under the control of the prime contractor) is not an easy task. Software engineering again comes to the rescue.

■ Increasing the productivity of people

As the manpower costs go up, the manpower has to be utilized effectively, continuous effort has to be made to increase the productivity of the individuals and teams. Software engineering provides the solutions.

Software engineering is a must for every organization—big or small. Even in small organizations, the days when development is carried out on ad hoc basis are gone, for an organization to grow, software engineering is the life line.

To summarize, today every business house has to aim for building "High Quality Software Products at Competitive Prices Just In Time" and there is no escape. To achieve this organizational goal, there is only one method—to follow software engineering principles. Every organization has to develop a "goal-oriented cybernetic system" (i.e., a system which is constantly improved based on the past experience) whereby the organization can achieve the above goal and also increase its productivity as well as productivity of its employees.

1.5 Is the Software Crisis Overcome?

Software engineering emerged as a discipline to overcome the software crisis. Is the crisis overcome now? No, not yet. Software projects continue to be crisis-oriented. Software project management in many organizations is still amateurish and very few tools or techniques are used even for managing very large software projects. Software engineers, in spite of learning the theory of software engineering during their school days, hardly practice it. Documentation continues to be considered a 'bad' job as a result of which if a person leaves in the middle of a project, it is difficult for others to continue the work. Due to lack of methodology in writing the source code, it becomes very complicated to maintain the code after it is delivered to the customer. Enough thrust is not given to software testing and hence buggy products are released into the market. Because of the cumulative effect of all these (and many more such) factors, the crisis continues.

A strong commitment to software engineering principles by the top management, software project managers and engineers is required so that software projects do not get into crisis.

One of the main reasons for the software crisis is lack of thrust for software testing. It is the test engineers who can contribute significantly to the software quality.

NOTE

1.6 THE SOFTWARE CHAOS

In spite of the fact that the software engineering emerged as a strong discipline in 1970's and many advances took place over the 30 years; even today, many software projects are executed in a chaotic manner. Major software projects resulted in huge losses, sometimes even loss of human life. Many projects result in cost overrun or time overrun or both. Sometimes, quality is compromised to deliver the product within the time and budget. Invariably in most of the projects, there will be immense mental tension on the working engineers and managers, leading even to mental disorders. Many startup companies, start with great dreams but disappear in no time. To summarize, software development is characterized by chaos, even today.

1.6.1 The Fiascoes in Software Development

There are many stories in the history of software development that teach us very important lessons. Here are some famous stories and the test engineers need to keep these stories in mind.

Patriot Missile

During the 1991 Gulf war, an Iraqi Scud missile hit an American army barrack killing many soldiers. An American Patriot missile could not track and intercept the Scud missile. The reason: a software bug in the Patriot missile. Whenever the tracking system of the Patriot was switched on, it measured the elapsed time from an internal clock in tenths of a second. This value was multiplied by 10 to get the time in seconds. The calculation was performed using 24-bit fixed-point registers. Hence, the value of 1/10 stored in a register was truncated to 24 bits whereas the exact value is 0.00011001100110011001100..... When the value is truncated, an error is introduced and this error accumulates over a period of time. The Patriot missile was switched on for about 100 hours and so the accumulated error was 0.34 second. Scud travels with a speed of 1,676 meters per second i.e., or more than half a kilometer in 0.34 seconds. As a result, the Patriot could not intercept the Scud. This incident indicates the care that needs to be taken while designing and testing mission-critical systems.

The Patriot Missile example shows how a small software bug, accumulation of error due to rounding off a number, can lead to a catastrophe.

Ariane 5

On June 4, 1996, European Space Agency launched the Ariane 5 satellite launch vehicle. Exactly 40 seconds after lift-off at an altitude of 3700 meters, the launcher exploded and became a ball of fire. The project, which was uninsured, costed US$ 500 million. What went wrong? In one of the embedded systems, a software exception caused the problem. A 64-bit floating-point number was to be converted into a 16-bit signed integer value. During one calculation, the converted integer value was more than the value that can be represented by a 16-bit signed integer. This caused an operand error. Yes, the software exception was handled, but badly. The specification of the exception handling routine was: to indicate the failure on the data bus, to store the context in the EPROM and to shut down the processor. The processor was shut down, and it created the chaos. The mishap can be attributed to lack of enough testing as well as the flaw in the software design, particularly in exception handling. This error is known as '500 million dollar software error' in the software literature [Jezequel 1997]. Interestingly, the software used in Ariane 4 was reused in Ariane 5, and Ariane 4 was a successful launch. The only difference is that in Ariane 5, this calculation was not at all required!

The failure of this project is a lesson for every software engineer—one line of code can cause irreparable damage.

Ariane 5 project illustrates the dangers associated with leaving some portions of the untested code in the software. The test engineers need to ensure that each and every line of the code is tested before releasing the software.

Mars Pathfinder

The NASA mission Pathfinder landed on the Mars on 4 July, 1997. The mission was successful—a perfect launch, a perfect landing on the Mars and lot of important data was sent to the earth. After a few days, the computing system started resetting intermittently and important data was not being received on the Earth. The on-board computer used a real-time operating system. Using an exact replica of the computer on the Earth, the debugging was done to find the fault.

Three tasks were running on the system—one with high priority, one with low priority, and one with medium priority. Intermittently, the task with medium priority was running for a long time, while the task with high priority was waiting for the task with low priority to complete. The task with low priority was not getting the CPU time because a higher priority task was running. Meanwhile, the watchdog timer, suspecting a deadlock, used to reset the processor. This problem was due to a bug in the inter-task communication module. Of course, the story ended in a positive note as the engineers were able to upload a modified file on to the Pathfinder.

The story of Pathfinder teaches us many lessons in software development. While doing the simulation studies, the engineers noticed such a problem before the launch of the Pathfinder, but they thought that the problem was due to a hardware glitch as it was observed only a very few times—we should not set aside even the occasional problems encountered. The engineers on the Earth could analyze and rectify the bug only because the debug code was also running on the computer of Pathfinder— sometimes the debug code is very important, we should not think that debug code is only for development, it is very useful for maintenance as well.

Mars Pathfinder is an excellent example to understand the complexity involved in testing real-time systems. The bad things are the bad design and the approach taken by some engineers when a problem was encountered while testing the software in the laboratory. The marvel is that the problem could be solved without someone flying to the Mars to upgrade the software in the field!

The field of software is full of such stories. Refer to [Glass 1999] for the lessons to be learned from 'computing calamities'. The calamities include products and projects that failed and organizations that failed.

Statistics reveal that nearly 74% of the software projects could not be completed within the time frame or within the budget or both [Jones 1994]. The problem can be due to (a) wrong estimation before starting the project or (b) the project could not be managed properly to complete it within the estimated time and budget. Many a time, the project is delivered within the time and budget, but compromised on quality, which is worse.

The competition, shortage of software professionals, short development time, need for high quality—these factors are making software development a highly challenging activity and calls for process orientation. In organizations which lack this process orientation, software development is a very painful process—fire-fighting is very common leading to burning of midnight oil by all the persons from top to bottom (yes, affecting their health, personal life and family life), tempers are lost in the times of crisis, misunderstandings creep in between the client and the developer, sometimes leading to battles in the courts of law, compromises in the quality leading to loss of life, loss of property, total failure of major missions, cyber crime in financial applications like banking, e-commerce, and so on.

The software engineers and project managers have two choices—to live with such painful process or to develop a process whereby the software development will be more of fun and challenge.

To make software development a fun-filled challenge, a creative activity that contributes to better quality of life, an intellectually satisfying job that makes the world a better place to live in—there is only one solution, a process-oriented and people-oriented software development.

Managing software projects, in a highly competitive environment with fast changing technologies and shortage of skilled workforce, has become the biggest challenge for all software organizations. The project team has to make every project a 'success'. But then, what is a successful software project? In the next section, we will define the criteria for the success of a software project.

1.7 Criteria for the Success of a Software Project

When do we say that a software project is successful? Success is a perception. After a project is completed, you can ask the team members and also some persons outside the team whether the project is a success. Do not be surprised if you get different answers. It is very difficult to get an objective answer to what a successful project is.

The four criteria for the success of a project are:
- The software must meet all the quality requirements.
- The software must be developed within the time frame.
- The software must be developed within the budget.
- The relations amongst the team members should be cordial during the project execution and after the project is completed.

We will study each of these criteria in detail.

1.7.1 Quality

The most important requirement of a software product is that it should meet the requirements of the customer. In addition to the user requirements, the management of the development organization may put additional requirements to ensure that the product is developed at a low cost and also to ensure that the software can be maintained at low cost. If the management wants to modify customized software to make it a generic product at a later date, additional requirement may be put such as portability. In general, the characteristics of a software product can be divided into

- Operational characteristics
- Transition characteristics
- Revision characteristics

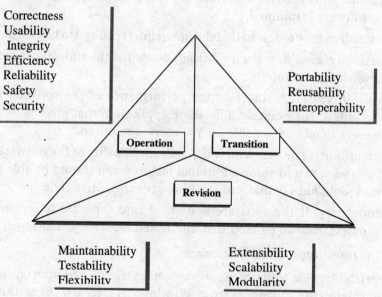

Correctness
Usability
Integrity
Efficiency
Reliability
Safety
Security

Portability
Reusability
Interoperability

Operation   Transition

Revision

Maintainability
Testability
Flexibility

Extensibility
Scalability
Modularity

Fig. 1.1 Software Quality Triangle

Software quality triangle, shown in Fig. 1.1, depicts these characteristics. Operational characteristics specify the requirements during the operation/usage. Transition characteristics specify the requirements for its usage in other hardware/operating system environments. Revision characteristics specify the requirements for making the changes to software easy.

The operational characteristics are:

- Correctness: The extent to which the software meets the specifications.
- Usability/Learnability: The effort/time required to learn the usage of the software. The usability of a well-designed GUI is very high compared to a menu-driven interface.
- Integrity: The software should not have side effects (like another application does not run when the software is invoked).
- Efficiency: Effective usage of the storage space, faster execution time etc.
- Reliability: The software should be defect-free and should not fail during the operation.
- Safety: The software should not be hazardous to environment/life.
- Security: The software should not have ill-effects on data/hardware.

The revision characteristics are:

- Maintainability: Easy to maintain so that time/effort required to remove defects in the software is minimal.
- Testability: Easy to test so that the time/effort required to test the software is minimal.
- Flexibility: Easy to make modifications so that the time/effort required for making modifications is minimal.
- Scalability: Easy to increase the performance of the software if the application demands it. For example, a database application that gives good response time for 10 users should be scalable for 100 users if required.
- Extensibility: The ease with which the functionality of the software can be enhanced. If you want to add some additional features, you should be able to do it easily, and you should not say that you would rewrite the entire code.
- Modularity: If the software is divided into separate independent parts (called modules) that can be modified, and tested separately, it has high modularity.

The transition characteristics are

- Portability: Ease with which software can be transferred from one platform to another platform (for example, from Windows NT to UNIX) without changing the functionality.
- Reusability: If portions of the software can be used in some other application with little or no modifications, the software is said to be reusable.

■ Interoperability: Ability to make the software exchange information with another system and make use of the information transparently.

Ideally, every software product must have all the above quality characteristics. However, depending on the application, only a subset of these characteristics may be required. Before starting the development of a software product, a requirements specification document is written clearly indicating all the quality requirements. After the product is developed, the software has to be tested to ensure that it meets the requirements of the customer and also the internal requirements. To differentiate between the two types of testing, the two terms 'validation' and 'verification' are used. Validation is used to check whether the software meets customer expectations. Verification is used to check whether the software conforms to all the specifications.

The customer is not bothered about the reusability or portability of the software as long as it meets his requirements. So, the customer independently carries out an acceptance testing of the software.

To meet the deadline given by the client, sometimes the software is delivered compromising on quality. This leads to increased maintenance costs. Generally the maintenance cost is much higher than the development cost. So, to make the software project a success, the first and foremost important requirement is the quality of the software.

The test engineer needs to understand the quality requirements of the product to be tested using the quality triangle. The testing has to be done to ensure that the software has the necessary quality attributes.

1.7.2 Time

To deliver the product within the time frame without compromising on quality is another criterion for the success of a project. Many clients are ready to pay more money if necessary but they do not like to compromise on time—after all time is money. But then, there is a problem. While giving the project proposal, the development time is estimated to be, say, 6 months. The client wants it in 3 months. To grab the order, in most cases, the manager will agree. Once the commitment is made to the client, it is the manager's responsibility to see that the project is completed within 3 months, then only the project is a success. Here, the perceptions differ—the manager may argue that even if it is delivered in 5 months, for him it is a success because it is within his initial estimate. But the fact remains that the customer is the ultimate reference. More than the project team's perceptions, the perception of the customer is important.

1.7.3 Budget

Project costing is an extremely complex process. While giving a project proposal to the prospective customer, it may not be possible to foresee each and every item to be costed. The initial estimate for the project cost may turn out to be erroneous for many reasons:

- The initial estimate of the number of people required may be incorrect.
- The initial estimate of time may be incorrect because of which penalty has to be paid.
- There may be unforeseen technical problems because of which additional personnel or external consulting services may be required.
- There may be changes in requirements due to which additional effort is needed.
- Due to oversight, costing under a particular head might not have been accounted.
- There may be changes in government rules as a result of which the cost would go up (e.g., increase in sales tax).
- Personnel leave in the middle of the project, because of which the schedule is likely to be affected.

The reasons can be many more. A meticulous planning and foresight are required to do the project costing. As experience is the best teacher in project costing, the project manager has to document all the factors that affect the project cost while executing each and every project. The process of cost estimation needs to be improved continuously.

Another important aspect in estimation is the risk items. During project proposal preparation itself, the manager has to analyze the likely risks and the corrective action to be taken and account for such costs as well. For instance, it is now common in some organizations for people to leave in the middle of the project. The manpower attrition is a risk item—the corrective action is to have backup personnel i.e., put additional personnel from the beginning of the project itself.

Note that the software has to be developed within the planned cost of development. If there is additional expenditure, it eats into the profit margin, which is not acceptable to the senior management.

1.7.4 Relationships

The software project manager has to ensure that cordial relations are maintained amongst all the people throughout the execution of the project. Sometimes, the project is completed as per schedule within the budget and quality software is delivered, but the relations are strained. The manager has to ensure that good relations are maintained between:

- Project manager and the team members

- Project manager and the top management
- Team members and the client/end users
- Development team and other teams such as quality team, test team etc.

It is a very challenging task for the manager to take all these groups of people along with him during the execution of the project. The most important element in managing the relations is 'expectations management'—how do you manage the expectations of these groups during the execution of the project? [Boehm 2000]. It is a complex task and many people opine that software project management is more of personnel management rather than technical management.

Consider a project, which involves development of a software product that will take the whole world by storm. The product is conceived and our businessman (the top management, as we call him/them) asks the project manager to bring out the product in just a few weeks. Generally, we like to give only good news to the top management, so we never say 'no' because most of the people do not like to listen to a no. The project manager says 'yes' knowing fully well that it cannot be done. If we keep the expectations of the people very high and suddenly drop them, it is a bad expectations management. One can imagine the problems that will be created by giving a commitment that cannot be fulfilled. Tempers are lost, sometimes jobs are lost, careers are ruined and the software development environment turns into a battlefield which leaves many 'dead'. Is it worth working on such projects?

Many project managers do not inform the clients the correct status of the project, but keep telling 'everything is fine, we will deliver as per schedule'. And, finally when the actual day of delivery arrives, the customer is informed that it is likely to take a few more days. This is a wrong strategy because raising the expectations and suddenly giving a shock is very dangerous.

We need to tell all the persons concerned, the client and the senior management, the reality of the development status as well as the issues related to quality of the software. Similarly, the manager has to get the right inputs from the engineers and make the engineers open up and express their opinions so that they give realistic dates for development and also the realistic picture of the quality of the software. Any issues related to the quality have to be resolved through discussions with the quality team and the test team rather than fighting endless battles.

It is very common during software project execution, for the project managers to shout at the engineers, the top management to shout at the project manager, the client threatening the project manager that he will cancel the order and so on. These unpleasant situations are due to lack of a process-oriented approach to software development on the one hand and due to improper relations management on the other hand.

Though relationship management is one of the most important tasks of a project manager, it is not given enough emphasis. But, one has to remember, a project can be considered a success only if at the end of it, everyone associated with the project is happy to have been associated with the project.

To summarize, a software project can be considered a success only when quality software is delivered within the time and within the budget and the execution goes smoothly without affecting the human relations.

> *In almost every organization, managing the relations between development team and testing team is a tough task. Test engineers should offer constructive criticism, by suggesting how the software can be improved, rather than just doing fault-finding.*
>
> NOTE

1.8 Process-Oriented Software Development

To make a project successful, software development cannot be done on an ad hoc basis. Without a process orientation, development leads to fire-fighting resulting in chaos. In spite of the stress that is given to the 'process' by the management, many projects are executed without defining, let alone following, a process. For a project to be successful, process orientation is a must. In this section, we will discuss briefly the process to be followed in software development.

1.8.1 The Software Process

As shown in Fig. 1.2, to develop a product, a process is defined. The process takes the raw material as input and produces a finished product.

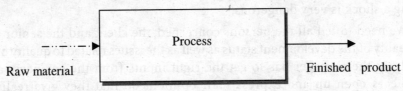

Raw material   Process   Finished product

Fig. 1.2 The Process

The process defines the various steps (or stages) to be followed to convert the raw material into the finished product. For example, to manufacture a car, the process defines the step-by-step procedure to assemble the various parts such as the chassis, engine, steering, tyres etc.

In the case of software, there is no raw material (rather, the human brain is the raw material). As shown in Fig. 1.3, the software process takes the problem definition as input and produces the software product.

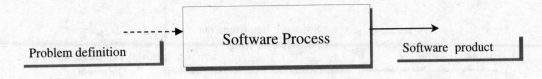

Fig. 1.3   The Software Process

As software development is a highly intellectual activity, it is very difficult to define precisely the software process. The process of software development is divided into various phases and in each phase, a set of activities is carried out to arrive at the end product.

1.9 Phases in Software Development Life Cycle

Each phase in the development process will have a defined input and a defined output. This divide-and-conquer strategy works well, as managing individual phases will be easier and monitoring will also be effective. The marketing department of an organization will carry out initial dialogue with the prospective client and get a project. Or, the organization may on its own, conceive a new project idea to develop a generic product (such as an operating system, database management software or an application software package). To start with, the feasibility analysis is done and then once it has been decided to take up the project, the development can be broadly categorized into the following phases:

- Software requirements engineering
- Software design
- Implementation
- Testing
- Maintenance

1.9.1 Software Requirements Engineering

In this phase, the requirements of the client are obtained, analyzed, documented and validated. Utmost care has to be taken by the project team to obtain the requirements of the client to the highest degree of accuracy. As shown in Fig. 1.4, the inputs to the requirements engineering process is the problem definition and the output is a validated Software Requirements Specifications (SRS) document.

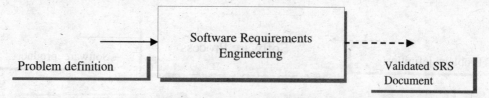

Fig. 1.4 The Process of Software Requirements Engineering

The project team members have to discuss with the client in detail on the exact functionality of the software and also the performance and other non-functional requirements. After that, these requirements have to be documented and a document called Software Requirements Specifications (SRS) has to be written. After necessary interactions with the client, it has to be ensured that the SRS document is as per the requirements of the client i.e., the document has to be validated.

Some of the mistakes made commonly are:

- To start the development work without even understanding the requirements correctly.

- Not to document the requirements and hence the requirements will be in the minds of some people who interacted with the client and when they leave the project halfway, the whole project will be in trouble.

- Whenever any changes are made to the requirements, not to incorporate them in the document as a result of which the changes are not known to all the team members.

- To accept a change asked by the client without analyzing the likely impact of the change on the project development time and budget.

It is not practical always to expect that the specifications will be frozen and assume that there will not be any changes. To the extent possible, all the requirements have to be documented and subsequently if any changes are to be made, a specific procedure has to be followed to ensure that all the team members are aware of the changes. Also, whenever a change is to be made, the impact of this proposed change on the time frame, budget and quality are to be analyzed.

Sometimes, an apparently small change in requirements may result in major changes in the design of the software. So, any change to be made to the specifications has to be discussed by the project team thoroughly and if the change turns out to be major in terms of the additional work to be done, the terms of the contract (time frame and budget) need to be re-negotiated.

So, the requirements engineering phase involves obtaining the requirements, documenting the requirements, validating the documented requirements and also defining the procedure for making the necessary changes in the requirements document.

For a test engineer, the SRS document is the reference. The testing has to be done to ensure that each and every specification given in the SRS document is tested.

1.9.2 Software Design

In this stage, the system design has to be carried out. The system consists of both hardware and software. The functionality of hardware and software are to be separated out. After that, the detailed design of hardware and software are to be carried out.

As shown in Fig. 1.5, the design process takes the SRS document as the input and the output is a validated design document.

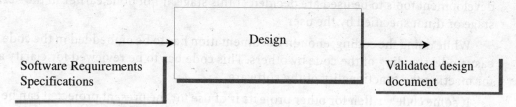

Fig. 1.5 The Design Process

Software design involves development of the architecture, design of the algorithms, and data structures. Unlike in other engineering fields, in software design, there are no fixed formulas. Software design is a highly intellectual activity involving exploration of different alternatives, studying the pros and cons of each alternative and choosing the best alternative based on some design criteria such as usability, performance, reliability etc. For user interface design, database design, real-time system design etc., different methodologies are to be followed and the process of design has to be documented. With the advent of Object-Oriented Technology (OOT), Object-Oriented Design (OOD) is catching up. Using a standard methodology such as UML (Unified Modeling Language), the design has to be documented.

The output of this phase is a design document giving the details of various modules and the details of logic and algorithms.

1.9.3 Implementation

In this phase, the design is converted into code. As shown in Fig. 1.6, the input to the implementation process is the design document and output is the source code. Ideally, the design document prepared by the software architects should be given to the programmers and the programmers should be able to do the coding. To achieve this, a very detailed design document has to be prepared, which is not very easy. So, the programmers need to constantly interact with the designers or the designers also need to actively participate in the implementation.

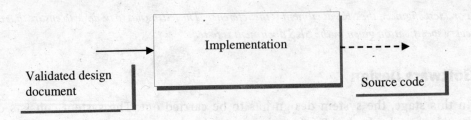

Fig. 1.6 The Implementation Process

The coding has to be done in such a way that the testing would be easier and later, the maintenance would be easier. The programming language to be used, the development tools to be used are decided at this stage, if not done earlier in the design stage or if not specified by the user.

While doing the coding, enough documentation has to be embedded in the code for easy understanding of the code by others. This code has to be reviewed for clarity and for meeting the functionality of the software.

If some code written for other projects is of use for the present project, it can be re-used resulting in reduced development time. However, enough care is to be taken while acquiring the code for reuse.

The output of this stage is the code in a given programming language, with each of the units (smallest code segments) tested.

> *The test engineers need to ensure that each and every line of the source code is tested. Using source code testing tools, this can be done; but the test engineers need to study the source code to do this.*

NOTE

1.9.4 Testing

Testing consumes the highest amount of time in the development life cycle, however, it is given the least importance by the development teams. The reason is that testing is difficult, difficult underlined.

The foremost thing in testing is to test the functionality of the software. In addition to functionality, the software has to be tested to ensure that it meets the performance requirements, the reliability requirements and other requirements such as portability, learnability (ease of use) etc.

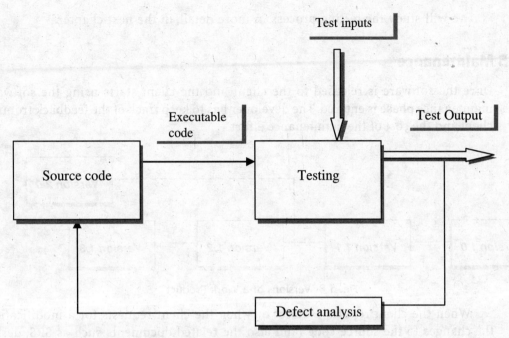

Fig. 1.7 The Testing Process

As shown in Fig. 1.7, the testing process is an iterative process. The source code is converted into an executable code and various test inputs are given. For every test input, the output is analyzed to check whether the program is functioning correctly. If there is a defect ("bug" is the commonly used word), the defect is reflected in terms of a wrong output (or no output). The defect is analyzed, and the source code is modified and again testing is carried out with the test inputs. This process is repeated till the source code is defect-free (or almost!).

In addition to testing the software in the laboratory, testing also needs to be done in the actual working environment (called beta testing). Sometimes, depending on the requirement, other types of testing such as stress testing (to test the software at the limits of its performance specifications) have to be done.

While testing the software, when defects are found, the source code has to be modified. Sometimes it may be necessary to modify the design or even the specifications. This makes software development an iterative process. A methodology has to be worked out so that the modifications to specifications, design, code etc. are done methodically.

For carrying out testing, the testing process is to be clearly defined, which involves development of a test plan, carrying out the testing as per the plan and documenting the test results in the form of a test report. The test plan has to specify the resources required for testing, the test tools to be used, the test cases (inputs to be given), the types of testing to be done etc.

The output of this stage is completely tested software, which meets the requirements specifications.

We will study the testing process in more detail, in the next chapter.

1.9.5 Maintenance

Once the software is released to the client and the client starts using the software, maintenance phase is entered. The developer has to keep track of the feedback from the client and the cost of the maintenance effort.

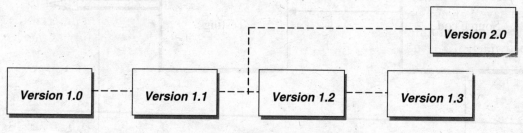

Fig. 1.8: Versions of a Work Product

When the client reports a defect or when the client requests for a modification, the changes to the source code (and also the related documents such as SRS, design document etc.) have to be done systematically. The work products (SRS, design document, source code etc.) have to be kept under 'configuration control'. As shown in Fig. 1.8, many versions of these documents may need to be generated. To start with, there will be version 1.0 from which version 1.1 will be generated. Version 1.1 may lead to two other versions—1.2 and 2.0. Unless a systematic procedure is followed to handle multiple versions, the work products will be unmanageable. Each version of the software work products has to be maintained with the required documentation. Making changes to the work products systematically is called configuration management.

The maintenance process involves configuration management of the work products, keeping track of the feedback from the client and also the effort spent on the maintenance.

The test engineers have to test the software thoroughly whenever a change is made to even a small portion of the code, because there is a possibility that a change in one portion of the code may affect the other portions of the software.

1.10 Software Development Life Cycle Models

The software product is first conceived, developed and then delivered. After delivery, the software may undergo changes—the client may find some defects, which need to be rectified; or the client may ask some enhancements. So, after development phase, there will be a maintenance phase till the software retires. This entire cycle is known as the life cycle of software development.

As we discussed earlier, we divide the development process into a number of phases such as requirements engineering, design, implementation, testing and maintenance. Each phase has a defined input and a defined output. This is a very simplistic model. It is not practical to use this model for development of software for all types of projects. For instance, if the requirements are not clear, it will be a futile exercise to write the SRS document. For research-oriented projects, it is difficult to even have a precise problem definition. To facilitate software development for different types of projects, different life cycle models have been proposed. We will discuss the most widely used life cycle models in this section.

1.10.1 Waterfall Model

The waterfall model is widely used for most of the commercial software development projects. This model is shown in Fig. 1.9.

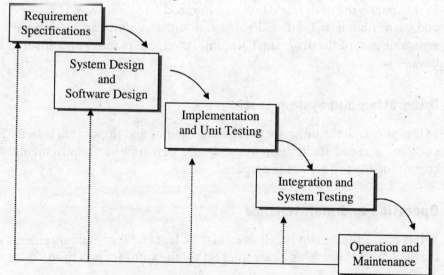

Fig. 1.9 Waterfall Model

In this model, the software development process is divided into five stages:

- Requirements specifications
- System design and software design
- Implementation and unit testing
- Integration and system testing
- Operation and maintenance

Requirements specifications

During this phase, the project team will work out in detail, the functionality and the likely limitations of the software product to be developed. A document will be prepared clearly indicating the requirements. It is called the Software Requirements Specifications (SRS) document.

System design and software design

During this phase, from the requirements specifications, the system design is carried out. System design implies hardware design and software design. The functionality of hardware and software are separated out and design of the software modules is worked out in detail. A test plan is also prepared describing the details of tests to be carried out on the system once development is completed.

Implementation and unit testing

In this phase, the design is converted into code. The software is divided into modules and each module is further divided into units. A unit can be defined as a logically separable part of the program. Each unit is tested separately and ensured that it has no bugs.

Integration and system testing

In this phase, all the units are combined together and the system is built. The complete software is tested for its functionality and performance requirements. A test report containing the test results is prepared.

Operation and maintenance

In this phase, the system is delivered to the client and if any enhancements are required, they are carried out. This phase goes on till the software is retired.

Outputs of stages in waterfall model

The attractive feature of waterfall model is that at the end of each stage, a visible output is available. The outputs at the end of each stage are given in Table 1.1.

Stage	Outputs
Requirements specifications	SRS document Draft user manual Maintenance plan
System design and software design	System design document Hardware design document Software design document Interface design document Unit test plan System test plan
Implementation and unit testing	Program code Unit test report
Integration and system testing	System test report Final user manual Working system
Operation and maintenance	$ (if the software is without any defects)

Table 1.1: Outputs at Different Stages in Waterfall Model

Advantages of waterfall model:

- Because of availability of well-defined outputs at each stage, the progress of the project will be evident to the management.

- Project monitoring, both by the internal management team and the client, is easy because of the visible outputs at each stage.

As it is a conceptually simple model, it is followed in a large number of organizations, particularly for commercial projects.

Limitations/disadvantages of waterfall model:

- For most of the projects, freezing the specifications is extremely difficult. In such cases, 'baseline approach' is followed. Baseline is defined as the certified output of one stage passed on to the next stage. The SRS document is written and even though there are some issues still to be resolved, version 1.0 of SRS (called the baseline document) is released and the design is taken up. While doing the design, if any changes are to be made in the SRS, a formal procedure is followed for making the changes on the baseline SRS document.

- For long-term projects (projects of duration one year and above), waterfall model requires freezing of the hardware. With fast developments in hardware technology, freezing the hardware may not be appropriate.

- If the client wants the developer to evolve specifications in a gradual manner, this model is not suitable.

When waterfall model is used, the test engineers can expect a reasonably mature software for testing. When bugs are found in the software, the test engineers need to analyze the reason for the bug and inform the development team to modify the SRS or design or source code. The involvement of test engineers from the beginning is advisable.

1.10.2 Prototyping Model

For some projects, it is very difficult to obtain the exact user requirements (for example, when the user is not IT-literate). In such cases, a prototype is built and demonstrated to the user. Based on the user's feedback, the SRS document is prepared. As shown in Fig. 1.10, the prototyping model is used for finalizing the SRS.

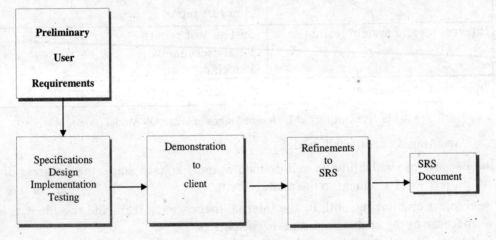

Fig. 1.10 Prototyping Model

It is important to differentiate between prototyping as applied to hardware and as applied to software. In hardware, prototyping is used to prove your design concepts. In software, prototyping is used to obtain the user requirements.

Prototype is generally developed at the cost of the developer, and not at the cost of the client. So, prototyping has to be done with minimal resources. Prototype is developed using prototyping tools such as scripting languages or Rapid Application Development (RAD) tools. When the prototype is demonstrated to the user, the user gets clarity of the functionality of the software and suggests required modifications. Prototyping is generally required to obtain user interface requirements. Based on the feedback, a more accurate SRS document can be prepared and the development work can start, using the waterfall model. For instance, if you have to develop software for a small bank, initially you can develop a prototype and demonstrate it to the bank employees. Based on their feedback, you can write the SRS document and then follow the waterfall model for development of full-fledged banking software.

Advantages of prototyping model:

- This is a good model for developing software for users who are not IT-literate.
- As SRS will be frozen after obtaining the feedback from the user, no changes are likely to be there in the requirements.
- When the client is not sure of the developer's strength in software development, the client can ask the developer to build a small prototype, which can be used to judge the capabilities of the developer.

Disadvantages of prototyping model:

- The prototype may not be of any use subsequently (that is the reason it is also known as throw-away prototype).
- The development cost has to be borne by the developer.

1.10.3 Evolutionary Development Model

In this approach, the system is built in stages. As shown in Fig. 1.11, the initial user requirements are obtained and the product is developed. The user validates the system and gives the feedback for enhancements. The product is refined based on the new requirements. This process is repeated till a user-acceptable product is built.

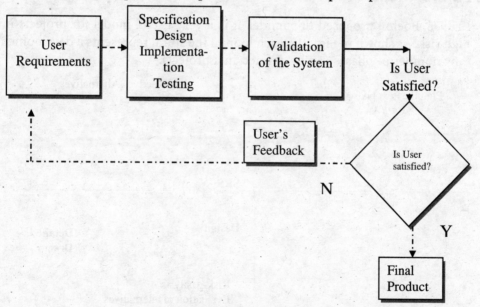

Fig. 1.11 Evolutionary Development Model

Advantages of evolutionary development model:

- This model is useful in exploratory programming (such as Artificial Intelligence applications) where it is difficult to frame the specifications.

- In case major problems are foreseen, the developer can stop the development after some iterations.

This model is very appropriate for research projects. For example, suppose you have to develop software for automatic speech recognition—the computer has to be made to understand the words spoken by you. Initially, a small vocabulary can be taken and the software can be developed. After achieving success, the vocabulary can be increased in stages. This approach is better than starting development of an unlimited vocabulary speech recognition system directly (and after two years, realizing that it is very difficult!).

Disadvantages of evolutionary development model:

- Because the project is open-ended, no time frame can be set.
- Project monitoring is difficult.
- Less visibility as compared to waterfall model.

Testing the software, when evolutionary development model is used, is a complex task. For every iteration of the development, the software has to be tested keeping in view the new specifications.

1.10.4 Spiral Model

In 1988, Boehm proposed this model. It is a very useful model for projects involving high risk. As shown in Fig. 1.12, each loop in the spiral represents a development phase (any number of phases can be defined in a project).

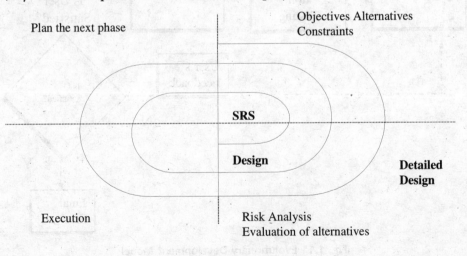

Fig. 1.12   Spiral Model

Each loop is split into four sections, each section to carry out a specific task:

1. To determine the objectives, alternatives, and constraints.
2. Risk analysis and evaluation of alternatives.
3. Execution of that phase of development.
4. Planning the next phase.

For each round of the spiral, one form has to be filled containing the following information.

Objectives: what are the objectives of this phase in terms of technical activities?

Alternatives: what are the alternatives available to achieve the objectives?

Constraints: what are the difficulties foreseen in the implementation?

Risk factors: what are the risk items and the impact of the risk items?

Risk resolution: how the risks can be resolved?

Results: what results have been achieved vis-à-vis the objectives?

Plans: what are the plans for the next phase?

Commitment: what are the commitments to the client and whether they can be fulfilled based on the results of this phase of development?

So, at the end of each spiral (phase), the management can review the status based on this form, and decide the future course of action.

Advantages of the spiral model:

■ This is a flexible model, the phases can be determined by an organization depending on the type and complexity of the project.
■ This model is suitable for high-risk projects.
■ Project monitoring is very effective as risk management is built into the model. Periodically, the project can be assessed for its risks vis-à-vis the progress and a decision can be taken at the end of each spiral regarding its continuation or otherwise.

Disadvantages of the spiral model:

■ This model is not suitable for low risk projects or projects without any risk.
■ It is a 'complicated' model for projects with clear SRS.

1.10.5 Synchronize-and-Stabilize Model

For developing software products that are highly innovative and with a very short development time, the preceding models cannot be applied. In such cases, the 'synchronize-and-stabilize' model, applied very effectively by Microsoft and Netscape [Cusumano 1999] would be very useful. This model is shown in Fig. 1.13.

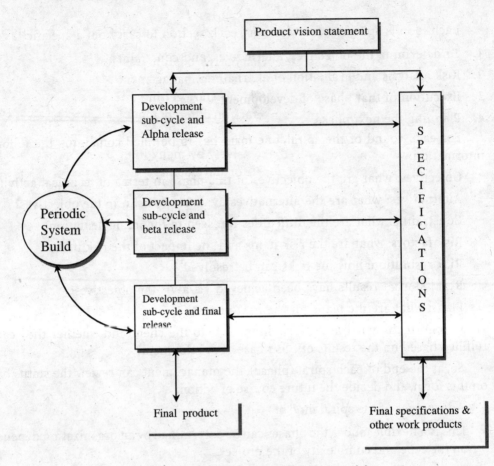

Fig. 1.13 Synchronize-and-Stabilize model

To start with, a vision statement for the product is prepared which gives the broad goals of the product. Based on this vision statement, and the inputs from market research, a document is prepared which lists out the important features to be incorporated, if necessary with prioritization (a draft specifications document). The development teams work in parallel on various modules and periodically integrate and test the code i.e., the code developed by different teams is 'synchronized'. Initially, the synchronization is done less frequently and at later stages very frequently, sometimes daily. These "periodic system builds" are tested for usability, functionality and reliability; and feedback is given to the development teams. During the total planned development time, three or four milestones are defined—these milestones are used to 'stabilize' the product. Three typical milestones are alpha release, beta release, and final release as shown in Fig. 1.13. This flexibility in the development approach coupled with early integration and testing gives a good 'feel' of the product in initial stages itself. Also, the feature prioritization helps in releasing a product with the most important functionality and also helps in meeting the time target.

The special feature of this model is that the specifications (and other work products) are complete only when the product is ready. However, after the alpha testing, the product can be demonstrated to the prospective customers and their feedback can be incorporated into the product. Also, from a management point of view, the model is attractive because the management can start getting a feel of the product from the beginning itself. Also, small teams work on different modules and integrate the modules periodically.

This model has been used extensively by many innovative product development organizations. It is the best model for development of products using cutting-edge technologies and with tight schedules.

Advantages of synchronize-and-stabilize model:

- Because of the intermediate 'releases' of the product, the product can be made feature-rich by incorporating the necessary feedback of the prospective customers.
- The periodic system building approach paves way for testing the software for both functionality and performance.
- The integration problems encountered in large projects using other models are eliminated in this model, again because of the periodic system building.
- Project monitoring will be easy as there are intermediate milestones, such as alpha release and beta release.

Disadvantages of the synchronize-and-stabilize model:

- The detailed specifications document will be made available only at the time of product release.
- Periodic system builds require a rigorous process to be defined for integration of various modules.
- A parallel independent testing team needs to be in place.

However, for innovative product development, the disadvantages mentioned above do not apply. To experiment with various alternatives and arrive at the right solution and get a good feel of the product from the beginning itself would be important for making a product that would make an impact.

 The test engineers play a very important role from the beginning of the project when synchronize-and-stabilize model is used for software development. Integration testing and system testing have to be done periodically, sometimes even daily.

1.10.6 Summary of Development Life Cycle Models

Table 1.2 gives a summary of the different models based on which a particular model can be selected for a specific project.

Development life cycle model	Features
Waterfall model	To be used when the SRS is clear. Simple and effective model for commercial projects with clear requirements. Project monitoring is effective as defined outputs are available at the end of each stage.
Prototyping model	Useful when the requirements are not clear. Prototyping generally at developer's cost. Good model to develop software for IT user organizations.
Evolutionary development model	Useful for research projects. Incremental building helps reduce risk for commercial projects.
Spiral model	Useful for high-risk projects. Complicated model for projects with clear specifications.
Synchronize-and-stabilize model	Useful model for highly innovative product development and projects with strict deadlines. Specifications will be available only at the time of releasing the product. Periodic system builds give a feel of the product from the beginning to the management.

Table 1.2 Summary of Software Development Life Cycle Models

1.11 The Management Processes

In addition to the process definition described earlier, a number of management processes have to be defined so that quality product is delivered. These management processes include:

■ Software Project Proposal Preparation: To give a proposal to the customer indicating the time frame and development cost.

■ Software Project Planning: To prepare a detailed plan for executing the project, clearly indicating the timeframe and effort required for each phase.

■ Training: To train the team members on the required skills and application domain.

■ Team Formation: To form the project team and ensure that there is a good coordination amongst the team members.

■ Project Monitoring and Tracking: To continuously monitor the progress of the project and take corrective actions through a defined review process. Reviews have to be conducted in every phase of development: SRS review, design review, code review, test results review etc.

1.12 Software Quality Assurance

To deliver quality software product, quality has to be assured in each and every phase of the development process. In many organizations, there will be a separate Software Quality Assurance (SQA) team that audits the work of the various development teams to ensure that the process definitions are followed strictly. In small organizations, the development engineers themselves need to do the quality assurance work. Whatever be the organizational structure, the most important point is that the output of each phase should be of very high quality. The SQA team is responsible to ensure that all the development teams follow the processes.

The output of a phase should not be described on qualitative terms—we should have quantitative measures. These quantitative measures or "metrics" will be discussed in the next section.

1.12.1 Metrics in Software Development

In every engineering discipline, measurement is an important activity. Just as we quantify weight, height etc. and use units such as gram, centimeter, to represent various parameters; in software engineering, measures (or metrics) are used to quantify various parameters. The software metrics help in

- Estimation of size and complexity of the project.
- Tracking the progress of the project.
- Analyzing the effectiveness of the software process and taking corrective action if necessary.
- Measuring the productivity of the people.

In software industry, it is said that you cannot manage what you cannot measure. For an effective management of the software projects, the metrics are very important. Some important software metrics are described in this section.

The Person Month

The effort required for execution of a project is measured in Person Months (PMs). If a person works for one month, the effort is one PM. If 6 people work on a project for one year, the effort is 72 PMs. Though the exact time a person works in a month may vary, on an average, 154 hours can be assumed. (22 days at the rate of 7 hours per day, excluding one hour for social formalities, gossip, tea breaks etc.)

If the complexity of the project is estimated in terms of PMs, it is easy to calculate the cost in terms of dollars, if the rate per person hour is known (or assumed).

Product Metrics

To estimate the size of a project is very difficult task. One accepted method of estimating the product size is using the metric KDSI (Kilo or Thousand Delivered Source Instructions) or Kilo Lines of Code (KLOC)—how many thousands of lines of code are required for the project excluding the comments.

Based on the KDSI, a project can be categorized as small, intermediate, medium, large or very large:

Small	<= 2 KDSI
Intermediate	>2 and <= 8 KDSI
Medium	> 8 and <= 32 KDSI
Large	> 32 and <= 128 KDSI
Very large	> 128 KDSI

In database management system (DBMS) projects, the project size can be measured in terms of number of tables, forms, and reports.

Productivity Metrics

The number of lines that can be written by a programmer in one hour can be used as a metric for measuring the productivity of the programmer i.e., the Delivered Source Instructions (DSI) per hour.

Using the size of the project in KDSI and the average productivity of the programmer, the time required to execute a project can be calculated as below.

Time required for execution of a project (in hours) = Total KDSI of the project / (average KDSI per hour)

Another metric used for productivity is the number of defects removed per hour by a programmer.

However, it needs to be mentioned that organizations should not judge the performance of individuals based on these metrics. These metrics must be used only to estimate the time required for the execution of the project or time required to remove the defects etc.

Quality Metrics

To measure the quality of the product, the following metrics can be used:

Number of defects found per KDSI (known as defect density)

Number of changes requested by the customer after the software is delivered.

MTBF (Mean Time Between Failures) i.e., the average time between failures.

MTTR (Mean Time to Repair) i.e., the average time required to remove a defect after it is detected.

To measure the quality of the output of a development phase, the SQA team has to define the metrics. For instance, during the requirements engineering phase, SRS document is written. Then design, implementation, and testing are done. While doing the design or implementation or while carrying out the testing, the SRS document may have to be changed. The number of changes made to the SRS document can be a metric to measure the quality of the requirements engineering process. Similar measures can be worked out for the design, implementation, and testing phases as well.

The SQA team has to define and measure the software metrics at every stage of software development.

NOTE

The product quality metrics are different from process quality metrics. The product quality metrics reflect the quality of the product whereas the process quality metrics reflect how well the process is defined.

1.12.2 Documentation

Many engineers dislike documentation work. However, the SQA team has to ensure that enough documentation is available at each stage of the project. The documents delivered at important milestones of a project are known as Work Products. Some important work products that need to be made available at various stages are:

- Project proposal
- Project agreement
- Project plan document
- Software requirements specification document
- Design document
- Configuration management document
- Test plan
- Quality assurance plan
- User manual
- Source code with enough on-line comments
- Test reports
- Maintenance manual

1.13 Quality Management Systems

When software development is sub-contracted to an organization, the prime contractor needs to ensure that the work is sub-contracted to a reliable organization, which can deliver quality software. So, the prime contractor has to ensure that the subcontractor has a defined quality system. To evaluate the effectiveness of the quality system, external auditing agencies will assess the quality system and certify it. The ISO 9000 standards and Capability Maturity Model Integration (CMMI) are two important Quality Management Systems that have been widely accepted in the software industry.

The management of every software development organization has to decide which quality system has to be implemented. If the organization has already obtained ISO 9000 or CMMI certification, for each project, the quality plan has to be in place based on these standards.

All the quality standards have the same underlying philosophy—to develop the software based on well-defined processes, with the necessary documentation; and ensure that every employee is committed to the quality improvement program. The quality standards should be considered as facilitators to the quality program of the organization rather than a hindrance. The management of every software development organization has to create a culture whereby the team-members work within a well-defined framework to develop quality software by giving thrust to quality at each and every stage of the development process.

The credit for the success of a project goes to the people who worked on the project and not to the processes. Similarly, the failure of a project is attributed to the people and not the processes. So, ultimately it is the people who are responsible for the success or failure of a project—and hence, the SQA team has to view the processes as facilitators for the development.

1.13.1 Quality Standards

Quality is the 'mantra' in the industry. To deliver a product that is the delight of the customer should be the main objective of the project manager, every team member as well as the senior management. To achieve this objective, quality standards come in handy. The management of every organization has to adapt quality standards so that quality is ensured in every product that is delivered. Implementation of quality standards also gives visibility to the organization. In this section, we will study the internationally accepted quality standards for software development.

Software engineering standards play an important role in defining the quality processes. There are nearly 250 software engineering standards developed by major standardization and professional bodies on various aspects—planning, testing, documentation, software metrics, Computer Aided Software Engineering (CASE), tool selection etc. [Pfleeger 1994].

British Standards Institute defines standard as "a technical specification or other document available to the public, drawn up with cooperation and consensus or general approval of all interests affected by it, based on the consolidated results of science, technology and experience, aimed at the promotion of optimum community benefits".

In any standardization process, measures (or metrics) play an important role. However, it is very difficult, in the field of software engineering, to obtain objective measures, and eliminate subjectivity completely. The quantity denoted by one liter of oil is same throughout the world, but the number of lines of code in a program may be different when measured by different organizations. Hence, the software engineering standards should be treated as guidelines for improving the quality of the software rather than a 'standard' that will have universal applicability.

There are international, national, and organizational standards. Most of the organizational standards are derived from national or international standards. For software engineering, ISO 9000 and Capability Maturity Model Integration (CMMI) are the most widely used international standards, which are described briefly in the following sections.

1.13.2 ISO 9000 Series Standards

The latest ISO 9000 series of standards of interest to software development organizations are:

ISO 9000:2000 Quality Management Systems—Fundamentals and vocabulary

ISO 9001:2000 Quality Management Systems—Requirements

ISO 9004:2000 Quality Management System—Guidelines for Performance Improvement

The quality management system to be developed as per ISO 9000 guidelines is used for quality assurance when the supplier has to demonstrate the capability to the customer. The supplier and customer can be internal to the organization (for example, the development team and the marketing team of an organization).

ISO9001:2000 standard gives the requirements to develop a quality management system. A summary of this standard with reference to software development is given next. The standard has 8 clauses.

Clause 1 Scope

The scope of the document is specified in this clause. This document defines the quality management system to deliver a quality product to the customer. This standard is applicable to all the organizations irrespective of the type, size or product/service being provided. Note that ISO 9000 is applicable to a variety of organizations—hotels, hospitals, hardware development organizations, manufacturing organizations, and also software development organizations.

Clause 2. Normative Reference

The references of this document are given in this clause. The important reference document is ISO 9000:2000, which describes the fundamentals and vocabulary.

Clause 3: Terms and definitions

The terms and definitions as specified in ISO 9000:2000 are given in this clause.

Clause 4.1 General requirements: The management must have a well-defined and documented quality management system that defines the processes to be followed to deliver a quality product or service. Using quantitative measures (metrics), the effectiveness of these processes has to be monitored and steps have to be taken for continual improvement of product and process quality. The processes should include both technical and managerial processes.

Clause 4.2 Documentation requirements: The documentation of quality management system includes:

- Quality policy
- Quality manual
- Detailed definition of procedures mentioned in the quality manual
- Quality records

The documentation need not be on paper (hard copy), it can be in computerized form (soft copy).

Clause 4.2.2 Quality manual: The quality manual should describe the processes to be followed for the entire software development life cycle. Alternatively, the quality manual can refer to other documents that give the details of the process definitions.

Clause 4.2.3 Control of documents: As it is likely that the documents related to the processes and projects will be changed periodically, it is necessary to establish a procedure for controlling the documents. Procedures have to be established so that there is clarity on who is the approving authority for a document, who is the authority to modify the documents and who is the authority to distribute the copies and to whom the copies have to be distributed. It is also necessary to establish procedures so that only the latest and relevant documents are made available.

Clause 4.2.4 Control of records: Once the quality management system has been established, it is also necessary to maintain records to give evidence to the external auditing agencies that the quality system is being effectively operational. Documented procedures have to be established to maintain such records.

Clause 5 Management Responsibility

Clause 5.1 Management commitment: The top management must have a written quality policy indicating its commitment to developing quality products and/or providing quality service to the customer. The management has to define measurable quality objectives to meet the customer requirements and communicate the quality objectives to all the employees. Periodic reviews have to be carried out to ensure that the quality objectives are met.

Clause 5.2 Customer focus: The ultimate goal of the management is to satisfy the customer. The management has to ensure that the customer's requirements are understood well and after completion of the project, the customer is satisfied with the product.

Clause 5.3 Quality Policy: Management's commitment is reflected by its quality policy. When you visit an ISO 9000 certified company, the quality policy is displayed at prominent locations. A typical quality policy is as follows:

"ICS is committed to quality products and services for the total satisfaction of the customers. Through continual improvement of processes in all phases of product life cycle, ICS will strive to attain reputation to provide high quality products in the emerging areas of Information Technology. Everyone at ICS will adapt, nurture and uphold the quality processes of the organization."

The quality of the policy has to be signed by the Chief Executive Officer (CEO) of the organization. Every employee of the organization should understand the spirit of the quality policy and commit himself/herself to the quality policy.

5.4 Planning

5.4.1 Quality objectives: Based on the quality policy, the management has to define quality objectives, such as increasing productivity, reducing defects etc. These objectives should be measurable.

5.4.2 Quality Management System planning: To meet the quality objectives, the management has to plan the quality management system by defining the details of the processes in the software development life cycle.

5.5 Responsibility, Authority, and Communication

5.5.1 Responsibility and authority: In many organizations, responsibility and authority are not clearly defined as a result of which the quality suffers. For instance, the project team does not know who is the deciding authority when a customer asks for change in specifications. The quality management system mandates that a clear organization chart is drawn, indicating the reporting structure and the responsibilities and authorities of each individual.

5.5.2 Management Representative: The management should appoint a Management Representative who has the responsibility and authority to implement the quality management system. He/she is the person who reports to the management on the effectiveness of the quality management system and also suggests necessary improvements. The management representative also interfaces with the external agencies such as external auditors.

5.5.3 Internal communication: Lack of proper communication among the teams and between the team members and the management leads to project delays and poor quality software. To avoid such problems, a proper procedure for internal communication should be established so that all the employees are in unison.

5.6 Management Review

5.6.1 General: The management has to periodically (say, every 3 months) review the quality policy, quality objectives and the quality manual to discuss the effectiveness and possible improvements. Records of such reviews have to be maintained.

5.6.2 Review inputs: For management review, the inputs have to be obtained from customers, external auditors, and internal auditors. The inputs can also be in the form of suggestions from the employees.

5.6.3 Review output: After the management review, the output will be action points in the areas of additional resources needed for effective quality management system implementation, process changes to be incorporated, improvements in the products etc.

6. Resource Management

6.1 Provision of resources: The management has to ensure that the resources necessary to implement the quality management system are in place.

6.2 Human resources

6.2.1 General: To deliver a quality product, the employees working on the project should have the competence. By selection of the right people and by imparting the necessary training, the management has to ensure that the people have the necessary competence.

6.2.2 Competence, awareness and training: The management has to ensure that each and every employee has the necessary understating of the quality, development processes and the products. Training has to be imparted based on the requirements of each individual, and the training records have to be maintained.

6.3 Infrastructure: The management has to provide the necessary hardware, software, testing tools and also supporting services such as communication facilities, Internet access etc. so that the employees can carry out their responsibility to meet the quality requirements.

6.4 Work environment: A congenial work environment is a must to deliver quality products and the management has to provide such a work environment.

7. Product Realization

7.1 Planning of product realization: The quality manual gives the overall processes to be followed in the organization. Based on the quality manual, for each product to be developed, a separate project plan has to be prepared. The project plan gives the details of the quality objectives to be met, processes to be followed, documents to be generated and the testing methodologies to be followed and the acceptance test criteria.

7.2 Customer Related Processes

7.2.1 Determination of requirements related to the product: The project team has to obtain the requirements from the customer and document them in the form of an SRS document. This document should give the details of functional and non-functional requirements.

7.2.2 Review of requirements related to the product: The project team has to ensure that the requirements of the customer are well defined, documented and can be implemented. Many times, because of communication gaps, the requirements of the customer will be different from what is written in the SRS document. So, the requirements have to be thoroughly reviewed by the customer and the project team so that there are no gaps between what the customer wants and what the developer understands. There should be a written agreement between the customer and the development organization on the requirements specifications.

7.2.3 Customer communication: The project team should formalize the procedure for communication with the customer; so that changes in the requirements, complaints etc. are handled effectively.

7.3 Design and Development

7.3.1 Design and development planning: The procedures for the design and development should be established which include defining interfaces, identifying inputs and outputs, review process, verification and validation of the design, and controlling the design changes. The sub-processes include development planning, design and implementation, testing and validation, and configuration management.

7.3.2 Design and development inputs: Inputs required for design and development of the product should be identified. These include the SRS document, design documents of other similar projects etc.

7.3.3 Design and development outputs: The outputs of the design and development phase should include the product that meets the requirements, product acceptance criteria, and the user manuals.

7.3.4 Design and development review: The project manager has to periodically review the design and development to ensure that work is progressing in the right direction and the end product will meet all the requirements as specified in the SRS. Any potential problems have to be identified and appropriate action has to be initiated. Records of the reviews have to be maintained.

7.3.5 Design and development verification: The project manager has to carry out the necessary verification of the design and development so that each and every requirement of the SRS is met. A document called Acceptance Test Procedure (ATP) has to be prepared and it should be ensured that the software is tested as per the ATP document.

7.3.6 Design and development validation: The project manager has to do a validation of the design and development to ensure that the project is being implemented as per the plan. Validation has to be completed before the product is delivered to the customer. Records of the validation results have to be maintained.

7.3.7 Control of design and development changes: During the design and development, a number of changes are likely in the SRS document, design document etc. that are already prepared. Whenever a change has to be made to any of the work products, the impact of the change has to be estimated and conscious decision has to be taken on implementing or discarding the change. Records of such changes are to be maintained.

7.4 Purchasing

7.4.1 Purchasing process: The products purchased must conform to the specified requirements. For ensuring this, there should be defined procedures for selection of suppliers and verification of purchased products.

7.4.2 Purchasing information: For purchasing a product, the manager has to specify the product specifications, the quality management system requirements (for example, whether the supplier should have ISO certification) and any other requirements such as installation, warranty, maintenance etc.

7.4.3 Verification of purchased product: At the time of giving the purchasing information itself, the project manager has to specify the acceptance test criteria for the proposed product and when the supplier gives the product, the verification has to be done as per this procedure.

7.5 Production and Service Operations

7.5.1 Control of production and service provision: Once the product is developed, it has to be delivered to the customers. If the product has to be delivered to multiple customers (as in the case of a generic product), proper planning has to be done to make multiple copies, installation, and later maintenance of the product. If any special equipment is required for production and maintenance, that also needs to be planned.

7.5.2 Validation of processes for production and service provision: In cases when the verification is not possible unless the product is installed in the customer premises, a process has to be established to obtain the feedback on the performance of the product from the customer and how the defects can be removed.

7.5.3 Identification and traceability: During all stages of production, delivery and installation, the product should be identified and traceable. For hardware products, a unique serial number is given. For multiple copies of the same software, a unique identification for each copy can also be given.

7.5.4 Customer property: For execution of some projects, the customer may give some of his property to the developer. For instance, the customer may give the required hardware to develop a device driver. In such cases, the development organization has to take proper care of the customer's property and if the property is lost or becomes unusable, it has to be reported to the customer.

In some cases, such as in the case of software maintenance projects, the customer may give the source code to be maintained. The source code is the intellectual property of the customer and proper care has to be taken to ensure that the intellectual property rights of the customer are not violated.

7.5.5 Preservation of the product: A process has to be defined for identification of the product, packaging, storage, and protection.

7.6 Control of monitoring and measuring devices: To ensure that the product meets the requirements, test and measuring instruments may be used such as oscilloscopes, protocol analyzers etc. It is necessary to ensure that these instruments are working well. Necessary procedures have to be established for this such as periodic calibration of the test equipment, to identify when the next calibration is due etc. If software test tools are used, it is necessary to ensure that these tools are functioning properly before using them to test the software.

8. Measurement, Analysis and Improvement

8.1 General: As discussed earlier, metrics play an important role in process improvement. Management has to define metrics for product quality and process quality and use these metrics to check on the process effectiveness and improvement. For instance, employee productivity is one metric. If the turnover per employee is rising steadily, this is a good indication that the organization is improving.

8.2 Monitoring and Measurement

8.2.1 Customer satisfaction: After all, customer satisfaction is the most important objective for any organization. The management has to define the metrics to measure the customer satisfaction. For instance, the number of complaints received from the customer on a product in a given period is one such metric.

8.2.2 Internal audit: An internal audit team has to be formed which audits the complete quality management system for its proper implementation across the organization. Necessary training has to be provided to the internal audit team on the auditing process. The auditors should not audit their own work. Based on the internal audit, the reports have to be generated which indicate the non-conformity, and follow up action is taken to correct the non-conformities. These internal audits have to be held at regular intervals, say every three months. Internal auditors should undergo a training program on the auditing process.

8.2.3 Monitoring and measurement of processes: Each process defined in the quality management system has to be monitored and its effectiveness is measured using metrics. For instance, the number of design changes is a metric to measure the design process. If the number is high, then the design process has to be refined to reduce the number of design changes.

8.2.4 Monitoring and measurement of product: For each product, metrics have to be defined such as number of non-conformities etc. so that this information can be analyzed to study the effectiveness of the product's processes.

8.3 Control of non-conforming product: If a product is found to be non-conforming to the requirements, appropriate action is to be taken to ensure that it is not delivered to the customer. If the non-conformity is known after delivery, it has to be reported to the customer. Records of non-conformities have to be maintained.

8.4 Analysis of data: The management has to collect data to study the effectiveness of the quality management system. This data can be from the customers, suppliers, process metrics, product metrics etc.

8.5 Improvement

8.1 Continual improvement: The management should aim at continually improving the organization's performance. To achieve this, the quality management system has to be continually improved based on the inputs such as customer feedback, external audit reports, internal audit reports, suppliers' feedback, product metrics, and process metrics. Quality policy, quality objectives, and quality manual need to be regularly reviewed and improved to achieve overall performance improvement.

8.5.2 Corrective action: When a product has non-conformities, the corrective action is taken to remove the defects. The cause for non-conformity has to be probed into and steps are taken to ensure that such causes do not recur. Records are maintained for the corrective actions taken.

8.5.3 Preventive action: Potential non-conformities are identified and preventive action is taken. Records of corrective actions serve as good inputs to take preventive actions. Records of preventive actions taken are maintained.

Time Table for ISO 9000 Certification

Software organizations that would like to obtain ISO 9001:2000 certification have to prepare a quality manual which gives the details of the development processes, prepare a quality plan for each project being executed, train all the employees on the processes, carry out internal audit and then make arrangements for auditing by the ISO 9000 certification bodies. A timetable for obtaining this certification is given next:

Month 1 to 3	Allocation of funds for quality certification
	All employees trained on quality processes
	Process documentation
Month 4	Hire certified quality auditor
	Audit existing process and recommendations
Months 5-6	Final quality manual preparation and audit the processes
Month 7	Send quality manual to certification body

Month 8   Review meetings on suggestions of the certification body
                Make changes as per recommendations
Month 9   Final on-site visit by the audit team and certification
        This is only an indicative timetable. Organizations can certainly do a faster job.

1.13.3 Capability Maturity Model Integration for Software Engineering (SW-CMMI)

The vision of Watts Humphrey, Capability Maturity Model (CMM) was developed to assess the capabilities of organizations in taking up large development projects of Department of Defense, USA. CMM addresses the process improvement in software development organizations. CMM identifies a set of guidelines that need to be implemented for producing quality software. The CMM framework has been accepted internationally as a very comprehensive framework for quality processes implementation.

Software capability is defined as "range of expected results that can be achieved by following a software process". The actual performance achieved by following these processes is known as Software Process Performance. "The extent to which a process is explicitly defined, managed, measured, controlled and effective" is defined as Software Process Maturity [SEI CMU 1994].

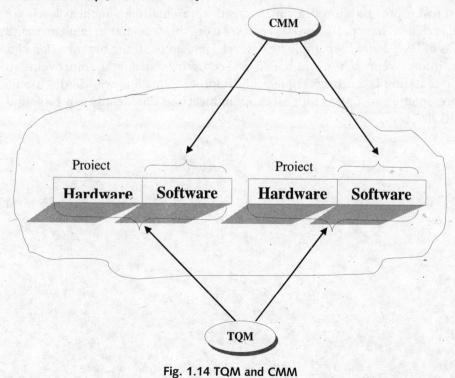

Fig. 1.14 TQM and CMM

In organizations that develop both hardware and software, Total Quality Management (TQM) has to be followed. As shown in Fig. 1.14, CMM addresses the management of quality of software aspects of the project i.e., CMM is confined to software quality management of the organization whereas TQM addresses both hardware and software quality management.

Software Engineering Institute has been developing Capability Maturity Models, since 1991, for a number of disciplines such as system engineering, software engineering, software acquisition, people management etc. A number of international standards bodies such as ISO also developed models/standards for assessing the quality systems of organizations. Capability Maturity Model Integration (CMMI) for Software Engineering is the result of SEI's efforts to develop an integrated improvement framework for the following standards for quality system management:

CMM for Software (SW-CMM) version 2.0 draft C

Electronic Industries Alliance Interim Standard (EIA/IS) 731

Integrated Product Development Capability Maturity Model (IPD-CMM) v0.98

CMMI framework is compatible with International Organization for Standardization/International Electro-technical Commission (ISO/IEC) 15504 Technical report for software process assessment.

In CMMI framework, there are two representations: staged and continuous. An organization can choose either staged representation or continuous representation for its software process improvement. In staged representation, 5 maturity levels are defined and each level has specific process areas. An organization has to implement the process areas of level 2 and then graduate to level 3 and so on. If the organization chooses the continuous representation, it can select its own order of improvement. Staged representation is a proven sequence of improvements and we will discuss the staged representation of CMMI for software engineering. The details can be found in [SEI CMU 2002].

Levels of Software Process Maturity

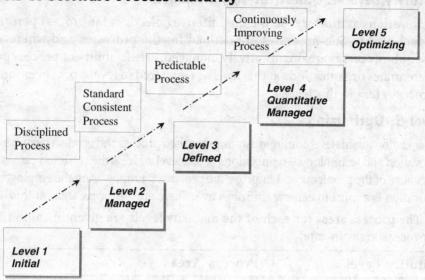

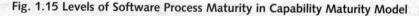

Fig. 1.15 Levels of Software Process Maturity in Capability Maturity Model

Based on the software process maturity, an organization can be at one of the 5 levels. The levels are shown in Fig. 1.15.

Maturity Level 1: Initial

Organizations at level 1 do not have any defined process. Such organizations are characterized by fire fighting, i.e., because of lack of clearly defined processes, everything is done at the last minute resulting in chaos. However, organizations at this level may be able to produce good results, mainly due to the 'heroics' of one or more people in the organization. Success solely is dependent on one or few highly competent people and if they quit the organization, the organization may collapse.

Maturity Level 2: Managed

Organizations at this level follow a defined process for execution of each project. The requirements are managed as per a defined process. Every project is planned and executed as per that plan. Hence a systematic procedure is followed to execute projects. Seven process areas are defined at this level and an organization is assessed as level 2 organization if it implements all these 7 process areas.

Maturity Level 3: Defined

Organizations at this level have a set of process definitions across the organization and processes related to a particular project are derived from the organization-wide processes. As compared to level 2 organizations, processes are more clearly defined and efforts are made to continuously improve the process definitions. Processes are consistent across the organization. Quantitative measures are used to find the effectiveness of the processes. There are 11 process areas at this level.

Maturity Level 4: Quantitatively Managed

Organizations at this level define quantitative objectives for process performance and product quality. Sub-processes are defined for the processes and wherever possible, these sub-processes are quantitatively managed. Predictability of process performance differentiates organizations at this level as compared to level 3 organizations. There are 2 process areas in this level.

Level 5: Optimizing

Organizations at this level continuously improve their process and product performance through innovation and technology. Organizations at this level address the common causes and find the root cause of the problems and improve the processes. Empowering the employees to bring in innovation is a must to achieve this objective. There are 2 process areas at this level.

The process areas for each of the maturity levels are given in Table 1.3. There are 22 process areas in total.

Maturity Level	Process Areas
1: Initial	
2: Managed	Requirements Management Project Planning Project Monitoring and Control Supplier Agreement and Management Measurement and Analysis Process and Product Quality Assurance Configuration Management
3: Defined	Requirements Development Technical Solution Product Integration Verification Validation Organizational Process Focus Organizational Process Definition Organizational Training Integrated Project Management Risk Management Decision Analysis and Resolution
4: Quantitatively Managed	Organizational Process Performance Quantitative Project Management
5: Optimizing	Organizational Innovation and Deployment Causal Analysis and Resolution

Table 1.3 CMMI Maturity Levels and Process Areas

Each of the process areas is described briefly in the following sub-sections.

Level 2 Process Areas

There are 7 process areas at this level.

Requirements Management

This process area addresses the issue of obtaining the requirements from the customer. Based on the customer requirements, the product requirements and product component (such as database) requirements are decided. If there are any inconsistencies in the requirements, they are identified and resolved. Any changes to the requirements are also managed using a defined process. Commitment is obtained from the engineers that the requirements can be met. Inconsistencies in project plan and work products are also identified.

Project Planning

This process area addresses the planning of the project—a very detailed project plan is prepared which contains all the details such as the estimates of time, effort and budget, identification of risk items and risk analysis, work products to be generated during the execution of the project, resources and training requirements etc. The project plan document is periodically reviewed and updated.

Project Monitoring and Control

This process area is to ensure that monitoring the project progress is done as per a defined process. Reviews are conducted to ensure that the plan is being followed and corrective action is taken if required. Risks, commitments, and project plan are reviewed and monitored periodically and appropriate corrective actions are taken in a timely manner.

Supplier Agreement and Management

When the product development involves purchase of third party software such as testing tools, RDBMS etc., a process is defined to identify the product components, select suppliers and evaluate the suppliers and for acceptance testing of the third party software. This process is followed to obtain the software components and integrate them into the product.

Measurement and Analysis

The management needs to be provided quantitative measures or metrics to monitor the effectiveness of a process or product. This process addresses this issue: identify metrics to be used, gather data, and measure the metrics and use the metrics for making decisions and taking corrective actions. Initially, the metrics are obtained at project level and then at organization level.

Process and Product Quality Assurance

This process area is to objectively evaluate the process and product quality. Non-compliance to the process or product quality is reported to the management and feedback is given to the development team. To objectively evaluate the quality, it is a general practice to have a separate quality assurance team though it is not mandatory.

Configuration Management

This process addresses the issue of ensuring that changes made to various work products are done according to a specific procedure i.e., to control changes.

Level 3 Process Areas

There are 11 process areas at this level.

Requirements Development

This process focuses on ensuring that the requirements of the software to be developed are captured, documented and validated. As a part of this process, the developer has to interact with the customer and obtain the customer requirements, identify the product requirements and product-component requirements and then validate the requirements. The product components are off-the-shelf software packages such as RDBMS, test tools etc. The customer may give the requirements in non-technical terms, these requirements need to be converted into technical documentation.

Technical Solution

Based on the requirements, the product is developed. The design, detailed design and implementation of the solution are the sub-processes of this process. To study the design alternatives, carry out a design and detailed design, obtain the off-the-shelf products if necessary, coding and unit testing, producing the necessary work products including user documentation form a part of this process.

Product Integration

The product is developed by integration of the different product components. By using formal testing methods, it is ensured that the product works correctly and it is delivered to the customer. So, the objective of this process is to integrate the verified product components, validate the product and to deliver the product to the customer along with all the necessary documentation.

Verification

Verification is the process to ensure that the work products meet their specifications. This is done throughout the life cycle of the project. After the product development is complete, testing is done to verify whether the product meets the customer requirements, product requirements, and product component requirements. Peer reviews play an important role in this process. If requirements are not met, corrective action is identified and implemented.

Validation

Validation is the process to test whether the product meets the customer requirements in the intended environment. In validation, customer/end users of the software are involved.

Organizational Process Focus

The objective of this process is to plan and implement an organization-wide process improvement program. Process performance objectives are defined such as productivity, defect removal rates and development time; areas for improvement are identified.

Organizational Process Definition

The existing processes being followed in the organization, which can be used across the organization, are documented. These are known as process assets. An asset library is maintained which is a collection of all the process related documents such as document formats, guidelines, checklists, life cycle models to be followed etc. How the overall process definition can be tailored for different projects is also documented. A measurement repository is also maintained which gives the historical data such as estimates and actual values of project duration, effort, defects removed etc.

Organizational Training

To ensure that the right people are assigned the right projects, training is of paramount importance. The management identifies the training needs of the people and trains them and also measures the effectiveness of the training program. The records of training are maintained.

Integrated Project Management

Based on the process definitions of the organization, the processes required for the specific project on hand are identified. A defined process is followed for the project management based on the processes defined for the organization. Project planning is carried out based on the process assets and the measurement repository. The project also should contribute to the process assets of the organization. Proper interface to the customer is done to resolve issues.

Risk Management

Risk management is an important process to prevent potential problems so that achieving the objectives is not jeopardized. It is a continuous activity throughout the project execution. A risk strategy is defined, risks are identified and analyzed, and plan to overcome the risks is implemented. For example, if some people are likely to leave in the middle of the project, it is a big risk item. The management has to work out how to overcome such a risk.

Decision Analysis and Resolution

In the course of project execution, alternative solutions may be available such as develop versus buy, which RDBMS to use, to take people on contract basis or on permanent basis, which life cycle development model to use etc. This process is to analyze the alternatives based on certain criteria using an evaluation process to arrive at the decision. The sub-processes are: evaluate alternatives, establish guidelines for decision analysis, establish evaluation criteria, identify alternative solutions and select a solution.

Level 4 Process Areas

Level 4 process areas focus on managing the processes and product development using metrics. For implementing the processes defined at this level, the people involved should be trained in statistical analysis and should have access to statistical analysis packages.

Organizational Process Performance

The objective of this process is to quantify the effectiveness of various processes defined for the development of a software product. Metrics for process quality and product quality are defined and data for the earlier projects are collected which can be used as the basis for predicting the expected results of the process performance for the future projects. As it may not be possible to quantify the effectiveness of all the sub-processes, only relevant sub-processes are selected for measuring the process performance. For instance, consider software project effort estimation process. If historical data is available for a number of projects, based on this data, a model can be developed which can be used for estimation of the future projects. However, if this model was developed for say, database application software, you cannot use the model for embedded software development! So, the estimation process needs to be improved to take care of the application domain as well.

Quantitative Project Management

At the start of a project, the project team will have some performance objectives for product performance and process performance. The objective of this process is to quantitatively manage the process to achieve product/process performance objectives. The manager should be able to predict that the project will meet the performance objectives using statistical techniques—i.e., the project should be statistically managed. For example, the project manager should be able to predict the percentage of time required for design, coding and testing for the project. This again can be done if models are developed based on the data of the earlier projects. The project manager has to set performance objectives, use the statistical models to predict the performance for the present project and check whether these predictions are correct or not by actually measuring the performance. Since it may not be possible to quantitatively manage all the processes, only some processes are selected for this activity.

Level 5 Process Areas

There are two process areas at this level.

Organizational Innovation and Deployment

The goal of the management is not just to put a quality system in place and to follow it verbatim, but to continuously improve the processes so that the business objectives are met. This process area addresses this continuous improvement: to improve product quality, process quality, productivity and customer satisfaction using innovation and new technologies. To achieve this objective, the management should actively involve all the employees and even customers to obtain suggestions and inputs for improvement. The innovation can be in technical aspects or managerial aspects.

Improvements can be in any of the phases of software development—planning, choosing the development life cycle models, using new technologies and tools, reuse strategies, new management techniques etc. Each suggestion for improvement has to be analyzed for cost, effort, time and cost-benefit analysis has to be carried out. A pilot study has to be carried out to ensure that the suggestion is likely to have a positive impact. The potential barriers to implement the suggestion also need to be studied—for instance, when a new technology is introduced, there may be opposition from some people who would resist change. Using objective measures, the impact of the suggestion has to be found out and if the suggestion is proved useful, it has to be implemented across the organization.

Causal Analysis and Resolution

The essence of this process is 'learn from history'. Based on the defects reported by the customers, quality assurance team members, or even the designers, the root cause of the defects has to be found out and recurrence of same or similar defects has to be prevented. This process helps in analyzing the cause of the defect and taking preventive measures so that the same defect does not recur in future. After all, prevention is better than cure.

Importance of CMMI

CMMI is the result of a combined effort of the industry, research and academic community. This model is compatible with other international standards and hence an organization that is assessed for CMMI can also get assessed for ISO 9000. CMMI is now finding wide acceptance with software development organizations across the world. Even if an organization does not have the resources to obtain the CMMI certification, the management can follow the guidelines of the framework to improve their process performance, product quality and employee productivity.

Software Engineering Institute developed the Personal Software Process (PSP) which defines the processes to be followed by individuals. The philosophy of PSP is simple: plan your work, track your work and analyze your work so that you will continuously improve yourself.

1.14 PROCESS CHANGE MANAGEMENT

A quality conscious organization must realize that the process defined for software development is not a static document that cannot be modified. Continuous process improvement—whereby the organization will improve its profitability, the individuals will improve their productivity, new technologies can be inducted into the organization—is a must for every vibrant organization.

The quality models and standards, ISO 9000 or CMMI, are also aimed at a continuously improving organization's capabilities. To continuously improve, one has to continuously learn. Such learning organizations will grow with changing times.

To change the process for betterment, the project manager has to define a process for process change management. Changes to the defined process should not be done on ad hoc basis, but using formal procedures. For instance, one engineer may come up with an idea of a new way of project estimation. He may claim that it is more accurate than the existing method. To prove the effectiveness of the new model, the model has to be studied along with the old model for at least a few projects and once the effectiveness is ascertained, then it can be introduced for all the other projects. Such a systematic way of process change management would help in ensuring that no errors are introduced in the process.

The process change has to be monitored and reviewed by the senior management. Employees should be encouraged and rewards can be introduced for suggestions on process change. Procedure for handling process change should be clearly defined:

1. Submission of proposal as to why the change is proposed—based on customer feedback, defect report analysis, benchmarking results, external auditor remarks or internal QA recommendations.

2. Evaluation of each proposal and documentation.

3. Decision on the priority of the proposal.

4. Implementation plan including responsibility and time frame.

5. Tracking the status of each proposal.

1.14.1 Quality Process Implementation Issues

The essence of ISO 9000 series standards and the CMMI framework is the same. Define a process, implement it and periodically review the process to check its effectiveness and based on the review of the results, improve the process. As the software development process is a highly complex activity, the process is divided into various sub-activities and each sub-activity (call it clause or Process Area, it does not matter), follow a defined methodology. As it is humanly not possible or advisable to rely on our memories all the time, we should document all these process definitions.

Unfortunately, in some organizations, management gives scope for 'process bureaucrats'. These guys insist on following the process documents blindly without any concern for the process improvement.

In some organizations that achieved CMMI Level 4 and 5, many employees suddenly become unhappy and they feel that the process is being given importance and not the people. Judy Bamberger says, "CMM is one of the most misunderstood pieces of technical literature in existence" [Bamberger 1997]. A culture needs to be developed whereby the engineers and managers get the 'essence' of CMM rather than a blind following of the process standards.

Large organizations working on large projects can afford to implement the CMMI or ISO 9000 standards though it results in lot of overheads. Certainly, many small organizations cannot afford nor do they want to obtain certification due to lack of resources. Even then, these organizations will be benefited by adapting these standards and if required suitably modifying them.

The project manager has to realize the importance of the quality standards and impress upon the team members the importance of following these standards. Standards implementation should be a culture rather than an add-on to the development.

1.14.2 Implementing Quality Standards in Small Organizations

The quality standards such as CMMI and ISO 9000 have been formulated to bring in process orientation for large-scale projects, executed by large organizations. The CMM framework, in particular, has been developed to assess the capabilities of subcontractors for large defense projects. To implement these quality standards, there will be lot of overhead. Additional people are required for the process engineering group, SQA group etc. Lot of documentation is involved for developing and maintaining organization-wide processes, and lot of administrative work is involved in maintaining the library for process documentation, configuration management etc. Most of the small organizations cannot afford this overhead as it eats away the profit margin. Small organizations working on small development projects, can avoid this overhead if they follow a customized software engineering methodology. In small organizations, everyone does everything—even senior level persons may be involved in coding. Small organizations work on high technology products and hence innovation and creativity are the key elements. Following standards with a bureaucratic approach hinders the creativity. Hence, small organizations need to tailor the quality standards for their specific needs [Computer 1999].

For working on small projects having a high technology orientation, the constitution of the project team is crucial. To reduce overheads, the project team will not be linked to a separate quality team or process team. The development team members themselves need to act as quality engineers and process engineers.

To summarize, quality standards provide the necessary framework for delivering quality software. Every organization, big or small, needs to understand the essence of these quality standards and follow them. Commitment of the management and also each and every employee to the quality of the product is a must.

Summary

In this chapter, software quality assurance is discussed in detail. The important points are summarized below:

- A project can be termed as successful when quality software is delivered to the customer within the time and the development is completed within the stipulated budget, without straining the human relations amongst the development team and between the client and the developers.

- The various characteristics that reflect the quality of a software product are depicted in the quality triangle. These characteristics are broadly divided into operational characteristics, revision characteristics, and transition characteristics.

- To deliver quality software, a systematic procedure has to be followed. Software engineering addresses this systematic procedure.

- Software engineering addresses the technical, managerial and administrative issues involved in software development.

- Software development can be broadly divided into the following phases: requirements engineering, design, implementation, testing and maintenance.

- Based on the type of project, one of the following software life cycle development models has to be chosen: waterfall model, prototyping model, evolutionary development model, spiral model or synchronize-and-stabilize model.

- ISO 9000 and CMMI address the quality management system to be followed in organizations to deliver quality software. The quality management system addresses the processes to be followed in development.

2 Software Testing Process

In this chapter

- Appreciate the importance and the details of the testing process
- Learn the various types of testing to be carried out on a software product
- Understand the different levels of testing
- Learn how to write a test plan and generate test cases
- Grasp the concept of software reliability
- Appreciate the difficulties involved in manual testing of software

In spite of the fact that software testing is a highly complex and time consuming activity, in most software projects, testing is not given the necessary attention. Statistics reveal that the nearly 30-40% of the effort goes into testing—irrespective of the type of project, whereas hardly any time is allocated for testing.

Software testing is a highly complex activity—it is even difficult to say when testing is complete. In addition to functional testing of the product in the laboratory, the software has to undergo many other types of testing for performance, reliability, usability, portability, stress etc., depending on the type of product and the requirements.

In this chapter, we will study the intricacies of software testing, the methodologies used in testing and the criteria for completion of testing. Based on these aspects, a rigorous testing process is developed to ensure that a high quality product is delivered to the customer and maintenance costs are reduced to the minimum.

2.1 Psychology of Testing

The psychology of the persons carrying out the testing will have an impact on the testing process [Meyer 1979]. Consider the following definition of testing:

"Testing is the process to prove that the software works correctly".

This definition sounds very good, but note that this is not a good definition of testing process. If the person who has developed the software carries out the testing, he/she will try to use this definition. This is the typical psychology of testing. The person who developed the software will only try to show that the software works correctly. So, he will give only those inputs for which correct results are obtained, or press only those keys by which the software does not crash. Recall your college days when you had to show your program to the professor in the lab exam. When your professor tries to give some input, you will quickly grab the keyboard and give the input yourself—suddenly your respect for your professor goes up! You know very well, for what inputs the program works and so you try to give only those inputs. If the professor gives some other input, your program will crash and you will lose your marks! Consciously, you are following this definition of testing. It is OK for your lab exam, but certainly such a psychology is not acceptable when your software has to work in a commercial environment. But then surprisingly, even practicing engineers try to use this definition while testing their software.

Now, consider the following definition:

"Testing is the process to prove that the software does not work".

Strictly, if the aim of the test engineer is to prove that the software does not work, then the testing process can be considered good. This type of psychology towards testing would bring out most of the defects. In fact, the SQA team and even the user/client teams try to use this definition while carrying out software testing. If your software performs well, then you can say that the software is very reliable.

When this definition is used, we encounter a practical difficulty—after how many days of testing one can say "yes, the software works"? If no bugs are found after say one week of testing, it does not mean that the software has no bugs at all. Many operating systems and commercial software packages which we use would not have been released at all into the market had this approach been followed.

So, a realistic definition of testing is

"Testing is the process to detect the defects and minimize the risk associated with the residual defects".

Once the software product has reached a mature stage of development, you start testing. Keep track of the number of bugs being detected and keep correcting the software. After a few days or weeks of testing, you come to the conclusion that the software is "good enough" to be released into the market i.e., there may be still some bugs undetected, but the risk associated with the residual defects is not very high. In such a case, you take a decision to release the software to the customer or into the market.

The objective of testing is to uncover as many bugs as possible. The testing has to be done without any emotional attachment to the software. If someone points out the bugs, it is only to improve the quality of the software rather than to find fault with you.

2.2 Verification and Validation

While doing the testing, the two terms verification and validation have to be differentiated. Barry Boehm defines these terms based on the answer to the following questions:

Verification: are we building the product right?

Validation: are we building the right product?

Validation is to check whether the software meets the customer expectations. Verification is to check whether the software conforms to specifications. Verification is done by the development team to ensure that the software is as per the specifications in the SRS document. Validation is carried out with the involvement of the client.

 Validation of the software is done to ensure that the software meets the requirements of the customer. Verification of the software is done to ensure that the software meets the specifications. Note that the customer/end users are involved in validation of the software. It is also important to differentiate between end users and client/customer. For example, if you are developing a library management system, the librarian is the client and the persons who issue the books, collect fines etc. are the end users.

2.3 Testing Team and Development Team

As discussed in the section on psychology of testing, the development team tries to prove that the software works correctly. To overcome the difficulty, in many organizations, the development team will be different from the testing team. This would ensure that the testing is done without any bias and maximum possible defects are found before the release of the software.

Because of the complexity of the testing, the test team must have sufficient manpower. In Microsoft Corporation, the ratio of development engineers to test engineers is 1:1. In NASA Goddard Space Flight Center, the ratio is 1:7 i.e., for every development engineer, there will be 7 test engineers. Hence, depending on the complexity of the project and criticality of the application, test team size will be different.

Large organizations can afford to have dedicated test teams for each project. However, in small organizations, it is very difficult to have such dedicated teams. Even then, the project manager has to make the software tested by people other than the developers. One possibility is to make another development team test the software. Alternatively, test engineers can be recruited on a part-time basis or on a limited time contract.

The test reports generated by the test team have to be looked into impartially by the project manager—the aim of the project manager is to ensure that the quality product is delivered and not to point the finger at the person whose module did malfunction.

Even if there is no separate QA/Testing team in your organization, it is desirable that the software is tested by people other than the developers. This will improve the quality of the software substantially.

2.4 Cost of Quality

The objective of every organization and every employee should be to deliver quality software. But then, quality does not come free. This cost of quality will have three important components [Humphrey 1997]:

Failure cost: Failure cost is the cost of fixing the bugs. At the time of releasing the software to the customer, if the software has many bugs, then you need to spend lot of money on the maintenance of the software. This is the failure cost. Your objective should be to reduce the failure cost to the maximum possible extent.

Appraisal cost: Appraisal cost is the cost of assessing whether the software has any bugs. This cost is the cost incurred on testing the software before releasing it to the customer. To reduce failure cost, you may increase the appraisal cost, but there is a limit to the amount of testing to be done.

Prevention cost: Prevention cost is the cost of modifying the process to avoid bugs. The project manager has to give a lot of thrust to the process so that the quality is built into the product in every stage of development. For instance, you may realize that the customer is reporting many bugs in the software. Instead of focusing only on removing the bugs or just increasing the effort on testing the product, a better option would be to find out the root cause and modify the process—the project manager can study whether introducing the software testing tools will help in better quality product. If so, the cost of the testing tools, the cost of training the engineers on these tools etc. will be the prevention cost.

2.5 Characteristics of Test Engineers

Many young software engineers think that testing is not a creative job. Contrary to this popular belief, testing is a very creative and challenging work. The test engineers need to understand the application well, study the software functionality in detail to find out where the bugs are likely to occur, study the code to ensure that each and every line of code is tested, create test cases in such a way that testing is done rigorously to uncover the hidden bugs and also ensure that the software is usable and reliable. All this has to be done very fast—testing engineers are given very less time in the whole life cycle of product development!

To take up testing of a software product, the test engineer needs to do the following:

- Understand the application domain: The software may be a Client/Server based database management system, or a telecom software, or data communication software, or embedded software, or process control software, a web site and so on. In your career as a test engineer, you may have to test software of various application domains. Before starting the testing, you need to understand the application, from an end-user point of view. You need to be a very fast learner of the application domain.

■ Learn about the development environment: Based on the application and the end user needs, the development environment varies—the operating system may be windows or Unix or Linux or Solaris; the programming language may be C, C++ or Java; some special tools would have been used to develop the software such as database engines, cross-compilers etc. You need to have flair to work on different development environments.

■ Learn how to use the application: The test engineer has to assume that he/she is the end user and run the application to get a feel of how the software works. Only then, he will be in a position to generate the test cases and also create automated test procedures.

■ Study the source code: If the test engineer is asked to validate the source code also, he needs to study the source code based on which the test case generation has to be done.

■ Study the requirements specifications document: The SRS document gives the functional, performance and reliability requirements of the software. The software has to be tested for all these requirements. You need to be "eagle-eyed" and look for detail while studying the specifications and check whether each requirement can be tested or not. If the SRS document says "the transaction response should be very fast"—it does not mean anything! You need to tell the person who wrote the specifications that the response time should be indicated, say 10 seconds. Then only you can test this performance requirement. Remember, software metrics are very important.

■ Study the acceptance test procedure: The ATP document gives the test plan based on which the user will validate the software. The test engineers need to carry out the testing as per the ATP document. The ATP document has to be prepared by the development team and the testing team in association with the customer representative.

The test engineers need to have an eye for the details, in other words, they need to be eagle-eyed. But then, they need to offer constructive criticism to improve the quality of the software rather than finding fault with the developers.

NOTE

2.6 Why Testing is Difficult?

Consider a simple example: to test a program which takes three numbers (for three sides of a triangle) as input and checks whether the sides form a triangle or not [Meyer 1979]. How do we test the program? We have to give different combinations of inputs (3 numbers) and check whether the program is working correctly. We need to give correct inputs (numbers which form a triangle) and wrong inputs (numbers which do not form a triangle) and ensure that the output is as expected. To give the correct numbers again, the numbers can be integers, floating point numbers or a combination of both. We also need to give characters and check the program (if you give single characters, it gives interesting output!). We need to give small integers (say, 10,12,3) and also big integers (568888, 9999999 etc). We need to give some inputs that have one or two 0's, and all zeros and check how the program is functioning. So, to carry out an exhaustive testing of such a simple problem, the input data to be given will be enormous. It takes nearly 2 hours to give all possible combinations and make sure that this program is ok!

Testing is difficult because:

- We need to test the software for both right and wrong inputs and check the functionality as well as the performance parameters.

- We need to give the inputs in such a way that each and every line of the code is tested.

- We need to give inputs randomly and check that the software never fails.

- We need to test the software as though a normal user is using it and check whether the necessary error messages, help etc. are provided.

- We need to test the software by simulating the actual environment. For example, if a database application has to be accessed by 100 users simultaneously, it is not enough if you test the software for 2 or 10 users and declare that the software is working fine.

- In many cases, it is not possible to test the software in actual environment. For example, how do you test the software used in a satellite launch vehicle or a missile? You need to do the entire testing only in a simulation environment.

As the complexity of the software increases, the time taken to do such exhaustive testing becomes enormous and exhaustive testing becomes humanly impossible.

To summarize, testing is difficult! To carry out the testing in a limited time with limited effort and resources, and try to bring out all the possible hidden defects is a challenging and intelligent task.

2.7 Levels of Testing

During the design stage, the software is divided into modules and each module is divided into units. This divide-and-conquer strategy is to make life simple (remember the old riddle: how do you eat an elephant? One bite at a time!).

Similarly, while testing, it is no good if one combines all the units into modules and all the modules into the system and then starts testing the entire system. A practical approach is to divide the testing process into different levels. To start with, each unit has to be tested separately, and then the modules have to be built from the units and the modules are tested. Then the modules are combined together and the system is built and tested.

As shown in Fig. 2.1, each level of testing is for testing a specific entity. Unit testing is done to test the source code. Integration testing is done to test the design. System testing is done to test the SRS. And, finally, the acceptance testing is done to test the client/user requirements.

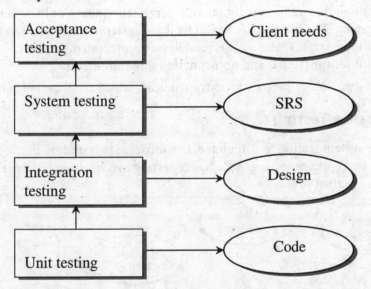

Fig. 2.1 Levels of testing

2.7.1 Unit Testing

A unit is the smallest entity in the software. Every unit has to be tested separately to check whether it is as per the specifications. As it is not possible to test a unit individually, additional piece of code may need to be written to test the units. Unit testing is normally done by the development engineers themselves.

2.7.2 Module Testing

A module is an independent entity in the software. The tested units are integrated into a module and each module is tested separately for the specifications.

For instance, if the software is a database management system, the modules can be database (back-end) and the user interface (front-end). The database can be tested separately using the Structured Query Language (SQL) commands to check correct data retrieval. However, validation of the front-end (forms) requires a database. So, after testing the back-end module, the front-end can be tested, after integration.

After completion of testing a module, a module-level test report has to be prepared. Once every module is working as per requirements, the next phase of testing will start i.e., integration and system testing.

2.7.3 Integration and System Testing

After the modules are tested, the modules can be integrated together. It is very difficult to integrate all the modules together and start testing, as it would be very difficult to do the debugging. The integration has to be done systematically by incremental building and testing in steps. Once all the modules are integrated together, system testing is carried out for functional and non-functional requirements.

For system testing, there are various approaches, which are discussed in the next section.

2.7.4 Acceptance Testing

After the system testing is completed, the software is tested by the client/user. This is known as acceptance testing. Acceptance testing can be done either at the developer's premises or client premises.

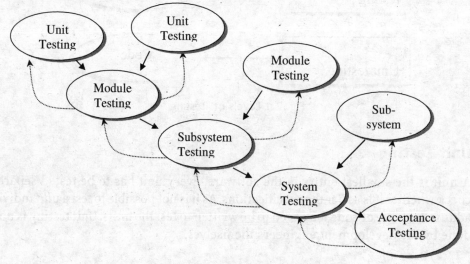

Fig. 2.2 Stages of Testing

The various stages of testing are shown in Fig. 2.2. Fig. 2.3 describes pictorially the complete testing process as discussed in this section.

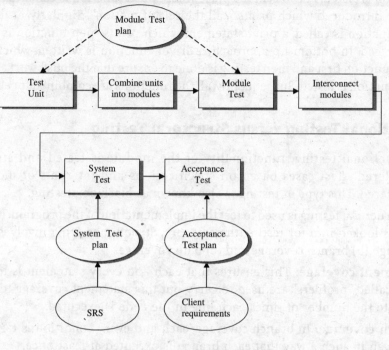

Fig. 2.3   Testing Process

2.8 Testing Approaches

In a large software project, it is impractical to integrate all the modules in one shot and start testing the software as a whole. The system has to be built in stages and the product has to be built incrementally carrying out testing on each incremented software. Such a systematic approach helps in easier debugging. The testing approaches discussed in this section help in achieving this objective.

2.8.1 Top-down Approach versus Bottom-up Approach

Top-down approach: In this approach, testing is done from top of hierarchy. Dummy routines called studs that simulate a module are introduced.

Bottom-up approach: In this approach, testing is done from bottom of hierarchy. Dummy routines called drivers are introduced that invoke the module.

Consider testing the software that implements a stack. The program contains a main function and functions to push and pop. In top-down approach, first the main function is tested. For this, in the place where push function is called, a print statement can be introduced which prints "call the push function". Similarly, at the point where pop function is called, a print statement which prints "pop function is called" can be introduced. In bottom-up approach, a driver function is written, which just calls the push function first and then testing is done to ensure that the push works well. Similarly, pop function is tested. Subsequently, all the functions are combined together and tested.

2.8.2 Functional Testing versus Structural Testing

In functional testing, functionality of the module is tested and structure is not considered. Test cases based on specifications and internals of modules are not considered. This type of testing is also known as black box testing.

Structural testing is used to test the implementation of the program. Here, the source code is looked into for testing the software. Structural testing involves (a) statement coverage (b) branch coverage and (c) path coverage.

Statement coverage: This ensures that each and every statement is tested. Software tools called "profilers" are used to carry out this statement coverage testing. Profilers indicate the number of times each line in the code is executed.

Branch coverage: In branch coverage, each and every condition is taken, and inputs are given in such a way that each branch is executed at least once.

E.g. if (a > 6 && b < 5)

To test this branch, inputs for a and b should be given in such a way that a > 6 is true and false; b < 5 is true and false.

Path coverage: To test loops, this is required. For example, the loop statement

for(i =0; i <= 100; i++)

is executed 101 times. Does the programmer really want 101 times or only 100 times? Invariably programmers make mistakes at the boundary values. So, testing has to be done at loop boundaries.

2.8.3 Mutation Testing

Mutation testing is required to ensure that the software does not fail. It is also a good debugging mechanism. After the software works correctly, mutation testing can be done to simulate wrong inputs.

In mutation testing, program is modified (or logic is changed) slightly to obtain mutants of the program. Different mutants are tested with the same test cases. If the mutant fails, and the actual program works correctly, confidence is gained in the program, and test cases are considered as good i.e., different mutants should give different results. Generally each mutant will have only one change. To produce mutants, mutation operators are defined. The mutation operators can be

Constant replacement

Variable replacement

Arithmetic operator replacement

Relational operator replacement

Goto label replacement

Consider the following code segment:

input y;

x = sin(y);

print x;

When you execute this program, you input a value for y and then check whether the value of sin (y) is displayed. If correct result is not obtained, a simple way of debugging the program is to create a mutant of the program. You can create the mutant by modifying the program as follows:

input y;

x = y;

print x;

Here, we removed the sine function. Now, when you execute the program, if the result is correct, we can isolate where the problem is: it is in the sine calculation. The mistake that is commonly done is not to give the value of the argument y in radians for sine calculation.

 Mutation testing is very useful for the developers to debug the programs. It is important to note that only one mutant has to be created at a time, for effective debugging.

2.8.4 Regression Testing

When a defect is reported in the software, the developer makes some change to the software to remove that defect. It is likely that the change made in the code may lead to another defect that may not be visible immediately. So, whenever a change is made to the source code, one has to ensure that there are no ill effects of the change on the other parts of the software. Regression testing is done precisely to ensure that change in one part of the software has no ill effect on other parts of the software.

Whenever a change is made to the source code, a set of pre-defined test cases has to be run to check whether any other portion of the software is affected.

For example, consider the following code segment:

```
input x;
y = x ** 2;
print y;
if (y == 100)
print "Alarm: x value is 10";
```

Initially, you wrote the program which takes a number as input, squares the number and checks whether the square of the number is 100 or not. If it is 100, it prints an alarm. Suppose later on, you change the logic and calculate the value of y as cube of x instead of square of x. You may simply change the second line as:

```
y = x * x * x;
```

Suppose you now test your program by giving some inputs 2, 6 and 8; and find that the program is working fine. Strictly, the program is not working fine, because you also need to change the if statement as follows:

```
if (y== 1000)
```

So, it is very important that even if you change one line of code, you need to test the software again thoroughly. This re-testing is called regression testing.

Whenever a change has to be made to the source code, the configuration management process has to be followed by all the engineers and the managers. Making changes without a defined process will result in chaos.

NOTE

2.9 Types of Testing

To release a quality product, the software has to be tested in such a way that it will meet all the requirements of the user. The software has to be tested in the actual environment in which the user will install the software. The software installations may differ—number of users, type of users, operating system, network environment etc. Based on these varying environmental requirements, the test plan has to be prepared in such a way that these issues are taken care of. We address these issues and study the various types of testing to be carried out on the software in this section.

2.9.1 Black Box Testing

In black box testing, the structure of the program is not considered at all. The software is considered as a black box to which defined inputs are given and from which defined outputs are obtained.

Since we are not worried about the internal structure of the program, we are only carrying out a functional testing. This method is generally followed while carrying out acceptance testing when the end user is not a software developer but only an IT user.

The test team has to carry out black box testing rigorously; the way the end user tests and uses the software. Initially, the testing has to be done in the lab (alpha testing) and then at the user site (beta testing). The durations of the alpha and beta testing are to be fixed during planning stage based on the complexity of the software and the number of functions to be tested.

Functional/regression testing tools can be used effectively to automate the testing process. The productivity of testing engineers will increase many times if these tools are used.

2.9.2 White Box Testing

In white box testing, the structure of the program is taken into consideration. The objective is to ensure that each and every line of the code is tested. Consider the example

```
if(i < 5 && j > 6)
        do this;
    else
            do that;
If the test case
    i = 3 and j = 7
```

is given as input, only the true condition is satisfied and the corresponding statements are executed. A test case that makes the condition false also needs to be given, such as i = 6 and j = 3.

White box testing is much more involved than the black box testing. Software utilities called "run time profilers" are extensively used which would give statistics on which statement is executed how many times. For developing highly reliable software, white box testing is a must.

2.9.3 Gorilla Testing

Imagine that the software developed by the team is given to a Gorilla for testing. The Gorilla will randomly press some keys (which may be irrelevant from software usage point of view) and statistically speaking, sometimes it may press the keys that are acceptable inputs.

This type of testing would bring out the defects when wrong input is given. Ideally, the software should not misbehave when wrong inputs are given. If the software fails, then the user will lose the confidence. Gorilla testing is used to check whether defensive programming has been done or not—through defensive programming, software is made to tolerate wrong inputs.

Consider the games software packages used by children (and some adults too!). Sometimes, when the child does not know what to do, the child will press some keys randomly. In such a case, the system should not hang. Hence, Gorilla testing is required to test user interfaces, particularly the application software used by non-IT users.

As it is very difficult to recruit a Gorilla for carrying out this type of testing, the test engineer can act as one! The testing process is simple, just keep pressing some keys randomly and check whether the software fails (the machine may hang, sometimes). If a wrong input is given, necessary error messages have to be displayed. If the system hangs, it is a major defect; if the error messages are not displayed, the error handling routines need to be improved.

For every software product, Gorilla testing is to be done without fail.

2.9.4 Beta Testing

Beta testing is carried out at the user's premises, in the absence of the development team. This brings to the fore some of the problems associated with the usability as well as performance. During the test plan formulation, the following aspects need to be decided:

- The number of beta test sites: The number depends on the type of the product. For a generic product that is to be released to the market on a very large scale, a large number of test sites are required to test the software under different environments (operating systems, users with different sophistication, users with different cultural backgrounds etc.) It is not surprising that for Windows 95, there were about 400,000 beta test sites. Sometimes, a limited beta testing is carried out with a small number of sites and then subsequently more sites are added.

- The environment required for the beta testing: The exact hardware and software configurations required need to be specified.

- The support services to be provided: During the beta testing, if the users encounter problems, they need to be provided with a help line. The support mechanism needs to be worked out and specified.

- Whether the beta test software is priced or free: If the beta testing is done on a reasonably mature product, it can be priced, perhaps at a lower price than the price of the end product.

- Defect reporting mechanism: When a user finds a defect, the mechanism for reporting the defect needs to be specified. One way is to give a feedback report periodically, sent to the customer support center. Other possibilities include informing as and when a defect is found, or giving a consolidated report at the end of the test period.

- Beta testing period: The testing period has to be fixed depending on the complexity of the product (can vary from 2 weeks to 2 months).

Some organizations announce a reward scheme: if a user at the beta test site reports a defect, he/she will be given a small reward (say, US$ 5). It creates a good motivation to the beta test site users, but be careful, if the product is not very mature, your organization may go bankrupt with this reward scheme.

2.9.5 Field Trial

Some products have to be tested on real conditions before releasing it in the market. Field trial facilitates testing the software in actual working environment. Field trial is similar to beta testing. Suppose you have developed messaging software that has to work on a satellite network. Initially, you will develop the software in the lab. You will test the software using dialup modems (as you cannot get a satellite link in your lab). After initial testing in the lab, the software has to be checked on the actual satellite link at the client's premises.

Before conducting the field trial, the test team has to make a detailed report on the requirements at the field. The project team has to prepare the hardware and software requirements for conducting the field trial.

A format for the field trial report also needs to be given which has to be filled up after the field trial.

A log sheet that gives all the problems encountered during the field trial has to be maintained with the following details:

Date

Preconditions (status of the software before the problem)

Description of the problem encountered

Post-condition (status of the software after the problem)

Impact (whether the software has become unusable or system has to be rebooted etc.)

The field trial duration has to be decided at the planning stage itself. During the field trial, a development team member has to be available at least on telephone or email for support activities.

Based on the field trial report, all the defects have to be removed and then the software can be released.

2.9.6 Performance Testing

Performance testing focuses on the performance parameters such as the transaction response time, throughput etc. For example, in database systems the response time relates to the time to obtain a report after clicking on a specific button. It may be difficult to specify the response times for each and every form/report, but the time that can be tolerated generally should be specified. For example, 30 seconds is a reasonable period, but not 2 minutes.

In real-time or embedded systems, the performance parameters are very significant. If the system demands that a particular job has to be completed within a stipulated time (e.g., measurement of temperature) and then another action has to be initiated (say, opening a valve), the timely response becomes critical. So, a performance requirement is "open the valve within 10 milliseconds if the temperature exceeds 40 degrees." Remember, if this performance requirement is not met, it may result in a catastrophe. Hence, performance testing is compulsory in process control and telecommunication software systems. For such systems, the specification document needs to specify the timing requirements. The design document should contain a detailed timing analysis. The test procedure needs to clearly indicate the details of the tests to be performed to ensure that the software (or the software/hardware combination) meets all the timing requirements.

In many real-time or embedded systems, the timing performance is a risk item. After spending lot of money on design and testing, the limitations of the system as regards the timing come into the fore. Particularly, for systems involving both hardware and software design, this issue needs to be studied in detail before the implementation starts. To ensure that the timing requirements are met, the functionality that goes into the hardware and software needs to be analyzed in detail.

In many projects, the client does not specify the timing constraints during the SRS stage, but introduces these requirements later on. This leads to major difficulties because, sometime the total design has to be changed to meet the performance requirements. Note that performance constraints are major risk items in many projects.

NOTE

2.9.7 Stress Testing

Stress testing is done to test the software at its limits of performance. For example, if the software is a DBMS package that is expected to give a response time within the specified limit for 16 simultaneous users, the software has to be tested while 16 users are using the database at the same time. Generally it is not done and the software is tested for 4 or 5 users and delivered to the client. When the client starts using the software in actual environment, the users have to wait for long time to get their reports (poor response times) and the client rejects the software.

Another type of stress testing is done on the resource requirement. If the RAM requirement is specified as 64 MB for a specific application, the software needs to be tested on machines with 64 MB also, not just the 128 MB machines on which the software was initially developed. It is worthwhile to test it on 32 MB and check the performance as well.

Stress testing is also to be done for systems that involve communication media. For instance, if the specification says that the communication link should have a minimum data rate of 56 Kbps, the system has to be tested with just that bandwidth.

The test set up for the stress testing needs to be defined as a part of the acceptance test plan.

2.9.8 Acceptance Testing

Acceptance testing is the most important testing as this decides whether the client approves the product or not. The criteria for acceptance testing should be done at early stages of product development. By the time the design is completed, a draft acceptance test plan has to be prepared and given to the client for approval. After discussions, the acceptance test plan has to be approved by both parties. The ATP should be very detailed, so detailed that if testing is done as per the ATP step by step, all the functionality and performance parameters are tested.

The format for the ATP is given in Table 2.1.

Acceptance Test Plan

Name of the project:

Reference of requirements document:

Reference of design document

Test set-up required for the acceptance testing

Types of testing to be carried out

Test for each functionality
    To test what
    Pre-conditions
    Post-conditions

Test cases (to be selected based on equivalence class partitioning, boundary value analysis and cause-effect graphs)

Test results (expected and actual)

Testing process deliverables

Test results
Deviations with respect to the specifications

Is the software meeting all the specifications? If not what are the deviations?

In case of deviations, the criticality of the deviations

In case the deviations cannot be rectified, what needs to be done (how to resolve the issues)

The final approving authority in case of differences of opinion

Client representative
Development team representative

Acceptance testing time frame

Resources allocated for acceptance testing

Testing personnel (developer side and client side)
Documentation personnel

Table 2.1 Acceptance Test Plan Format

During the project planning stage itself, the testing team has to identify the various types of testing to be carried out on the software. The test engineers need to be involved in the requirements engineering stage itself.

2.10 Test Plan

The test plan, containing the details of the testing process, has to be prepared during the project planning stage itself. This plan should contain all the details of required resources, the testing approaches to be followed, the testing methodologies, the test cases etc. This section will address these aspects of the test plan.

2.10.1 Test Oracles

Oracle is a repository of knowledge. In earlier days, people used to go to a place, known as an oracle, where the God in the form of a statue, used to be present. The people go to the statue and tell their problems and the God (the priest who is hiding beneath the statue) answers the person and gives a solution. Such places are called oracles.

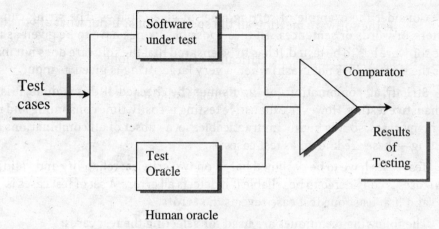

Fig. 2.4 Test Oracle

Test oracles are the people (or machines) used to check the correctness of the program for the given test cases as shown in Fig. 2.4. Human test oracles are used extensively if the program does not work. A common way is to give the program and the input test data to a friend and ask him to derive the output from the program. Your friend acts like a computer, goes through the code step by step as per the input data and arrives at the output. If this output is same as that expected, then the program can be said to be correct, otherwise there is a defect in the software.

The automated testing tools act as test oracles. Whatever the human oracle does is automated through a software program.

NOTE

2.10.2 Test Cases

Test cases can be defined as sets of input parameters for which the software will be tested. As shown in Fig. 2.5, test cases are selected, the program is executed and the results are compared with the estimated results.

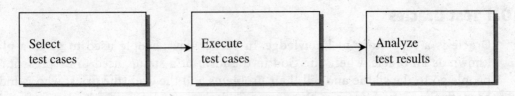

Fig. 2.5 Testing Process using Test Cases

Consider the example of sorting a set of given strings. The string can be simply letters, or words or sentences. All these possible strings have to be given as inputs and the software has to be tested. It has to be ensured that the software does not malfunction (or the system does not crash) when a very large string is given as input.

Strictly, all combinations of inputs must be checked. If this is done, it is known as exhaustive testing. However, exhaustive testing is costly, time consuming and impossible in many cases, so it is highly impracticable. So, a subset of all combinations is used for testing—these are known as test cases.

Test cases have to be designed based on two criteria: reliability and validity. A set of test cases is considered to be reliable if it detects all errors. A set of test cases is considered as valid if at least one test case reveals the errors.

The following techniques are used for selecting the test cases:

Equivalence class partitioning: In this technique, all the possible valid inputs and valid outputs are identified. The test cases consist of both valid inputs and invalid inputs. (Refer to the example on testing software to check whether three numbers form a triangle).

Boundary value analysis: Values that are on the boundary of the equivalence classes are "high yield" test cases. Consider the example

```
for (i = 0; i < n; ++i) {
}
```

$i = n-1$ is one boundary value, because there is a likelihood that the programmer would have made a mistake: `i < n   or i <= n?`

Cause effect graphing: In this approach, for each cause (inputs), effect (actions) is identified and a cause effect graph is drawn. Consider an example of withdrawal form verification in a bank account.

Example. C1: account number is correct

C2: signature matches

C3: enough money

A1: give money

A2: inform not enough money

A3: print fraud case

Each of the causes (C1 to C3) can be true or false. For the various combinations of these causes, the action or effect can be A1 or A2 or A3. So, the test cases have to be generated in such a way that all the three causes are true and false. For each test case, it has to be checked whether the right action is being taken.

Using these three approaches, the test cases have to be generated. Depending on the type of application you need to generate the test cases. Hence, you need to study the application to be tested (known as Application Under Test or AUT) in detail for test case generation. We will study in the subsequent chapters, how to generate test cases for various types of applications such as calculator software, database software, web sites etc.

Generation of the test cases is the most interesting and challenging task of test engineers. Testing tools help in fast execution of the test cases, but provide very little help in generating good test cases.

2.10.3 Test Plan Format

Before taking up the testing, a test plan has to be prepared. It is preferable if the test plan is prepared during the planning stage itself and revised just before the testing process starts (as the issues involved in testing will be clearer after the coding is completed). A template for the test plan is given in Table 2.2. The ATP document discussed in the previous section can be derived from this test plan.

Test Plan

Project name:

Estimated start date for testing   Estimated end date for testing

Actual start date for testing   Actual end date for testing

Estimated effort in person hours /person months

Test set-up (including the hardware, software environment), other peripherals required, any special tools required and any test equipment required (such as oscilloscopes etc.)

Test personnel and their responsibility

Types of testing to be carried out (functional, structural, alpha testing, beta testing, Gorilla testing, usability testing, field trial, performance testing, stress testing etc.)

For each type of testing, the test cases have to be specified.

Testing tools to be used

Test schedule for each type of testing

Test cases to be executed for regression testing

Defect report (in the following format)

S. No.
Defect found
Type of defect
Classification of the defect (critical, major, minor)
Status of the defect (new, remove, defect removal has been approved by QA manager)
Time for removal of defect
Stage when the defect was injected
Stage when the defect was removed

How defects are classified and what are the criteria for completion of testing

Tools to be used for managing the testing process

Table 2.2 Test Plan Format

The system testing has to be carried out as per the test plan and the test results report has to be generated.

Test plan is the most important document that brings in a process-oriented approach to testing. Automated test management tools help a lot in achieving this process-oriented approach. ATP document can be derived from the test plan.

2.11 Criteria for Completion of Testing

Surprisingly, it is very difficult to say when the testing phase is complete and when the product can be released. As you keep testing the software, it may happen that you keep getting a defect—and this process may go on forever. On the other hand, you may not detect any defect, but what is the guarantee that there is no hidden defect? And, that defect may show its effect on the day the software is delivered to the customer. See the irony, after all the effort of developing and testing the software, you are not sure whether it is ready for shipment! This proves our point once more: "testing is difficult". Instead of relying on gut feeling, we need to arrive at a scientific method to declare that the testing is complete and the product is ready for shipment.

2.11.1 When is Testing Complete?

It is very difficult to say when testing is complete. Three criteria used in practice for completion of testing [Pressman 1994] are:

- When you run out of time.
- When you run out of money.
- Based on statistical criteria.

In practice, unfortunately, the first two criteria are followed. During the planning stage, certain time and money (or effort) are allocated for the testing process. The test team keeps testing the software, and when they run out of time (or money), the product is delivered (to avoid the penalty for late delivery). Most managers do not realize that this is a very dangerous practice because if the software fails at customer's site, the reputation of the organization is at stake.

A more practical approach for declaring that the testing is complete is to use the third criterion. After the coding is completed, and testing begins, initially many defects are detected. Slowly, the number of defects found in a given time (say, in a day or week) keeps reducing. The graph showing the number of defects found every week will be as shown in Fig. 2.6. If the number of defects found per week remains less than a pre-defined threshold consecutively for three weeks, then the software can be considered a mature product and released to the client.

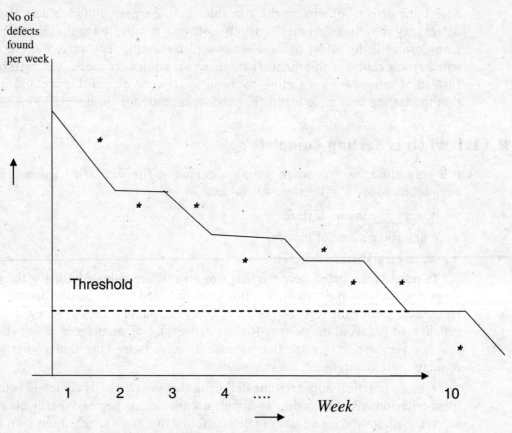

Fig. 2.6   'Completion of testing' based on Defects Found per Week

Taking a decision on 'when testing is complete' is very difficult. A systematic approach to tracking the bugs found and analyzing the bug reports will help in making this decision.

2.11.2 Classification of Defects

All defects are not of the same type. Some defects may result in system crash. Some defects may be very minor (such as a spelling mistake in an error message). So, the defects need to be classified based on its impact on the functionality of the software. The defects can be classified as

- Critical
- Major
- Minor

Critical defects result in a system crash, or the application may not be useable at all if this type of defect occurs. In a time critical application, if the timing is not within the limits or if the response time is not within limits; then also the defect can be termed as critical. Inconsistent performance of the application is also a critical defect.

Major defects will not lead to a system crash, but may result in some portions of the application difficult to use, such as difficult navigation of the menus.

Minor defects can be tolerated, such as lack of help for some functionality, a spelling mistake in an error message, incorrect ordering of control buttons in a GUI etc.

While recording the defects in a defect log sheet, the severity of the defects also needs to be noted down. If a critical defect is present in the code, then the software is not ready for delivery. Only a few major defects are allowed. Similarly, a threshold needs to be kept on the number of minor defects. As the threshold depends on the application, the project manager/test team member has to use his judgment in fixing the thresholds on major and minor defects.

After analyzing the test report, the project manager needs to decide whether the software is ready for delivery or not.

Different organizations use different methods for classification of defects. The classification may also differ from application to application. The test plan has to clearly bring out the classification approach.

2.12 Software Reliability

A number of reliability analysis models are available to predict the reliability of the software, in terms of the number of defects still remaining in the software [Wood 1996]. This metric is very useful to decide when to deliver the product or when to release the product into the market, particularly when the software is highly complex. The software reliability models generally follow one of the trends as shown in Fig. 2.7. Fig. 2.7a shows the 'concave model' and Fig. 2.7b shows 'S-shaped model'. The assumption made in arriving at these models is that during initial stages, testing is not as efficient as at later stages (not necessarily a true assumption) and hence there is an increase in the rate of defect detection. In Fig. 2.7c, the two-stage model curve is shown, this model is applicable when significant functionality is added to the software during the testing process (which is normally the case!).

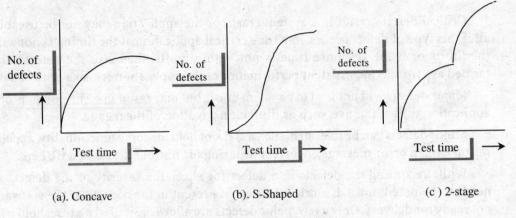

Fig. 2.7   Software Reliability Curves

The software reliability models are still at a theoretical level and studies are being carried out at academic institutions. Very few organizations use them in practice for obtaining the reliability figures. The most important reliability figures are MTBF (Mean Time Between Failures), MTTR (Mean Time To Repair) and MTTF (Mean Time To Fail). The relation between these three values is shown in Fig. 2.8.

While carrying out the testing process, the values of MTBF, MTTR and MTTF need to be recorded and if these values are within the limits only, the product can be considered as 'ready for release'.

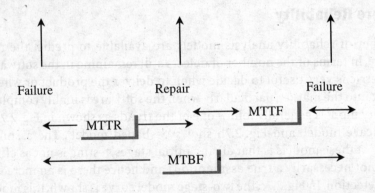

Fig. 2.8   Relation between MTBF, MTTR & MTTF

To obtain the values of MTBF, MTTR, and MTTF is difficult. You need to keep track of the total time for testing by all the test engineers). For example, let us say, the software is tested for about 1000 hours and during that time, the software failed twice. So, the MTBF value is 500 hours. After the failure, if it takes 5 hours to rectify the problem on an average, the MTTR is 5 hours. After the rectification, again if it fails after 495 hours, the MMTF is 495 hours. If the testing time is more, you get more accurate values for these parameters.

The software reliability models have to be developed using the defect analysis during the testing phase and maintenance phase. Based on these models, the reliability estimation models can be evolved in the organization. Organizations, which would like to improve their process based on quantitative measures, need to apply the reliability models as a part of their quality improvement process.

2.13 Manual Testing and its Limitations/Drawbacks

In many organizations, software testing is carried out manually. After the product reaches a mature stage, the test team generates various test cases and manually tests each and every feature. If a defect is found, the software is modified. Again, using the test cases, the software is tested. Such a manual testing is not advisable for the following reasons:

- Manual testing is very time consuming. The same set of operations need to be done repeatedly, and hence the test engineers are likely to get bored when the testing has to be done repeatedly.

- Regression testing has to be done to ensure that changes in one portion of the software have no ill effects on other portions of the software. The entire testing process needs to be repeated whenever a change is made to any portion of the software.

- To do performance testing, many resources are required, both computers and people. For example, to test a Client/Server application, the client software has to be run on different machines and one person has to test each client application to test the performance of the software when multiple users use the same software simultaneously. On the other hand, automated tools facilitate running the software from a single client machine, resulting in savings in terms of infrastructure and manpower.

- Manual testing is error-prone because test engineers become bored when testing has to be done repeatedly. For instance, to test a web site, each and every link has to be checked. In manual testing, the test engineer is likely to miss some links.

- Even to manage the testing process is complicated as the testing has to be planned, bugs have to be tracked and reliability analysis has to be performed. Automated test tools help in managing the testing process effectively.

Summary

In this chapter, the details of testing process are discussed. Here are the important points to be remembered:

- Testing is the most important and time consuming phase in software development and a systematic approach has to be followed to test software.

- Development engineers try to test the software in such a way that they want to prove that the software works correctly. However, the test engineers need to focus on uncovering as many bugs as possible. Hence, it is important to have a separate test team to objectively evaluate the software.

- Testing has to be done at different levels: unit testing is done to test the basic units of software, module testing is done to test each module separately; integration testing is done while integrating different modules and system testing is done to test the system as a whole.

- The various tests to be carried out are: black box testing, white box testing, beta testing, field trial, and acceptance testing.

- A detailed test plan has to be prepared indicating the types of tests to be carried out, testing environment, resources required and test cases.

- In addition to functional testing, the software has to be tested for its performance requirements, reliability requirements and other requirements such as portability, maintainability etc.

- The software is accepted by the customer based on acceptance testing. Acceptance Test Procedure (ATP) document has to be prepared by the QA team in association with the customer and the testing has to be done as per this procedure.

- As manual testing is very laborious and time consuming, it is advisable to use automated test tools.

3 ▪ Software Testing Tools: An Overview

In this chapter

- Appreciate the need for automated testing tools
- Understand the requirements of testing tools
- Get to know the various categories of testing tools and their functionality
- Learn how to select a testing tool

Software testing tools are of immense use to develop quality software. In this chapter, we will study the various categories of testing tools and their functionality.

3.1 Need for Automated Testing Tools

As we discussed in the previous chapter, manual testing is time-consuming, error-prone and requires lot of infrastructure and manpower. All these drawbacks can be overcome if the testing process is automated. The testing tools reduce manual testing to a large extent and the testing can be done automatically. Using these tools has many advantages:

- Once the software is ready for testing, the functionality of the software can be tested repeatedly to improve the quality and reliability.
- Testing can be done unattended, for example, during nighttime and during holidays.
- When the software has to be tested in different environments (different hardware platforms, different operating systems, using different browsers etc.), the labor involved can be reduced.
- Performance testing can be done without the need for many computers and many test engineers. The test tools simulate multiple users on a single machine. As compared to manual testing, finding out transaction response times when multiple users access the same application will be very easy.
- Testing process can be planned and managed effectively using these tools. **97**

- Test reports can be generated automatically for later analysis and corrective action.
- Testing can be done using tools that are available to test not only generic applications such as database applications and web sites, but also for DLLs, Visual Basic Programs, Siebel software, Power Builder software, databases, stand-alone Java applications etc.
- The testing process can be managed efficiently—the planning can be done systematically, the tests can be scheduled efficiently, and the bug tracking can be done effectively.

 Hence, using automated test tools results in:

- Improvement in the quality and reliability of the software.
- Drastic reduction in time, effort, and money spent on testing.
- A systematic approach to the testing process.
- Efficient management of the testing process even if the teams are at different geographical locations.

3.2 Taxonomy of Testing Tools

A wide variety of software testing tools are available to cater to the different types of software, different programming languages, and to carry out different types of testing. These testing tools can be broadly divided into the following categories:

- Functional/Regression testing tools
- Source code testing tools
- Performance testing tools
- Java testing tools
- Embedded software testing tools
- Network protocol testing tools
- Configuration management/bug tracking tools
- Testing management tools

Functional/Regression Testing Tools: These tools are used to test the application software and web applications such as web sites. As majority of the applications involve Graphical User Interface (GUI), the tools test the GUI objects and functionality automatically. These tools carry out black box testing. Client/Server applications, Enterprise Resource Planning (ERP) software packages such as SAP,

Customer Relations Management (CRM) software packages such as Siebel, web sites etc. can be tested for functionality using these tools. Whenever a change is made to the software, the software needs to be retested and hence these tools are also called regression testing tools. Compuware's QACenter, Segue Software's SilkTest, IBM Rational's Robot, Mecury Interactive's WinRunner belong to this category.

Source Code Testing Tools: These tools check the source code of the application software. The testing is white box testing and hence the implementation details are taken into consideration. A number of tools are available for checking line coverage, branch coverage, and path coverage. For instance, the profilers display the number of times each line is executed. The test engineer can study the profiler output to find out which portions of the code are not executed and then create test cases in such a way that the lines, which were not executed earlier, can be executed. Tools are also available to test whether the source code is compliant to the standard coding guidelines and to generate the metrics such as number of non-commented lines, number of commented lines, number of functions etc. Some tools check the portability of the code. For example, the code written in C is not portable if operating system dependent features are used. The 'lint' utility in Unix/Linux systems checks the portability of C code. Some application software source code testing tools are: AutomatedQA's AQtime, Parasoft's Insure++, and Telelogic's Logiscope.

Performance Testing Tools: These tools are used to carry out performance testing or stress testing. These tools are very useful to test how the application works when multiple users access the application simultaneously. The application can be for example, a database or a web site. These tools simulate multiple users on a single machine and hence you do not need many machines and many test engineers to do the performance testing. AutoTester's AutoController, Compuware's QALoad, Mercury Interactive's LoadRunner, Segue Software's SilkPerformer, IBM Rational's Performance Tester, Apache JMeter belong to this category. Some other specialized tools in this category are Argogroup's MonitorMaster for testing mobile applications that use WML and XHTML, Short Messaging Service (SMS) and Multimedia Messaging Service (MMS); IBM Rational's Prevue-X and Prevue-ASCII for X-windows and ASCII terminal emulators.

Java Testing Tools: As Java has become a popular programming language in recent years, a number of tools are available exclusively for testing Java applications. These tools are for testing applications written in Java programming language and for testing Java classes. Jemmy is an open source library to create automated tests for Java GUI applications. JMeter of Apache is another open source software to do performance testing. Parasoft's jtest is used for Java class testing.

Embedded Software Testing tools: Testing embedded software is a very challenging task as the timing requirements for these applications are very stringent. In embedded systems, the code has to be optimized so that it occupies the minimum memory. IBM Rational Test Real Time is the widely used test tool in this category.

Network Protocol Testing tools: As computer networks are becoming widespread, testing networking/communication software has attained lot of importance in recent years. A number of tools are available for testing networking and communication protocols. Many test instrumentation vendors such as Agilent Technologies, Rhode & Schwartz etc. supply protocol analyzers which generate the necessary protocols based on international standards such as ITU-T standards. netIQ's ANVL (Automated Network Validation Library) is to test routers and other networking products. This software generates packets in correct and incorrect formats to test the networking software. netIQ's Chariot is a network performance testing tool.

Configuration Management/Bug Tracking Tools: In large software development projects, configuration management is a very important process. Also, when the test engineers report bugs, the managers have to track these bugs and ensure that all the bugs are removed. To facilitate this activity, good workflow management software is important. Many such tools, which are web-based are available. Bugzilla's Bugzilla is an open source defect tracking system. Samba's Jitterbug is a freeware defect tracking system. IBM Rational Software's Clear DDTS is a change request management software. GNU's GNATS is a freeware bug tracking and change management software. Segue Software's SilkRadar is an issue tracking and bug tracking software. Microsoft Excel is also used extensively for bug tracking. In Unix/Linux/Solaris systems, utilities are available for version and release control of source code—these utilities are Source Code Control System (SCCS) and Revision Control System (RCS).

Software Testing Management Tools: These tools help in managing process-oriented software testing. Using these tools, the QA manager can create a formal test plan, allocate resources, schedule unattended testing, track the status of various bugs/activities etc. AutoTester's AutoAdviser, Compuware's QADirector, QIS's QCIT, Segue Software's SilkPlan Pro, IBM Rational Test Manager, Mercury Interactive's TestDirector are some such tools.

NOTE

If your organization is planning to introduce testing tools for the first time, you need to evaluate the commercially available tools for your specific application. Your choice for a specific tool is dependent on the application to be tested, hardware and software environment as well as the types of testing to be done.

3.3 Functional/Regression Testing Tools

In functional testing of software, the functionality of the software is tested without bothering about the source code and implementation details. For example, consider the standard calculator software that is available on your Windows system. The GUI of the standard calculator is shown in Fig. 3.1.

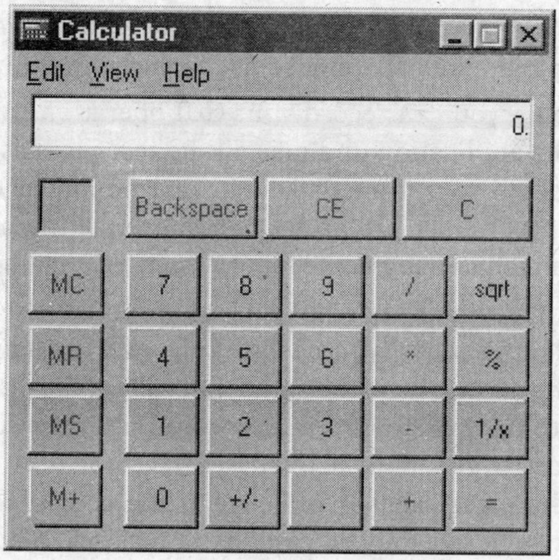

Fig. 3.1: Standard Calculator GUI

To test the functionality, you will do some calculations and find out whether you are getting the correct answers. You may type in '4 * 5 =' and the correct answer 20 is displayed. You go on giving inputs and check the answers. If the expected result matches with the actual displayed result, your calculator software is working OK. While you are testing the software, you need to give test cases in such a way that all the buttons in the GUI are tested. So, you need to generate the test cases. Table 3.1 shows some test cases and the expected result. Note that we have chosen the test cases in such a way that each and every button on the GUI is pressed at least once. Some test cases are chosen in such a way that the calculations give an error output message (for example, finding the square root of a negative number).

Test Case	Expected Output
4 1/x	0.25
-6 sqrt	Err: "Invalid input for function"
4 C	Clears the Display
1.2 * 3	3.6
5 / 2.0	2.5
7 + 8 – 9	6
600 * 2 %	12
2, MS, C, MR	2
MC, 2, M+, 3, M+, C, MR	5

Table 3.1: Test Cases for testing the Standard Calculator

While you are still in the development stage, your software is not likely to work perfectly, and for some test cases, you may get wrong results. During the course of development, you need to test the software many times using the above test cases. If you do it manually, it takes lot of time, and yes, you will get bored. The functional/ regression testing tools are of immense use in such situations.

Using these tools, you can record your GUI operations. While running the testing tool, you invoke the application and give all the test cases as input. Automatically, the testing tool will record your inputs—keystrokes and mouse clicks—and then the tool will create a script. The script can be run subsequently and hence you are saved botheration of manually giving these inputs again and again.

Consider another example of testing a login process. In many applications, initially a login screen will appear and you need to type in a username and a password. Only users who are authorized to use the application will be allowed to enter the application. Assume that a user is given the username 'john' and password as 'mary'. To test this simple GUI, you need to generate the test cases. The specification says that the username and the password are case-sensitive. Hence, if the user types "John", it is an invalid username. You can generate the test cases as shown in Table 3.2.

Input: user name	Input: password	Expected output
john	mary	Login successful
John	Mary	Login unsuccessful
John	[no password typed]	Login unsuccessful
JOHN	MARY	Login unsuccessful
John	John	Login unsuccessful

Table 3.2: Test Cases for Login Screen

As you can see, life is tough for a testing engineer. Just to test a login screen, you need to generate a good number of test cases. The development engineer, during the initial stages of development, would give his software with lot of bugs (the login will be successful if the password field is left blank). Every time, he modifies the software, you need to run all the above test cases and check whether the software still has any bugs. Obviously, if you record the test using a tool, the test script can be run repeatedly.

Now, testing the login screen is much more complicated. When a user enters his login name and password, the software will check in a database whether a valid username and password are entered. So, the login name can be not only john, but also donald, bush, prasad and so on. It is not possible to generate test cases by entering so many usernames and passwords manually. Testing tools provide a beautiful mechanism through "data driven testing". In data driven testing, the username and password are considered as variables, the values these variables can take can be obtained from a database and the testing is carried out. Data driven testing is one of the most important features of these testing tools. As a test engineer, your job is just to create the test script with the variable names and then you can run the test in unattended mode (and go to a movie with your friend, and by the time you come back, your test report is ready).

While testing the software in unattended mode, we get into another problem. Suppose, for an application, the user has to first login, then update a database table and then logout. You created the test cases for all the three functions. Suppose that the software fails at login stage itself—should you continue to run the test or stop the test. The testing tools provide you an option either to continue testing or stop testing. The application can be made to recover automatically to a specified state. This feature is called recovery management. You will appreciate the power and beauty of all these features of these testing tools in the subsequent chapters.

The following tools, which are widely used in the software industry, are discussed in detail in this book:

- Mercury Interactive's WinRunner
- Segue Software's SilkTest
- IBM Rational SQA Robot

 All functional/regression testing tools operate in a similar fashion. They capture the user interactions with the GUI (keyboard entries and mouse clicks) and automatically create a test script. The script can be run repeatedly without the need for interacting with the GUI again and again.

3.4 Performance Testing Tools

In Client/Server (C/S) applications, many users access the server application (such as a database) simultaneously. In such a case, the software has to be tested for its performance. Consider a database application. When only one user accesses the database, the transaction response time to query the database and obtain the report is say, 10 seconds. When 10 users access the database simultaneously, what will be the response time—10 seconds or 40 seconds? When 1000 users access the database simultaneously what will be the response time—10 seconds or 10 minutes? No user will accept a few minutes of response time. Generally, in the SRS document, the response time will be specified. How do you test the software to find out the response time when say 100 users are simultaneously accessing the database? As shown in Fig. 3.2, you need to connect 100 client systems and then put 100 test engineers on the job and use a communication network such as a Local Area Network (LAN) or a Wide Area Network (WAN). Your company will go bankrupt by the time you complete the testing! An economical approach is to use performance testing tools which will do the job with minimal infrastructure and minimal number of persons.

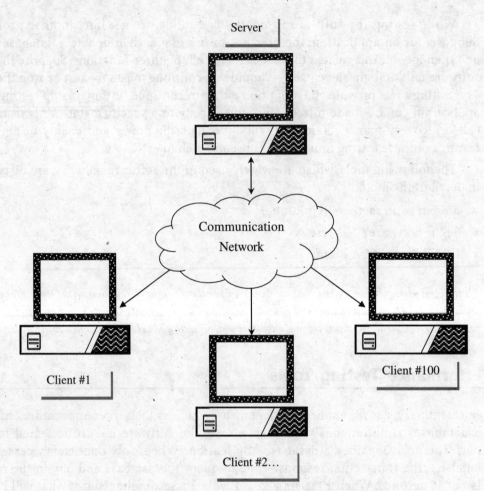

Fig 3.2: Performance Testing of a Client/Server Application

The performance testing tools functionality is shown in Fig. 3.3. The server application continues to run on the server. But only one or a few clients will be running the client application but on these client machines, many virtual users are simulated, effectively simulating an environment in which 100 users access the database.

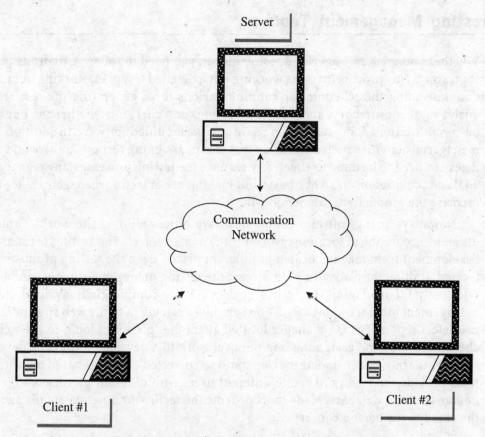

Fig 3.3: Performance Testing Using Automated Tools

Today's many enterprise applications such as ERP software, web services, web sites, CRM software etc. need to be tested for performance testing. Performance testing is also called load testing or stress testing. These tools display the performance of the application using graphs and charts so that analysis will be easy. For instance, you can plot a graph which shows the response time as a function of the number of simultaneous users who access the database.

The following performance tools, widely used in the software industry, are covered in this book:

- Mercury Interactive's LoadRunner
- Apache's JMeter

The performance testing tools create virtual users on the same machine and hence with minimal infrastructure you can simulate multi-user environment.

NOTE

3.5 Testing Management Tools

Whether you are a m ager or a test engineer, you need to follow a rigorous process for testing. This process involves working out a detailed test plan, working out the test cases, deciding the schedule for running various tests, generating the test reports, analyzing the test reports and tracking the bugs and checking whether the bugs have been removed and doing regression testing on the modified software. In addition, many managerial activities such as forming test teams, assigning responsibilities and target dates etc. need to be done to effectively manage the testing process. Many managers do all these activities on an ad hoc basis; but making use of testing management tools will increase the productivity tremendously.

Nowadays, many software companies have offices all over the world. Groups at different geographical locations work on the same project. The testing team and the development team may be located at different places. Even the testing groups may be located at different places. In such a case, the testing management tools can be used effectively for managing the testing process. Many commercially available testing management tools are web-based. A test engineer can log in to the web site and update the defect report. The QA manager located at another place can login to the web site, check the status and assign the bug removal work to a developer. After the developer removes the bug, he can update the bug status to 'corrected'. The web-based management tools provide the facility to create different users with different privileges to read or update the bugs database. Many tools provide the facility to generate emails and send the email to the person concerned.

Testing management tools facilitate all these process-oriented activities to be done systematically. We will study how to use Mercury Interactive's TestDirector for managing the testing process.

 Testing management tools can be integrated with other testing tools (functional/regression testing tools and performance testing tools). However it is advisable to obtain the complete test suite from the same vendor rather than one tool from one vendor and another tool from another vendor.

3.6 Source Code Testing Tools

Source code testing tools are specific to the programming language used for developing the software. As Unix/Linux is nowadays used for software development extensively, we will study the following tools in this book:

- Lint, a utility used to test the portability of the code.

- Line profilers used to do the timing analysis. These profilers find out the execution time for the entire program as well as for individual function calls.
- SCCS and RCS, source code configuration management tools.

Source code testing tools differ from programming language to programming language. These tools can be used for checking whether coding guidelines are being followed or not by the development engineers. Some tools also give coding metrics such as the total number of commented lines, ratio of commented lines to uncommented lines etc.

3.7 How to Select a Testing Tool?

Does your organization require an automated testing tool? This question can be very easily answered, if you spend some time and analyze the existing scenario in your organization:

- Are your customers happy with the software delivered by you? If they are unhappy and you get many reports on the bugs detected, the testing process needs to be improved a lot. Certainly, you need to consider the option of using a testing tool. The amount of effort and money you will be spending on corrective maintenance will be much more than the cost of buying the testing tools.

- If your customers are happy with the software you have delivered, find out the effort, time and money spent on the testing phase. The productivity of the people can be increased many fold by using the tools. The test engineers can do a more productive work in generating the test cases, rather than unproductive 'data entry' work by giving manual inputs.

- How many testing engineers are leaving your organization? If the manpower attrition rate is very high, then the most likely reason is that they were getting bored doing repetitive things. Testing tools remove the manual work and the test engineers will enjoy the testing process.

- Using manual testing, you can never bring out a quality product if performance testing is a part of the requirements. If performance testing has to be done on your software, tools come in handy.

- If your organization believes in a process-oriented approach to testing, testing tools will be of immense use.

- If your project teams are located at different places, a web-based management tool will be very effective for an efficient management of the testing process.

Once you decide to use testing tools, you need to make a choice based on the following criteria:

- What types of testing have to be done on the software? Invariably, most of the application software packages need to be tested for functionality. As the software is likely to be modified, regression testing is also a must. Hence, you need to get functional/regression testing tools.

- If your software is a C/S application or a web application, you may need to do load testing. In such cases, you need to use a performance testing tool as well.

- Some vendors integrate testing management tools along with the above tools. Alternatively, some vendors supply a separate module at additional cost for testing management.

- Once the types of testing tools required are decided, you need to obtain the tool for the environment in which the software runs. Your application may be running only in Windows, or only in Unix (or its variants such as Linux, Solaris etc.). Sometimes you may have to run the software in different platforms. In such cases, you need to check whether the testing tool supports such environments.

- Testing tool vendors also give tools that support testing for proprietary software packages such as Siebel, SAP etc.

- If you need to test the source code as well, you need to buy the source code testing tools.

- If you working on a very large software development project, tracking the bugs is a major issue. Bug tracking tools need to be used in such a case.

- If your organization is keen on implementing process-oriented testing, testing management tools are a must. If the project teams are at different places, a web-enabled testing tool will be of great use.

- A number of open source testing tools are now available. The main attraction of these tools is that they are free. However, you may not get technical support for such tools.

Summary

In this chapter, we presented an overview of the software testing tools. The important points to be noted are:

- Use of automated testing tools has many attractions: better quality product can be delivered to the customer; time, effort, and money spent on testing can be drastically reduced; productivity of the test engineers can be increased many fold and the entire testing process can be streamlined.

- Functional/regression testing software tools are used to carry out black box testing of the software. Using these tools, the functionality of the software can be tested automatically by recording the GUI operations and automatically replaying these operations to carry out unattended testing. Data driven testing and recovery management are the two important features of these tools.

- Performance/load testing software tools are used to carry out the testing by simulating multiple users on one or few machines. Such a testing is required to be done on Client/Server applications, distributed applications and web sites.

- Source code testing tools are used for carrying out white-box testing. These tools test the statement coverage, path coverage, and branch coverage. Tools are also available for profiling, calculating coding metrics etc.

- Test management tools facilitate a process-oriented test management by providing such facilities as test scheduling, generation of test cases, generation of test reports, bug tracking etc.

- The widely used functional/regression testing tools are: Mercury Interactive's WinRunner, Segue Software's SilkTest, and IBM Rational's Robot.

- The widely used performance testing tools are: Mercury Interactive's LoadRunner, Segue Software's SilkPerformer, and IBM Rational's Performance Tester.

- The widely used test management tools are: Mercury Interactive TestDirector, Segue Software's SilkPlan Pro, and IBM Rational's Test Manager.

4 | WinRunner

In this chapter

- Understand the features of WinRunner
- Learn how to use WinRunner for functional/regression testing
- Learn how to create the test scripts for unattended testing
- Understand how to do synchronization of tests cases
- Learn how to use data driven wizard and GUI checkpoints
- Learn how to do rapid testing

WinRunner is a very powerful automated testing tool for functional/ regression testing. In this chapter, we will study how to use WinRunner through case studies and illustrative examples.

4.1 Overview of WinRunner

Mercury Interactive's WinRunner is a testing tool to do functional/regression testing. Using WinRunner, you can record GUI operations. While recording, WinRunner automatically creates a test script. This test script can be run automatically later on for carrying out unattended testing. The important aspects of WinRunner are:

- You can do functional/regression testing of a variety of application software written in programming languages such as PowerBuilder, Visual Basic, C/C++, and Java. You can also carry out the testing on ERP/CRM software packages.

- You can do the testing in all flavors of Windows operating systems and different browser environments such as Internet Explorer and Netscape Navigator.

- You can record the GUI operations in the 'record' mode. WinRunner automatically creates a test script. This test can be modified if required and can be executed later on in unattended mode. The recovery manager enables the application to be brought to a known state in case there is a problem during the unattended testing. Rapid Test Script Wizard creates the test scripts automatically.

- You can add checkpoints to compare actual and expected results. The checkpoints can be GUI checkpoints, bitmap checkpoints and web links.

- It provides a facility for synchronization of test cases.

- Data Driver Wizard provides the facility to convert a recorded test into a data driven test. So, you can replace data with variables within a test script. For example, you can test a login process by taking the input for username and password fields from a database.

- Database checkpoints are used to verify data in a database during automated testing. The records that are inserted, deleted, modified, or updated will be highlighted so that you can ensure database integrity and transaction accuracy.

- The Virtual Object Wizard of WinRunner is used to teach WinRunner to recognize, record, and replay custom objects.

- The reporting tools provide the facility to generate automatically the test reports and analyze the defects.

- WinRunner can be integrated with the testing management tool TestDirector to automate many of the activities in the testing process.

4.2 Testing an Application using WinRunner

After installing the WinRunner on your computer, invoke the WinRunner application:

- Start → Programs → WinRunner → WinRunner

The opening screen of the WinRunner application is displayed, prompting you to select one of the three options:

- New Test: To create a new test script
- Open Test: To open an existing test script
- Quick Preview: To view the quick preview of WinRunner

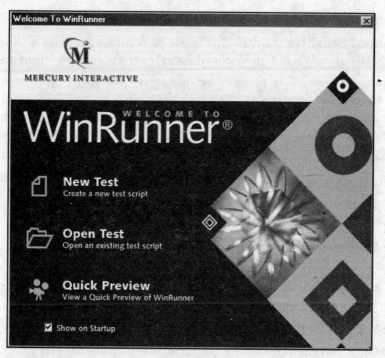

Fig. 4.1

You can select the Quick Preview to get a good understanding of this tool. You can run the sample application given along with this tool to understand the intricacies of this tool.

4.2.1 Recording Test Cases

To test any application, first you can run the application and understand its operation. Then, you can invoke WinRunner, again run the application and record the GUI operations. During the recording mode, WinRunner will capture all your actions, which button you pressed, where you clicked the mouse etc. You need to work with the application as usual and perform all the actions to be tested. Once the recording is completed, WinRunner generates a script in TSL (Test Script Language). You can run this test script generated by WinRunner to view the results. The test results will show whether the test has passed or failed.

Once the required actions are recorded, the application should be brought back to the "Base state" (initial state).

There are two modes of recording:

1. **Context Sensitive mode:** This mode of recording is used when the location of the GUI controls (i.e. X and Y coordinates) or the mouse positions are not necessary.

2. **Analog mode:** This mode of recording is used when the mouse positions, the location of the controls in the application, also play an important role in testing the application. This mode of recording has to be used to validate bitmaps, testing the signature etc.

The procedure for recording a test case is as follows:

Step 1: Open a new document: File → New (or) Select "New Test" from the WinRunner's Welcome screen.

Step 2: Open (run) the application to be tested.

Step 3: Start recording a test case.

Create →   Record – Context Sensitive (or) click on the toolbar's "Record" button once, to record in Context Sensitive mode.

Step 4: Select the application to be tested by clicking on the application's title bar.

Step 5: Perform all the actions to be recorded.

Step 6: Once all required actions are recorded, stop the recording.

Create → Stop (or) Click on the toolbar's "Stop" button to stop the recording WinRunner generates the script for the recoded actions.

There are two modes for generating the test cases: "Global GUI map file mode" and "GUI map file per test mode". By default, it is in "Global GUI map file mode".

■ In Global GUI map file mode, you have to explicitly save the information learnt by WinRunner. WinRunner saves it in a file with extension ".gui".

When you have to run a test, you need to load the corresponding GUI map file; otherwise it will not be able to recognize the objects in the test case and displays an error message.

■ In GUI map file per test mode, WinRunner automatically saves the information it has learnt from the application.

It is always preferred to work in Global GUI map file mode.

The procedure for saving the GUI map file in Global GUI map file mode is as follows:

Step 1: Record a test case by following the preceding procedure.

Step 2: Open the GUI Map Editor window as shown in Fig. 4.2.

Tools → GUI Map Editor

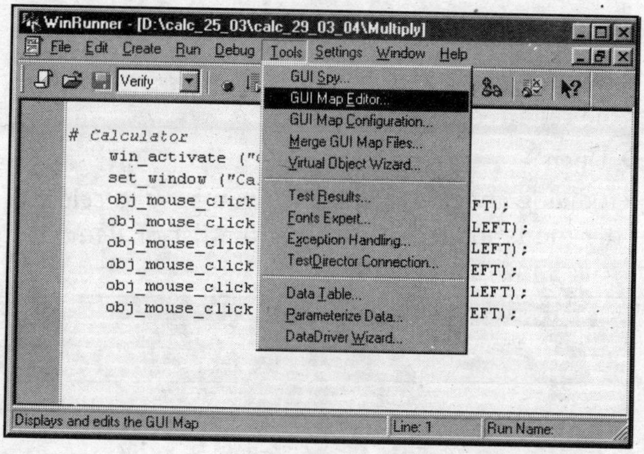

Fig. 4.2

Step 3: On selecting the GUI Map Editor, the screen as shown in Fig. 4.3 is displayed.

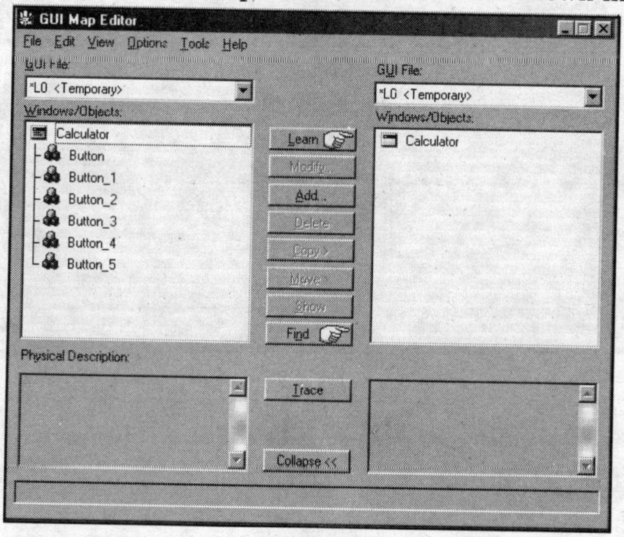

Fig. 4.3

Step 4: Save the GUI Map file.

File → Save As

A File dialog appears and you need to enter the filename.

Step 5: Close the GUI Map Editor window.

The procedure for loading the GUI map file is as follows:

Step 1: Open the GUI Map Editor.

Tools → GUI Map Editor

Step 2: Close all the opened GUI Map files

File → Close All

Step 3: Select the required GUI Map file

File → Open

A File Open dialog appears from which you have to select the GUI map file to be loaded. Once the file is loaded, it displays the list of items it has learnt during the recording phase as shown in Fig. 4.4.

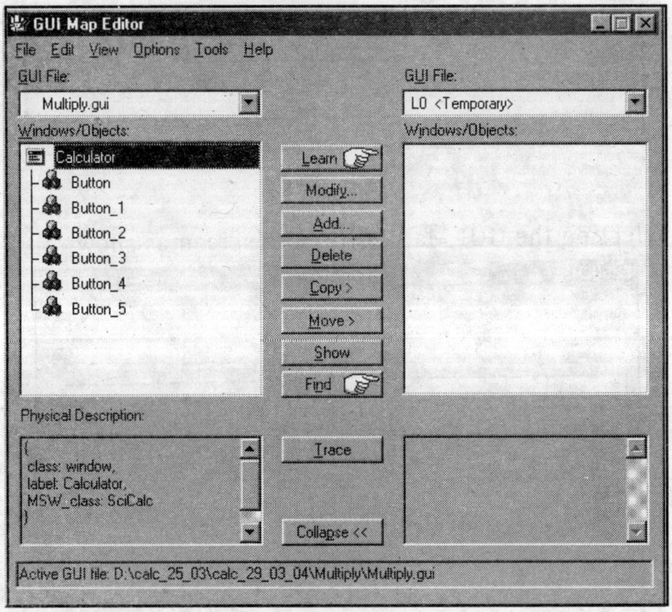

Fig. 4.4

The procedure for running a test case is as follows:

Step 1: Open the test script to be executed.

Step 2: Run the test

Run → Run from top (or) press F5 to run the test.

WinRunner executes the generated script and displays the results in the Test Results window.

We will now illustrate using WinRunner to test the "Standard Calculator" application available on your Windows system. You can invoke the calculator application from the desktop Start → Programs → Accessories → Calculator. The GUI of the "Calculator" application is shown in Fig. 4.5.

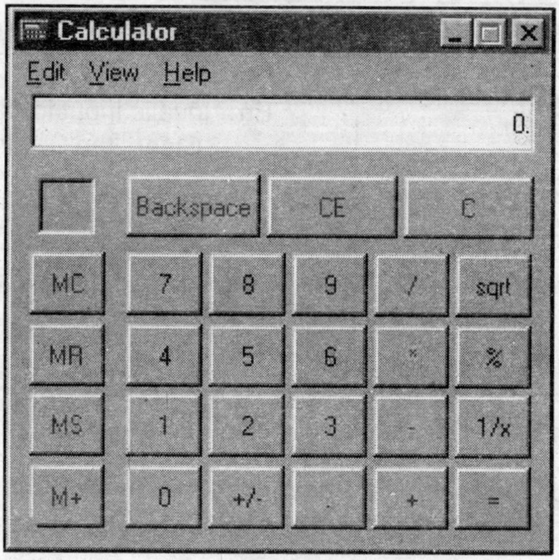

Fig. 4.5

The symbols on the buttons of Calculator application represent the following functions:

+ :   To perform addition

- :   To perform subtraction

* :   To perform multiplication

/ :   To perform division

. :   Decimal point

sqrt: To find square root of a number

% :   To find percent

1/x :   To find inverse of a number

MC :   To clear the memory

MR :   To recall from memory

MS :   To save in the memory

M+ :   To add to the memory

C :   To clear the current calculation

CE :   To clear the displayed number

Backspace: To remove left most digit

+/- :   To give sign to a number (positive or negative)

To test the complete functionality of the application, we need to generate test cases in such a way that all the buttons are made use of. We need to generate some test cases which will give correct output and also some test cases which will give error messages. Table 4.1 table gives such test cases and the expected output for each test case.

Test Case	Expected Output
4 1/x	0.25
- 6 sqrt	Err: "Invalid input for function"
4 C	Clears the Display
1.2 * 3	3.6
5 / 2.0	2.5
7 + 8 − 9	6
600 * 2 %	12
2, MS, C, MR	2
MC, 2, M+, 3, M+, C, MR	5

Table 4.1 Test Cases and Expected outputs for testing the Calculator.

To test the functionality of the application perform the following steps:

Test Case #1: To test the Inverse operation (inverse of 4 using 1/x button)

Step 1: Open WinRunner application.

Step 2: Open Calculator application.

Step 3: Create a new document as shown in Fig. 4.6.

File → New or Click ⬜ (New) on tool bar or press Ctrl+N

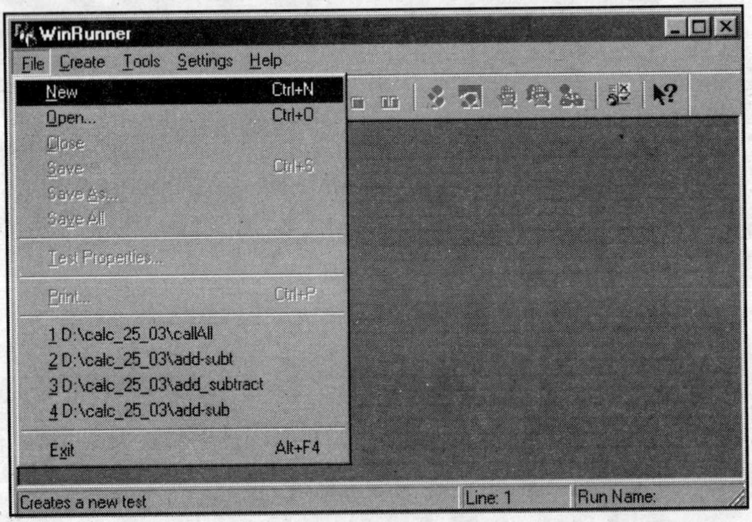

Fig. 4.6

Step 4: Start recording

Create → Record-Context Sensitive (or) press F2 (or) Click ● on the toolbar

Click the (Record-Context Sensitive) button on the toolbar of WinRunner as shown in Fig. 4.7 or Select "Record – Context sensitive" option from the "Create" menu as shown in Fig. 4.8.

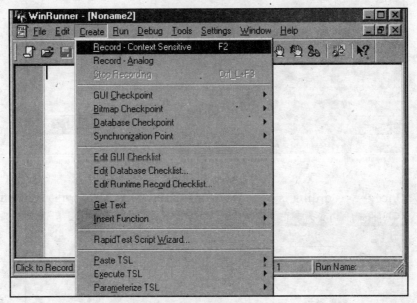

Fig. 4.7

Fig. 4.8

Step 5: Select the Calculator application and start recording the actions.

- Click "4" on the Calculator
- Click the "1/x" button on the Calculator to find the inverse of 4.
- The result, 0.25 will be displayed on the Calculator.

Step 6: Stop the Recording process.

   Create → Stop Recording (or) Click (Stop) on toolbar

Click (Stop Recording) button on the toolbar of WinRunner as shown in Fig. 4.9 or
   Select the "Stop Recording" option from the "Create" menu as shown in Fig. 4.10.

Fig. 4.9

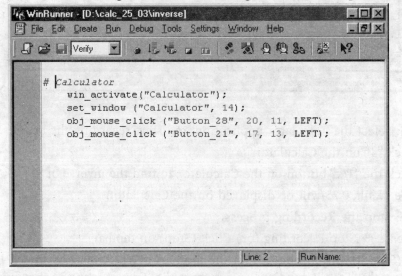

Fig. 4.10

Step 7: Once the recording is over, WinRunner generates TSL Script as shown in Fig. 4.11.

Fig. 4.11

```
# Calculator
    win_activate("Calculator");
    set_window ("Calculator", 14);
    obj_mouse_click ("Button_28", 20, 11, LEFT);
    obj_mouse_click ("Button_21", 17, 13, LEFT);
```

Step 8: Save the file as "inverse" in the selected folder.

File → Save

In the "Save" dialog box that appears, save the test script with name "inverse".

Step 9: Run the test script generated by WinRunner.

Run → Run from Top or press F5 or Click (Run from Top) on the toolbar

Click the (Run from Top) button on the toolbar of WinRunner as shown in Fig. 4.12 or select the "Run from Top" option from the "Run" menu as shown in Fig. 4.13.

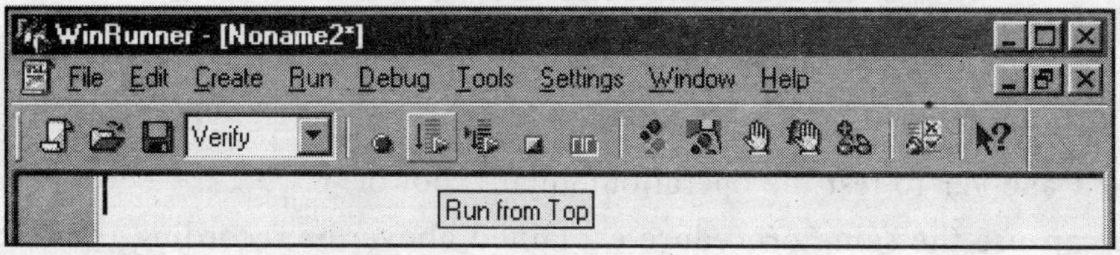

Fig. 4.12

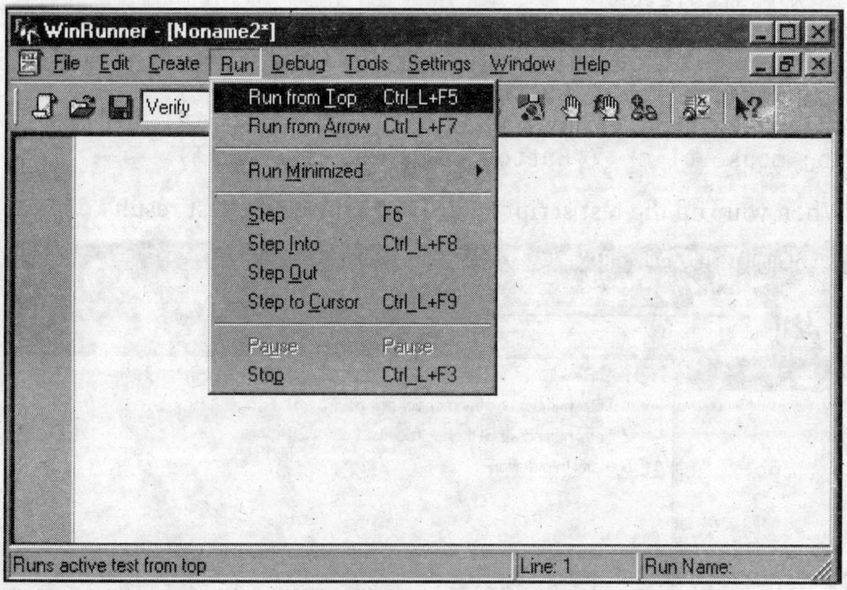

Fig. 4.13

Step 10: After executing the TSL statements, WinRunner generates test results as shown in Fig. 4.14. The Results column indicates whether the test has "Passed" or "Failed". The test results also give useful information such as the name of the test case, the line numbers in the test script and the time taken for executing the test case.

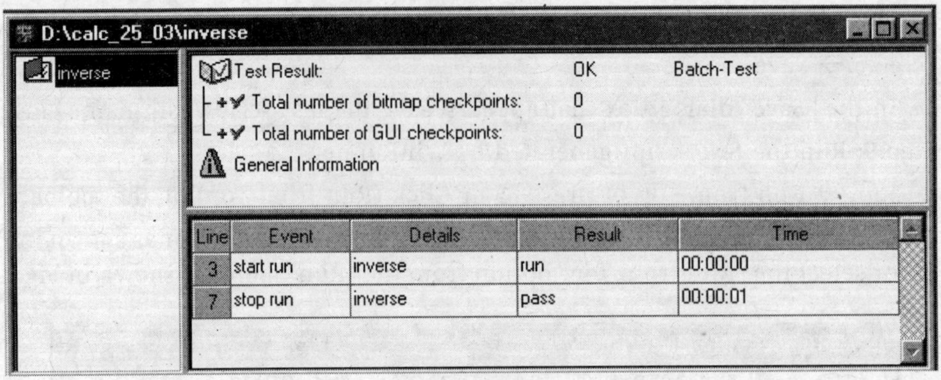

Fig. 4.14

Test Case #2: To test the operation Square root of -6.

You can use the same procedure explained above for recording the test case. The
following test script will be generated:

```
    # Calculator
win_activate ("Calculator");
set_window ("Calculator", 1);
obj_mouse_click ("Button_38", 20, 12, LEFT);
obj_mouse_drag ("Button_35", 10, 15, 11, 14, LEFT);
obj_mouse_click ("Button_60", 20, 11, LEFT);
```

When you run the test script again, you can see the test results, as in Fig. 4.15.

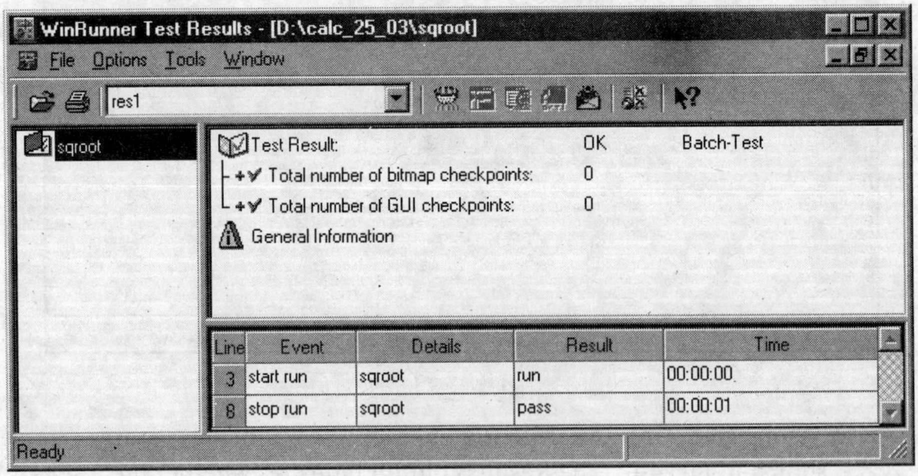

Fig. 4.15

Test Case #3: To clear the display after performing some operations. For this test
case, the following script will be generated:

```
# Calculator
win_activate ("Calculator");
set_window ("Calculator", 3);
obj_mouse_click ("Button_37", 13, 23, LEFT);
obj_mouse_click ("Button_59", 34, 19, LEFT);
```

Again, you can run the test script and observe the test results (Fig. 4.16).

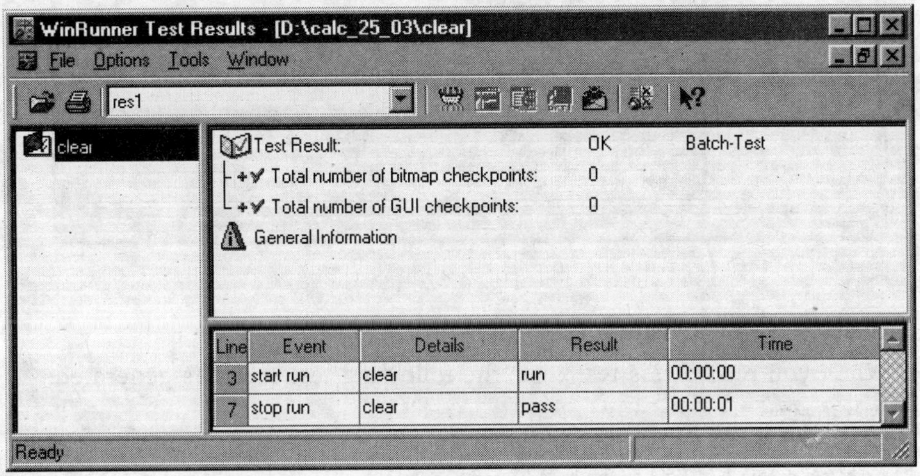

Fig. 4.16

Test Case #4: Multiplication of two numbers. (1.2 * 3)

When you record this test case, the following test script is generated:

```
# Calculator
    win_activate ("Calculator");
    win_move ("Calculator", 489, 176);
    set_window ("Calculator", 5);
    obj_mouse_click ("Button_29", 11, 15, LEFT);
    obj_mouse_click ("Button_40", 16, 13, LEFT);
    obj_mouse_click ("Button_34", 26, 12, LEFT);
    obj_mouse_click ("Button_43", 10, 4, LEFT);
    obj_mouse_click ("Button_39", 20, 9, LEFT);
    obj_mouse_click ("Button_50", 23, 19, LEFT);
```

The test results are shown in Fig. 4.17.

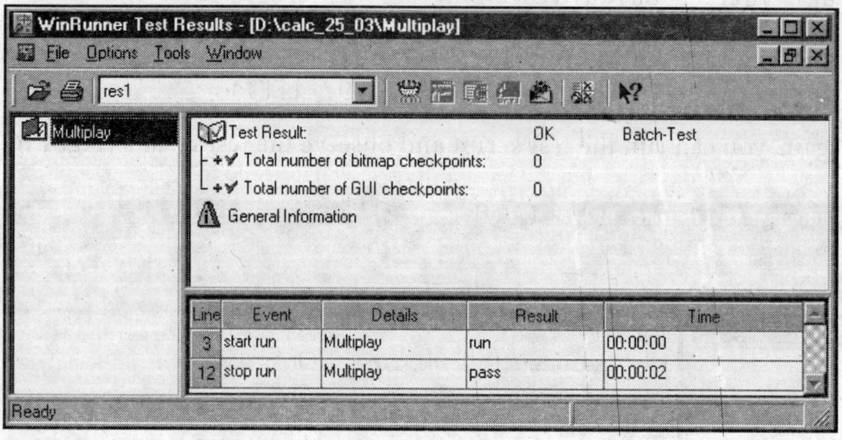

Fig. 4.17

Test Case #5: Division of two numbers. (5 / 2.0)

When you record this test case, the following test script is generated:

```
# Calculator
win_activate ("Calculator");
set_window ("Calculator", 7);
obj_mouse_click ("Button_33", 25, 14, LEFT);
obj_mouse_click ("Button_42", 22, 11, LEFT);
obj_mouse_click ("Button_34", 19, 16, LEFT);
obj_mouse_click ("Button_40", 18, 19, LEFT);
obj_mouse_click ("Button_30", 19, 10, LEFT);
obj_mouse_drag ("Button_50", 19, 19, 18, 19, LEFT);
```

The corresponding test results screen is shown in Fig. 4.18.

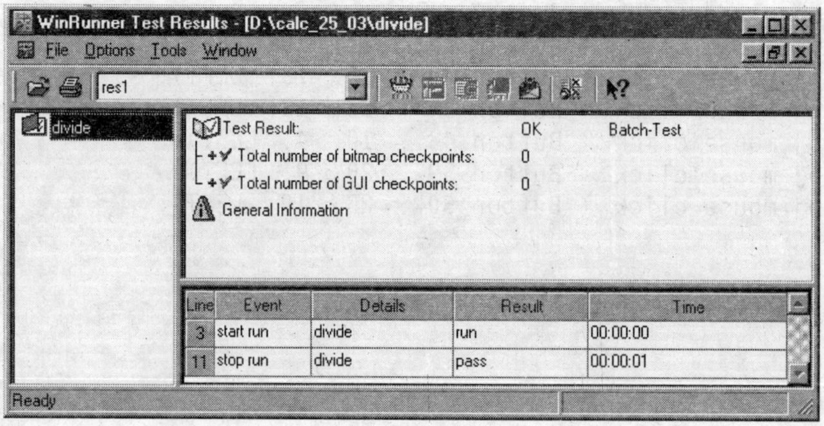

Fig. 4.18

Test Case #6: To test the operation (7 + 8 − 9)

The following test script is generated:

```
# Calculator
win_activate ("Calculator");
set_window ("Calculator", 7);
obj_mouse_click ("Button_27", 17, 14, LEFT);
obj_mouse_click ("Button_45", 12, 20, LEFT);
obj_mouse_click ("Button_32", 12, 17, LEFT);
obj_mouse_drag ("Button_44", 22, 11, 23, 11, LEFT);
obj_mouse_click ("Button_37", 19, 13, LEFT);
obj_mouse_drag ("Button_50", 16, 16, 17, 16, LEFT);
```

The test results screen is shown in Fig. 4.19.

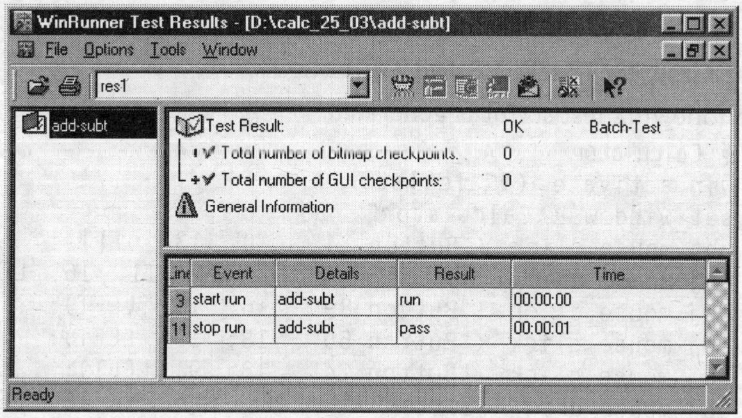

WinRunner Test Results - [D:\calc_25_03\add-subt]

File   Options   Tools   Window

add-subt

Test Result:		OK	Batch-Test
Total number of bitmap checkpoints.		0	
Total number of GUI checkpoints:		0	
General Information			

Line	Event	Details	Result	Time
3	start run	add-subt	run	00:00:00
11	stop run	add-subt	pass	00:00:01

Ready

Fig. 4.19

Test Case #7: To test the operation 2% of 600.

The following test script is generated:

```
# Calculator
win_activate ("Calculator");
set_window ("Calculator", 1);
obj_mouse_click ("Button_38", 23, 14, LEFT);
obj_mouse_dbl_click ("Button_30", 13, 4, LEFT);
obj_mouse_click ("Button_43", 15, 14, LEFT);
obj_mouse_click ("Button_34", 19, 12, LEFT);
obj_mouse_click ("Button_61", 14, 19, LEFT);
```

The test results screen is shown in Fig. 4.20.

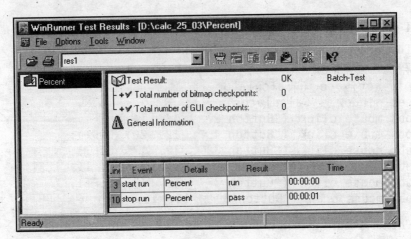

Fig. 4.20

Test Case #8: To test MS and MR buttons.

The following test script is generated:

```
# Calculator
win_activate ("Calculator");
set_window ("Calculator", 2);
obj_mouse_click ("Button_34", 10, 13, LEFT);
obj_mouse_drag ("Button_45", 10, 16, 11, 16, LEFT);
obj_mouse_click ("Button_39", 16, 11, LEFT);
obj_mouse_click ("Button_50", 18, 19, LEFT);
obj_mouse_click ("Button_24", 18, 9, LEFT);
obj_mouse_drag ("Button_59", 25, 19, 25, 18, LEFT);
obj_mouse_click ("Button_23", 8, 13, LEFT);
```

The test results screen is as shown in Fig. 4.21.

Fig. 4.21

Test Case #9: To test M+ and MR buttons.

The following test script is generated:

```
# Calculator
    win_activate ("Calculator");
    set_window ("Calculator", 2);
    obj_mouse_click ("Button_6", 27, 9, LEFT);
    obj_mouse_click ("Button_2", 17, 15, LEFT);
    obj_mouse_click ("Button_7", 16, 19, LEFT);
    obj_mouse_click ("Button_4", 22, 20, LEFT);
    obj_mouse_click ("Button_7", 15, 17, LEFT);
    obj_mouse_click ("Button_8", 19, 13, LEFT);
    obj_mouse_click ("Button_9", 22, 19, LEFT);
```

The test results screen is as shown in Fig. 4.22.

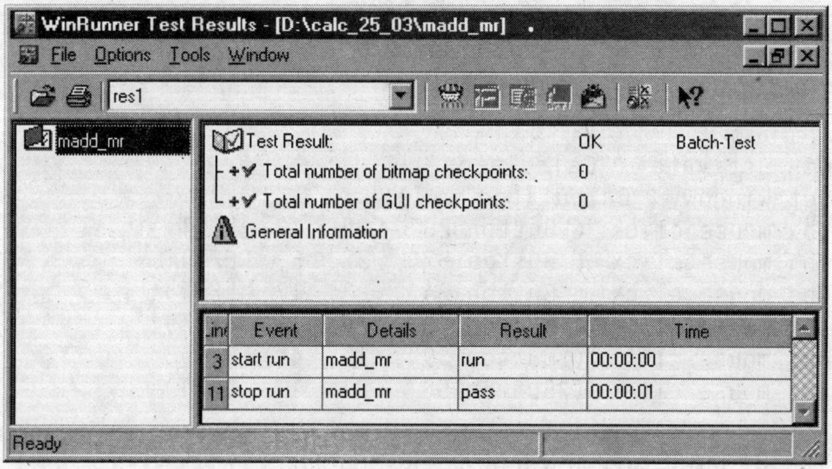

Fig. 4.22

Test Case #10: To test MC button

The following test script is generated:

```
# Calculator
win_activate ("Calculator");
set_window ("Calculator", 3);
obj_mouse_click ("Button_37", 13, 23, LEFT);
obj_mouse_click ("Button_59", 34, 19, LEFT);
```

The test results screen is shown in Fig. 4.23.

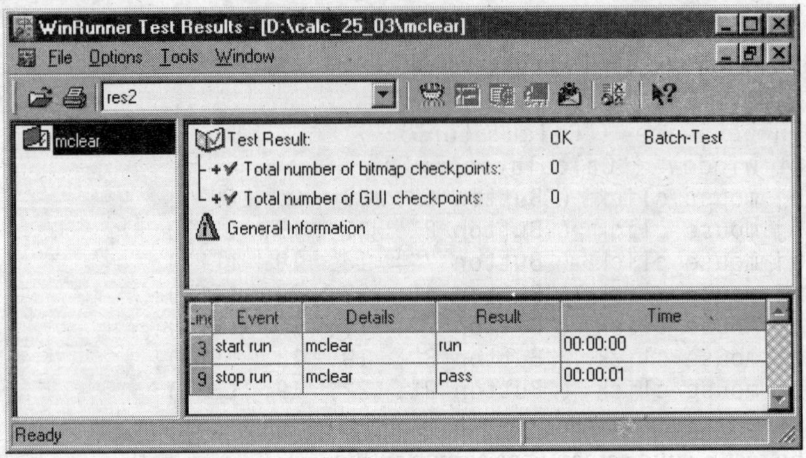

Fig. 4.23

Test Case #11: To test the Backspace

The following test script is generated:

```
# Calculator
win_activate ("Calculator");
set_window ("Calculator", 1);
obj_mouse_click ("Button_28", 20, 12, LEFT);
obj_mouse_click ("Button_57", 37, 5, LEFT);
obj_mouse_click ("Button_34", 23, 17, LEFT);
obj_mouse_click ("Button_45", 24, 16, LEFT);
obj_mouse_click ("Button_39", 19, 4, LEFT);
obj_mouse_click ("Button_50", 21, 17, LEFT);
```

The test results screen will be as shown in Fig. 4.24.

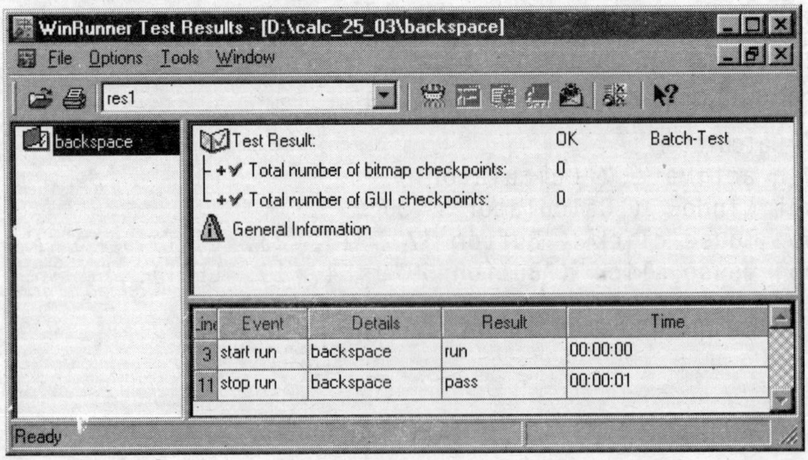

Fig. 4.24

If you want to repeatedly execute the preceding test cases, it will be very time consuming. You can call the test cases using the "call" function as illustrated below.

4.2.2 Calling the Test Cases using "call" Function

The "call" function can be used to execute a series of test cases without any user interaction. The syntax of call function is:

call <test-case name> for example, call test1();

- Create a new document
- Write the following test script
- Save the file as "callAll"
- Execute the test case

All the preceding test cases can be combined into one file as follows:

```
call  inverse();
call  sqroot();
call  clear();
call  Multiplay();
call  divide();
call  add_subtract();
call  Percent();
call  ms_mr();
call  madd_mr();
call  mclear();
call  backspace();
```

When you execute this test script, all the earlier test cases are executed in one shot. The test results screen will be as shown in Fig. 4.25. As you can see from the table, the "Details" column gives the various test cases executed. The "Result" column shows whether the test has passed or failed. The "Time" column gives the time taken to execute the test case.

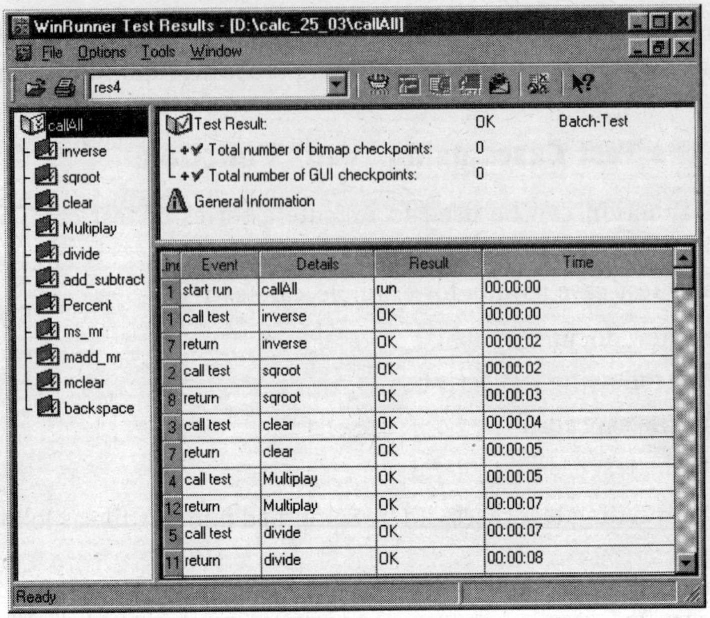

Fig. 4.25

When you have to retest the application using the same test cases, you can run the script in unattended mode. You can save the script in a file and run the script at specified time.

This feature of WinRunner is extremely useful for regression testing. When you are developing the software, you need to run the same set of test cases many times. So, you can run the application once, generate the test script and then keep doing the regression testing. Obviously, the productivity of the test engineers will be very high when this tool is used.

4.3 Test Script Language (TSL)

Test Script Language (TSL) is a scripting language with syntax similar to C language. There are 4 categories of TSL functions. Each category of functions is for performing specific tasks: These categories are as follows:

- *Analog functions*: These functions are used when you record in Analog mode, a mode in which the exact coordinates of the GUI map are required.

- *Context sensitive functions*: These functions are used where the exact coordinates are not required.

- *Customization functions*: These functions allow the user to improve the testing tool by adding functions to the Function Generator.

- *Standard functions*: These functions include all the basic elements of programming language like control flow statements, mathematical functions, string related functions etc.

The most frequently used functions in each category are as follows:

- *click:* To click a mouse button.

    Syntax: click(mouse_button,[time])

    mouse_button – specify LEFT, RIGHT or MIDDLE

- *dbl_click:* To double click a mouse button.

    Syntax: dbl_click(mouse_button,[time])

    mouse_button – specify LEFT, RIGHT or MIDDLE

- *get_x:* To get the current x coordinate of the mouse pointer.

    Syntax: get_x();

    Return value: integer

- *get_y:* To get the current y coordinate of the mouse pointer.

    Syntax: get_y();

    Return value: integer

- *wait_window:* Waits for a window bitmap to appear for synchronizing the test procedure.

    Syntax: wait_window(time, image, window, width, height, x, y [, relx1, rely1, relx2, rely2])

- *get_text:* To read the text from the screen specified by the location.

    Syntax: get_text(location);

    The location can be x1, y1, x2, y2 or x ,y or ()(no location).When no location is specified, it considers the point closest to the mouse pointer.

- *button_check_info:* To check the value of the button property.

    Syntax: button_check_info (Button, property, property_value);

    Button – Name of the button

    Property - The property to be checked

    Property_value - The property value

- *button_check_state:* To check the state of the radio button or check box.

    Syntax: button_check_state (button, state);

    Button - Name of the button.

    State - The state of the button (1 for ON and 0 for OFF)

- *button_get_info:* Returns the value of a button property.

    Syntax: button_get_info (button, property, out_value);

Button - Name of the button.

Property - The property of the button to be retrieved.

Out_value – The variable where the retrieved property value will be stored.

■ *button_get_state:* To get the state of a radio button or check button.

Syntax: button_get_state (Button, Out_state);

Button - The name of the radio button or check button.

Out_state - The variable where the retrieved state of the button will be stored.

■ *button_press:* clicks on a push button.

Syntax: button_press (Button);

Button - The logical name of the button.

■ *button_set:* To set the state of a radio or check button.

Syntax: button_set (Button, State);

Button - The name of the button.

State - The state of the button.

The state of the button can either be ON, OFF, DIMMED or TOGGLE (toggles between ON and OFF).

■ *button_wait_info:* Waits for the value of a button property.

Syntax: button_wait_info (Button, Property, Value, time);

Button - The name of the button.

Property - The property of the button

Value - The value of the property

Time - The time interval before the next statement to be executed.

■ *ddt_close:* To close the data table file.

Syntax: ddt_close (data_table_name);

Data_table_name – name of the data table.

■ *ddt_close_all_tables:* To close all open tables.

Syntax: ddt_close_all_tables();

■ *db_disconnect:* To disconnect from the database and end the database session.

Syntax: db_disconnect (Session_name);

Session_name – The logical name of the database.

■ *ddt_get_row_count:* To retrieve the number of rows in a data table.

Syntax: ddt_get_row_count (Data_table_name, out_rows_count);

Data_table_name – The name of the data table.

out_rows_count – The variable in which the row count is stored.

- *ddt_get_current_row:* To retrieve the current row from the data table.

  Syntax: ddt_get_current_row (Data_table_name, out_row);

  Data_table_name – The name of the data table.

  Out_row – The variable that stores the output row from the data table.

- *ddt_next_row:* To point to the next row in the data table.

  Syntax: ddt_next_row (Data_table_name);

  Data_table_name – The name of the data table.

- *ddt_open:* To create or open a data table file so that WinRunner can access it.

  Syntax: ddt_open (Data_table_name [, Mode]);

  Data_table-name – The name of the Data table.

  Mode – The mode in which the table has to be opened. The various modes are: DDT_MODE_READ (read-only) or DDT_MODE_READWRITE (read or write).

- *edit_check_info:* To check the value of an edit object property.

  Syntax: edit_check_info (Edit, Property, Property_value);

  Edit - The logical name of the edit object.

  Property – The property to be checked.

  Property_value – The values of the property.

- *edit_delete:* To delete the contents of an edit object.

  Syntax: edit_delete (Edit, Start_column, End_column);

  Edit - The logical name of the edit object.

  Start_column - The column where the text starts.

  End_column – The column where the text ends.

- *obj_check_gui:* To compare the current GUI object data to expected data.

  Syntax: obj_check_gui (Object, Checklist, Expected_results_file, Time);

  Object - The logical name of the GUI object.

  Checklist - The name of the checklist defining the GUI checks.

  Expected_results_file - The name of the file that stores the expected GUI data.

  Time – Specifies the delay between the previous input and the next input.

- *win_check_gui:* To compare the current GUI data to expected GUI data for a window.

  Syntax: win_check_gui (Window, Checklist, Expected_results_file, Time);

  Object - The logical name of the GUI object.

  Checklist - The name of the checklist defining the GUI checks.

  Expected_results_file - The name of the file that stores the expected GUI data.

  Time – Specifies the delay between the previous input and the next input.

- *list_activate_item:* To activate an item in a list.

  Syntax: list_activate_item (List, Item [, Offset]);

  List – The logical name of the list.

  Item – The item to be activated in the list.

  Offset – The horizontal offset of the click location in pixels.

- *menu_get_info:* To return the value of a menu property.

  Syntax: menu_get_info (Menu, Property, Out_value);

  Menu – The logical name of the menu.

  Property – The property to be checked.

  Out_value – The variable in which the value of the specified property is stored.

- *menu_get_item:* To return the contents of a menu item.

  Syntax: menu_get_item (Menu, Item_number, Out_contents);

  Menu - The logical name of the menu.

  Item_number - The numerical position of the item in the menu.

  Out_contents - The output variable to which the value of the designated menu item is assigned.

- *obj_check_bitmap:* To compare an object bitmap to an expected bitmap.

  Syntax: obj_check_bitmap (Object, Bitmap, Time [, x, y, width, height]);

  Object - The logical name of the GUI object.

  Bitmap - A string expression that identifies the captured bitmap.

  Time – The time interval for which the application waits for the expected bitmap

- *obj_check_gui:* To compare the current GUI object data to expected data.

  Syntax: obj_check_gui (Object, Checklist, Expected_results_file, Time);

  Object - The logical name of the GUI object

  Checklist - The name of the checklist defining the GUI checks.

  Expected_results_file - The name of the file that stores the expected GUI data.

  Time – The delay between the previous input and the next input.

Test Script Language (TSL) is a C-like procedural programming language. It has constructs like statements, comments, constants, variables, mathematical operators, control statements, and functions.

4.4 GUI MAP File

In WinRunner, if you run a test case without loading the corresponding GUI Map file, it generates an error as it fails to identify the controls used in the test cases. This is illustrated with an example here.

Suppose you have recorded a test case for "inverse" function for the Calculator application and forgot to save its GUI Map file. When you close the test case and again open it to run the test case, an error message is generated as shown in Fig. 4.26.

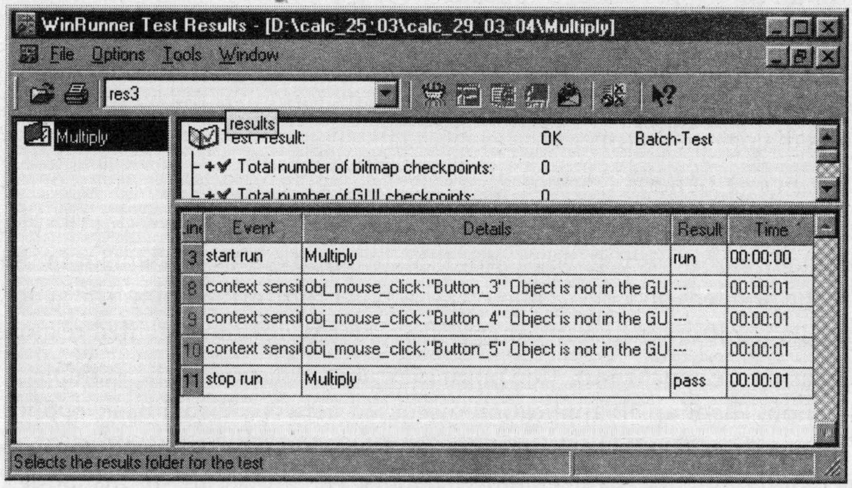

Fig. 4.26

Even if you save the GUI Map file but forget to load the corresponding GUI Map file mode, it generates the error message as shown in Fig. 4.26.

WinRunner may generate some ambiguous or wrong results but not errors if the application is not brought back to base state before trying to run the application. It is always advisable to bring the state of the application to base state while "Recording".

The other important features of WinRunner application are as follows:

1. Synchronization of test cases
2. Data driven testing
3. Rapid testing
4. GUI checkpoints

We will demonstrate these features with illustrative examples in the following sections.

4.5 Synchronization of Test Cases

In WinRunner, it takes by default one second to execute the next statement. But sometimes there may be a case where the WinRunner has to wait for a few seconds to accept the data from the user or wait till the current operation is completed, before executing the next statement.

The Synchronization is required in the following cases:

- When data has to be retrieved from the database.
- When a progress bar has to reach 100%.
- To wait till some message appears.

Though, by default, WinRunner takes one second to execute the next statement, it is possible to change the default time to any desired value. Changing the value of the "Timeout for Checkpoints and CS Statement" option in the Run tab of the General option's dialog can do this.

Settings → General Options

In such a case, it will affect the entire application and as a result the entire process of testing becomes very slow. To avoid this, we find out the statement in the test script where the problem may occur and create a synchronization point. The synchronization point tells WinRunner to wait for specified interval for the specified response.

Creating the synchronization point is explained here with the example of a database application. The EmpDB application discussed here is a Visual Basic application and is available on the CDROM that accompanies this book. This application is used to create, open, modify, and delete the employee details. The procedure for installing this sample application is given in Appendix E. The first screen of EmpDB is shown in Fig. 4.27.

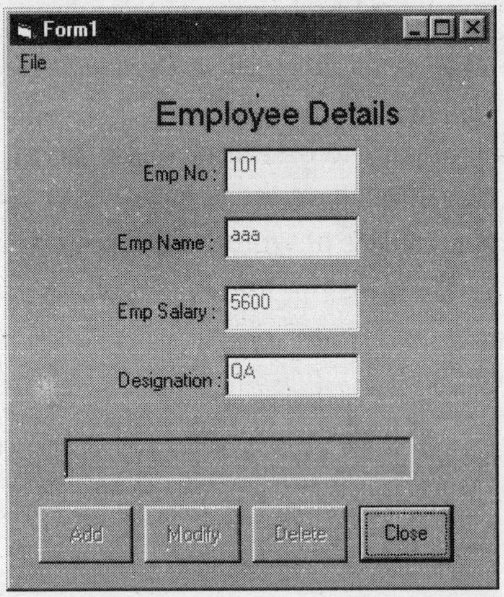

Fig. 4.27

Creating the Test Case

Step 1: Open WinRunner application and create a new test case.

Step 2: Open the EmpDB application.

Step 3: Start recording the test case in Context Sensitive mode

Create → Record – Context Sensitive or click the button from WinRunner toolbar.

Step 4: Create a new Employee record as shown in Fig. 4.28.

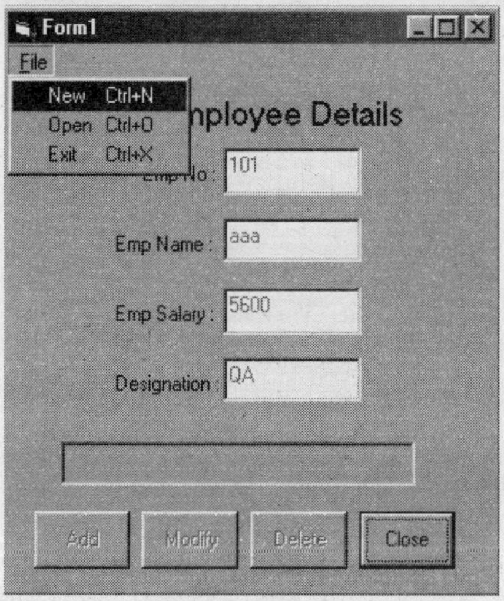

Fig. 4.28

Step 5: When you click "New" menu option, a dialog is displayed where the Emp No. is automatically incremented and prompts you to enter the remaining details such as Emp Name, Emp Salary, Designation as shown in Fig.4. 29.

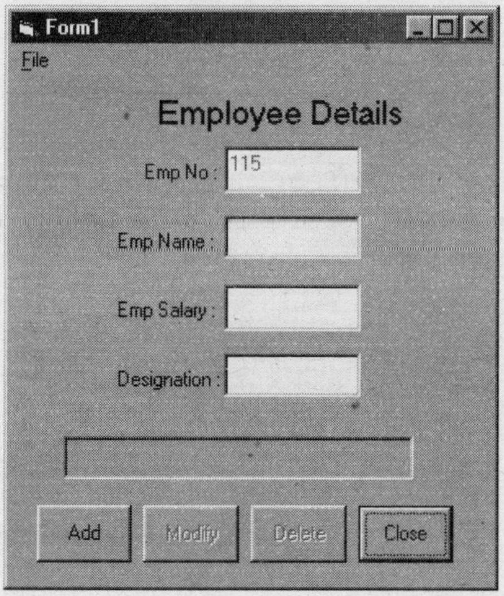

Fig. 4.29

Step 6: After entering all the details click on "Add" button to insert the record into the database as shown in Fig. 4.30.

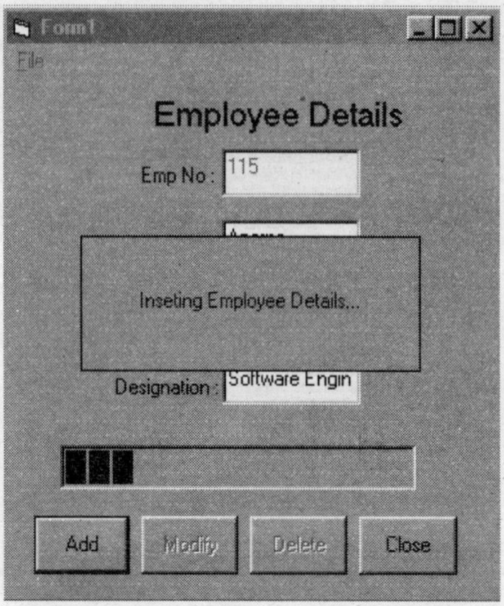

Fig. 4.30

Step 7: When the insertion is completed, "Insert Done" message appears in the status bar as shown in Fig. 4.31.

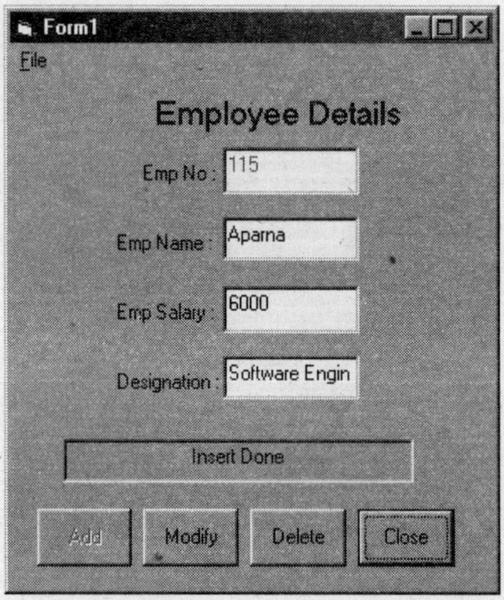

Fig. 4.31

Step 8: Select File → Exit and close the EmpDB application.

Step 9: Stop the recording process.

Create→ Stop Recording or click the button on the WinRunner toolbar.

Step10: Save the test script with name "sync_before". The test script is displayed as shown in Fig. 4.32.

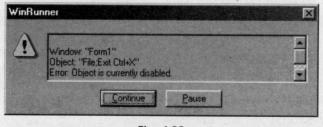

Fig. 4.32

Step 11: Run the test case by selecting "Run from Top" option from the Run menu or Click button on WinRunner toolbar. An error message, as shown in Fig. 4.33 appears because WinRunner fails to select the menu option "File – Exit". The error occurred because WinRunner did not wait until the insertion action is completed. Click "Pause" button.

Fig. 4.33

If you click on the "Continue" button, it executes the remaining lines in the test script and displays the error report as shown in Fig. 4.34.

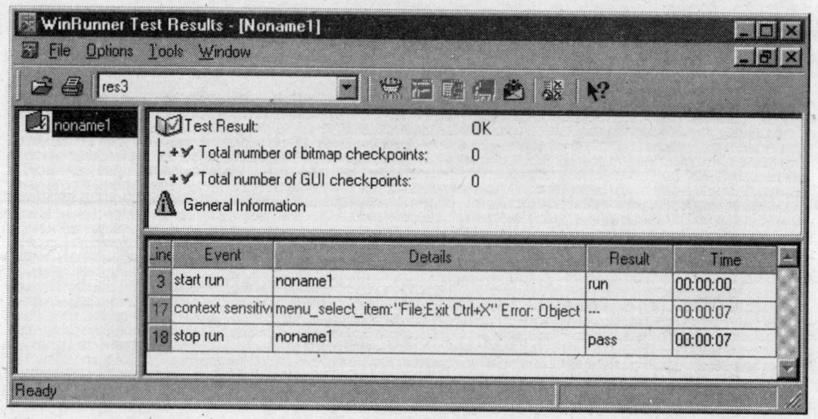

Fig. 4.34

To avoid such kind of problems, synchronizing the test cases is required. WinRunner application captures the bitmap image of the "Insert Done" and when you run the test script, it waits for the "Insert Done" message to appear in the status bar.

Synchronizing the Test Cases

We will now create a synchronization point into the test script shown in Fig. 4.32.

Step 1: Open the test script if it is closed.

File → Open and select the "sync_before" file.

Step 2: Place the cursor at the point where the test has to be synchronized.

Insert a line after the statement

obj_mouse_click ("Add", 49, 12, LEFT);

as our aim is to make the WinRunner application wait till the insertion is over.

Step 3: Insert a synchronization point as shown in Fig. 4.35 to make WinRunner wait until the insertion is completed.

Create → Synchronization Point → For Object/Window Bitmap

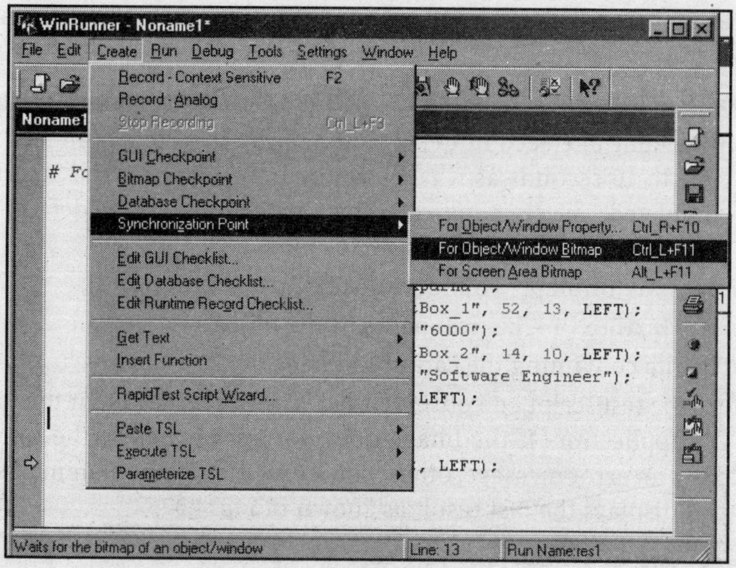

Fig. 4.35

Step 4: Use the pointer to select the "Insert Done" status message in the EmpDB dialog as shown in Fig. 4.36.

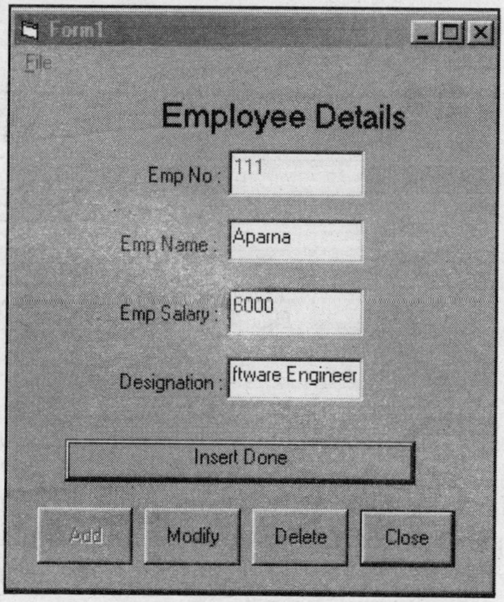

Fig. 4.36

Once you select the status message, it inserts the following statement into the test script:

```
obj_wait_bitmap("ThunderRT6TextBox_4","Img1",1);
```

Step 5: By default one-second delay time will be inserted. Manually change the wait time to 10 seconds as it takes about 10 seconds for the insertion action to be completed. The time indicated by you is added to the default time interval. So totally WinRunner waits for 11 seconds.

obj_wait_bitmap("ThunderRT6TextBox_4","Img1",10);

ThunderRT6TextBox_4 – Logical name of the object.

Img1 – The file containing the captured image

Step 6: Run the test script and observe that, WinRunner waits for the image to appear in the application. If the image does not appear before the timeout time, it displays an error message; otherwise it executes all the statements in the test script and displays the test result as shown in Fig. 4.37.

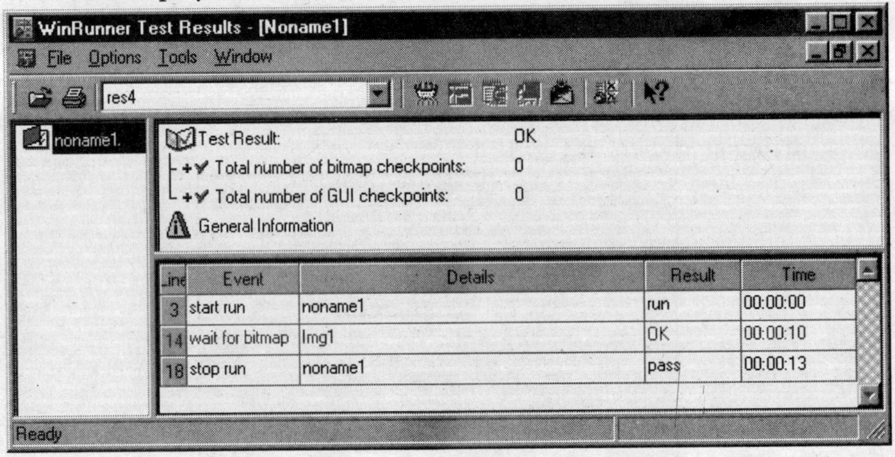

Fig. 4.37

4.6 Data-Driven Testing

Once the test script is created, we may sometimes want to check how the test script behaves for multiple data. This can be done by creating that many number of test cases and by running each test case individually, which is a very tedious process. In such cases we make use of Data-Driver wizard. This involves 3 steps.

- Inserting the statements to open and close the data table.
- Retrieving the data from the data table.

■ Replacing the static values (for example, the employee name) with the variables containing the retrieved value from the data table. This is known as parameterizing the test.

Converting the test case to Data-Driven test

Step 1: Create a new test case for inserting one record in the EmpDB application and synchronize it.

Step 2: Open the DataDriver Wizard. It then selects the entire test script and displays the DataDriver wizard window as shown in Fig. 4.38.

Tools → DataDriver Wizard

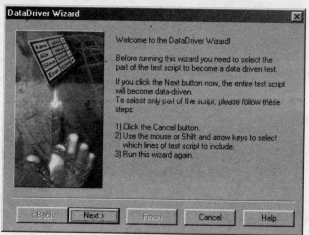

Fig. 4.38

Click "Next".

Step 3: Create the data table.

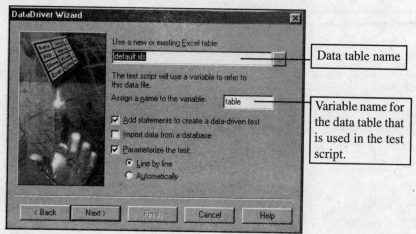

Fig. 4.39

Enter new or select the existing name of the data table. Here, we are taking the data from an Excel table and hence the name of the table has .xls extension. Select the "Add Statements" check box to add the code to the test script. Click the "Next" button.

Step 4: Select the data that has to be parameterized by creating a new column in the data table as shown in Fig. 4.40.

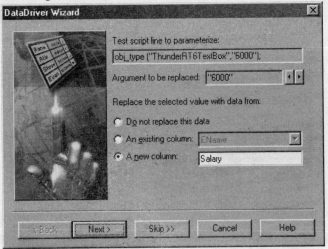

Fig. 4.40

Select "A new column" radio button and enter the column name as "Ename". This will create a new column in the data table with column name as "Ename". Click next.

Step 5: Select "A New column" radio button and enter the column name as "Salary" as shown in Fig. 4.41.

Fig. 4.41

Step 6: Create another column with name "Designation" as shown in Fig. 4.42. Click "Next"

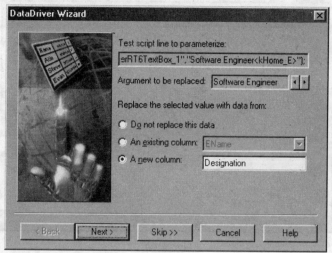

Fig. 4.42

Step 7: Once the data has been parameterized, it displays the screen shown in Fig. 4.43.

Fig. 4.43

Check the "Show data table now" to enter the values in the data table for which the test has to be executed as shown in Fig. 4.44.

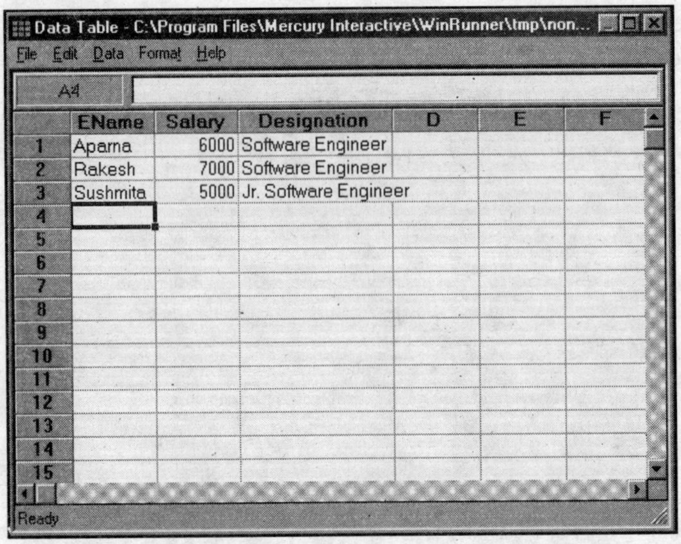

Fig. 4.44

WinRunner adds all the statements required for opening, closing the data table and also for retrieving the values from the data table. It also replaces the static values with the variables containing values retrieved from the data table as shown below.

```
table = "table.xls";
rc = ddt_open(table, DDT_MODE_READ);
if (rc!= E_OK && rc != E_FILE_OPEN)
    pause("Cannot open table.");
ddt_get_row_count(table,table_RowCount);
for(table_Row = 1; table_Row <= table_RowCount; table_Row ++)
{
    ddt_set_row(table,table_Row);

    # Form1
        win_activate ("Form1");
        set_window ("Form1", 8);
        menu_select_item ("File;New Ctrl+N");
obj_mouse_drag ("ThunderRT6TextBox", 33, 13, 34, 14, LEFT);
        obj_type ("ThunderRT6TextBox", ddt_val(table, "EName")&"
<kTab>");
        obj_type ("ThunderRT6TextBox_1",ddt_val(table,"Salary"));
        obj_mouse_click ("ThunderRT6TextBox_2", 24, 9, LEFT);
obj_type ("ThunderRT6TextBox_2", ddt_val(table, "Designation"));
        obj_mouse_click ("Add", 31, 23, LEFT);
        obj_wait_bitmap("ThunderRT6TextBox_3", "Img1", 9);


}
ddt_close(table);
```

Step 8: Run the test. It will insert all the records specified in the data table and displays the test results as shown in Fig. 4.45.

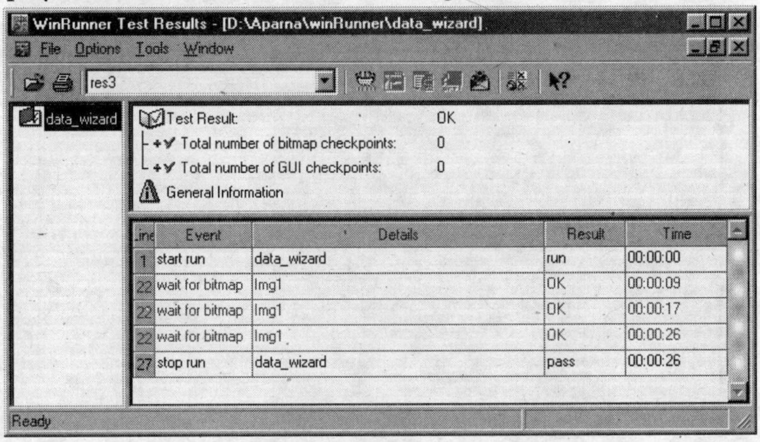

Fig. 4.45

Data driven testing simplifies the testing process as you can just generate one test case with constants, and then replace these constants with variables. This type of testing is very important for most database applications.

NOTE

4.7 RAPID TEST SCRIPT WIZARD

The Rapid test script wizard is the fastest way of performing the test process. It systematically opens up all the windows in the application, stores the learnt information in the GUI Map file and generates the test cases based on the information learnt from the application. It is possible to apply these tests only on those applications, which open windows upon performing some task (like clicking a button, selecting the menu item etc). Let us apply this wizard on the Calculator application whose GUI is shown in Fig. 4.46.

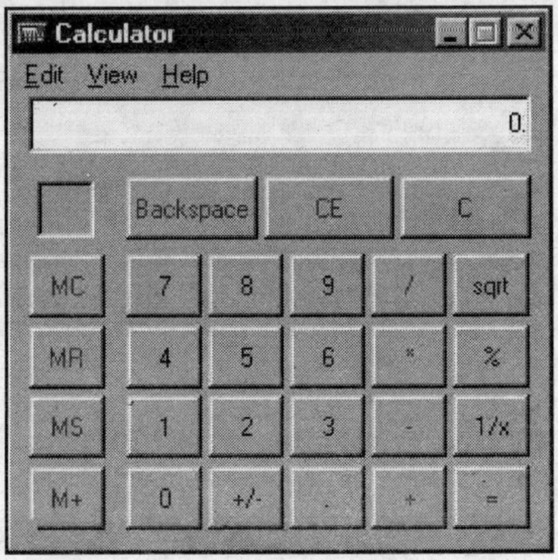

Fig. 4.46

Step 1: Open the RapidTest Script Wizard as shown in Fig. 4.47.

Create → RapidTest Script Wizard

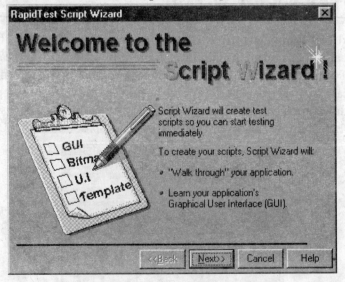

Fig. 4.47

Step 2: When you select the "RapidTest Script Wizard" option, it displays the "Welcome" screen of the RapidTest Script wizard as shown in Fig. 4.48.

Fig. 4.48

Click "Next" to walkthrough the wizard.

Step 3: When you click on "Next" button, the dialog shown in Fig. 4.49 is displayed, prompting you to select the application to be tested.

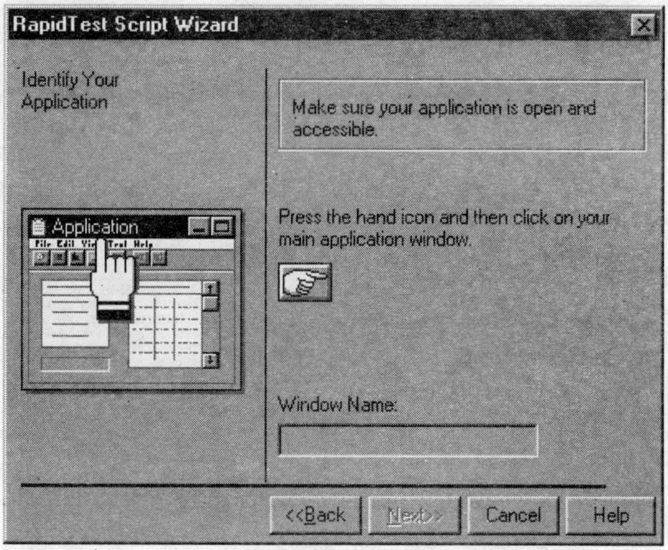

Fig. 4.49

Press the  button and click on the main application's title bar. This will capture the title of the window and displays it on the "Window Name:" label as shown in Fig. 4.50.

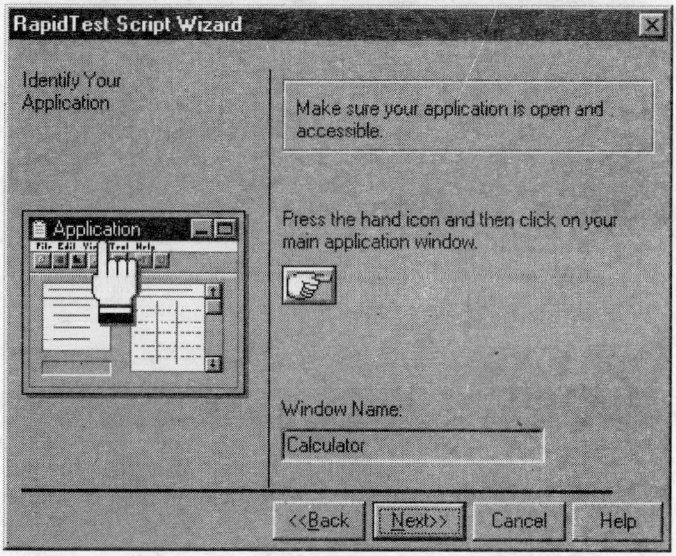

Fig. 4.50

Click the "Next" button.

Step 4: Select the tests to be performed by the Rapid script wizard on the application as shown in Fig. 4.51.

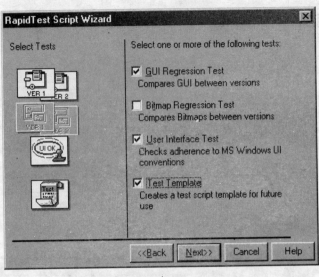

Fig. 4.51

Step 5: When you click "Next" button, it asks you whether to pause before learning the next window. To pause, check the "Pause to confirm for each window" checkbox as shown in Fig. 4.52.

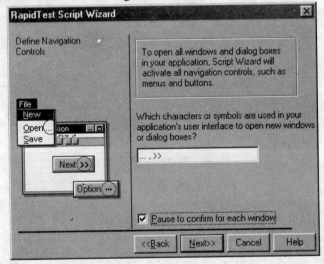

Fig. 4.52

Click "Next" to proceed further.

Step 6: WinRunner now prompts you to select the learning flow. By default it is set to "Express" where it learns the entire application using WinRunner defaults.

If "Comprehensive" is selected, then it pauses after each window allowing you to provide the learning flow information. Set it to "Express" as shown in Fig. 4.53.

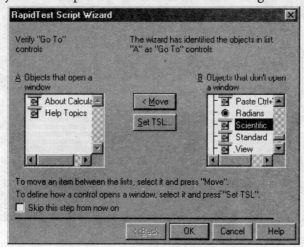

Fig. 4.53

Click "Learn" button to allow WinRunner learn the application.

Step 7: When you click the "Learn" button, it starts learning the main window of the application and displays the list of items it has learnt by categorizing them into "Objects that open a window" and "Objects that don't open a window". If WinRunner fails to identify any control or menu option which results in opening another window, then you can explicitly select the control name from "Objects that don't open a window" and click on "Move" button to move them to "Objects that open a window" as shown in Fig. 4.54.

Fig. 4.54

Click "OK" button to allow WinRunner learn the resulting windows by clicking on the items just selected one after the other. It pauses before learning the next window as shown in Fig. 4.55. Click "OK" to proceed.

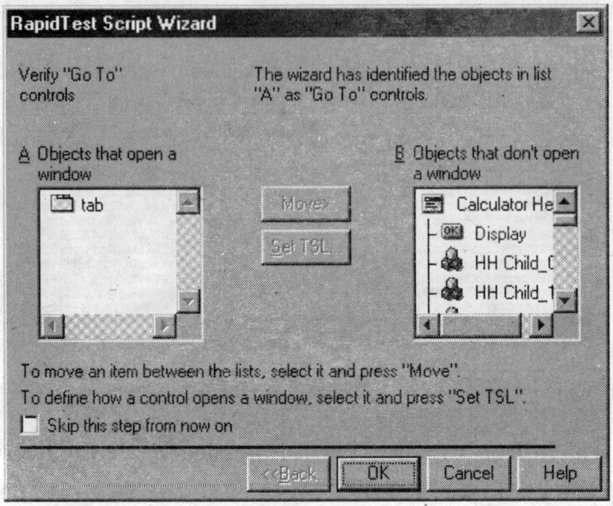

RapidTest Script Wizard

Verify "Go To" controls

The wizard has identified the objects in list "A" as "Go To" controls.

A Objects that open a window

☐ tab

B Objects that don't open a window

- Calculator He
  - Display
  - HH Child_0
  - HH Child_1

Move>

Set TSL

To move an item between the lists, select it and press "Move".
To define how a control opens a window, select it and press "Set TSL".

☐ Skip this step from now on

[<<Back] [OK] [Cancel] [Help]

Fig. 4.55

Step 8: After it learns all the windows, it asks you whether to start this application whenever you invoke WinRunner. Select the default option as shown in Fig. 4.56.

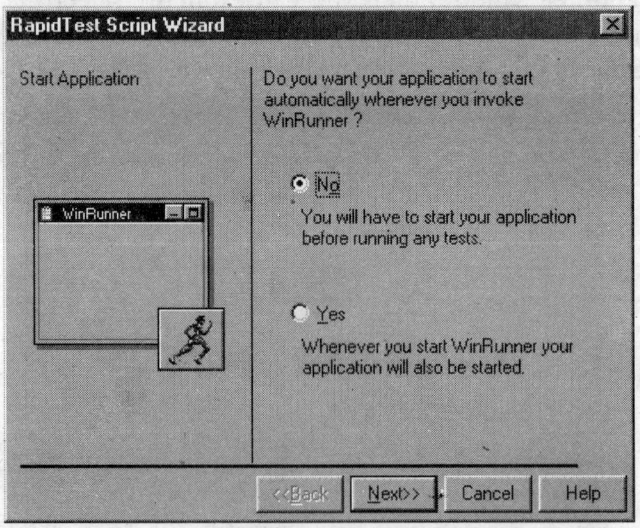

RapidTest Script Wizard

Start Application

Do you want your application to start automatically whenever you invoke WinRunner ?

WinRunner

◉ No
You will have to start your application before running any tests.

○ Yes
Whenever you start WinRunner your application will also be started.

[<<Back] [Next>>] [Cancel] [Help]

Fig. 4.56

Click "Next" to proceed further.

Step 9: All the information that WinRunner learns about the application is stored in a file "myinit". Select the location where the file has to be stored and click "Next" as shown in Fig. 4.57.

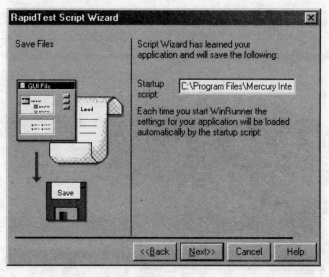

Fig. 4.57

Step 10:WinRunner prompts you to specify the location where the GUI Regression test, User Interface test and the Test Template are to be stored. Enter some names or leave the default names as shown in Fig. 4.58.

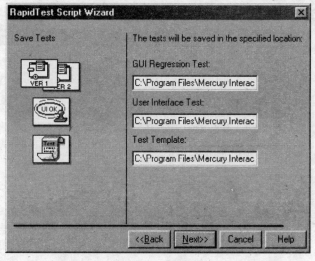

Fig. 4.58

Step 11:Once the RapidTest Script Wizard successfully learns all the windows in the application, it displays the screen shown in Fig. 4.59.

RapidTest Script Wizard
Congratulations !
GUI
Bitma
U.I
Template
Your tests will be displayed in the WinRunner window.
Use the "Run" command from the WinRunner menu to execute a test.
<<Back
OK
Cancel
Help

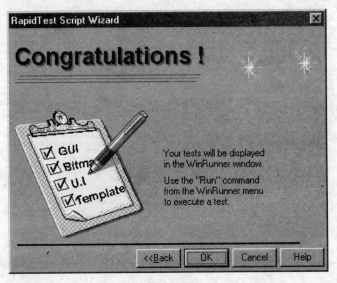

Fig. 4.59

When you click "OK" button, it generates the test script automatically for all the three tests i.e., GUI Regression, User Interface and Test Template as shown in Fig. 4.60.

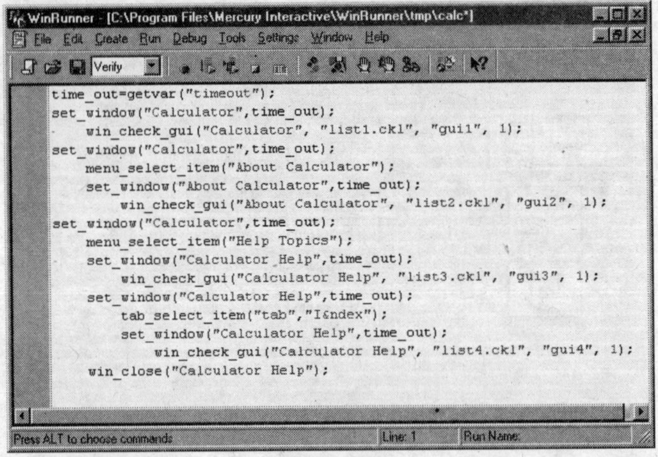

WinRunner - [C:\Program Files\Mercury Interactive\WinRunner\tmp\calc*]
File Edit Create Run Debug Tools Settings Window Help
Verify
time_out=getvar("timeout");
set_window("Calculator",time_out);
win_check_gui("Calculator", "list1.ckl", "gui1", 1);
set_window("Calculator",time_out);
menu_select_item("About Calculator");
set_window("About Calculator",time_out);
win_check_gui("About Calculator", "list2.ckl", "gui2", 1);
set_window("Calculator",time_out);
menu_select_item("Help Topics");
set_window("Calculator Help",time_out);
win_check_gui("Calculator Help", "list3.ckl", "gui3", 1);
set_window("Calculator Help",time_out);
tab_select_item("tab","I&ndex");
set_window("Calculator Help",time_out);
win_check_gui("Calculator Help", "list4.ckl", "gui4", 1);
win_close("Calculator Help");
Press ALT to choose commands
Line: 1
Run Name:

Fig. 4.60

Step 12:Run the test script and analyze the test result. The test will fail as shown in Fig. 4.61.

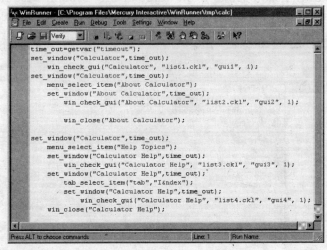

Fig. 4.61

Why the test failed?

RapidTest script wizard does not provide statements in the test script for closing the windows. In the preceding example, WinRunner opened the "About Calculator" dialog and without closing the "About Calculator" dialog, it is trying to set focus to the "Calculator" window and as a result the test fails as shown in Fig 4.61.

To overcome this, manually you need to close the previous window before trying to open the next window. To close the "About Calculator" window before setting the focus onto "Calculator", insert the following statement

```
win_close("About Calculator");
```

```
time_out=getvar("timeout");
set_window("Calculator",time_out);
    win_check_gui("Calculator", "list1.ckl", "gui1", 1);
set_window("Calculator",time_out);
    menu_select_item("About Calculator");
    set_window("About Calculator",time_out);
        win_check_gui("About Calculator", "list2.ckl", "gui2", 1);

        win_close("About Calculator");

set_window("Calculator",time_out);
    menu_select_item("Help Topics");
    set_window("Calculator Help",time_out);
        win_check_gui("Calculator Help", "list3.ckl", "gui3", 1);
    set_window("Calculator Help",time_out);
        tab_select_item("tab", "I&ndex");
        set_window("Calculator Help",time_out);
            win_check_gui("Calculator Help", "list4.ckl", "gui4", 1);
    win_close("Calculator Help");
```

Fig. 4.62

After including the "win_close" statements for all the required windows, again run the test.

While learning the windows, WinRunner stores the images of the windows internally and creates a checkpoint for each image automatically. When the user runs the test script, if any of the windows does not match the captured image, it will give "Mismatch" error and as a result the test fails.

In our example, consider the "About Calculator" dialog as shown in Fig 4.63.

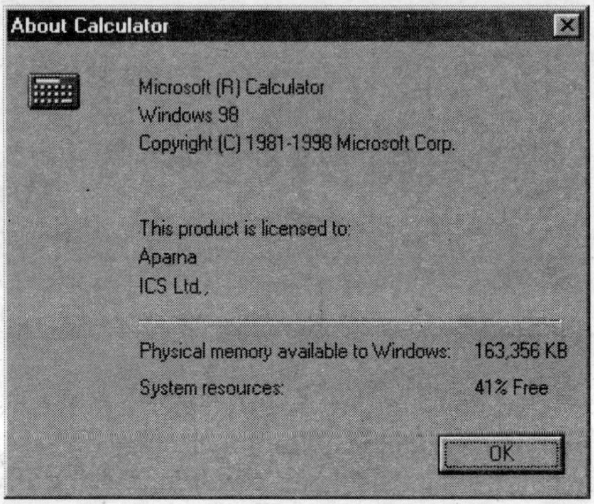

Fig. 4.63

In this dialog the "System resources" may vary. While learning this window, the "System Resources" was "71% Free" but while running, if this value changes, then WinRunner will find mismatch as the image will not match the captured image and as a result the test fails. So see to it the value of the "System Resources" is "71% Free" and then run the test script. It will then display the result as shown in Fig. 4.64.

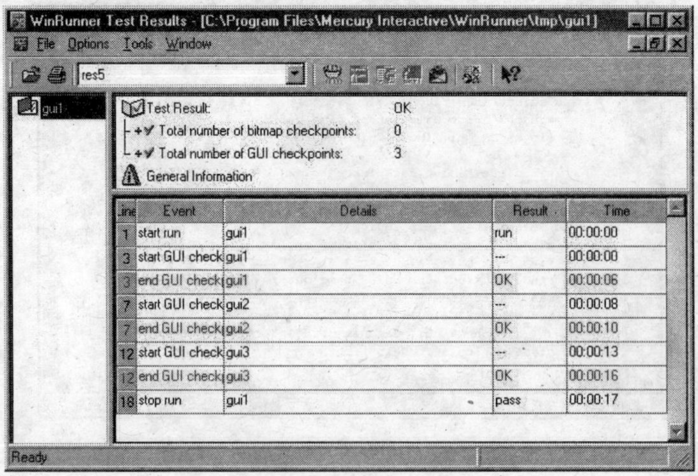

Fig. 4.64

4.8 Mapping Custom Object to a Standard Class

A custom object is an object that does not belong to any of the standard classes used by WinRunner. By default, WinRunner learns such objects under "Object" class. All the operations performed on custom objects are recoded using "obj_mouse_" statements. In such cases, it is required to make WinRunner map the custom object to one of the standard classes by making use of the "GUI Map Configuration". For example, if the application contains a custom edit control, WinRunner identifies it as an Object class instead of "edit" class. In such a case, mapping the custom control is a must.

The procedure to map the custom object to a standard class is as follows:

Step 1: Select the "GUI Map Configuration" as shown in Fig. 4.65.

Tools → GUI Map Configuration

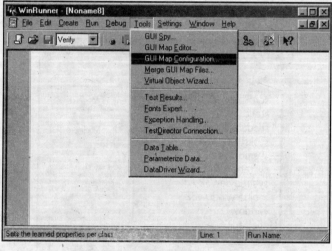

Fig. 4.65

Step 2: On selection of "GUI Map Configuration", it displays the dialog shown in Fig. 4.66.

Fig. 4.66

Step 3: Click the "Add" button. This will display the dialog as shown in Fig. 4.67. To select the custom control that has to be mapped to standard class, click on the button and select the custom control from the application. The name of the custom control object appears in the "Class Name".

Fig. 4.67

Step 4: Click "OK" to close the "Add Class" dialog. The name of the selected custom control is now added to the Class List in the "GUI Map Configuration" preceded by "U" indicating the user defined control as shown in Fig. 4.68.

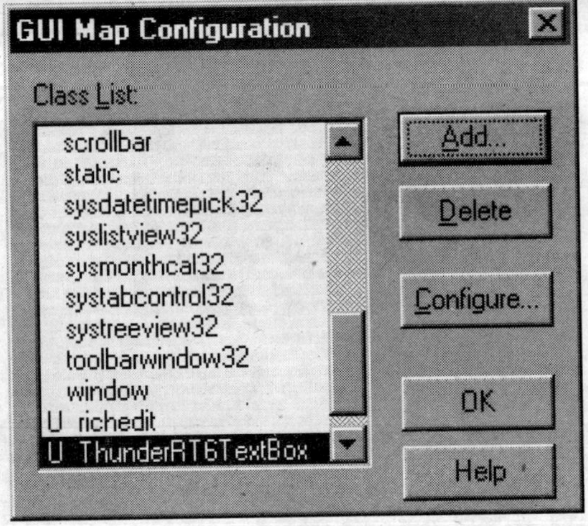

Fig. 4.68

Step 5: Click the "Configure" button to map the custom control to a standard class. It will display the "Configure Class" as shown in Fig. 4.69.

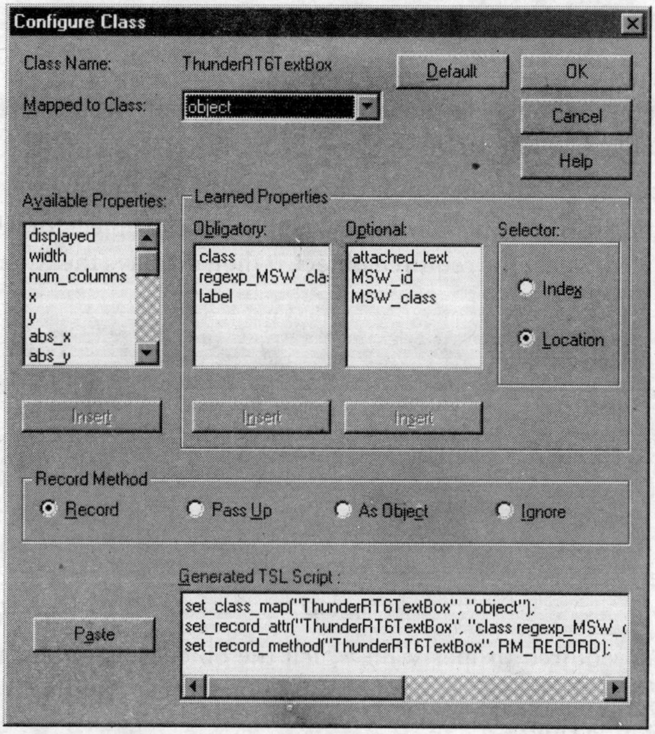

Fig. 4.69

Select the class to which the custom control has to be mapped from the "Mapped to Class". It displays the Available Properties, Learned Properties of the selected class. Click "OK" button.

Step 6: Click "OK" button to close the "GUI Map Configuration" window.

4.9 Checking GUI Objects

It is possible to check the behavior of the objects in the application by creating the GUI Checkpoints. The GUI Checkpoints help to find the defects in the application, by examining the objects.

If the application contains any custom objects that do not fall under any of the standard classes, then the custom object has to be mapped to the required standard class before creating the checkpoint, as explained in the previous section.

Checking a Single property

In order to check a single property of one particular object (for example, if you want to check whether a button is enabled or disabled), you need to create the checkpoint for a single object as follows:

- Go to Create → GUI Checkpoint → For Single Property

On selecting this option, it prompts you to select the object for which the checkpoint has to be created. Select the required object. It then displays the "Check property" dialog as shown in Fig. 4.70.

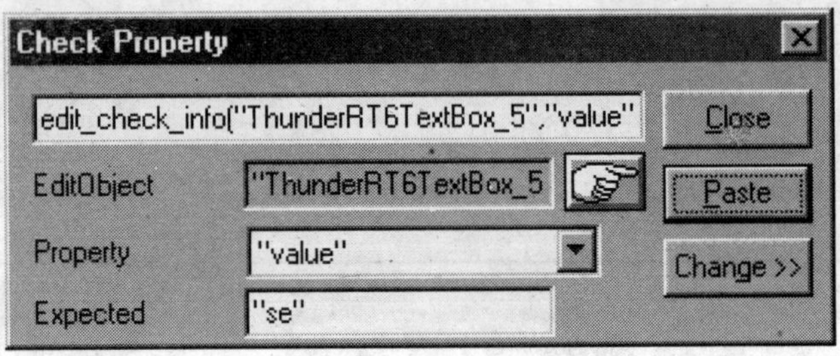

Fig. 4.70

Select the required property, on which the object has to be checked, by selecting a value from the "Property" combo box. WinRunner automatically assigns the default values to that function.

For example, if you want to create the checkpoint for an edit control where you want to check that except for one value i.e. "se", if you enter any other value, it should generate error. In such cases, select the Property as "value" and in the Expected field enter the string "se" as shown in Fig. 4.70. When you run the test script, the test fails if you enter any value other than "se".

Checking a Single Object

If you want to create checkpoint for multiple properties of a single object, then you need to follow the procedure given next. Let us consider the EmpDB application to create checkpoint for multiple properties of a single object. Consider the case where you want to create a checkpoint for the "Designation" field in the EmpDB application. If you enter any other designation except for "Software Engineer", it should display error. To create a checkpoint on the "Designation" field follow the steps below.

Step 1: Create a new test.

File → New

Step 2: Open the EmpDB application

Step 3: Start Recording in Context Sensitive mode.

Create → Record – Context Sensitive

Step 4: Insert a record into EmpDB
- File→New
- Enter all the fields
- Click "Add" to insert the record

Step 5: Synchronize the test (Refer to the section *Synchronization of test cases* for details)

Step 6: Stop Recording

    Create → Stop Recording

Step 7: Place the cursor where the "Designation" field has to be validated.

Step 8: Create a GUI Checkpoint for the object/window as shown in Fig. 4.71

Create → GUI Checkpoint → For Object/Window

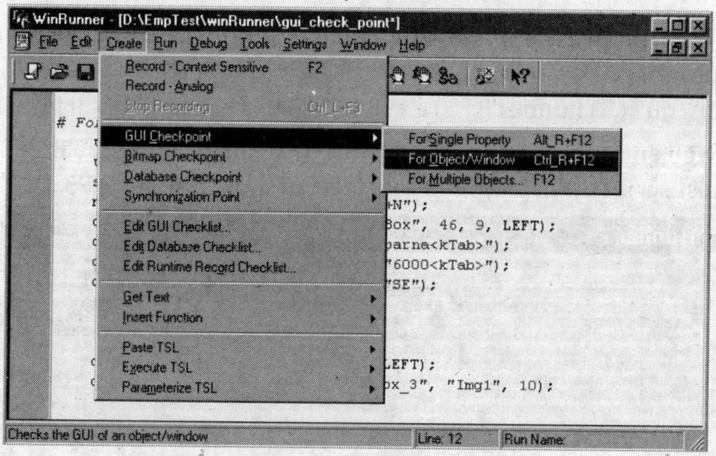

Fig. 4.71

Step 9: Double-click on the object on which the checkpoint has to be created.

Step 10. When you double click on the object, the "Check GUI" dialog appears which displays all the available properties of the control. Since we want to compare the text of the control, double click on the "Expected value" of "Compare" property. This will display "Edit Expected value" dialog prompting you to enter the expected value. Enter "Software Engineer" as shown in Fig. 4.72. Change the other properties on which checkpoints have to be created, if required.

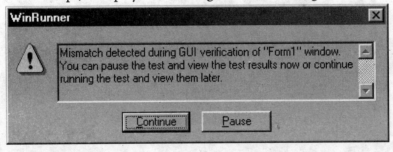

Fig. 4.72

Step 11: This will insert the following statement in the test script where the cursor is pointing.

```
obj_check_gui("ThunderRT6TextBox","list1.ckl","gui1",1);
```

Step 12: If you enter the Designation as "SE" instead of "Software Engineer" and run the test script, it displays the message as shown in Fig. 4.73.

Fig. 4.73

When you click the "Continue" button, it executes the remaining statements of the test script and finally displays the test result as shown in Fig. 4.74.

Fig. 4.74

Step 13: Now manually change the value of the "Designation" to "Software Engineer" as shown in Fig. 4.75.

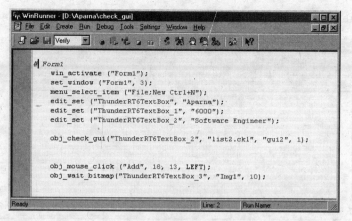

Fig. 4.75

Step 14: Run the test script. The test result is shown in Fig. 4.76.

Fig. 4.76

Checking for Multiple Objects

The checkpoints can also be created for multiple objects. To create checkpoints for multiple objects, select "For Multiple objects" as shown in Fig. 4.77.

■   Create → GUI Checkpoint → For Multiple objects

Fig. 4.77

- "Create GUI Checkpoint" dialog box appears as shown in Fig. 4.78.

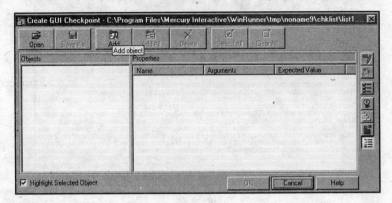

Fig. 4.78

- Click the "Add" button. The mouse pointer changes to a pointing hand. Click the objects on which the checkpoints have to be created. Once all the required objects are selected, right-click to come out and change all the required properties.

  There are three modes in which the application can be executed as shown in Fig. 4.79.

- Verify mode
- Debug mode
- Update mode

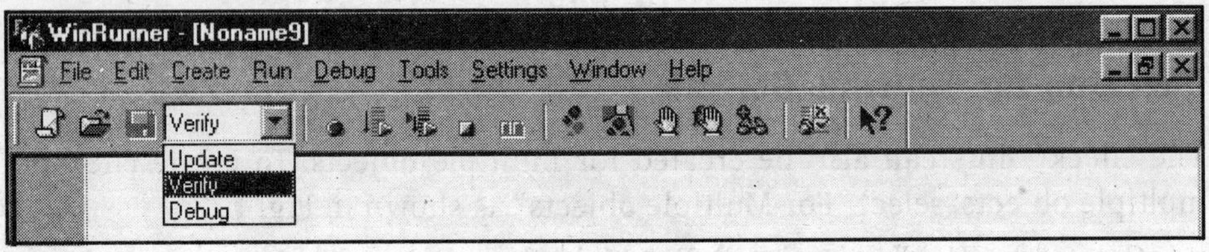

Fig. 4.79

Verify mode: By default, it is in "Verify" mode. This mode is used to run the test script. Each time WinRunner encounters GUI Checkpoints, it compares the current value with the expected value that was captured earlier. If a mismatch occurs i.e., the current value does not meet the expected value, then an error is generated.

Debug mode: This mode is used to check the values of the variables during runtime, to monitor the variables. This mode helps us to find the defects in the application. The results of the test are stored in a Debug folder that can be deleted after the test is over.

Update mode: This mode is used to change the expected value that you might have assigned during the creation of checkpoint for one or more objects. Just set the mode to "Update" and run the test script. The values you enter this time become the expected values.

Checkpoints are extensively used in database applications to check the database integrity and consistency of the fields.

Summary

This chapter presented the details of using WinRunner through two case studies (a) calculator and (b) database application. The important points to be noted are:

- To carry out functional testing, you need to generate the test cases and run the test cases. While running these test cases, you can record the interaction with the GUI. WinRunner, while recording, automatically creates a test script.
- WinRunner uses a scripting language called Test Script Language (TSL).
- TSL is a C-like procedural programming language with statements, constants, variables, functions, control structures etc. You can modify the test scripts generated by WinRunner to suit your application.
- The test script can be executed repeatedly for regression testing.
- You can synchronize various test cases. If the second test case has to be executed say, after completion of the first test case only, then you can set the delay by modifying the test script. By default, the delay between execution of two statements in the test scripts is one second.
- Using data driver wizard, you can do data–driven testing. This facility is useful when you test a database application for multiple inputs.
- WinRunner automatically learns the objects of a GUI and creates the test script using Rapid Test Script Wizard.
- GUI checkpoints are used to check the GUI object properties.
- Database checkpoints can be used to verify the database entries and to ensure data consistency and integrity.
- Custom objects can be mapped to standard classes using GUI map configuration.

5 | Silk Test

In this chapter

- Learn the features of SilkTest
- Know how to test an application using SilkTest
- Grasp the 4Test scripting language details
- Gain knowledge of creating automated test suite for unattended testing of applications
- Learn how to do data-driven testing and create checkpoints.

5.1 Overview of SilkTest

Segue Software's SilkTest can be used for testing a variety of applications such as

- Standalone Java, Visual Basic, and Win32 applications
- Web sites written in DHTML, HTML, XML, JavaScript, ActiveX, Applet, using Internet Explorer and Netscape Navigator.
- Dynamic Linked Libraries (DLLs)
- AS/400 and 3270/5250 applications
- PowerBuilder applications
- Databases

Here are some of the most important features of SilkTest:

- To facilitate unattended testing, SilkTest has an in-built customizable recovery system. So, while automated testing is in progress, even if the application fails in between, automatically the test continues without halt.
- It has an object-oriented scripting language called 4Test; using the scripts written in 4Test, an application can be tested on different platforms.
- It can access the database and validation can be done.

- For test creation and customization, workflow elements are available
- Test planning, management and reporting can be done by integration with other tools of Segue Software.

 The 4Test scripting language used in SilkTest is a powerful 4th Generation Language (4GL). In addition to the data types of C language, it allows user defined types as well. It is a true object-oriented language with support for inheritance.

5.2 Architecture of SilkTest

When you test an application GUI, you manipulate the GUI objects such as windows, menus, buttons, etc. using mouse clicks and keyboard. SilkTest interprets these objects and recognizes them based on its class properties and methods that uniquely identify them. SilkTest simulates the operations done by the user (mouse clicks and keyboard entries) and verifies the expected results automatically.

SilkTest has two components that execute as separate processes:

- Host software
- Agent software

The machine on which the host software component runs is called the host machine. Host software is the component that is used to develop test plans and test scripts. You can create test scripts, edit them, compile them, run the scripts and then debug them.

The agent software is the component that interacts with the GUI of your application. The agent software drives and monitors the Application Under Test (AUT). It translates the commands in the 4Test script into GUI specific commands. The AUT and the agent software have to run on the same machine. Each GUI object has a unique match to the 4Test object.

Silk Test testing process involves the following four steps:

- Creating a test plan
- Recording a test frame
- Creating test cases
- Running test cases and interpreting these results

5.3 Testing an Application Using SilkTest

To start testing an application in SilkTest, follow the steps given below.

Step 1: Start SilkTest.

          Start → Programs → SilkTest → SilkTest

Step 2: In SilkTest, the Quick Start Wizard is displayed automatically. It can also be invoked by selecting "New" option from File menu.

File → New and select the Quick Wizard icon.

The Quick Start Wizard helps you in executing the above-mentioned four steps fast. Invoke the wizard by selecting QuickStart Wizard icon as shown in Fig. 5.1.

Fig. 5.1

Step 3: On clicking the "Quick Start wizard" icon, the dialog box shown in Fig. 5.2 opens.

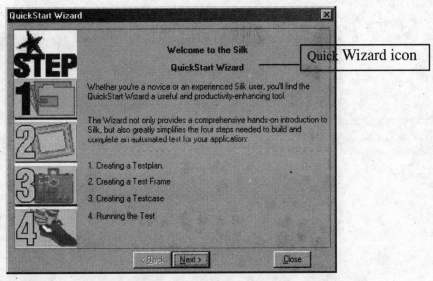

Fig. 5.2

Step 4: Click "Next" to proceed further. The dialog shown in Fig. 5.3 is displayed. By default the name of the test plan is given as "Sample".

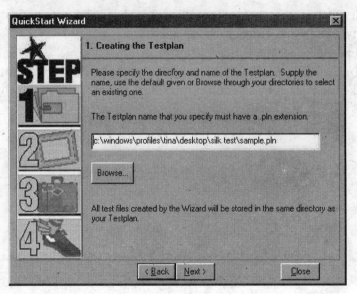

Fig. 5.3

Browse the folder where the test plan has to be saved and enter the name of the test plan. The test plan will have the extension ".pln". Click the "Next" button to proceed further.

Step 5: On clicking the "Next" button, the dialog shown in Fig. 5.4 is displayed.

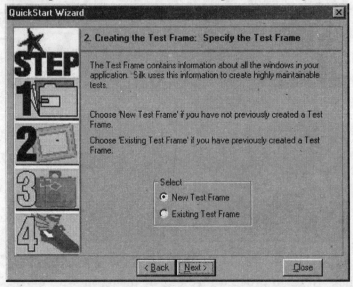

Fig. 5.4

Select the "New Test Frame" option and click the "Next" button.

Step 6: Quick Start Wizard lists all the running applications (which are not minimized).

Let us now see how to perform testing using SilkTest. Let us consider the "Calculator" application for the testing purpose.

Step 7: Open the "Calculator" application, and click on the tittle bar of the Quick Start Wizard window. The Calculator is now added to the list of applications, as shown in Fig. 5.5.

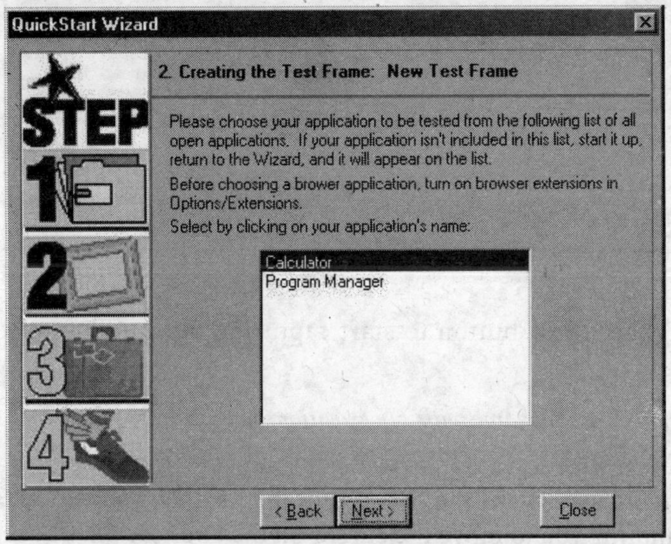

Fig. 5.5

Select the Calculator and Click Next.

Step 8: The test plan is successfully completed. The next step is to create the TestFrame. To capture the Calculator window, click on the Calculator window.

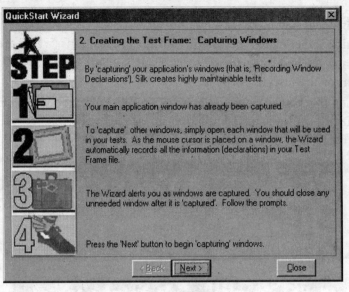

Fig. 5.6

Click the "Next" button to start capturing the windows of the application.

 The test plan will have a filename with .pln extension. The test script source code will have .t extension.

Step 9: When the user clicks the "Next" button, the dialog shown in Fig. 5.7 is displayed prompting you to move the cursor on the application, whose windows are to be captured.

Fig. 5.7

When you move the mouse pointer on a window, the wizard records all the declarations SilkTest needs, in a file called frame.inc (saved in the same directory of your testplan). The ".inc" file contains the test script that is automatically generated by the QuickStart wizard. The screen shown in Fig. 5.7 is displayed. You should make sure that all the windows are opened so that the wizard records all the declarations.

Step 10: Once all the windows in the application are captured, click the "Return to Wizard" button to return to the "Quick Start wizard".

Step11: The dialog shown in Fig. 5.8 is displayed.

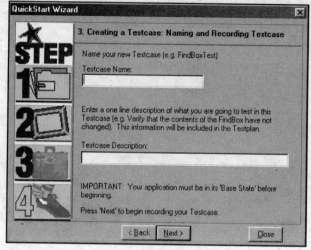

Fig 5.8

Enter the Testcase name and Testcase Description, which helps you understand the purpose of the test case. Click Next to record the test case.

Step 12: The record status dialog as shown in Fig. 5.9 is displayed. Start recording the actions. All the events that are performed are recorded. To pause the recording, click "Pause Recording" and to again begin recording click "Resume Recording".

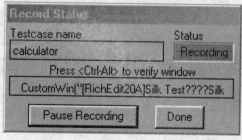

Fig. 5.9

Once all the actions to be tested are recorded, click "Done" button to stop the recording.

Step 13: When you stop the recording Quick Start Wizard displays the "Creating a Testcase" dialog. It displays the Testcase name and Testcase Description as shown in Fig.5.10.

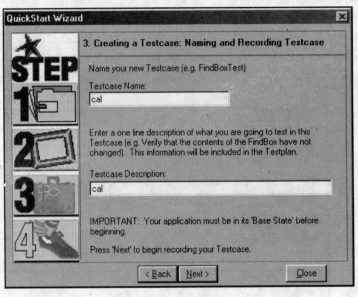

Fig. 5.10

Step 14: When you click the "Next" button the wizard displays "Running the test" dialog as shown in Fig 5.11.

Fig 5.11

If you click on the "Run Test" the test case will not be saved. Hence click the "Next" button.

Step15: The "Congratulations!" dialog is displayed as shown in Fig. 5.12. It displays details of the test recorded.

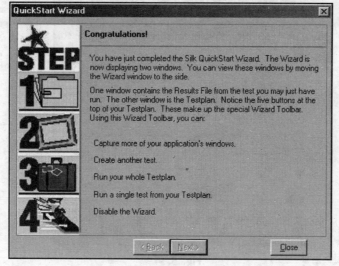

Fig 5.12

Step 16: Select the Testcase and click the [button] button to run the test case as shown in Fig. 5.13.

Fig. 5.13

Wizard reports the result, whether the test has passed or failed. The result of your script is saved in .res file and the testplan is saved in .pln with the corresponding test plan name.

Wizard sets the application state to DefaultBaseState (initial state).

Till now we have described the general procedure of how to record test case, execute it and then interpreting the results. Now we will demonstrate a few test cases. Here we use the standard calculator for our testing purpose. So in order to test the application (Calculator) efficiently, design your test cases so that each and every button in the GUI is pressed at least once.

The GUI of the standard calculator application is shown in Fig. 5.14.

Fig. 5.14

To test this application, we generate the test cases as shown in Table 5.1. For each test case, the expected result is also given in this table.

Test Case	Expected Output
4 1/x	0.25
-6 sqrt	Err: "Invalid input for function"
4 C	Clears the Display
1.2 * 3	3.6
5 / 2.0	2.5
7 + 8 − 9	6
600 * 2 %	12
2 + 3, MS, MR, C	Memory gets stored, recalled and then cleared
62345 backspace	6234

Table 5.1 Test cases and expected output for testing Calculator

While testing non-browser applications, you need to disable the browser extensions on the host machine as the recovery system works differently for browser applications and non-browser applications.

Test case #1: To test the Inverse operation (inverse of 4 using 1/x button)

Step 1: Open the Silk Test – Quick Start Wizard.

Step 2: Open the "Calculator" application.

Step 3: Follow the steps to capture the windows of the Calculator application as specified in the *"Testing an Application Using SilkTest"* section.

Step 4: Start recording the following steps:

- Click "4" on the Calculator
- Click the "1/x" button on the Calculator to find the inverse of 4.
- The result, 0.25 will be displayed on the Calculator.

Step 5: Stop the recording by clicking "Done" button on the "Record Status" window.

Step 6: Follow the steps of the Quick Start wizard.

Step 7: Select the "Byx" test case and click the [button] button to run the test.

Step 8: The results of the test case are displayed as shown in Fig. 5.15.

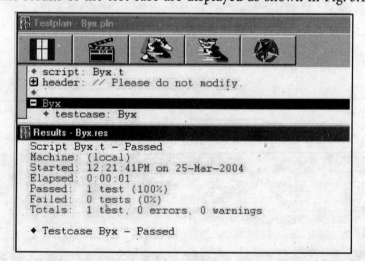

Fig. 5.15

The wizard gives the time, date, elapsed time, percentage of test passed, as shown in Fig. 5.15.

You can view the test script generated by the wizard. To view this, click on the in the "Byx.pln" window. It displays three files under "header" section "usepath", "usefiles", "framefile". Open the file specified at the section to see the events that are recorded as shown in Fig. 5.16.

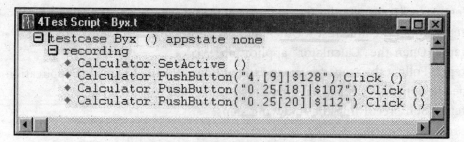

Fig. 5.16

Test Case #2: To test the operation Square root of -6.

The test script shown in Fig. 5.17 is generated:

Fig. 5.17

The test result is displayed as shown in Fig. 5.18.

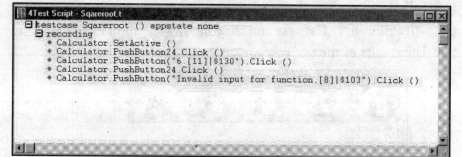

Fig. 5.18

Test Case #3: To Clear the display after performing some operations.

The test script generated is shown in Fig. 5.19.

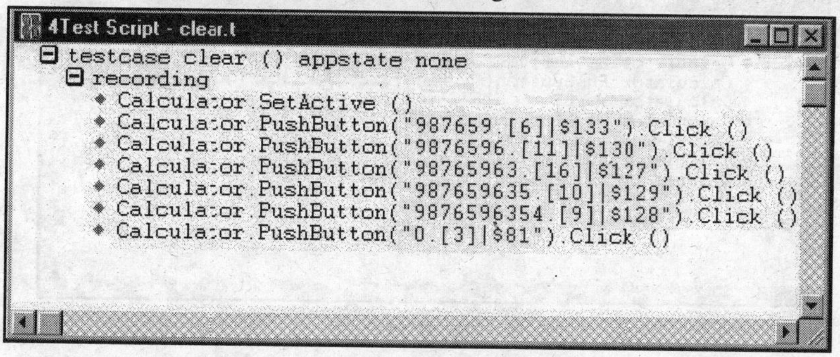

```
4Test Script - clear.t                                    _ □ ×
□ testcase clear () appstate none
  □ recording
    ◆ Calculator.SetActive ()
    ◆ Calculator.PushButton("987659.[6]|$133").Click ()
    ◆ Calculator.PushButton("9876596.[11]|$130").Click ()
    ◆ Calculator.PushButton("98765963.[16]|$127").Click ()
    ◆ Calculator.PushButton("987659635.[10]|$129").Click ()
    ◆ Calculator.PushButton("9876596354.[9]|$128").Click ()
    ◆ Calculator.PushButton("0.[3]|$81").Click ()
```

Fig. 5.19

When this test script is executed, the test results are as shown in Fig. 5.20.

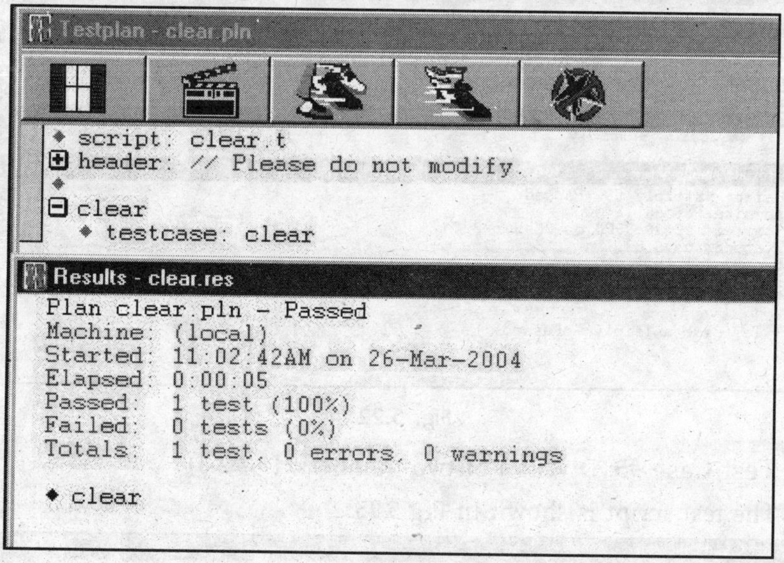

```
Testplan - clear.pln

  ◆ script: clear.t
  ⊞ header: // Please do not modify.
  ◆
  □ clear
    ◆ testcase: clear

Results - clear.res
Plan clear.pln - Passed
Machine: (local)
Started: 11:02:42AM on 26-Mar-2004
Elapsed: 0:00:05
Passed:  1 test (100%)
Failed:  0 tests (0%)
Totals:  1 test, 0 errors, 0 warnings

◆ clear
```

Fig. 5.20

Test Case #4: Multiplication of two numbers. (1.2 * 3)

The test script generated is shown in Fig. 5.21.

```
4Test Script - multiply.t                                    _□×
testcase multiply () appstate none
  recording
    ◆ Calculator.SetActive ()
    ◆ Calculator.PushButton("1.[14]|$125").Click ()
    ◆ Calculator.PushButton25.Click ()
    ◆ Calculator.PushButton("1.2[15]|$126").Click ()
    ◆ Calculator.PushButton("1.2[12]|$91").Click ()
    ◆ Calculator.PushButton("3.[16]|$127").Click ()
    ◆ Calculator.PushButton("3.6[20]|$112").Click ()
```

Fig. 5.21

The test results will be as shown in Fig. 5.22 when this test script is executed.

```
Testplan - multiply.pln                                      _□×

◆ script: multiply.t
⊞ header: // Please do not modify.
◆
□ multiply
   ◆ testcase: multiply

Results - multiply.res                                       _□×
Script multiply.t - Passed
Machine: (local)
Started: 02:38:39PM on 25-Mar-2004
Elapsed: 0:00:03
Passed:  1 test (100%)
Failed:  0 tests (0%)
Totals:  1 test, 0 errors, 0 warnings

◆ Testcase multiply - Passed
```

Fig. 5.22

Test Case #5: Division of two numbers. (5 / 2.0)

The test script is shown in Fig 5.23.

```
4Test Script - divide.t                                      _□×
testcase divide () appstate none
  recording
    ◆ MainWin("Calc*|$C:\WINDOWS\CALC.EXE").SetActive ()
    ◆ MainWin("Calc*|$C:\WINDOWS\CALC.EXE").PushButton("5.[10]|$129").Click ()
    ◆ MainWin("Calc*|$C:\WINDOWS\CALC.EXE").PushButton("5.[7]|$90").Click ()
    ◆ MainWin("Calc*|$C:\WINDOWS\CALC.EXE").PushButton("2.[15]|$126").Click ()
    ◆ MainWin("Calc*|$C:\WINDOWS\CALC.EXE").PushButton("#25|$85").Click ()
    ◆ MainWin("Calc*|$C:\WINDOWS\CALC.EXE").PushButton("#23|$124").Click ()
    ◆ MainWin("Calc*|$C:\WINDOWS\CALC.EXE").PushButton("2.5[20]|$112").Click (
```

Fig. 5.23

The test results are shown in Fig. 5.24.

Testplan - divide.pln
script: divide.t
header: // Please do not modify.
divide
testcase: divide
Results - divide.res
Script divide.t - Passed
Machine: (local)
Started: 02:52:34PM on 25-Mar-2004
Elapsed: 0:00:01
Passed: 1 test (100%)
Failed: 0 tests (0%)
Totals: 1 test, 0 errors, 0 warnings
Testcase divide - Passed

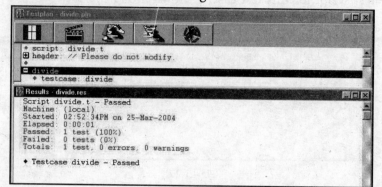

Fig. 5.24

Test Case #6: To test the operation (7 + 8 – 9)

For this test case, the test script is as shown in Fig. 5.25.

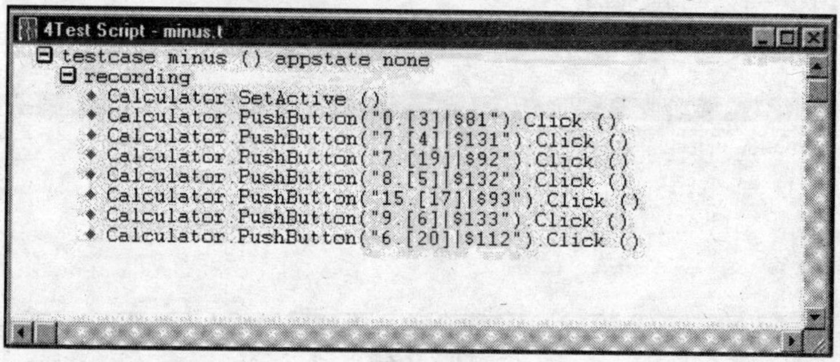

4Test Script - minus.t
testcase minus () appstate none
recording
Calculator.SetActive ()
Calculator.PushButton("0.[3]|$81").Click ()
Calculator.PushButton("7.[4]|$131").Click ()
Calculator.PushButton("7.[19]|$92").Click ()
Calculator.PushButton("8.[5]|$132").Click ()
Calculator.PushButton("15.[17]|$93").Click ()
Calculator.PushButton("9.[6]|$133").Click ()
Calculator.PushButton("6.[20]|$112").Click ()

Fig. 5.25

The test results for this test case are shown in Fig. 5.26.

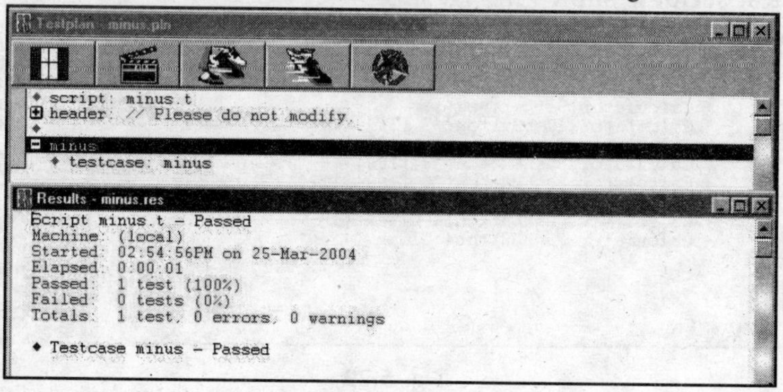

Testplan - minus.pln
script: minus.t
header: // Please do not modify.
minus
testcase: minus
Results - minus.res
Script minus.t - Passed
Machine: (local)
Started: 02:54:56PM on 25-Mar-2004
Elapsed: 0:00:01
Passed: 1 test (100%)
Failed: 0 tests (0%)
Totals: 1 test, 0 errors, 0 warnings
Testcase minus - Passed

Fig. 5.26

Test Case #7: To test the operation 2% of 600.

The test script for this test case is shown in Fig. 5.27.

```
4Test Script - percentage.t                              _ □ ×
⊟ testcase percentage () appstate none
  ⊟ recording
    ◆ Calculator.SetActive ()
    ◆ Calculator.PushButton("6.[11]|$130").Click ()
    ◆ Calculator.PushButton23.Click ()
    ◆ Calculator.PushButton23.Click ()
    ◆ Calculator.PushButton("600.[12]|$91").Click ()
    ◆ Calculator.PushButton("2.[15]|$126").Click ()
    ◆ Calculator.PushButton("12.[13]|$109").Click ()
```

Fig. 5.27

The test results are shown in Fig. 5.28.

```
Testplan - percentage.pln                                _ □ ×
 [||]     [🎬]      [👟]       [🏃]        [🌐]

◆ script: percentage.t
⊞ header: // Please do not modify
◆
⊟ percentage
  ◆ testcase: percentage

Results - percentage.res                                 _ □ ×
Script percentage.t - Passed
Machine: (local)
Started: 03:03:41PM on 25-Mar-2004
Elapsed: 0:00:01
Passed: 1 test (100%)
Failed: 0 tests (0%)
Totals: 1 test, 0 errors, 0 warnings

◆ Testcase percentage - Passed
```

Fig. 5.28

Test Case #8: To test MS, MR and MC buttons.

The test script is shown in Fig. 5.29.

```
4Test Script - m_s_r_c.t                                 _ □ ×
⊟ testcase m_s_r_c () appstate none
  ⊟ recording
    ◆ Calculator.SetActive ()
    ◆ Calculator.PushButton("2.[15]|$126").Click ()
    ◆ Calculator.PushButton("2.[19]|$92").Click ()
    ◆ Calculator.PushButton("3.[16]|$127").Click ()
    ◆ Calculator.PushButton("5.[20]|$112").Click ()
    ◆ Calculator.PushButton16.Click ()
    ◆ Calculator.PushButton10.Click ()
    ◆ Calculator.PushButton4.Click ()
```

Fig. 5.29

The test results are shown in Fig. 5.30.

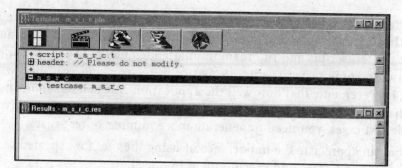

Fig. 5.30

Test Case #9: To test the Backspace.

The test script is given in Fig. 5.31.

```
4Test Script - backspace.t
testcase backspace () appstate none
  recording
    Calculator.SetActive ()
    Calculator.PushButton("4.[9]|$128").Click ()
    Calculator.PushButton("0.[1]|$83").Click ()
    Calculator.PushButton("6.[11]|$130").Click ()
    Calculator.PushButton("6.[19]|$92").Click ()
    Calculator.PushButton("2.[15]|$126").Click ()
    Calculator.PushButton("8.[20]|$112").Click ()
```

Fig. 5.31

The test result is shown in Fig. 5.32.

```
Testplan - backspace.pln

  script: backspace.t
  header: // Please do not modify.
  backspace
    testcase: backspace

Results - backspace.res
Script backspace.t - Passed
Machine: (local)
Started: 03:07:33PM on 25-Mar-2004
Elapsed: 0:00:01
Passed:  1 test (100%)
Failed:  0 tests (0%)
Totals:  1 test, 0 errors, 0 warnings

  Testcase backspace - Passed
```

Fig. 5.32

So, we have completed using all the buttons in the Calculator. Since, you are testing a standard application which does not have any bugs, all the tests have passed. When the software is in development stage, you need to give these test cases repeatedly and keep testing the software given by the development team. In such cases, you don't need to keep entering the test cases manually; you can create the test scripts and run them in unattended mode. Even if the application fails in between some tests, it will automatically recover and continue with other test cases. However, note that how well the application is tested depends on how well you design the test cases. Even for the calculator application, we have given only some sample test cases, you need to generate more number of test cases.

You can appreciate the importance of using the tool for repeated testing. You can store all the test cases and execute them in one shot.

5.4 The Test Scripting Language

When you are recording the application, the test script is automatically generated. The test script used in SilkTest is called 4Test.

There are basically four classes to which these methods belong

1. AgentClass
2. AynWin
3. ClipboardClass
4. CursorClass

Few important methods that you will come across in test scripts are listed below.

1. **Accept (): closes the dialog box and accepts the values specified there.**
Syntax: dialogbox.Accept()

2. **ClearText (): removes all text from the text field.**
Syntax: textfield.ClearText()

3. **Click (): Clicks a mouse button on the push button.**
Syntax: pushbutton.Click ([iButton, iXpos, iYpos, bRawEvent])
iButton: The number of the button to click. (Optional)
iXpos: The horizontal coordinate to click. (Optional)
iYpos: The vertical coordinate to click. (Optional)
bRawEvent: Specifies playback mechanism. (Optional)

4. **Close (): Closes the window.**
Syntax: window.Close ([bCloseConfirm, bSetActive])
bCloseConfirm: TRUE to close confirmation boxes (Optional)
bSetActive: TRUE to set window active before closing.(Optional)

5. **Close Windows (): closes all windows of the application except the main window.**

   Syntax: mainwindow. CloseWindows ([bTrace])

   bTrace: TRUE to log of all windows closed. (Optional)

6. **Exit (): terminates the application.**

   Syntax: mainwin.Exit ()

7. **GetActive (): returns the active window in the application.**

   Syntax: wActive = mainwin.GetActive ()

   wActive: The active window.

8. **GetCloseWindows (): returns the windows that must close to return the application to base state.**

   Syntax: IwWindow = mainwin.GetCloseWindows ()

   IwWindows: The list of windows to close.

9. **GetFocus (): returns the control with the input focus**

   Syntax: wFocus = GetFocus ()

   wFocus: The returned control

10. **Invoke (): invokes the application.**

    Syntax: mainwin. Invoke ()

11. **SetActive (): makes the windows active.**

    Syntax: window.setActive ()

12. **Wait (): waits for the specified cursor and returns the value of elapsed time.**

    Syntax: nSeconds = Cursor. Wait (Cursor, n Timeout [, nNoChange])

    nSeconds   The seconds waited for the cursor.

    Cursor   The type of cursor to wait for. CURSOR

    nTimeout   The time to wait for cursor to change

    nNoChange   How long the cursor must remain (Optional)

13. **VerifyActive (): verifies that the window is active.**

    Syntax: window. VerifyActive ()

14. **Start (): invokes the application and waits for the main window to appear.**

    Syntax: mainwin.Start (sCmdLine)

    SCmdLine :The command for running the application

15. **Size (): resizes the window.**

    Syntax: window. Size (iWidth, iHeight)

    iWidth: The new width of the window

    iHeight : The new height of the window

NOTE

The various extensions for the script files are as follows: .t is for source script file, .o is for object file, .s for suite file and .res for results file.

5.5 CHECKPOINTS

The checkpoints are created to check the behavior of the object. We create a checkpoint on the object for a specific property that is to be tested. Checkpoints help us to determine whether the objects return the expected results or not so that we can find out if there are any defects in our application.

We use the checkpoint to check whether the expected output is achieved or not with the input provided. For instance, if the static text does not match the expected value, SilkTest raises an exception.

To illustrate the use of checkpoints, we will use a database application. This application's executable code is given in the CDROM that accompanies this book. The procedure for installing this sample application on your system is given in Appendix E. This application has a data table which can be updated using a form. The GUI is shown in Fig. 5.33. This form contains the following fields: Employee number, Employee name, Employee salary, and Designation. You can add, modify, and delete records from the database.

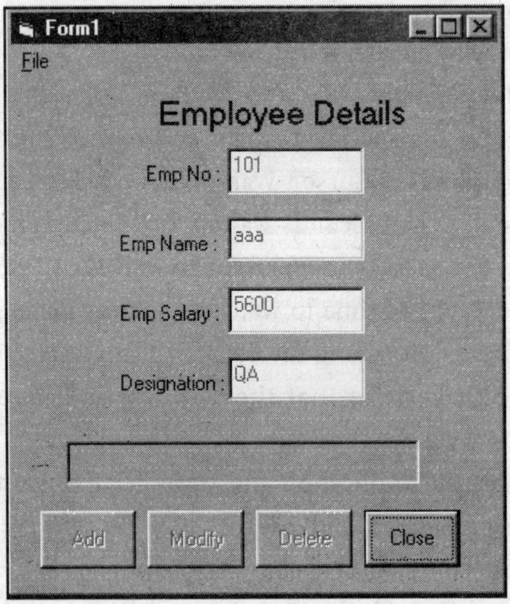

Fig. 5.33

Window Checkpoint

We will use the "Window Checkpoint" to test the caption of the window with a static value. When a form gets activated the caption should be "Form1" (in our case) and if a mismatch occurs, it should generate an error. For this purpose, there is a function called window. VerifyCaption, which verifies the window caption with a static caption.

 Window checkpoints can be used to test many aspects of GUI such as to test whether all text fields start with a capital letter or not, to test whether the caption of the window starts with a capital or not etc. You can create a checklist for GUI testing and then create a test script to test whether the GUI is as per this checklist.

To Verify the Caption of the Window

Step 1: Record a test case.

Step 2: Open the test script (".inc" file)

Step 3: Insert the following statement after the "SetActive()" statement as shown in Fig. 5.34.

```
Form1.VerifyCaption ("Form1")
```

Step 4: Run the test case

SilkTest will now check the caption of the window that is displayed. If the caption does not match with "Form1", it displays an error "Verify caption failed".

```
4Test Script - sample.t                                    _ □ ×
⊟ testcase check () appstate none
  ⊟ recording
      ◆ Form1.SetActive ()
      ◆ Form1.VerifyCaption ("Form1")
      ◆ Form1.ThunderRT6TextBox2.Click (1, 16, 9)
      ◆ Form1.ThunderRT6TextBox2.TypeKeys ("t")
      ◆ Form1.ThunderRT6TextBox2.TypeKeys ("i")
      ◆ Form1.ThunderRT6TextBox2.TypeKeys ("n")
      ◆ Form1.ThunderRT6TextBox2.TypeKeys ("a<Tab>")
      ◆ Form1.ThunderRT6TextBox3.TypeKeys ("5")
      ◆ Form1.ThunderRT6TextBox3.TypeKeys ("0")
      ◆ Form1.ThunderRT6TextBox3.TypeKeys ("0")
      ◆ Form1.ThunderRT6TextBox3.TypeKeys ("0<Tab>")
      ◆ Form1.ThunderRT6TextBox4.TypeKeys ("S")
```

Fig. 5.34

The above test case will pass as the caption of the window is "Form1". But if the user tries to match the caption of the window as "Form", then it will display an error message "Verify caption failed" as shown in Fig. 5.35.

```
Results - sample.res                                    [_][□][x]
Script sample.t - 1 error                              [Maximi]
Machine: (local)
Started: 06:55:19PM on 02-Apr-2004
Elapsed: 0:00:01
Passed: 0 tests (0%)
Failed: 1 test (100%)
Totals: 1 test, 1 error, 0 warnings

⊟ Testcase check - 1 error
  *** Error: Verify caption failed - got "Form1", expected "Form"
  Occurred in Form1.VerifyCaption
  Called from check at sample.t(4)
```

Fig. 5.35

Command to create window checkpoint:

Command: window.VerifyCaption

Action: Verifies the caption of the window.

Syntax: window.VerifyCaption(sCaption)

Variable	Description
Caption	The caption you expect the window to have STRING.
Example	Window.VerifyCaption ("CorrectCaption")

VerifyCaption checks whether the caption of a window has the expected value.

Checkpoint on Text Field

Suppose you want to create a checkpoint for a text field. That is, if you enter any text other than the expected text, it should display an error. For example, if the employee name is "Dustu", and if you enter any name other than "Dustu", it generates an error. When you record a test case on EmpDB application, the script will be generated as shown in Fig. 5.36. Since the text field value is not stored in a single statement, Textfield checkpoint cannot be created.

```
⊟ recording
   ✦ Form1.SetActive ()
   ✦ Form1.VerifyCaption ("Form1")
   ✦ Form1.ThunderRT6TextBox2.Click (1, 29, 8)
   ✦ Form1.ThunderRT6TextBox2.TypeKeys ("t")
   ✦ Form1.ThunderRT6TextBox2.TypeKeys ("i")
```

Fig. 5.36

When you try to create a checkpoint for this test case, it will generate an error.

" Verify value is not defined for window Form1 ThunderRT6TextBox2"

To avoid this situation, we have to make SilkTest learn the declarations of our application, this is nothing but addition of custom objects to SilkTest.

Step 1: Start the application.

File → New

New dialog shown in Fig. 5.37 appears.

Fig. 5.37

Step 2: Select the "Test Frame" radio button and Click OK.

Step 3: The "New Test Frame" dialog appears as shown in Fig. 5.38. The dialog allows you to create a test frame for an application displayed in the application list box. The application list box displays all applications that are in active state. If you application is not listed, click "Cancel", and open the application.

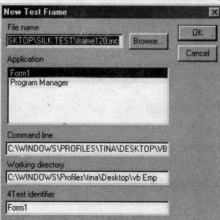

Fig. 5.38

The default .inc file is displayed. This .inc file denotes an include file which stores declarations. You can browse to edit the path. Click "OK". It displays 4test declarations for the main window and all the menu items as shown in Fig. 5.39.

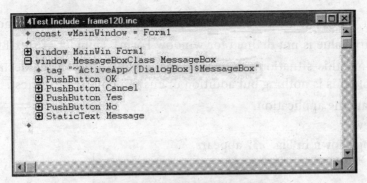

Fig. 5.39

Step 4: Select "Window Declarations" from Record menu.

Record → Window Declarations

The "Record Window Declarations" dialog is displayed as shown in Fig. 5.40.

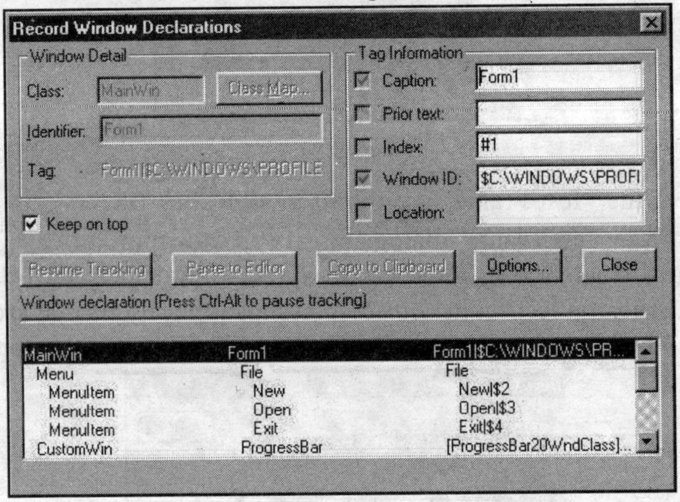

Fig. 5.40

Make sure that "EmpDB" application is active.

Step 5: Place mouse pointer on the text box opposite to the "Emp Name" label on the EmpDB application.

The class field contains the Custom Win and the Identifier field contains the ThunderRT6TextBox as shown in Fig. 5.41.

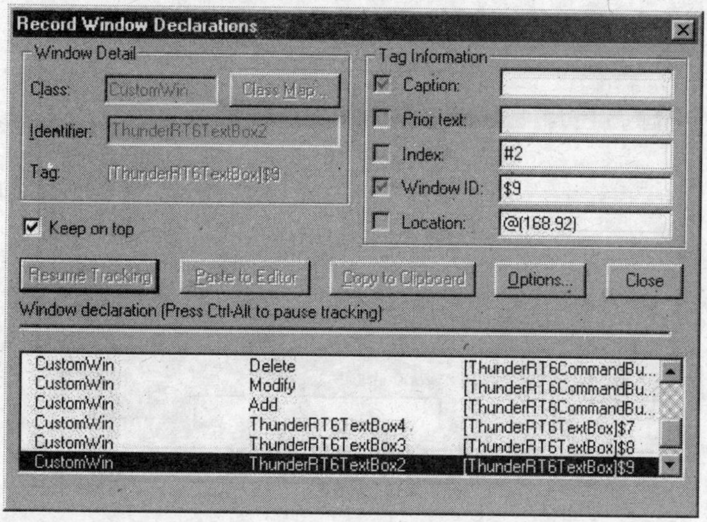

Fig. 5.41

Step 6: Press Ctrl+Alt.

The "Window Detail" becomes enabled. Click "Class Map" button to customize the object.

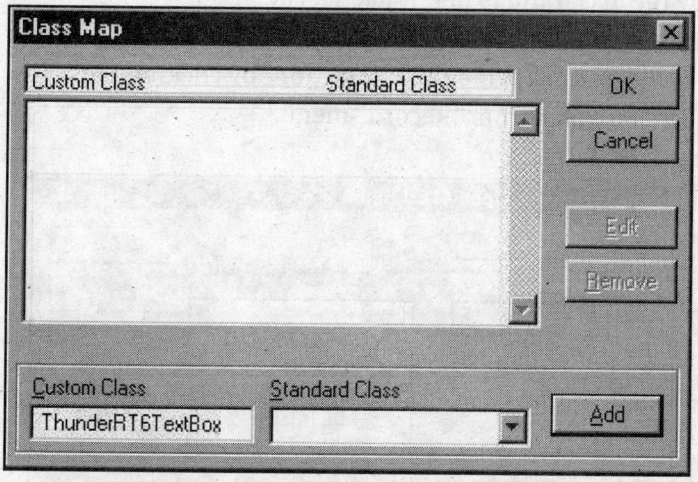

Fig. 5.42

In Fig. 5.42, notice that Custom Class text field contains ThunderRT6TextBox. Now you can select the "TextField" from the Standard Class drop-down list box and click the "Add" button.

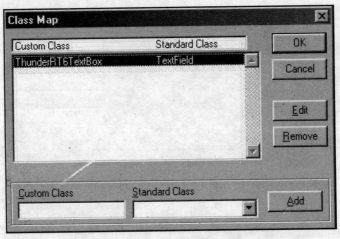

Fig. 5.43

As shown in Fig. 5.43, the Class Map view indicates that the Custom Class is ThunderRT6TextBox and Standard Class is TextField. Hence, the object ThunderRT6TextBox is customized as TextField. To close the "Class Map" dialog click the "OK" button.

Step 8: Copy the declarations that it had learnt:

Click "Copy to Clipboard" button

Step 9: Close the "Record Window Declaration" by clicking the "Close" button.

Step 10: Select "Testcase" from "Record" menu.

Record → Testcase

Fig. 5.44

Enter the File name with .t extension. A message will appear "4TestScript.t does not exist. Would you like to create it?" click "Yes" to create it. Click the "OK" button.

Step 11: Start Recording by clicking the "Start Recording" button on the window shown in Fig. 5.45.

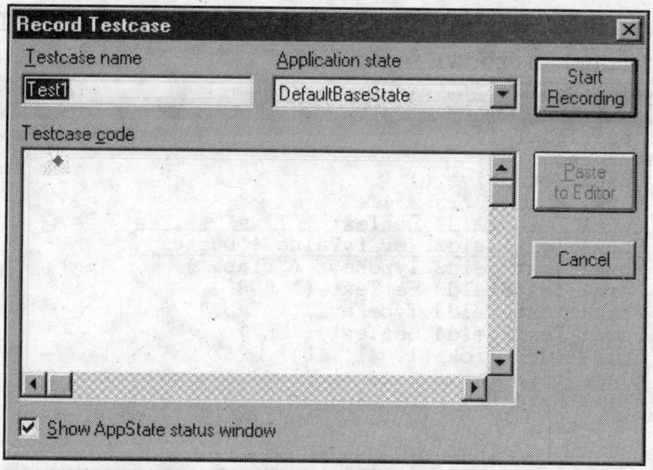

Fig. 5.45

Step 12: Select "New" option from the File menu to add a record into the database.
File → New

Enter the values in the Form1 window i.e., Emp name, Emp salary, Emp
Designation and click the "Add" button to insert the record.

Step13: When you have finished recording Click "Done" button, shown in
Fig. 5.46.

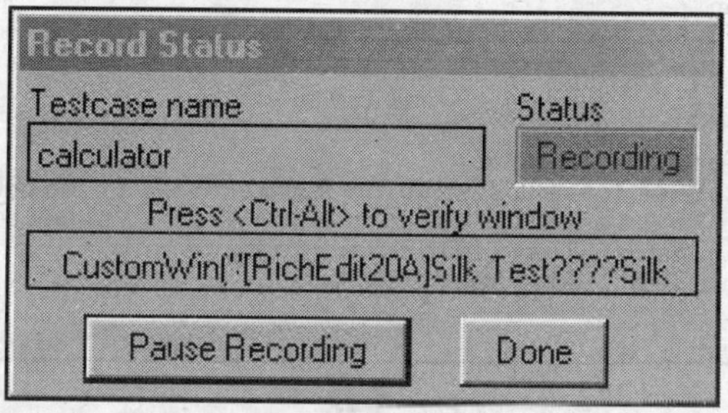

Fig. 5.46

Step 14: When you record the actions, the "Paste to Editor" button gets enabled.
Click "Paste to Editor" button to add the test script of the recorded
actions into the ".t" file.

Step 15: Select "Run" from the Run menu to run the test case.

Result window is automatically displayed.

Example:

■ Suppose you want to create a checkpoint for the "EmpName". To verify the
"EmpName", we need to create checkpoint for the "EmpName". In order to do
this, add the following code:

"Form1.TextField2.VerifyValue ("Dustu")" after the "Form1.TextField2.SetText ("tina")" statement as shown in Fig. 5.47.

```
4Test Script - ckeck.t                                    _ □ ×
⊟ testcase Test1 ()
  ⊟ recording
    ◆ Form1.SetActive ()
    ◆ Form1.Move (371, 39)
    ◆ Form1.TextField2.SetText ("Tina")
    ◆ Form1.TextField2.VerifyValue ("Dustu")
    ◆ Form1.TextField2.TypeKeys ("<Tab>")
    ◆ Form1.TextField3.SetText ("5000")
    ◆ Form1.TextField3.TypeKeys ("<Tab>")
    ◆ Form1.TextField4.SetText ("SE")
    ◆ Form1.Add.Click (1, 41, 18)
    ◆ Sleep (5)
    ◆ Form1.File.New.Pick ()
```

Fig. 5.47

If the employee name is different from "Dustu " (expected value), it generates an error. In this case the expected value is "Dustu " and the recorded "EmpName" is "Tina". Hence SilkTest generates an error as shown in Fig. 5.48.

```
Results - check.res                                       _ □ ×
Script check.t - 1 error
Machine: (local)
Started: 12:58:41PM on 02-Apr-2004
Elapsed: 0:00:01
Passed:  0 tests (0%)
Failed:  1 test (100%)
Totals:  1 test, 1 error, 0 warnings

⊟ Testcase Test1 - 1 error
  *** DefaultBaseState is setting Form1 active, MainWin("Reco
  *** Error: Verify text failed - got "Tina", expected "Dustu
  Occurred in Form1.TextField2.VerifyValue
  Called from Test1 at check.t(4)
```

Fig. 5.48

Command to create Text field checkpoint:

Action: Verifies the text of the text field.

Syntax: object.VerifyValue (Expected)

Variable	Description
Expected	The text you expected.

You can also verify the appearance of a GUI object using bitmap comparison feature. Bitmap comparison fails if the window frame widths are different, window positions are different, if the colors are different or the screen resolutions are not the same.

5.6 Data-Driven Test Cases

Look at the following test case

```
testcase Test1()
recording
Form1.TextField2.SetText ("Tina")
Form1.TextField2.TypeKeys ("<Tab>")
Form1.TextField3.SetText ("5000")
Form1.TextField3.TypeKeys ("<Tab>")
Form1.TextField4.SetText ("SE")
Form1.Add.Click (1, 29, 15)
Sleep (5)
Form1.File.New.Pick ()
```

The above test case tests only one out of the many possible sets of input data. In order to test all possible inputs, you have to manually record all the test cases and run them. Even for a small application, this creates a huge number of test cases, so the procedure becomes time consuming.

SilkTest uses *Data-Driven Test cases* to run a set of test cases. Data-Driven test case is applied on a test case which has passed for at least one set of data. For that one set of data, the inputs given are constant values. These constant values are replaced by variables in data-driven tests.

The procedure to create a data-driven test case is as follows:

Step 1: Record a test case for one data set.

Step 2: Identify the data type of each recorded data value, i.e. the data values appear inside the parentheses at the end of a 4Test statement.

```
testcase Test1()
recording
Form1.TextField2.SetText ("Tina")
Form1.TextField2.TypeKeys ("<Tab>")
Form1.TextField3.SetText ("5000")
Form1.TextField3.TypeKeys ("<Tab>")
Form1.TextField4.SetText ("SE")
Form1.Add.Click (1, 29, 15)
Form1.File.New.Pick ()
```

In this case, we have only STRING data type for Name, Salary, and Designation.

Step 3: Define data type for the data used in the test case.

Step 4: Add a record variable to the list of parameters for the test case. The list of parameters is specified between the parentheses after the name of the test case. If you want to test the cases with 3 data sets the code will look like

```
list of DATADRIVEN lsData = {...}
  {"Dustu","15000","SE"}
  {"Tina","5000","SE"}
  {"Deebendu","20000","SE"}
```

Step 5: Replace each data value in the test case with the appropriate field from the record. In 4Test, fields in records are indicated with the dot (.) operator.

Data elements used by the test case:

```
type DATADRIVEN is record
STRING   Name   //Text to type in document window
STRING   Sal
STRING   Design
```

You also have Boolean data type.

So, the revised test case is as follows:

```
  testcase Test1(DATADRIVEN Data)
  recording
  Form1.TextField2.SetText (Data.Name)
  Form1.TextField2.TypeKeys ("<Tab>")
Form1.TextField3.SetText (Data.Sal)
Form1.TextField3.TypeKeys ("<Tab>")
Form1.TextField4.SetText (Data.Design)
Form1.Add.Click (1, 29, 15)
Sleep (5)
Form1.File.New.Pick ()
```

To pass the data to the Data-Driven test cases, we have a main function main ()

// 1. Declare a variable to hold current record

// 2. Store all data for test case in a list of records

// 3. Call the test case once for each record in the list.

Finally, the code will be as shown in Fig. 5.49.

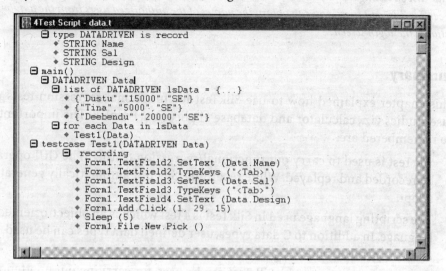

```
4Test Script - data.t
type DATADRIVEN is record
    STRING Name
    STRING Sal
    STRING Design
main()
    DATADRIVEN Data
    list of DATADRIVEN lsData = {...}
        {"Dustu","15000","SE"}
        {"Tina","5000","SE"}
        {"Deebendu","20000","SE"}
    for each Data in lsData
        Test1(Data)
testcase Test1(DATADRIVEN Data)
    recording
        Form1.TextField2.SetText (Data.Name)
        Form1.TextField2.TypeKeys ("<Tab>")
        Form1.TextField3.SetText (Data.Sal)
        Form1.TextField3.TypeKeys ("<Tab>")
        Form1.TextField4.SetText (Data.Design)
        Form1.Add.Click (1, 29, 15)
        Sleep (5)
        Form1.File.New.Pick ()
```

Fig. 5.49

Here "for" loop is used to execute the test for all 3 test inputs.

The syntax for the for loop is: for each item in expr statement

Variable	Description
item	A variable name.
expr	An expression that evaluates to a list or a set.
statement	A single statement or a series of statements.

Step 6: When you select Run option from Run menu

Select Run → Run

The main function will be executed first, and it will run the test case for each data set in lsData (the list of DATADRIVEN records) as shown in Fig. 5.49 and the results will be displayed as shown in Fig. 5.50.

```
Results - data.res
Script data.t - Passed
Machine: (local)
Started: 12:10:26PM on 05-Apr-2004
Elapsed: 0:00:23
Passed:  3 tests (100%)
Failed:  0 tests (0%)
Totals:  3 tests, 0 errors, 0 warnings

Testcase Test1 ({"Dustu", "15000", "SE"}) - Passed
Testcase Test1 ({"Tina", "5000", "SE"}) - Passed
Testcase Test1 ({"Deebendu", "20000", "SE"}) - Passed
```

Fig. 5.50

Data-driven testing simplifies the testing process significantly. For example, if you have to test a login screen for different users, you can obtain the names of the authorized users from the database and then validate the login screen.

Summary

This chapter explained how to use SilkTest for functional/regression tests using two case studies viz., calculator and database application, EmpDB. The important points to be remembered are:

- SilkTest is used to carry out functional/regression testing. The GUI operations can be recorded and replayed. While recording, SilkTest automatically generates the test script.
- The scripting language used in SilkTest is 4Test which is an object-oriented scripting language. In addition to C data types, user defined data types can be used. It also has all the control structures of C language.
- The test scripts created by SilkTest can be used for carrying out unattended testing and regression testing.
- You can create data-driven tests. In data-driven testing, you replace constant values by variables. The variables can be defined in the script or they can be obtained from a database.
- You can use the checkpoint features to check the GUI and database applications. For example, you can test the present status of a GUI button using a GUI checkpoint. You can also check the validity of the input data by making a comparison between the input values and the allowed values.

6 | SQA Robot

In this chapter

- Learn how to do functional/regression testing using SQA Robot
- Understand how to do synchronization of test cases
- Learn how to add GUI and database checkpoints

IBM Rational SQA Robot is a powerful functional/regression testing tool. In this chapter, we will study how to test applications using this tool. We will demonstrate the features of this tool using two case studies: calculator and a database application.

6.1 Overview of SQA Robot

SQA Robot is a tool from IBM Rational for carrying out functional/regression testing. This tool is a part of the test suit that contains:

- SQA Manager, to manage testing process.
- SQA Robot, for functional testing/regression testing of applications written in VB, Delphi, C++, Java etc., ERP packages as well as using Integrated Development Environments (IDEs) such as Visual Studio, Visual Age, Jbuilder.
- LoadTest, to test networking and web applications.
- SiteCheck, to check web sites.
- PurifyPlus, to check code coverage for C and C++ and to analyze the performance of the code as well as to detect bottlenecks in the code.

Similar to the other functional testing tools we discussed earlier, SQA Robot can be used to record the test cases. SQA Robot automatically generates a test script which can be stored and executed. You can do synchronization of test cases and also introduce GUI and database checkpoints.

SQABasic or Visual Basic is used as the test procedure scripting language If you know Visual Basic, it is very easy to understand the script generated by SQA Robot. Only SQABasic scripting language supports virtual user procedures.

6.2 Testing an Application using SQA Robot

Starting SQA Robot: Opening the SQA Robot application

- Go to Start → Programs → SQA Suite → SQA Robot

This displays the Login screen of the SQA application as shown in Fig. 6.1, prompting you to enter the User ID and password. By default the User ID is displayed as "ADMIN". If the user logs in as "ADMIN", there is no need to enter the password.

Fig. 6.1

Once you login into the application, the screen shown in Fig. 6.2 is displayed.

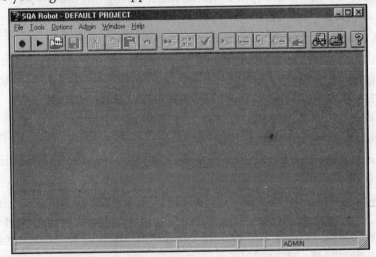

Fig. 6.2

6.2.1 Recording Test Cases

You need to have a clear idea about the sequence of operations to be performed to test the Application Under Test (AUT). You need to work with the application as usual and perform all the actions to be tested. SQA Robot keeps track of all the actions performed by you and generates a script. The procedure for recording the test cases is as follows:

- Open the application to be tested.
- Create a new test procedure as shown in Fig. 6.3.

  Admin → Test Procedure

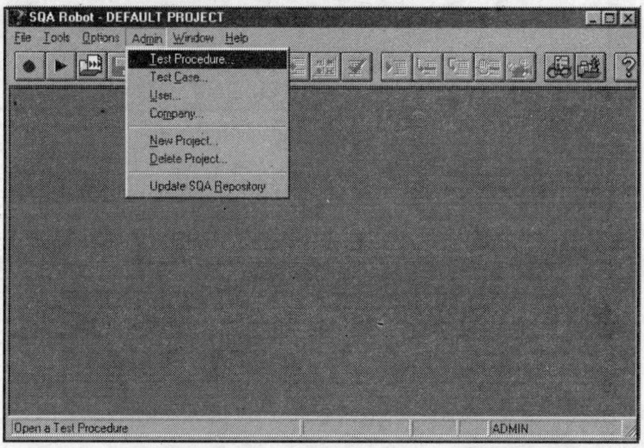

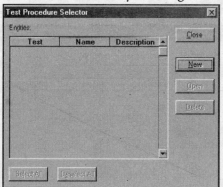

Fig. 6.3

- This displays a "Test Procedure Selector" dialog as shown in Fig. 6.4 prompting you to create a new Test Procedure by clicking on the "New" button.

Fig. 6.4

- When you click "New" button, the dialog shown in Fig. 6.5 is displayed prompting you to enter the Test Procedure Name, its Description and Author name.

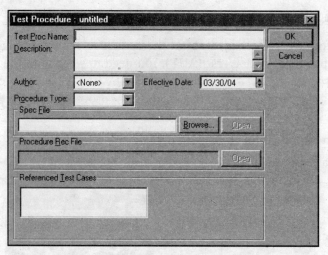

Fig. 6.5

- After entering the required details, if you click "OK" button, it prompts you to enter the ID for the new test procedure as shown in Fig. 6.6.

Fig. 6.6

- The ID of the test procedure need not be same as the name of the Test Procedure.
- Once you create a test procedure and specify the ID for the test procedure, it adds the details to the list box of the Test Procedure dialog as shown in Fig. 6.7.

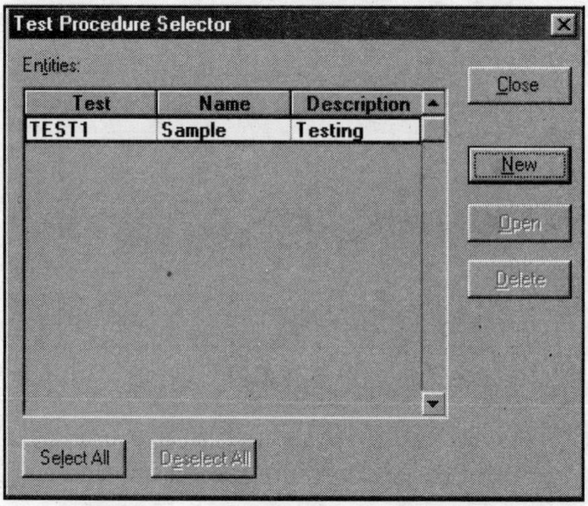

Fig. 6.7

- Now the new test procedure is created successfully and you can start recording the actions to be tested by following the procedure given below.
- Start recording the actions to be tested

  Select File → Record Test Procedure or click [●] on the toolbar

Click the [●] button on the toolbar of the SQA Robot as shown in Fig. 6.8 or select "Record Test Procedure" option from the "File" menu as shown in Fig. 6.9.

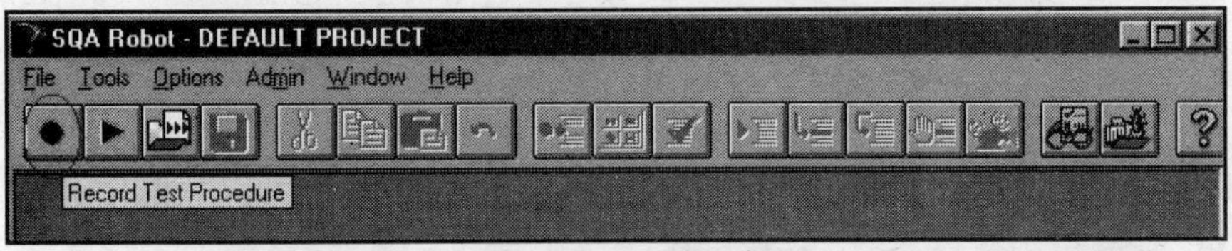

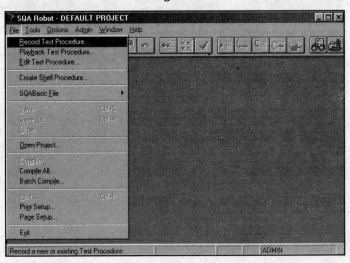

Fig. 6.8

Fig. 6.9

- Once you click the "Record Test Procedure", the dialog shown in Fig. 6.10 is displayed prompting you to select the Test Procedure name from the "Available Test Procedures" list. Select the Test Procedure name "TEST1". On selecting the Test procedure name, its details would be displayed automatically.

Fig. 6.10

- Once you select the required test procedure name, the Record toolbar is displayed as shown in Fig. 6.11.

Fig. 6.11

- Now you need to perform all the actions to be recorded.
- Once all the required actions are recorded, click on the "Stop" button shown in Fig. 6.11.
- SQA Robot generates the script and stores it in a ".rec" file with default path "C:\SQAREPO\DEFPROJ\PROCS".

6.2.2 Running the Test Procedure

- Select "Playback Test Procedure" from "File" menu or click button on toolbar. Select the "Playback Test Procedure" from the "File" menu as shown in Fig. 6.12 or click the button to run the test procedure as shown in Fig. 6.13.

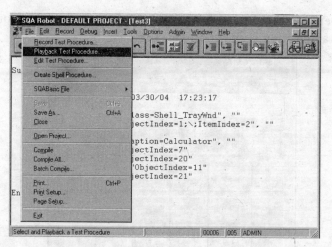

Fig. 6.12

Fig. 6.13

■ Once you run the test procedure, it repeats all the actions performed by you while recording and displays the test results in a "SQA Log viewer" as shown in Fig. 6.14.

Fig. 6.14

Let us perform the testing process on "Calculator" application. The GUI of the "Calculator" application is shown in Fig. 6.15.

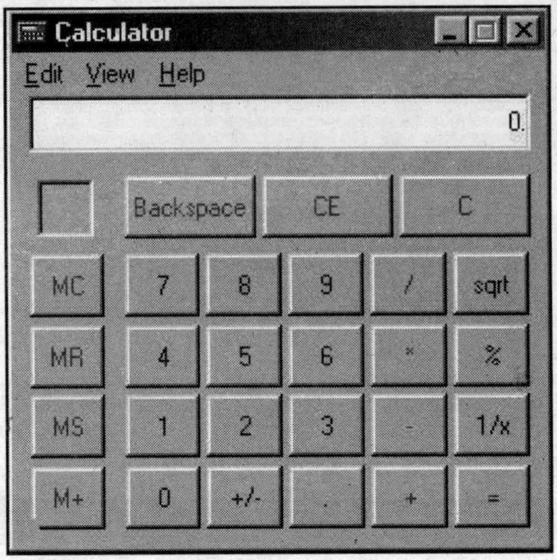

Fig. 6.15

The symbols on the buttons of Calculator application represent the following functions:

+	:	To perform Addition
-	:	To perform Subtraction
*	:	To perform Multiplication
/	:	To perform Division
.	:	Decimal point
sqrt	:	To find square root of a number
%	:	To find percent
1/x	:	To find inverse of a number
MC	:	To clear the memory
MR	:	To recall from memory
MS	:	To save in the memory
M+	:	To add to the memory
C	:	To clear the current calculation
CE	:	To clear the displayed number
Backspace	:	To remove left-most digit
+/-	:	To give sign of the number(positive or negative)

To test the complete functionality of the application, we need to generate test cases in such a way that all the buttons are made use of. We need to generate some test cases which will give correct output and also some test cases which will give error messages. Table 6.1 gives such test cases and the expected output for each test case.

Test Case	Expected Output
4 1/x	0.25
-6 sqrt	Err: "Invalid input for function"
4 C	Clears the Display
1.2 * 3	3.6
5 / 2.0	2.5
7 + 8 − 9	6
600 * 2 %	12
2, MS, C, MR	2
MC, 2, M+, 3, M+, C, MR	5

Table 6.1 Test Cases and Expected Output for Calculator Application

To test the functionality of the application, perform the following steps:

Test Case #1: To test the Inverse operation (inverse of 4 using 1/x button)

Step 1: Create a new test procedure

Admin → Test Procedure

Step 2: Enter the Test Proc Name as "inverse", give the description and select the Author as "ADMIN" as shown in Fig. 4.16 and click the "OK" button.

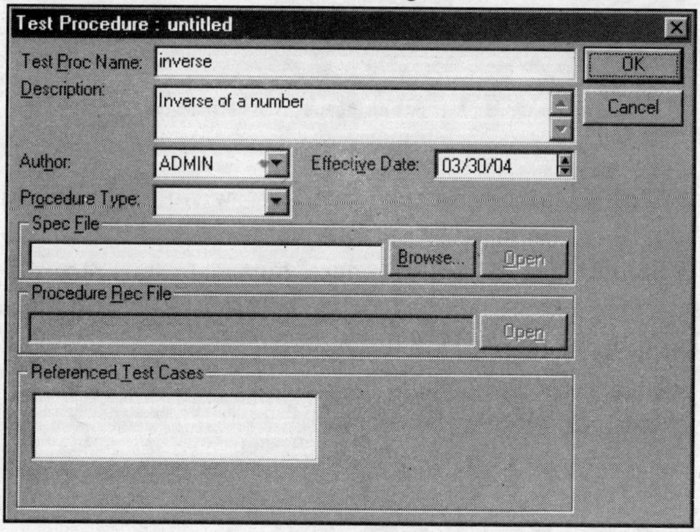

Fig. 6.16

Step 3: You are prompted to enter the ID for the test procedure. Give the ID as "INVERSE" as shown in Fig. 4.17 and click the "OK" button.

Fig. 6.17

Step 4: SQA Robot adds the newly created test procedure to the list box in the "Test Procedure Selector" as shown in Fig. 6.18.

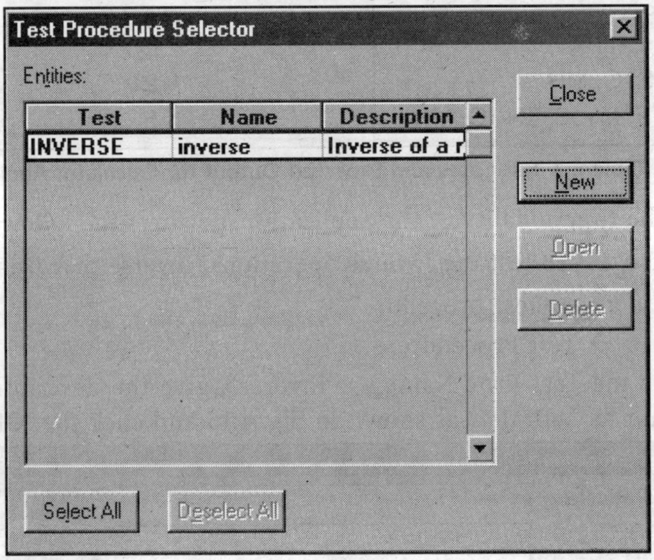

Fig. 6.18

Step 5: Close the "Test Procedure Selector" window by clicking the "Close" button.

Step 6: Click on the "Record Test Procedure" button to start recording. It prompts you to select the test procedure name. Select "INVERSE" from the list box as shown in Fig. 6.19 and click "OK" button.

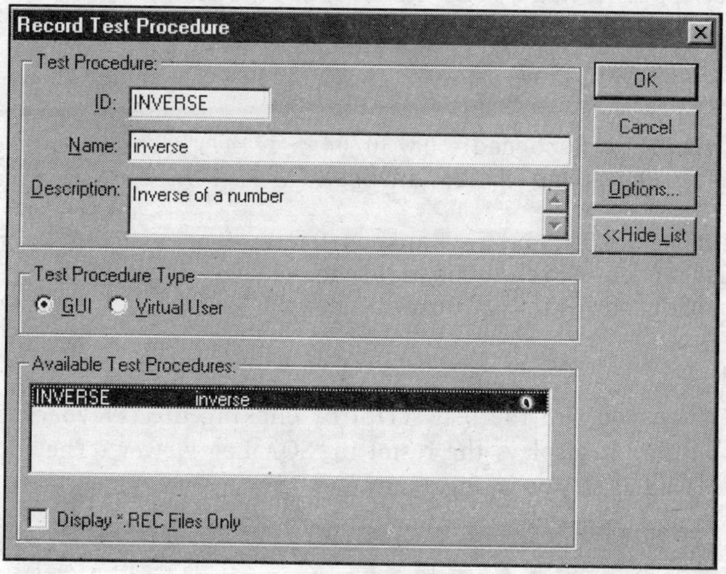
Record Test Procedure
Test Procedure:
ID: INVERSE
Name: inverse
Description: Inverse of a number
OK
Cancel
Options...
<<Hide List
Test Procedure Type
GUI
Virtual User
Available Test Procedures:
INVERSE inverse
Display *.REC Files Only

Fig. 6.19

Step 7: Click "4" on the Calculator.

Click the "1/x" button on the Calculator to find the inverse of 4.

The result, 0.25 will be displayed on the Calculator.

Step 8: Stop recording by clicking on the "Stop" button on the Record toolbar.

Step 9: SQA Robot generates the script as shown in Fig. 6.20.

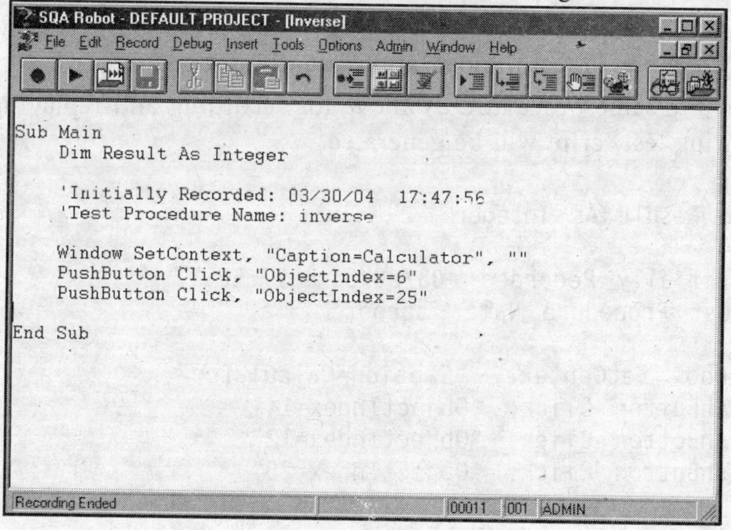
SQA Robot - DEFAULT PROJECT - [Inverse]
File Edit Record Debug Insert Tools Options Admin Window Help
Sub Main
Dim Result As Integer
'Initially Recorded: 03/30/04 17:47:56
'Test Procedure Name: inverse
Window SetContext, "Caption=Calculator", ""
PushButton Click, "ObjectIndex=6"
PushButton Click, "ObjectIndex=25"
End Sub
Recording Ended
00011 001 ADMIN

Fig. 6.20

The test script generated by SQA Robot is as follows:

```
Sub Main
      Dim Result As Integer

      'Initially Recorded: 03/30/04   17:47:56
      'Test Procedure Name: inverse

      Window SetContext, "Caption=Calculator",  ""
      PushButton Click, "ObjectIndex=6"
      PushButton Click, "ObjectIndex=25"

End Sub
```

Step 10: When you run the test script by clicking the "Playback Test Procedure" button, it displays the result in "SQA Log viewer". The results will be displayed as shown in Fig. 6.21.

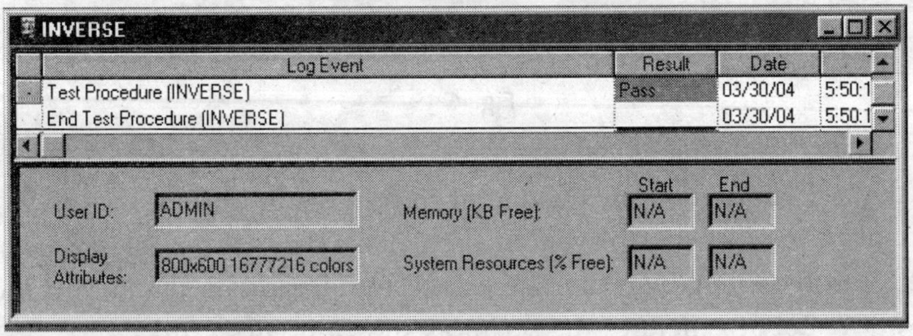

Fig. 6.21

Test Case #2: To test the operation Square root of -6.

Follow the same procedure as above for recording and replaying the test case. The following test script will be generated.

```
Sub Main
      Dim Result As Integer

      'Initially Recorded: 03/30/04   17:52:37
      'Test Procedure Name: sqroot

      Window SetContext, "Caption=Calculator",  ""
      PushButton Click, "ObjectIndex=14"
      PushButton Click, "ObjectIndex=12"
      PushButton Click, "ObjectIndex=26"

End Sub
```

When you execute this test script, the result will be as shown in Fig. 6.22.

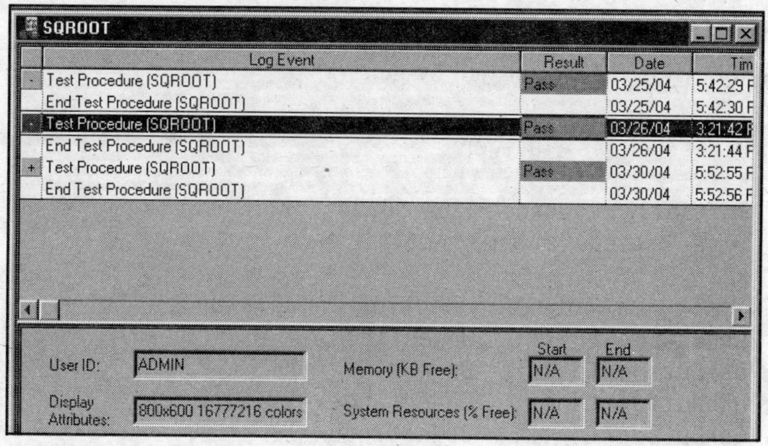

Fig. 6.22

Test Case #3: To Clear the display after performing some operations.

The following test script will be generated:

```
Sub Main
    Dim Result As Integer

    'Initially Recorded: 03/30/04 17:55:16
    'Test Procedure Name: clear

    Window SetContext, "Caption=Calculator", ""
    PushButton Click, "ObjectIndex=6"
    PushButton Click, "ObjectIndex=24"
End Sub
```

When this test script is executed, the result will be as shown in Fig. 6.23.

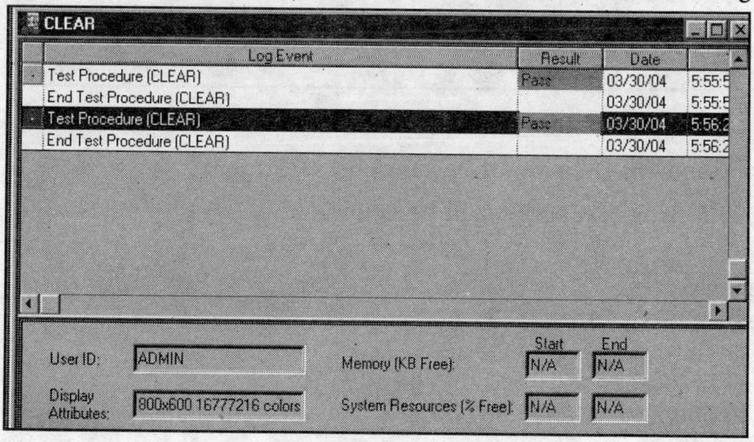

Fig. 6.23

Test Case #4: Multiplication of two numbers. (1.2 * 3)

The following test script will be generated:

```
Sub Main
    Dim Result As Integer

    'Initially Recorded: 03/30/04   17:57:49
    'Test Procedure Name: multiply

    Window SetContext, "Caption=Calculator", ""
    PushButton Click, "ObjectIndex=7"
    PushButton Click, "ObjectIndex=16"
    PushButton Click, "ObjectIndex=11"
    PushButton Click, "ObjectIndex=18"
    PushButton Click, "ObjectIndex=15"
    PushButton Click, "ObjectIndex=21"

End Sub
```

When the test script is executed, the result will be as shown in Fig. 6.24.

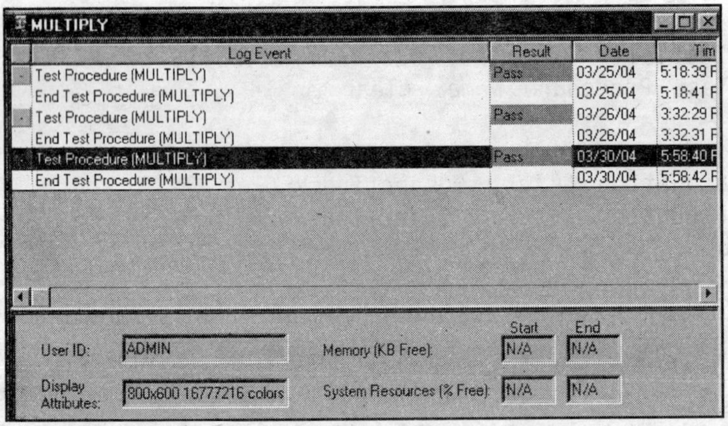

Fig. 6.24

Test Case #5: Division of two numbers. (5 / 2.0).

The following test script will be generated:

```
Sub Main
Dim Result As Integer

'Initially Recorded: 03/30/04 17:59:55
'Test Procedure Name: divide
```

```
Window SetContext, "Caption=Calculator", ""
PushButton Click, "ObjectIndex=10"
PushButton Click, "ObjectIndex=17"
PushButton Click, "ObjectIndex=11"
PushButton Click, "ObjectIndex=16"
PushButton Click, "ObjectIndex=8"
PushButton Click, "ObjectIndex=21"

End Sub
```

The output will be as shown in Fig. 6.25 when this test script is executed.

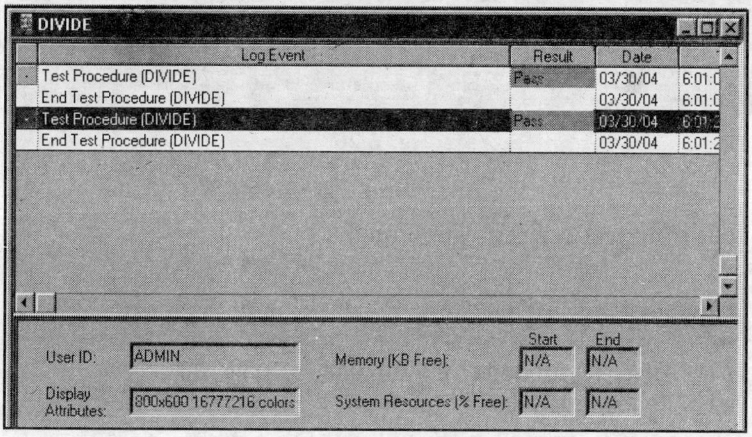

Fig. 6.25

Test Case #6: To test the operation $(7 + 8 - 9)$

The test script generated is as follows:

```
Sub Main
    Dim Result As Integer

    'Initially Recorded: 03/30/04   18:02:42
    'Test Procedure Name: add_sub

    Window SetContext, "Caption=Calculator", ""
    PushButton Click, "ObjectIndex=5"
    PushButton Click, "ObjectIndex=20"
    PushButton Click, "ObjectIndex=9"
    PushButton Click, "ObjectIndex=19"
    PushButton Click, "ObjectIndex=13"
    PushButton Click, "ObjectIndex=21"

End Sub
```

The result screen will be as shown in Fig. 6.26 when this test script is executed.

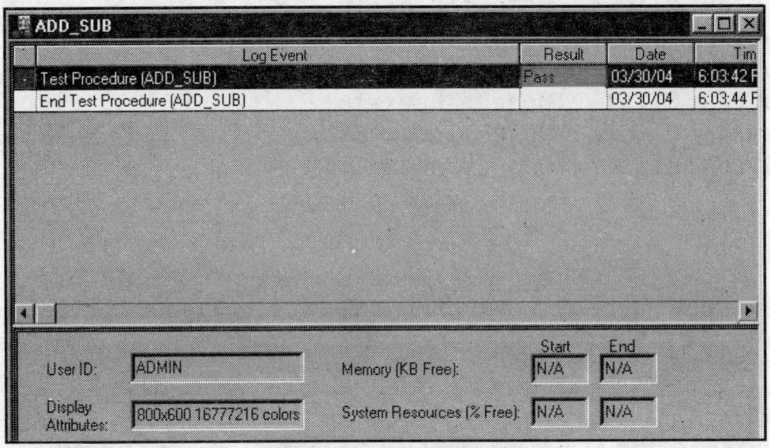

Fig. 6.26

Test Case #7: To test the operation 2% of 600

The following test script is generated.

```
Sub Main
    Dim Result As Integer

    'Initially Recorded: 03/30/04   18:05:00
    'Test Procedure Name: percent

    Window SetContext, "Caption=Calculator", ""
    PushButton Click, "ObjectIndex=14"
    PushButton DblClick, "ObjectIndex=8"
    PushButton Click, "ObjectIndex=18"
    PushButton Click, "ObjectIndex=11"
    PushButton Click, "ObjectIndex=27"

End Sub
```

When this test script is executed, the test results will be as shown in Fig. 6.27.

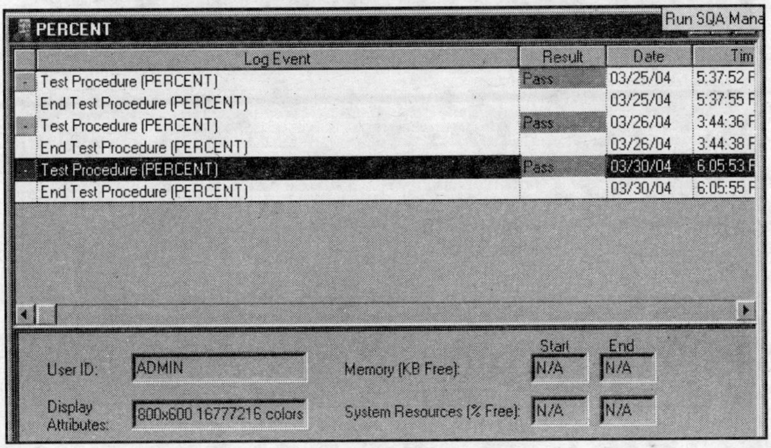

Fig. 6.27

Test Case #8: To test MS and MR buttons.

The following test script will be generated:

```
Sub Main
    Dim Result As Integer

    'Initially Recorded: 03/30/04   18:07:21
    'Test Procedure Name: ms_mr

    Window SetContext, "Caption=Calculator", ""
    PushButton Click, "ObjectIndex=11"
    PushButton Click, "ObjectIndex=3"
    PushButton Click, "ObjectIndex=15"
    PushButton Click, "ObjectIndex=3"
    PushButton Click, "ObjectIndex=24"
    PushButton Click, "ObjectIndex=2"

End Sub
```

The test results will be as shown in Fig. 6.28.

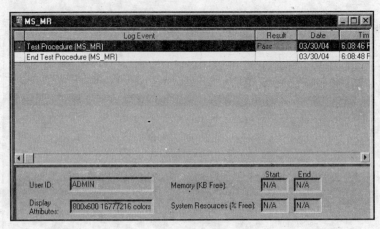

Fig. 6.28

Test Case #9: To test M+ and MR buttons.

The test script generated will be as follows:

```
Sub Main
    Dim Result As Integer

    'Initially Recorded: 03/30/04   18:10:30
    'Test Procedure Name: madd_mr

    Window SetContext, "Caption=Calculator", ""
    PushButton Click, "ObjectIndex=1"
    PushButton Click, "ObjectIndex=11"
    PushButton Click, "ObjectIndex=4"
    PushButton Click, "ObjectIndex=15"
    PushButton Click, "ObjectIndex=4"
    PushButton Click, "ObjectIndex=24"
    PushButton Click, "ObjectIndex=2"

End Sub
```

The test results will be as shown in Fig. 6.29.

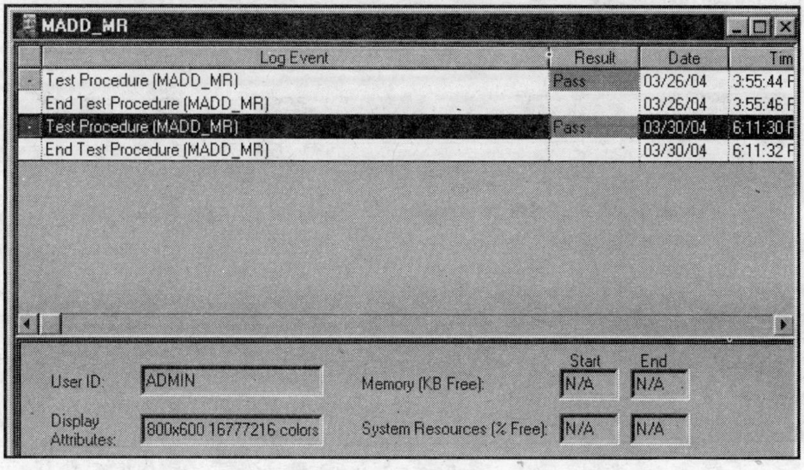

Fig. 6.29

Test Case #10: To test the Backspace.

When this test case is executed and recorded, the following test script is generated.

```
Sub Main
    Dim Result As Integer

    'Initially Recorded: 03/30/04   18:12:52
    'Test Procedure Name: backspace

    Window SetContext, "Caption=Calculator",  ""
    PushButton Click, "ObjectIndex=6"
    PushButton Click, "ObjectIndex=22"
    PushButton Click, "ObjectIndex=14"
    PushButton Click, "ObjectIndex=20"
    PushButton Click, "ObjectIndex=11"

End Sub
```

Execution of this test script produces the test result shown in Fig. 6.30.

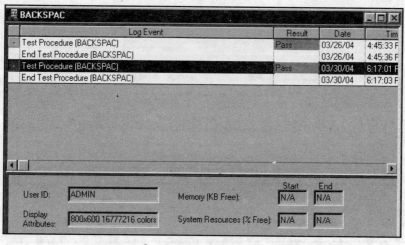

Fig. 6.30

6.2.3 Calling the Test Procedures using "CallProcedure" Function

Step 1: Create a new test procedure and save it as "Testcall".

Step 2: Click the "Record Test Procedure" button

Step 3: It displays the Record toolbar. Now click on the "Insert Action" button of SQA Robot Record as shown in Fig. 6.31.

Fig. 6.31

Insert Action

Step 4: Clicking on the "Insert Action" button will invoke "SQA Robot Insert" window.

Click on the "Call Test Procedure" button as shown in Fig. 6.32.

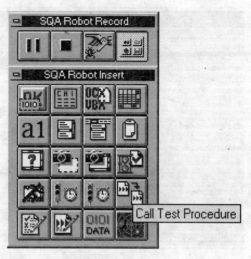

Fig. 6.32

Step 5: When you click on the Call Test Procedure button, it will prompt you to select the test procedure to be inserted as shown in Fig. 6.33.

Fig. 6.33

Step 6: Checking the "Run Now" button will run the called test procedure once before inserting into the test script. Unchecking it will just insert it into the script.

Step 7. Run the "Testcall" test script. It will internally call the inserted test scripts and displays the result of each called test procedure as shown in Fig. 6.34.

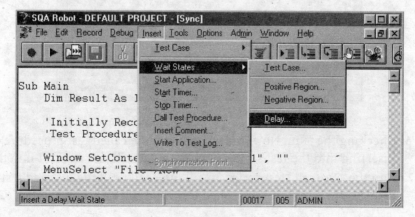

Fig. 6.34

6.3 Synchronization of Test Procedures

SQA Robot takes the delay time as 20 seconds by default i.e. it automatically waits for 20 seconds before executing the next statement in the test procedure. Hence SQA Robot automatically implements the process of synchronization. If you want to change the default delay time, then you can do it by following the steps given below.

Step 1: Open the "Delay Interval" dialog as shown in Fig. 6.35.

Insert → Wait States → Delay

Fig. 6.35

On selecting this option, the "Delay Interval" screen as shown in Fig. 6.36 is displayed.

Fig. 6.36

Step 2: Enter the required delay interval (in milliseconds) and click on the "OK" button to incorporate the delay in the application.

If you change the delay interval manually by following the above-specified procedure, then SQA Robot waits for the specified time interval before executing the next statement in the test procedure. This is not an efficient way, as it slows down the entire process of testing. If a particular action requires waiting for more than the default timeout time, it is better to synchronize only that action rather than increasing the delay interval manually. This can be done by creating a "Positive Wait state" or "Negative Wait state".

- **Positive wait state:** When the "Positive wait state" is defined, SQA Robot waits until the selected region matches the area in the application that is tested. If a match occurs before the timeout time, the next statements will be executed, otherwise, it displays an error message and the test fails.

- **Negative wait state:** When the "Negative wait state" is defined, SQA Robot waits until the selected region *does not* match the area in the application that is tested.

We illustrate the synchronization process using a database application. The EmpDB application, given in the CDROM, can be used. The procedure for installing this sample application is given in Appendix E.

In EmpDB application, it takes around 10 seconds to insert a record into the database. In such cases it is not required to create synchronization point. But to discuss this feature, first manually change the delay interval to 5 seconds and follow the steps below to create the synchronization point.

Step 1: Create a new test procedure. Give the test procedure name as "Sync"

Admin → Test Procedure

Step 2: Start Recording the actions

File → Record Test Procedure

Step 3: Insert a record into the database in the EmpDB application

- File → New

- Enter all the fields and click the "Add" button to insert the record into the Database

Step 4: Stop recording

Click the "Stop" button in the Record toolbar.

Step 5: Place the cursor at the point where that action has to be synchronized. In the present example, place the cursor after clicking the "Add" button. It is at this point the synchronization is required, as SQA Robot should wait till the insertion is completed before going for the next statement. Place the cursor after the following statement in the test procedure.

```
GenericObject Click, "Text=Add", "Coords = 11, 12"
```

Step 6: Create the Synchronization point as shown in the Fig. 6.37.

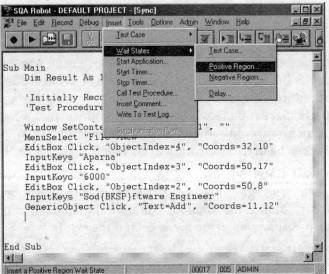

Fig. 6.37

This displays the "Region Image Capture" window as shown in Fig. 6.38.

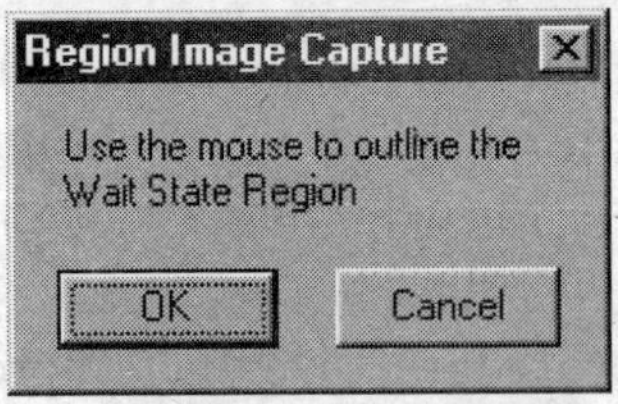

Fig. 6.38

Click the "OK" button to capture the image.

Step 7: The mouse pointer changes into a "Cross Lines". Now, you need to select the region for which SQA Robot should wait before executing the next statement.

Step 8: Use the mouse pointer to select the region "Insert Done". Then SQA Robot waits for this image to appear in the EmpDB application before executing the next statement.

Step 9: SQA Robot will now insert the following statement into the test procedure

```
Result   =   RegionTC (WaitPositive,   "",   "Name=Sync.W06;
Wait=10,4;Coords=289,381,496,403")
```

Step 10: Change the Wait time to 10 seconds in the test procedure. SQA Robot will wait for 10 seconds for the image to appear in the EmpDB application. If the image does not appear within the timeout time, then SQA Robot generates an error and as a result, the test fails.

Step 11: Run the test procedure.

File → Playback Test Procedure.

6.4 Creating Checkpoints

If you want to check whether the properties of the object in the application match the expected value or not, then you need to create the checkpoint on that object and enter the expected values for the required properties to be tested.

Let us consider the EmpDB application in which we now create a checkpoint for the "Designation" field. The test should fail if you enter any text other than "Software Engineer". This can be done by following the steps given below:

Step 1: Create a new test procedure

Admin →Test Procedure

Step 2: Start Recording

File → Record Test Procedure

Step 3: Insert a record into the EmpDB database.

File → New

Enter all the fields and click the "Add" button to insert the record into the Database.

Step 4: Stop Recording.

Click the "Stop" button on the Record toolbar.

Step 5: Synchronize the test procedure if needed. (Refer to *Synchronization of Test Procedures* for details)

Step 6: Place the cursor at the point where the checkpoint has to be created.

Step 7: Create the checkpoint as shown in Fig. 6.39.

Insert → Test Case → Object Properties

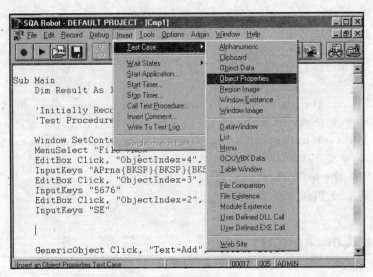

Fig. 6.39

When you select this option, it displays the "Define an Object Properties Comparison Test Case" dialog. Enter the Case ID, Case Name, its Description as shown in Fig. 6.40. Click the "OK" button.

Fig. 6.40

Step 8: The mouse cursor changes to a pointing hand. Click on the object in the application for which the checkpoint has to be created. Click on the "Designation" editbox in the EmpDB application. On selecting this, "Object Properties Test Case" dialog appears as shown in Fig. 6.41, which displays all the available properties of the selected object in the "Properties" list box. In case of "Designation" field, it displays the properties of the EditBox.

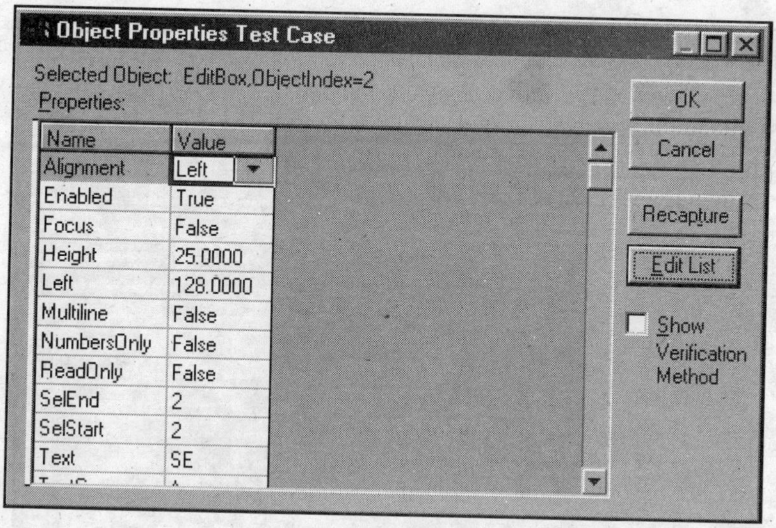

Fig. 6.41

If all the properties of the object are to be checked then enter the expected values for the properties and click the "OK" button. In case of EmpDB, we want to check only the "Text" property. To select the required properties, click the "Edit List" button. It will display the "Edit Property List" dialog, which contains two list boxes "Available Properties" and "Selected Properties". Select all the properties except for the "Text" property and click the "Remove" button to move the unwanted properties to the "Available Properties" list box as shown in Fig. 6.42. Click "OK" button.

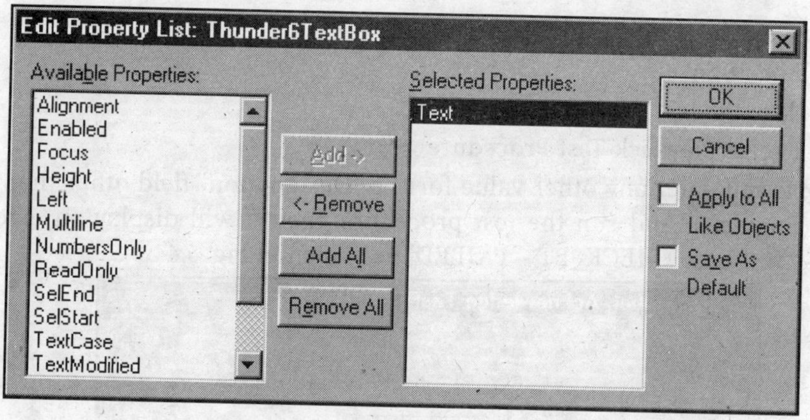

Fig. 6.42

Step 9: Only the "Text" property will be added to the "Properties" list. Change the property "Text" value to "Software Engineer" as shown in Fig. 6.43 and click the "OK" button.

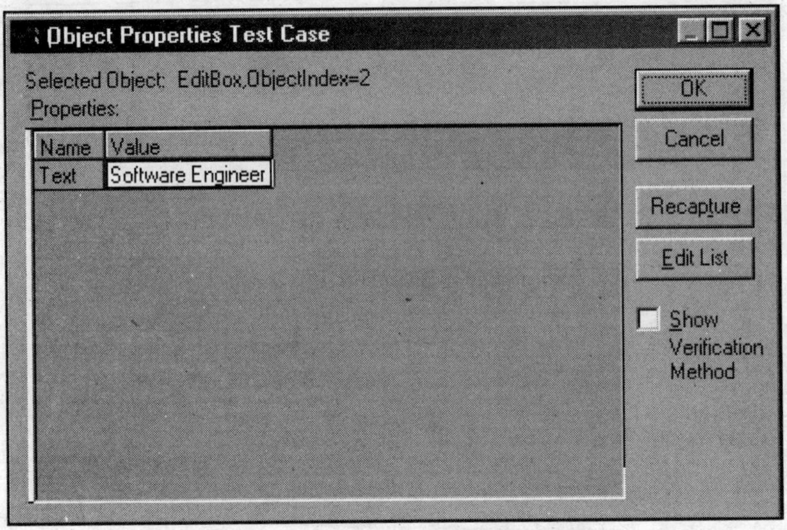

Fig. 6.43

Step 10: The code for comparing the property value with the expected value is added to the test procedure.

```
Window SetTestContext, "Caption=Form1", ""
    Result = EditBoxTC (CompareProperties, "ObjectIndex=2",
"CaseID=CHECK_PT")
    Window ResetTestContext, "", ""
```

Step 11: Save the test procedure.

File → Save

Step 12: Run the test procedure.

File → Playback Test Procedure

Step 13: If you enter any other value for the "Designation" field other than "Software Engineer" and run the test procedure, then it will display an error message "Test Case CHECK_PT – FAILED" as shown in Fig. 6.44.

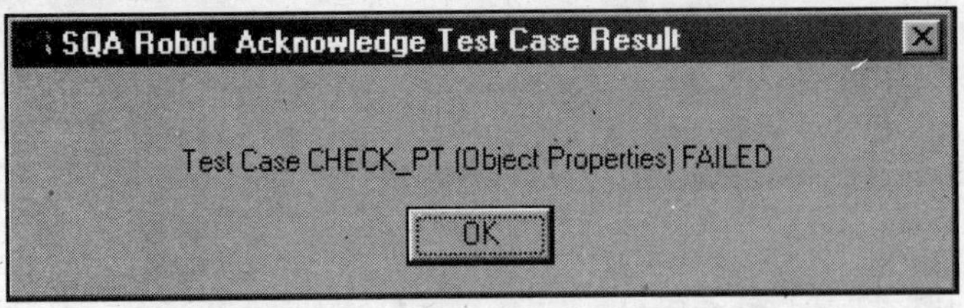

Fig. 6.44

When you click the "OK" button, SQA Robot executes the remaining statements and displays the test result as shown in Fig. 6.45.

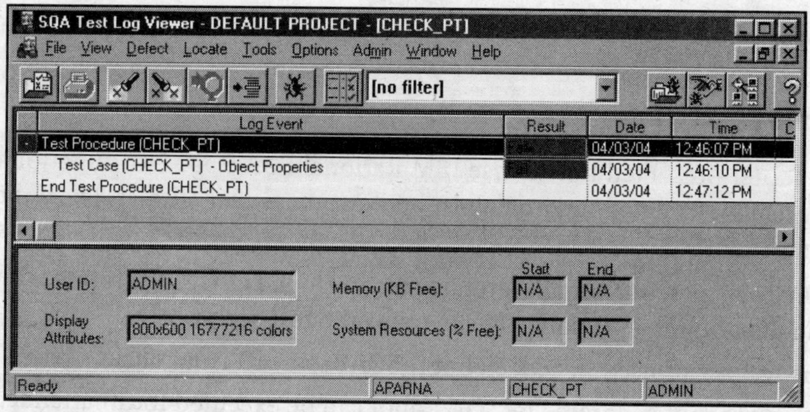

Fig. 6.45

Step 14: If you enter the "Designation" field in the EmpDB application as "Software Engineer" and run the test procedure, then it displays a message "Test Case CHECK_PT – PASSED" as shown in Fig. 6.46

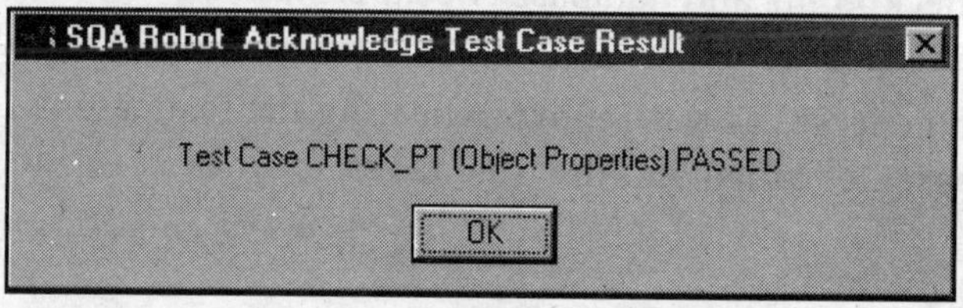

Fig. 6.46

Step 15: When you click the "OK" button, it executes the remaining statements and displays the test results as shown in Fig. 6.47.

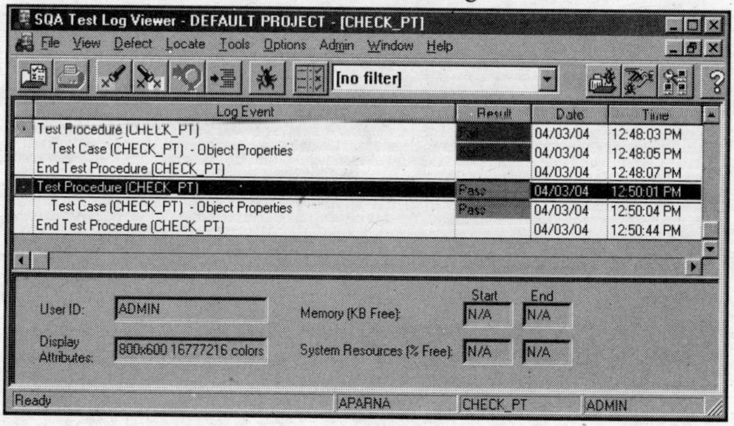

Fig. 6.47

The database checkpoints have to be used to check the database integrity and consistency.

Summary

This chapter presented how to use IBM Rational SQA Robot for functional/regression testing using calculator and a database application as case studies. The important points to be noted are:

- SQA Robot is a functional/regression testing tool. The GUI operations can be recorded and SQA Robot automatically generates the test script.

- The test script used in SQA Robot is SQABasic or Visual Basic.

- The test script generated by SQA Robot can be executed for unattended testing and regression testing.

- You can synchronize different test cases. The delay between execution of two statements can be changed to suit your application needs.

- The GUI checkpoints and database checkpoints are used to check the state of a GUI object or to check the validity of a particular field in a database.

- SQA Robot generates a test report indicating the test cases executed, whether each test has passed or failed and the time taken for the execution.

7 ▪ LoadRunner

In this chapter

- Learn how to use LoadRunner to carry out performance/load testing
- Understand how to evaluate the performance of web-based applications
- Grasp the performance requirements of web-based applications

To test the performance requirements such as transaction response time of a database application or response time in the case of multiple users accessing a web site, LoadRunner is an excellent tool that reduces the infrastructure and manpower costs. In this chapter, we will study how to use LoadRunner through a case study.

7.1 Overview of LoadRunner

Mercury Interactive's LoadRunner is used to test the Client/Server applications such as database management systems and web sites. As we discussed in Chapter 3, to study how the application performs when multiple users access the application requires lot of infrastructure and manpower, if testing tools are not used. Using LoadRunner, with minimal infrastructure and manpower, performance testing can be carried out. LoadRunner simulates multiple transactions from the same machine and hence it creates a scenario of simultaneous access to the application. So, instead of 'real' users, 'virtual' users are simulated. With virtual users simultaneously accessing the application, LoadRunner accurately measures and analyzes the performance of the Client/Server application.

In LoadRunner, we divide the performance testing requirements into various scenarios. A scenario is a series of actions that are to be tested. LoadRunner creates Virtual users (abbreviated Vusers). The Vusers submit the requests to the server. Vuser script is generated and this script is executed for simulating multiple users.

For demonstrating the features of LoadRunner, we will use an application "Weather India" which gives information about the weather in various cities in India. It is a web-based application with hyperlinks such as Weather Basics, Weather Phenomenon, and Weather Forecasting. This application is available on the CDROM that accompanies this book. You need to install the application in your system before proceeding further for using it with LoadRunner. The weather information is internally stored in an MS Access database. Note that the LoadRunner is installed on a Windows NT system and the web site is accessed from a Windows 95/98 client. The client makes a HTTP connection to the server and gets the web site. The detailed procedure for installing this sample application is given in Appendix E.

Virtual user script (abbreviated Vuser Script) describes the actions performed by a virtual user.

7.2 Creating Vuser script using Virtual User Generator

For creating the Vuser script, follow the steps given below:

Step 1: Start the Virtual User Generator

Start → Programs → LoadRunner → Virtual User Generator

Step 2: LoadRunner displays the welcome screen as shown in Fig. 7.1.

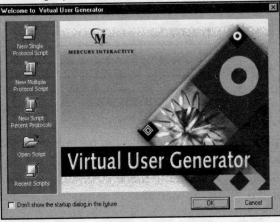

Fig. 7.1

Step 2: Click the "New Single Protocol Script" button. It displays the list of protocols as shown in Fig. 7.2. Select the "Category" under which the application to be tested falls. In case of our example, select the "Web (HTTP/HTML)" option and click "OK" button.

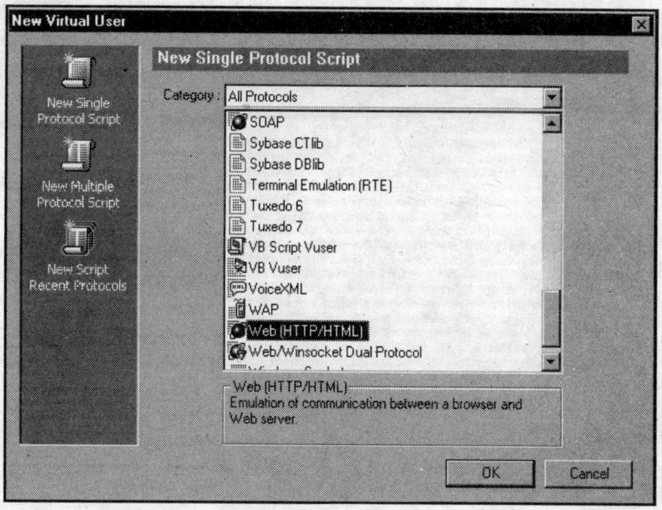

Fig. 7.2

Step 3: When you click the "OK" button, it displays the dialog as shown in Fig. 7.3.

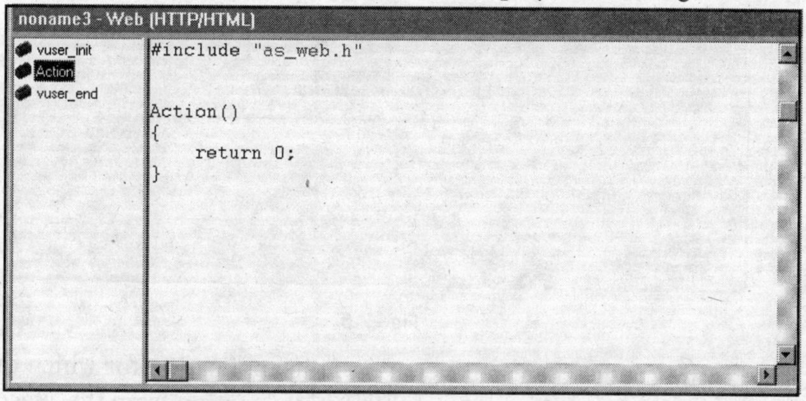

Fig. 7.3

The Virtual user script is divided into 3 sections: Vuser_init, Actions, Vuser_end.

Vuser_init: These actions are performed when the Vuser is loaded or initialized.

Actions: These actions are performed when the Vuser is in "Running" state.

Vuser_end: These actions are performed when the Vuser finishes or stops.

You can select the section before or while the recording is under progress.

Step 4: Select the "Actions" section. Click the ⬤ Start Record button or select the "Start Recording" option from the "Vuser" menu as shown in Fig. 7.4.

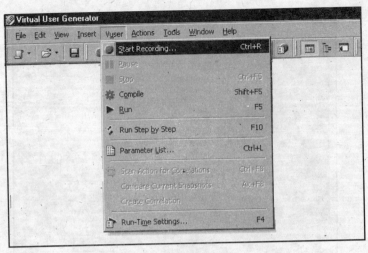

Fig. 7.4

Step 5: On selecting "Start Recording" option, it displays the "Start Recording" dialog as shown in Fig. 7.5.

Fig. 7.5

This prompts you to enter the "URL" of the application for which the test has to be performed. Enter the URL and select the "Action" section from the "Record into Action" combo box as shown in Fig. 7.5 and click the "OK" button.

Note that you need to give the URL based on where you installed the application.

Step 6: LoadRunner now opens the specified URL and a "Recording Toolbar..." appears as shown in Fig. 7.6.

Fig. 7.6

LoadRunner is now in the "Recording" mode. Perform the actions that are to be recorded such as clicking on a link to obtain the weather information for a particular city. Once all the actions are recorded, stop the recording by clicking the "Stop" button in the Recording toolbar.

Step 7: LoadRunner generates the script for the actions that are recorded as shown in Fig. 7.7.

```
noname3 - Web [HTTP/HTML]
  vuser_init    #include "as_web.h"
  Action        Action()
  vuser_end     {
                    web_url("main1.htm",
                        "URL=http://aparna/weather/main1.htm",
                        "Resource=0",
                        "RecContentType=text/html",
                        "Referer=",
                        "Snapshot=t1.inf",
                        "Mode=HTML",
                        EXTRARES,
                        "Url=indiamap1.gif", ENDITEM,
                        LAST);

                    lr_think_time( 84 );

                    web_url("cityweather.asp",
                        "URL=http://aparna/weather/cityweather.asp?city1
                        "Resource=0",
                        "RecContentType=text/html",
                        "Referer=",
                        "Snapshot=t2.inf",
```

Fig. 7.7

Vuser Scripts can be generated by using a number of tools such as WinRunner, VuGen, QuickTest etc. which together form a testing suite of Mercury Interactive Corporation.

Step 8: Save the Test Script.

File → Save

Step 9: Run the script.

Click the ▶ button to run the test script or click the "Run" from "Vuser" menu or press F5.

Vuser → Run

Step 10: Once the execution is completed, examine the "Execution log" to see whether the script ran without errors or not.

Step 11: The test results are displayed in the "Test Results" window, which contains various sections: "Vuser_init_summary", "Iteration", "Vuser_end_summary".

The Results Summary Report is shown in Fig. 7.8, the Iteration Report is shown in Fig. 7.9 and Vuser_end Summary Report is shown in Fig. 7.10.

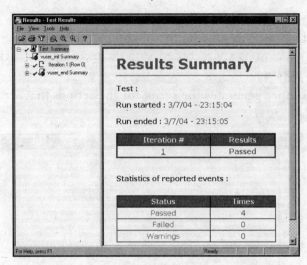

Fig. 7.8

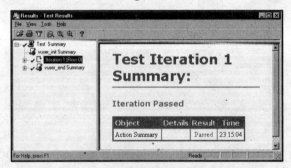

Fig. 7.9

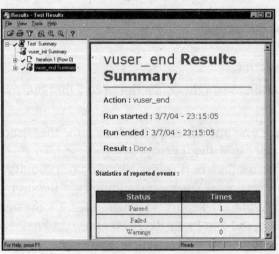

Fig. 7.10

Transaction time indicates the time taken by the server to respond to a request made by the client. LoadRunner creates "rendezvous points" wherein multiple virtual users are made to perform a particular task exactly at the same time. "Rendezvous" means meeting point.

7.3 Creating Virtual Users Using Loadrunner Controller

LoadRunner Controller is used to create the virtual users who replace the human users to test the performance of the application. By default, it creates 10 virtual users who will access the application simultaneously and tests the load on the application. It is also possible to increase the number of virtual users. Let us now create virtual users for the web-based application for which we have already generated the test script using the LoadRunner Virtual User Generator.

Fig. 7.11

To create the Virtual users and test the performance of the "Weather India" application whose home page is shown in Fig. 7.11, follow the steps given below.

Step 1: Start the Load Runner - Controller

    Start → Programs → LoadRunner → Controller

Step 2: On starting the Controller, it displays the screen as shown in Fig. 7.12.

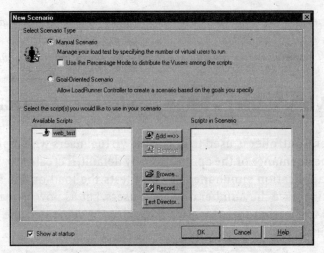

Fig. 7.12

Select the "Manual Scenario" option and the required test script from the "Available Scripts" list and click the "OK" button.

Step 3: From the "LoadRunner Controller Scenario1" dialog, click the "Generator" button or select the "Load Generators" from the "Scenario" menu. "Load Generators" dialog is opened as shown in the Fig 7.13.

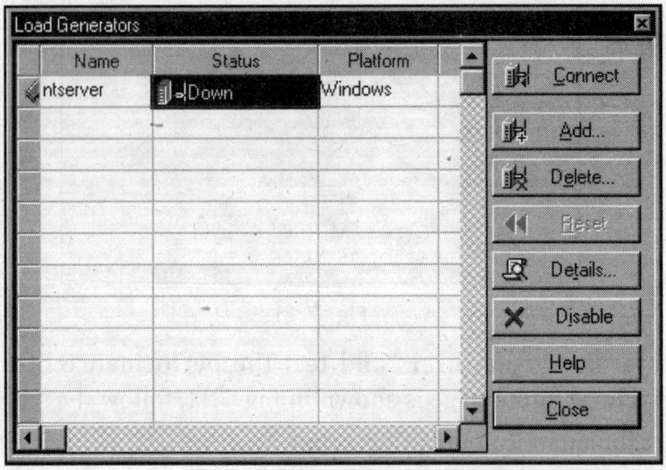

Fig. 7.13

Click the "Add" button to add a generator, or double-click the "Status" column of the default host details, which displays the "Load Generator Information" as shown in Fig. 7.14.

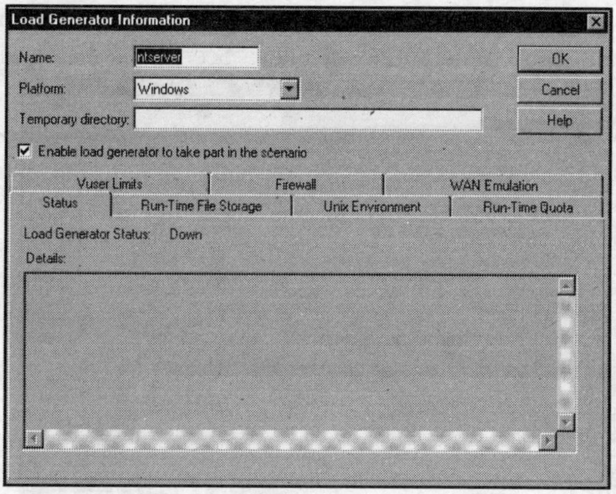

Fig. 7.14

Host Name refers to the identity of the system. Enter the name of the system in this field. Select the platform (in case of our example select "Windows") and click the "OK" button.

Step 4: In the "Load Generators" dialog, click the "Connect" button to change the status of the load generator from "Down" to "Ready" and click the "Disconnect" button to change the status of the load generator from "Ready" to "Down".

Step 5: Click "Close" button to close the "Load Generators" dialog.

Step 6: In the "Load Runner Controller – Scenario1" dialog, click the "Add Group" to create the group for the virtual users. It then displays the "Add Dialog" as shown in Fig. 7.15.

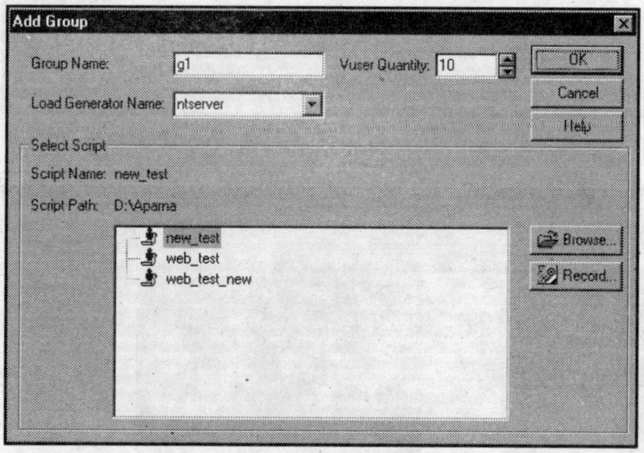

Fig. 7.15

Enter the group name as "g1", select the host name from the "Load Generator Name" and select the test script from the "Select Script" list box that has to be tested. Enter the number of virtual users to be created in the "Vuser Quantity" and click the "OK" button.

Step 7: The Group "g1" will be displayed along with its host name and the number of virtual users in the "Load Generator Controller – Scenario1" dialog as shown in Fig. 7.16.

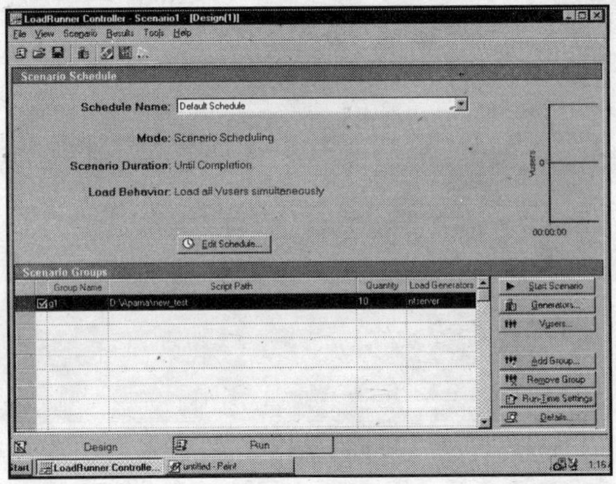

Fig. 7.16

Step 8: Click "Vuser" button to view the virtual users. Initially all the users are in "Down" State as shown in Fig. 7.17. Select all the users and right click to select the "Initialize Vuser/s" option as shown in Fig. 7.18.

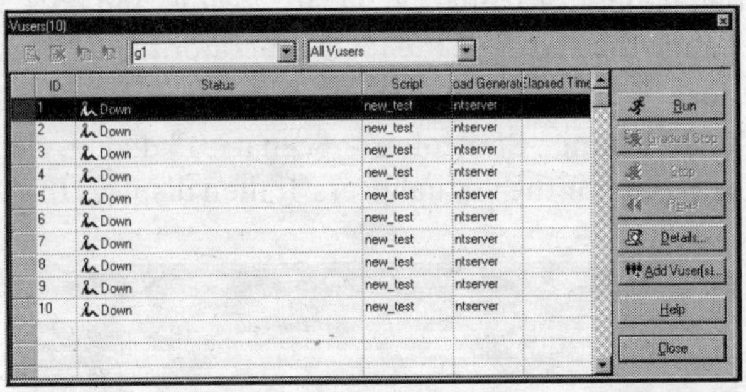

Fig. 7.17

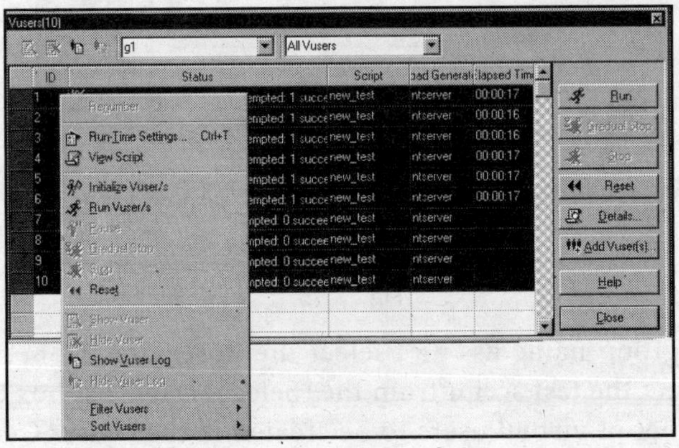

Fig. 7.18

All the Vusers will change their state from "Down" - "Initializing" - "Ready" mode. Now to run the Vusers, again select all the Vusers, right click and select "Run Vuser/s" or click the "Run" button. The status of the Vusers will change from Ready - Running – Done. Passed or Done. Failed.

Step 9: Once all the Vusers complete the execution of the script, it displays which user has passed the test and which has not, as shown in Fig. 7.19.

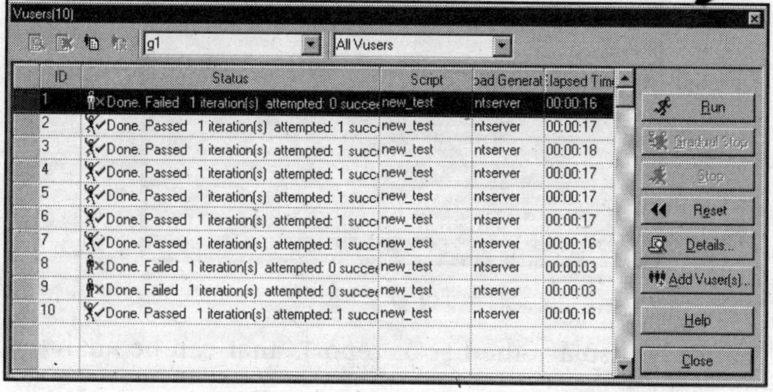

Fig. 7.19

If only 5 Vusers are allowed to test the "Weather India" application simultaneously, then all the Vusers successfully complete the test as shown in Fig. 7.20. This means that the "Server" that is processing the requests is not able to take the load of all the 10 users at a time.

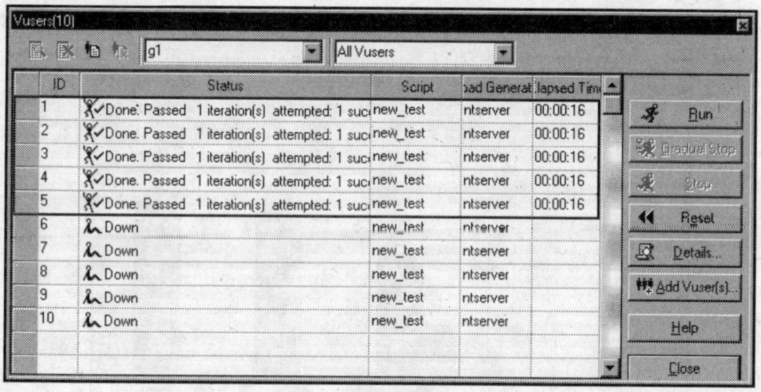

Fig. 7.20

Step 10: Click the "Close" button to close the "Vusers" window.

Step 11: Analyze the test results.

Tools → Analysis

Load Runner internally opens the "Load Runner Analysis". It displays "LoadRunner Analysis" dialog as shown in Fig. 7.21.

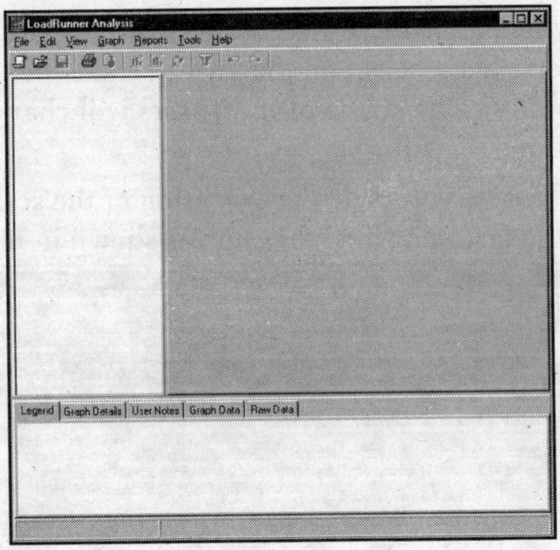

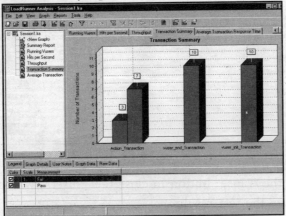

Fig. 7.21

It automatically displays the list of reports that can be analyzed. You can obtain the following reports:

- Running Vusers
- Hits per second
- Throughput
- Transaction summary
- Average transaction response time

Step 12: Analyze the results by studying graphs shown in Fig. 7.22 which shows the transaction summary report.

Fig. 7.22

The Transaction Summary report specifies the number of Vusers that passed and failed the various sections of the script i.e. Action, Vuser_init, Vuser_end in the form of Bar graph.

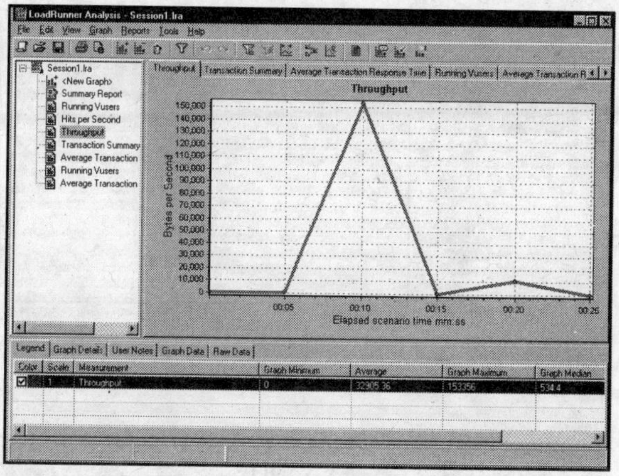

Fig. 7.23

Fig. 7.23 gives the Throughput Report. The Throughput Report shows the rate at which the Vusers run the script and produce the test results.

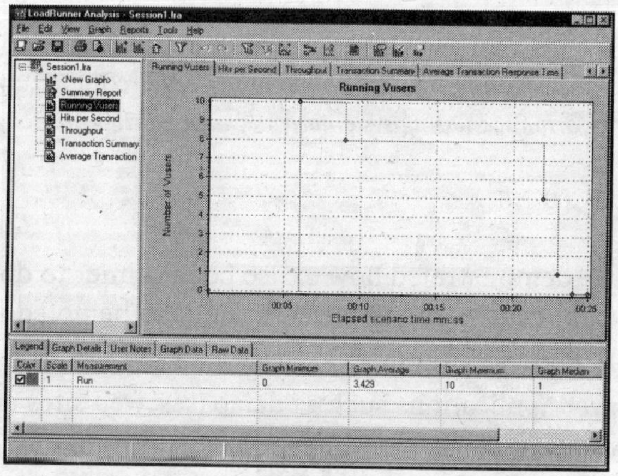

Fig.7.24

"Running Vusers" report, shown in Fig. 7.24, describes the elapsed time for each user in mm:ss format

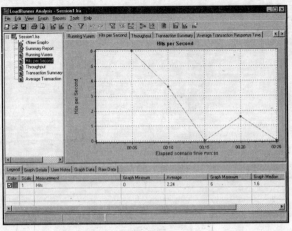

Fig. 7.25

Fig. 7.25 shows the graph which indicates the number of requests made by the user per second.

You can integrate WinRunner and LoadRunner with TestDirector to carry out functional/regression testing as well as performance testing systematically using a rigorous testing process.

Summary

In this chapter, we demonstrated how to use LoadRunner to do performance testing of a Client/Server application. The important points to be noted are:

- Mercury Interactive's LoadRunner can be used for carrying out performance testing of Client/Server applications such as databases, web sites etc.
- To test the performance of an application, LoadRunner generates virtual users i.e., it simulates the actions of real users simultaneously accessing the application.
- To generate the virtual users, Virtual user script has to be created by recording the interaction with the application GUI.
- From a single machine, a number of virtual users can be created and the application can be tested for its performance parameters.
- The performance test report gives the various performance parameters such as average transaction time, throughput, hits per second etc.
- LoadRunner can be integrated with testing management tool such as TestDirector to carry out unattended performance testing.

8 ▪ JMeter

In this chapter

- Learn the important features and capabilities of JMeter
- Learn how to do performance testing of a database application
- Learn how to do performance testing of a HTTP connection for web site access.

Due to the immense popularity of web-based applications, testing these applications has now gained a lot of importance. Particularly, performance testing of applications, such as e-commerce, web services etc., is of paramount importance as multiple users access the service simultaneously. In this chapter, we will study how to do performance testing of web-based applications using JMeter, an open source performance testing tool.

8.1 JMeter Overview

The Apache JMeter is an open source testing tool used to test the performance of the application when it is under heavy load. It can be used to test both static and non-static data. It puts heavy load on the server, tests the performance and analyzes the results when many users access the application simultaneously. First you need to identify the category under which the application falls. Some of these categories are:

- FTP Request
- HTTP Request
- JDBC Request
- Java object request
- LDAP Request

The CDROM that accompanies this book contains the folder "JMeter" from which the tool can be installed on your system. The procedure for installing JMeter is given in Appendix E. In the next section, we will illustrate the use of JMeter through a case study, to test a web site.

243

Using Apache JMeter, we will test the web site "Weather India". This web site developed using Active Server Pages (ASPs) and MS Access as database. We need to test the performance of this application for its database and the HTTP connection. Hence, this test is divided into two cases: JDBC test and HTTP test. This application is available on the CDROM that accompanies the book. You need to install the JMeter and this application before proceeding further. You can also run the sample application of JMeter to get a good understanding of its capabilities.

JDBC requests are, issued by multiple users to access a database using Java Database Connectivity (JDBC). Hyper Text Transfer Protocol (HTTP) requests are sent from the client to the server when a web site is accessed.

8.2 JDBC Test

Let us now consider the "Weather India" application. It is a web-based application, which accesses data from the table called "cityweather" of "weather.mdb" (MS Access file). We will demonstrate how to use Apache JMeter to test the performance of the database server (.mdb file), when multiple users try to access the database simultaneously.

The first step is to create a JDBC Test Plan. The test plan includes the following sections:

1. Creation of Thread Group
2. Adding the JDBC Requests
3. Adding Listeners to View/Store Results
4. Saving the Test Plan
5. Running the Test Plan

8.2.1 Creating the Thread Group

Step 1: When you initially start the JMeter application, it displays the dialog shown in Fig. 8.1. By default, the tree structure contains two elements: Test Plan and Work Bench.

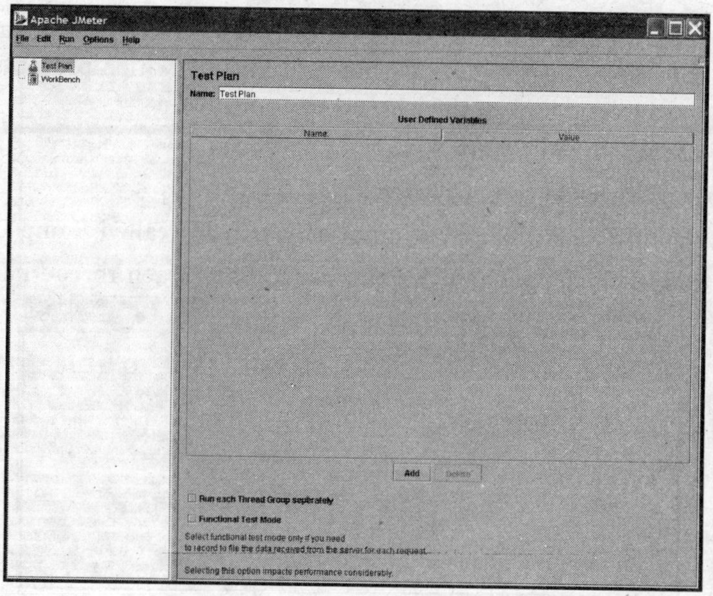

Fig. 8.1

Step 2: To create a Thread Group, right click on the "Test Plan" and select Add→ Thread Group as shown in Fig. 8.2.

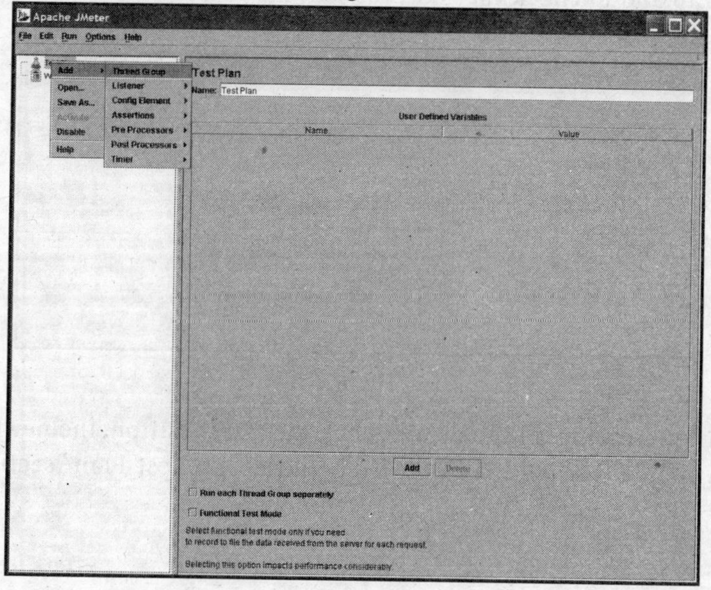

Fig. 8.2

The Thread Group has to be created under the "Test Plan" section.

Step 3: On adding the "Thread Group", it displays the "Thread Group" details on the right side of the window as shown in Fig. 8.3, which prompts you to enter all the details related to the Thread Group, such as

- Name of the Thread Group
- Number of Threads to be created
- Delay time between the execution of each thread (called Ramp-Up period).
- Loop Count which specifies the number of times each thread has to be executed.

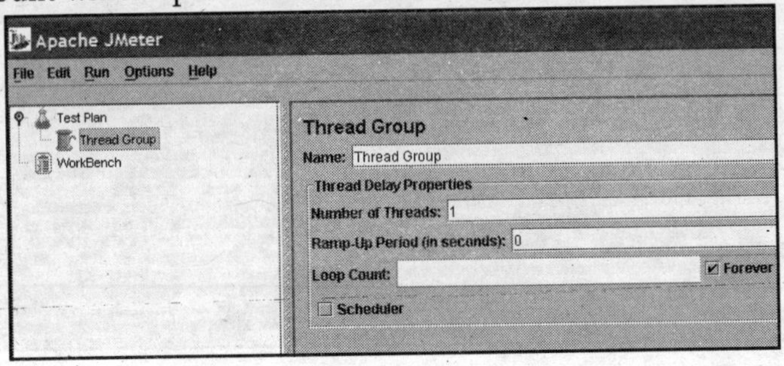

Fig. 8.3

Enter the Thread Group name as "Weather Jdbc Users", Number of Threads to be created as 10 and uncheck the "Forever" checkbox and enter the "Loop Count" as 3 as shown in Fig. 8.4.

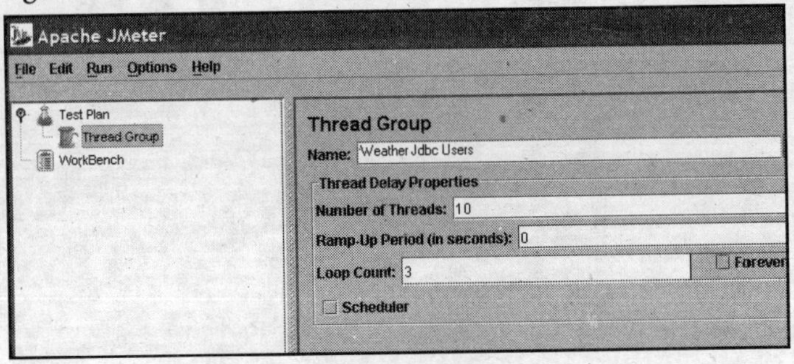

Fig. 8.4

Step 4: After entering all the details, click the "Add" button, the newly created Thread Group will be added to the Tree under the "Test Plan" section.

8.2.2 Creating the JDBC Requests

Now add the various requests to be made, to the Thread Group we just created.

Step 1: Select the "Weather Jdbc Users" Thread Group from the tree structure. Right click on it to add the JDBC Request as shown in Fig. 8.5.

Add → Sampler → JDBC Request

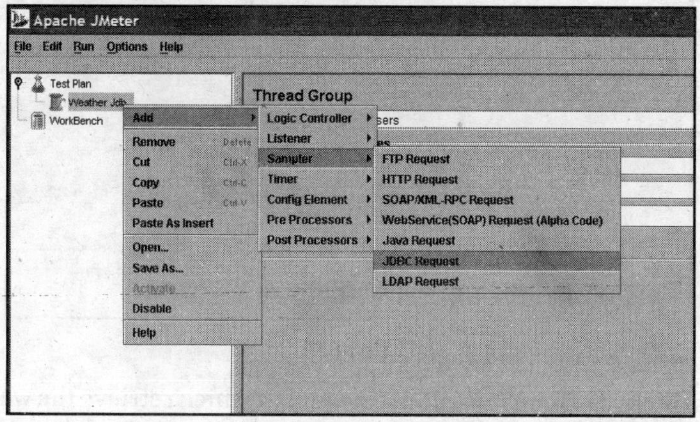

Fig. 8.5

Step 2: When you select the "JDBC Request" option, it displays the "JDBC Request" details at the right side work area as shown in Fig. 8.6.

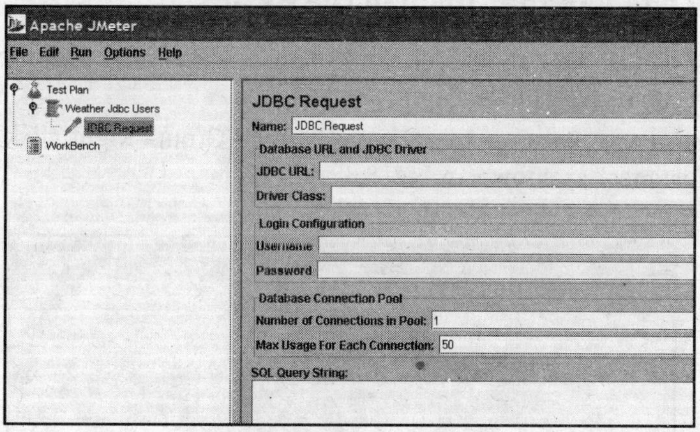

Fig. 8.6

- Enter the name of the JDBC Request as "City Weather JDBC Request1".
- Enter the JDBC URL as "jdbc:odbc:weather" where "weather" is the DSN (Data Source Name) of the "weather" database.

■ Enter the "Driver Class" as "sun.jdbc.odbc.JdbcOdbcDriver as this is the default driver for Java based applications.

■ Give the query string that has to be executed.

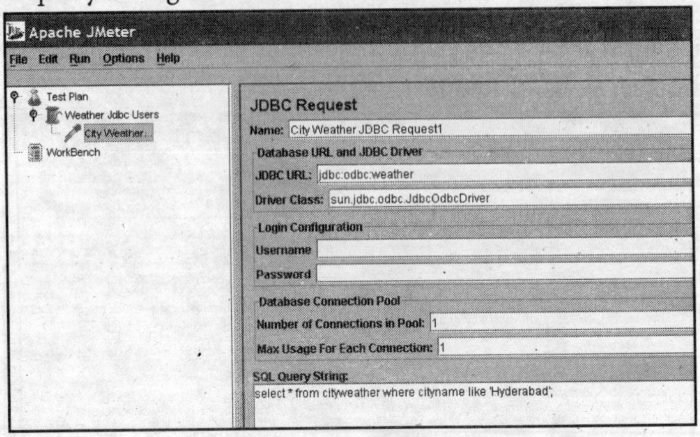

Fig. 8.7

Similarly create some more JDBC Requests, which retrieve the weather information of some more cities like "Pune", "Jaipur", "Chennai" etc. by providing the corresponding query strings.

8.2.3 Adding Listeners that Display the Result

This helps you to view the results and to store the results in a file. To add listeners, follow the steps given below:

Step 1: Select the "Weather Jdbc Users" Thread Group. Right click on it and add the "Listener" as shown in Fig. 8.8.

Add → Listener → Graph Results

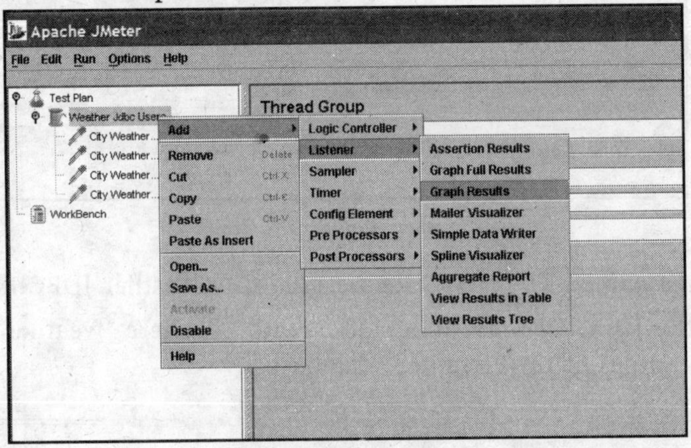

Fig. 8.8

Step 2: On selecting this option, the "Graph Results" section will be added to the "Weather Jdbc Users" Thread Group. Enter the name of the Listener as "Weather Graph Results".

8.2.4 Saving the Test Plan

To Save the Test Plan

File → Save

It will display the Save Dialog box, enter a File name and click on Save button.

8.2.5 Running the Test Plan

To Run the Test plan

Run → Start

The "Start" option of "Run" menu will now be disabled and the "Stop" option will be enabled. If the small square on the upper-right hand of the "Graph Results" dialog is in green color, it indicates that the application is in "Running" Mode as shown in Fig. 8.9.

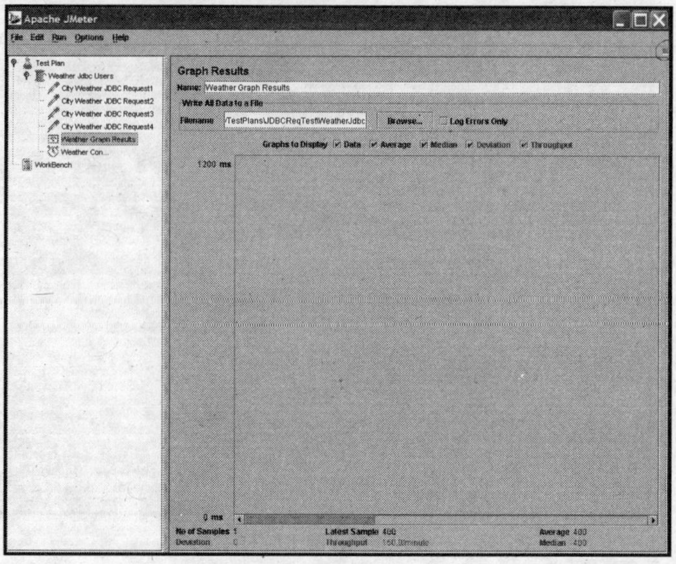

Fig. 8.9

If you stop the execution in between by selecting the "Stop" option from the "Run" menu, then it displays the message shown in Fig. 8.10.

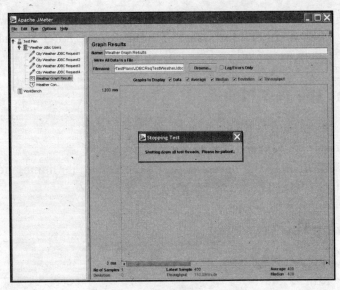

Fig. 8.10

Fig. 8.11 displays the results that are generated by the Graph Listener after executing the requests.

Fig. 8.11

8.2.6 Inserting the Timer

JMeter, by default, does not pause between the requests. But it is recommended to put some time-interval before processing the next request. Timer is used to specify the delay between each request.

Till now we have tested the application without introducing any delay between the requests. We now introduce some delay and perform the tests again. There are 4 types of timers. We will make use of the "Constant Timer".

To insert the timer into the test plan, the procedure is as follows:

Step 1: Insert the Timer as shown in Fig. 8.12.

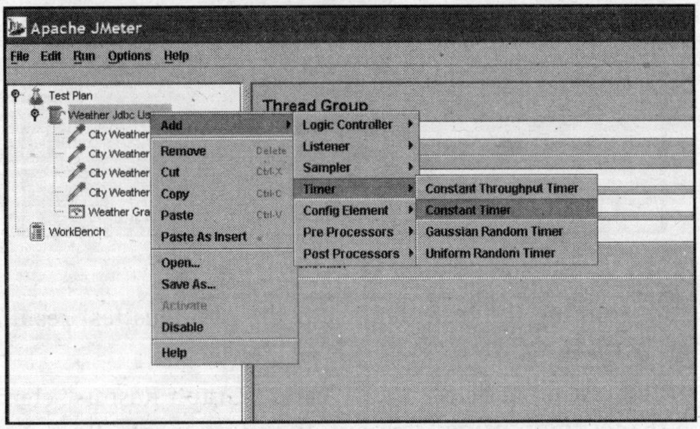

Fig. 8.12

The "Constant Timer" waits for the specified amount of time before processing the next request.

Step 2: On selecting "Constant Timer", the dialog shown in Fig. 8.13 is displayed.

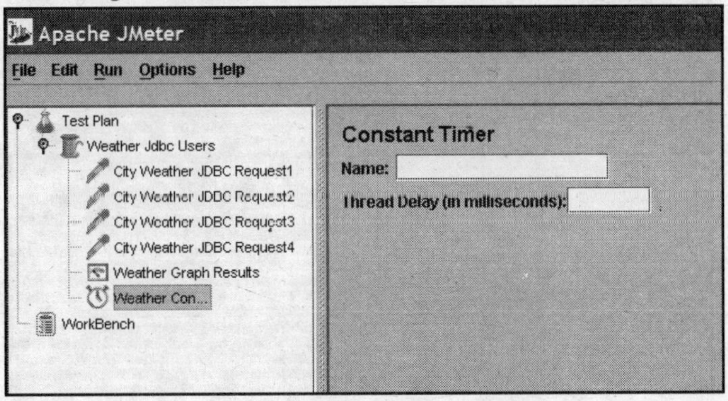

Fig. 8.13

Enter the name of the Timer as "Weather Constant Timer" and the delay time as 300 milliseconds as shown in Fig. 8.14.

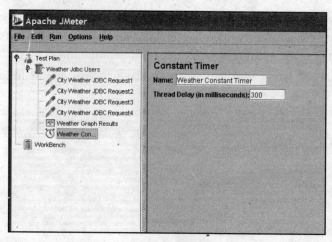

Fig. 8.14

Step 3: Before running the test plan, clear the previous test results.

Run → Clear

Step 4: Run the test plan: Select the "Weather Graph Results" element from the tree, run the test plan using Start option in Run menu (Run → Start) and examine the test results as shown in Fig. 8.15.

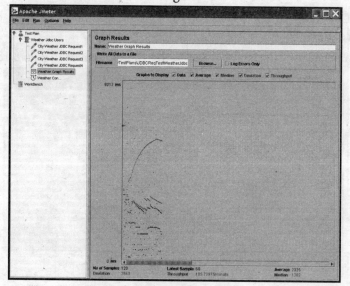

Fig. 8.15

8.3 HTTP Test

In this section we will consider the "Weather India" web application to test the HTTP load on the web server (Personal Web Server).

To start with, we need to create a HTTP Test Plan. The test plan includes the following sections:

1. Creation of Thread Group
2. Adding the HTTP Requests
3. Adding Listeners to View/Store Results
4. Saving the Test Plan
5. Running the Test Plan

8.3.1 Creating the Thread Group

Step 1: When the user initially starts the JMeter application, it displays the dialog shown in Fig. 8.16. By default, the tree structure contains two elements: Test Plan and Work Bench.

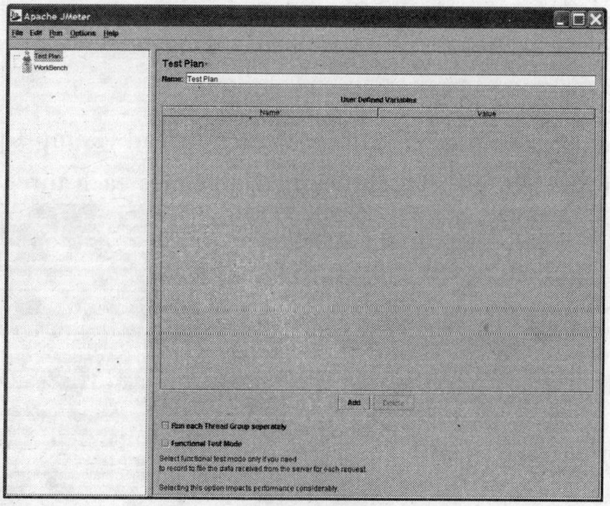

Fig. 8.16

Step 2: To create a Thread Group, right click on the "Test Plan" and select Add → Thread Group as shown in Fig. 8.17.

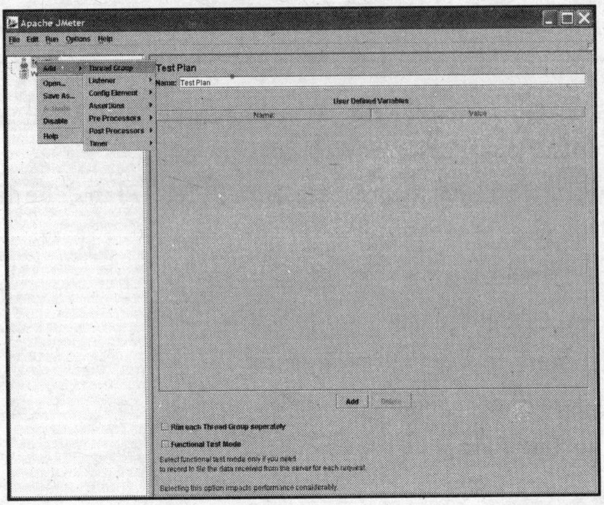

Fig. 8.17

The Thread Group has to be created under the "Test Plan" section.

Step 3: In adding the "Thread Group", "Thread Group" details are displayed on the right side of the window as shown in Fig. 8.18, which prompts you to enter all the details related to the Thread Group like:

- Name of the Thread Group
- Number of Threads to be created
- Delay time between the executions of each thread (Ramp-Up period).
- Loop Count which specifies the number of times each thread has to be executed.

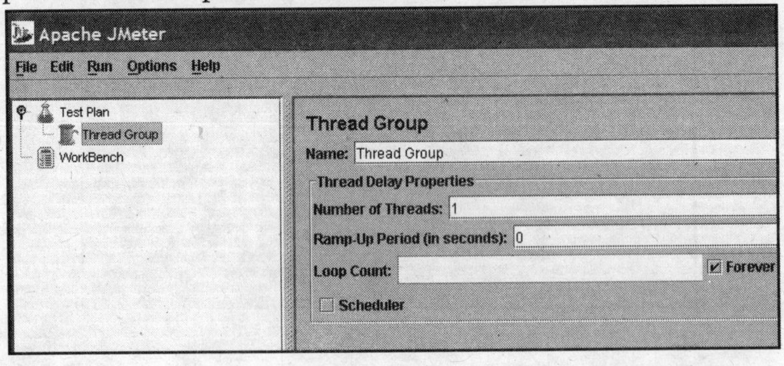

Fig. 8.18

Enter the Thread Group name as "Weather Http Users", Number of Threads to be created as 10 and uncheck the "Forever" checkbox and enter the "Loop Count" as 3 as shown in Fig. 8.19.

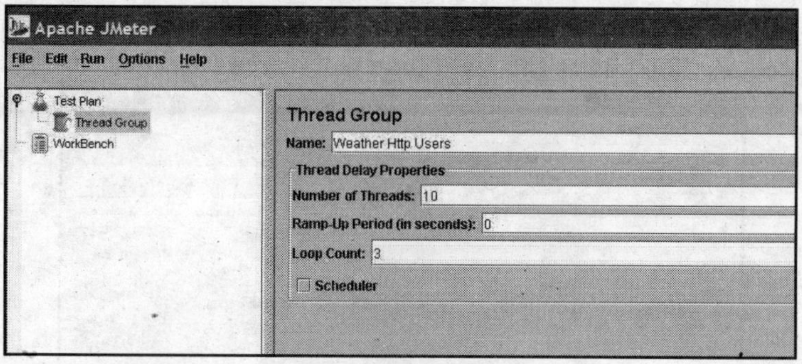

Fig. 8.19

Step 4: Once you enter all the details and click the "Add" button, the newly created Thread Group will be added to the Tree under the "Test Plan" section.

8.3.2 Creating the HTTP Requests

Add the various requests to be made, to the Thread Group we just created. Here we can add directly the HTTP Requests or we can add the HTTP defaults and then add the HTTP Requests. We will add four different Http requests to the thread group, "Weather Http Users".

Step1: Select the "Weather HTTP Users" Thread Group from the tree structure. Right click on it to add the Http Request as shown in Fig. 8.20.

Add → Sampler → HTTP Request

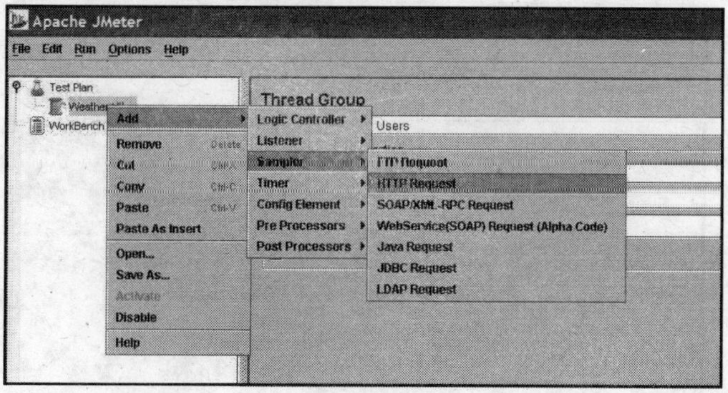

Fig. 8.20

Step 2: When you select the "HTTP Request" option, it displays the "HTTP Request" details at the right side work area as shown in Fig. 8.21.

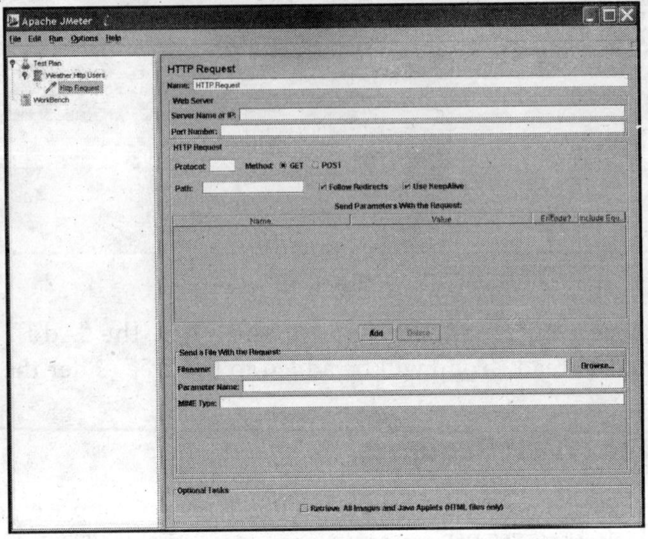

Fig. 8.21

- Enter the name of the HTTP Request as "Main Page".
- Enter the Server Name or IP as your System's IP address or System name (on which the Personal Web Server is running).
- Enter the Path as "/weathermain.htm".

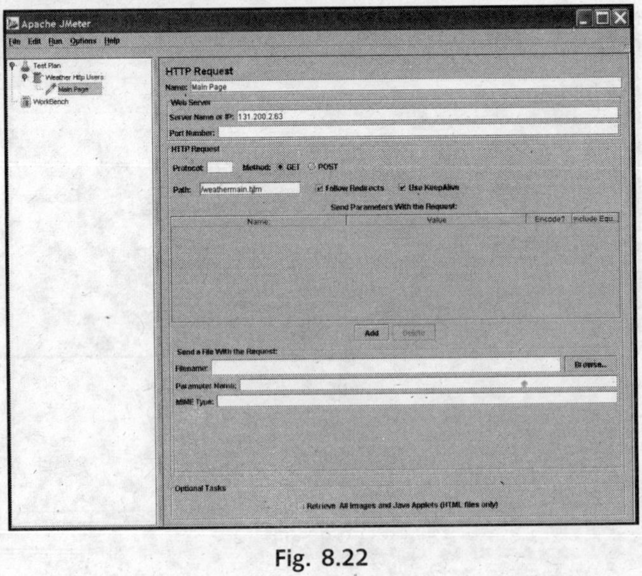

Fig. 8.22

In Fig. 8.22, the Server Name or IP address is given as 131.200.2.63. This is the IP address of the system on which the software was tested. You need to replace this address with the IP address of your system.

Similarly we will add three more HTTP Requests, repeat Step1 and Step2 for each request.

Second Request:

- Enter the name of the HTTP Request as "Weather Basics".
- Enter the Server Name or IP as your System's IP address or System name (on which the Personal Web Server is running).
- Enter the Path as "/weather/weather_basics.htm".

Third Request:

- Enter the name of the HTTP Request as "Weather Phenomenon".
- Enter the Server Name or IP as your System's IP address or System name (on which the Personal Web Server is running).
- Enter the Path as "/weather/weather_phenomenon.htm".

Fourth Request:

- Enter the name of the HTTP Request as "Weather Forecasting".
- Enter the Server Name or IP as your System's IP address or System name (on which the Personal Web Server is running).
- Enter the Path as "/weather/weather_forecasting.htm".

8.3.3 Adding Listeners that Display the Results

This helps you to view the results and to store the results in a file. To add listeners, follow the steps given below:

Step 1: Select the "Weather Http Users" Thread Group. Right click on it and add the "Listener" as shown in Fig. 8.23.

Add → Listener → Graph Results

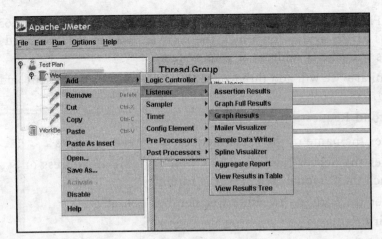

Fig. 8.23

Step 2: On selecting this option, the "Graph Results" section will be added to the "Weather Http Users" Thread Group.

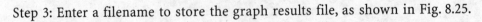

Fig. 8.24

Step 3: Enter a filename to store the graph results file, as shown in Fig. 8.25.

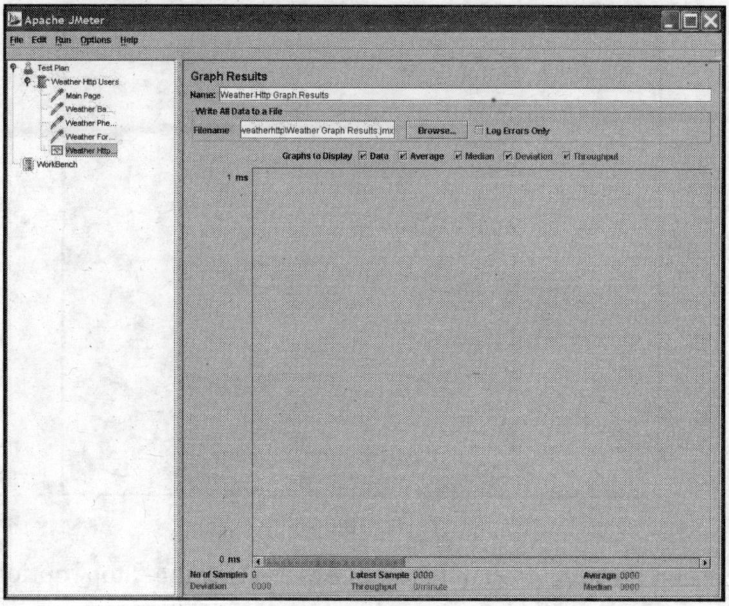

Fig. 8.25

8.3.4 Saving the Test Plan

To Save the Test Plan

File → Save

The Save Dialog box is displayed. Enter a filename and click on the Save button.

8.3.5 Running the Test Plan

To Run the Test plan

Run → Start

The "Start" option of "Run" menu will now be disabled and the "Stop" option will be enabled. If the small square on the upper-right hand of the "Graph Results" dialog is in green color, it indicates that the application is in "Running" Mode as shown in Fig. 8.26.

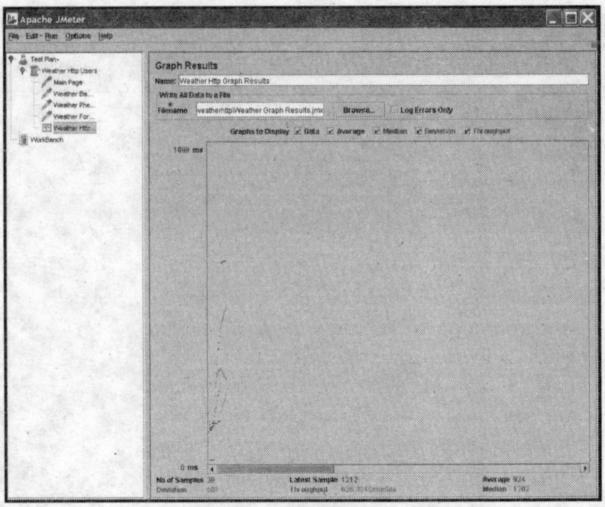

Fig. 8.26

If you stop the execution in between by selecting the "Stop" option from the "Run" menu, then it displays the message shown in Fig. 8.27.

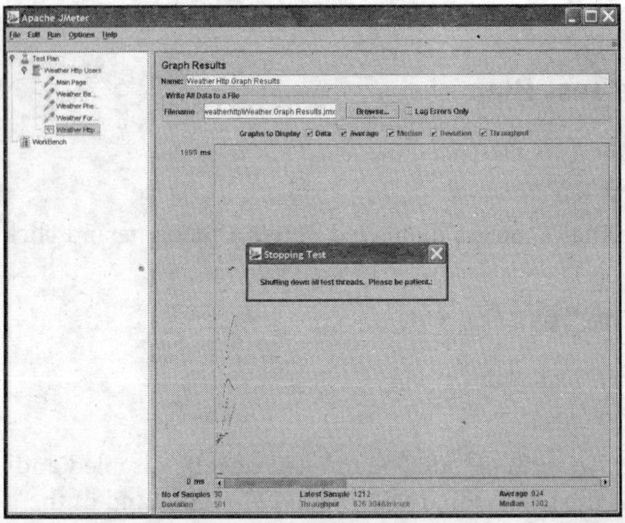

Fig. 8.27

Fig. 8.28 displays the results that are generated after execution of the requests without any user interaction.

While analyzing the performance reports for both JDBC and HTTP tests, you need to study the performance requirements as specified in the SRS document. For example, if there is a considerable delay in the HTTP request processing, you need to find out the reason for the delay—it can be due to the server being slow or the communication link being slow.

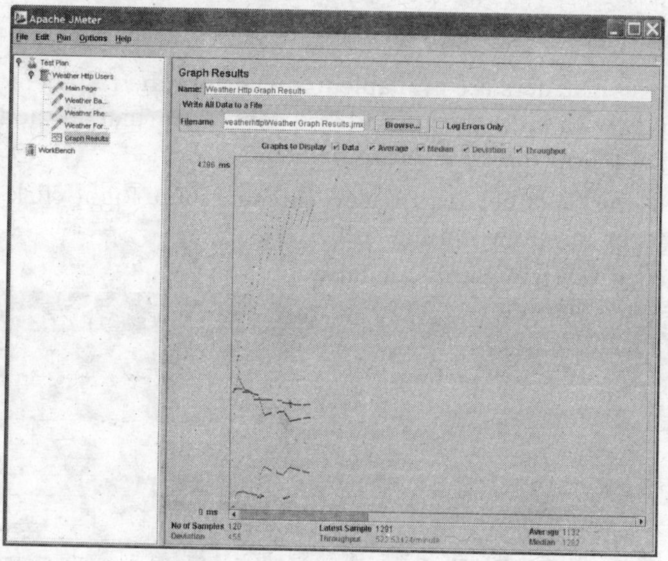

Fig. 8.28

8.3.6 Inserting the Timer

Insert the Timer as explained in "Creating a JDBC Test Plan" section. Fig. 8.29 shows the graph results after introducing a "Constant Timer" in the "Weather Http Users" thread group.

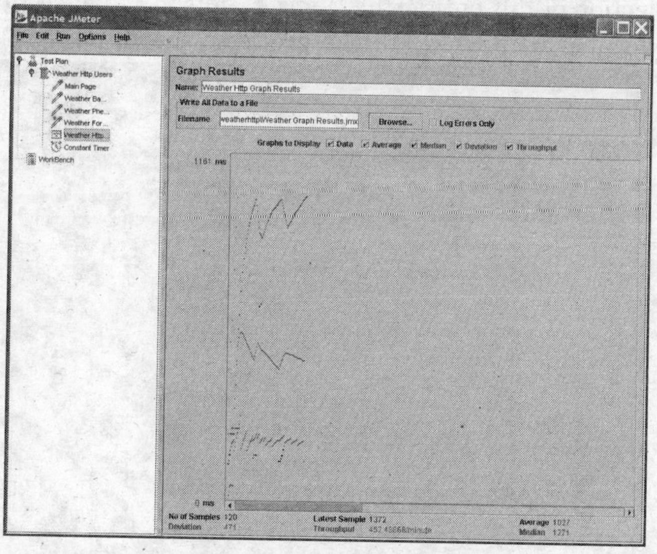

Fig. 8.29

8.3.7 Viewing the Results in a Tabular Format

In JMeter, many Listeners are available to view/store the results of test plans. We will demonstrate how to view the results in a tabular format. To add "View Results in Table" listener, follow the steps given below:

Step 1: Select the "Weather Http Users" thread group. Right click on it and add the "Listener" as shown in Fig. 8.30.

Add → Listener → View Results in Table

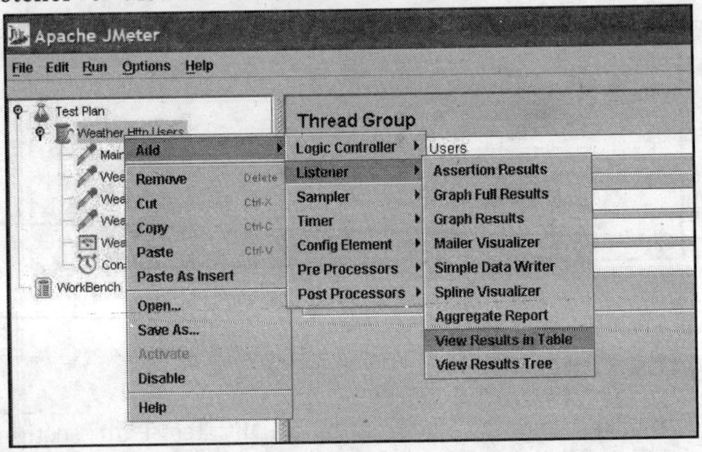

Fig.8.30

Step 2: On selection of this option, the "View Results in Table" section will be added to the "Weather Http Users" thread group as shown in Fig. 8.30.

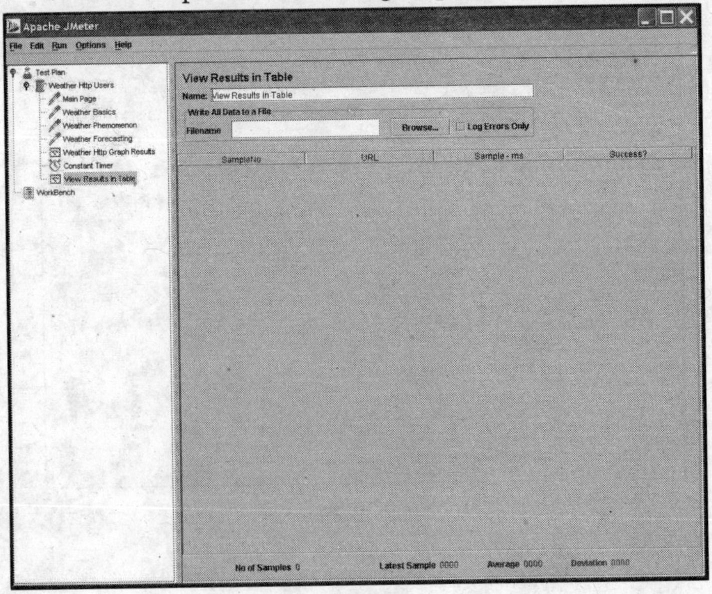

Fig.8.31

Step 3: Enter a File name to store the table results to a file, as shown in Fig. 8.31 and Fig. 8.32.

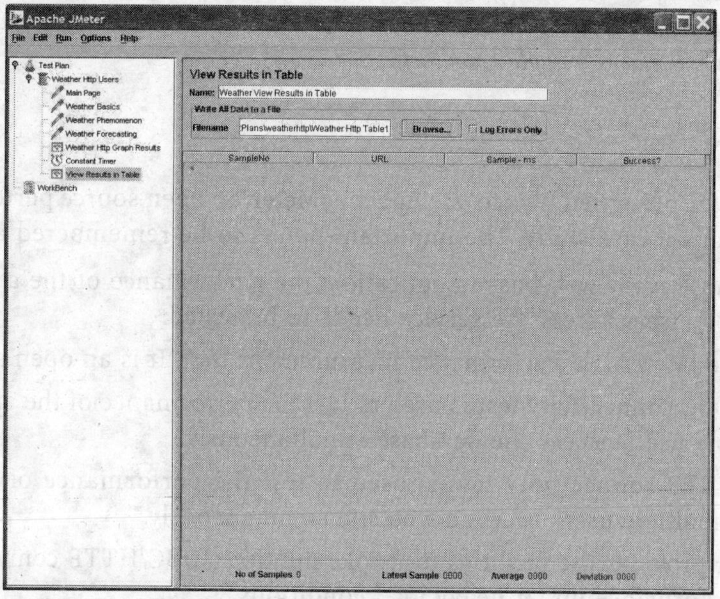

Fig.8.32

Run the Test plan to View the Results in table:

To Run the Test plan: Run → Start.

Fig. 8.33 shows the "View Results in Table" screen after running the test plan.

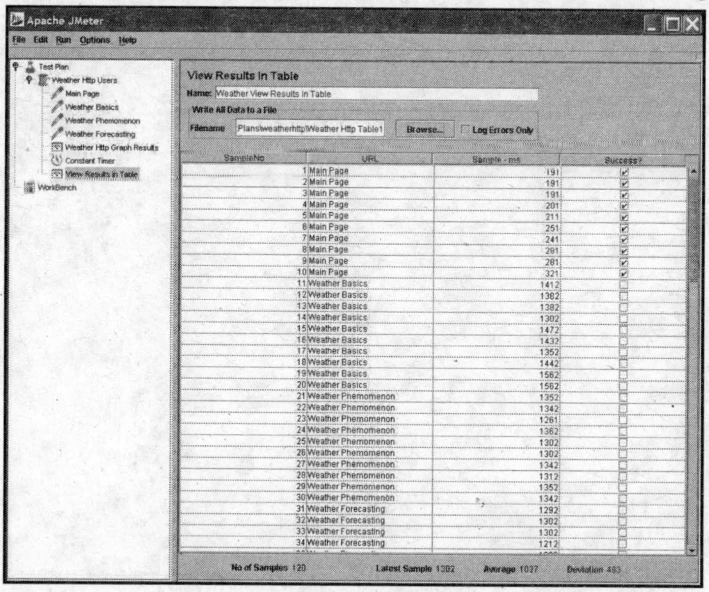

Fig. 8.33

In most of the Internet-based applications and Client/Server applications such as e-commerce, CRM software, ERP software, web services etc., testing the performance for both JDBC connectivity and HTTP connectivity is very important as multiple users simultaneously access the service and performance degradation will make the application ineffective.

Summary

This chapter, presented how to use Apache JMeter, an open source performance testing tool, through a case study. The important points to be remembered are:

- In almost every web-based application, the performance of the application when multiple users access the service needs to be tested.
- Apache JMeter is a performance measurement tool. It is an open source software.
- The JDBC connectivity test is used to test the performance of the application when multiple users access the database simultaneously.
- The HTTP connectivity test is used to test the performance of the application when multiple users access a web site simultaneously.
- JMeter provides the facilities to invoke multiple JDBC/HTTP connections and test the performance under heavy load conditions.
- JMeter provides a number of listeners to generate various test reports. These test reports can be analyzed for performance parameters such as the transaction response time and throughput.

9 ┊ TestDirector

In this chapter

- Get an overview of capabilities of test management tools
- Understand the important features of TestDirector
- Learn how to create test plan
- Learn how to execute the test plan
- Grasp the details of bug tracking and bug analysis

To deliver quality product, the testing process has to be managed efficiently. Testing management tools come in handy in such situations. Mercury Interactive's TestDirector is a powerful tool for managing the testing process. In this chapter, we will study the details of this testing management tool.

9.1 TestDirector Overview

Nowadays every organization is giving lot of importance to process-oriented software development. To deliver quality software, the testing process has to be very well defined and managed. Mercury Interactive's TestDirector is an excellent tool for managing the testing process effectively. As it is a web-based tool, it is very easy to use. Also, even if the development team and testing team are located at different places, the testing process can be managed very effectively. The important features of TestDirector are listed below:

- It is a web-based tool (the earlier versions being Client/Server based) and hence it facilitates distributed testing.
- As testing the software is linked to the requirements of the software, it provides the feature of linking the software requirements to the testing plan.
- It provides the features to document the testing procedures.
- It provides the feature of scheduling the manual and automated tests—the testing can be done during nighttimes or when the system load is less.

- It provides the feature of setting groups of machines to carry out testing. For example, if you want to test the software on both Windows and Linux machines, you can group the machines based on their OS.
- It keeps a history of all the test runs.
- The audit trail feature allows keeping track of changes in the tests and test runs.
- It keeps a log of all defects (or bugs) found and the status of each bug can be changed by authorized persons only.
- It provides the feature of creating different users with different privileges (e.g., developer, tester, QA manager, beta tester etc.).
- It generates test reports and analysis for the QA manager to decide when the software can be released into the market.

 Test engineers need to study the requirements of the software in detail. The requirements define what needs to be tested. Hence SRS document gives the testing objectives. TestDirector provides the feature of linking the tests with the requirements.

9.2 Testing Management Process

While using the TestDirector, the testing management process can be defined using the following four steps:

- Testing Requirements
- Design and develop tests
- Run the tests in manual mode or automatic mode
- Analyze the defects
  Accordingly, TestDirector use can be divided into four phases:
- Test requirements management
- Test planning
- Test execution
- Test results analysis

9.2.1 Test Requirements Management

Requirements Manager is used to link the requirements with the tests to be carried out. Each requirement in the SRS has to be tested at least once. In the SRS, the functional requirements and performance requirements are specified. Functional requirements are generated from use-case scenarios. Performance requirements are dependent on the application—for example, transaction response time or maximum number of users that are allowed to access a database or a web site. These requirements are referred to as Service Level Objectives (SLOs).

9.2.2 Test Planning

In test planning, the QA manager does a detailed planning and addresses the following issues:

- Hardware and software platforms on which the testing has to be carried out.
- The various tests to be performed (functional/regression testing, performance testing, source code testing etc.).
- Time schedule for conducting the tests.
- Roles and responsibilities of the persons associated with the project. For example, a test engineer can report a bug, he cannot remove a bug (even if he is capable of doing it!).
- Procedure for running the tests (manual or automatic).
- Various test cases to be generated.
- Procedure for tracking the progress of the testing.
- Documents to be generated during the testing process.
- Criteria for completion of testing.

During the test planning stage itself, test design is done which involves defining the sequence of steps to execute a test in manual testing. This is the most challenging task for test engineers as the test cases have to be created intelligently to uncover the possible bugs. The test engineers also identify the common test scripts that can be reused to test different modules and map the workflow between tests.

The test plan is communicated to all the test engineers and also the development team.

TestDirector can be integrated with other tools such as WinRunner and LoadRunner. Hence, the test scripts generated using these tools can be incorporated in the test plan.

9.2.3 Test Execution

The actual testing is carried out based on the test cases generated, either manually or automatically. In the case of automated testing, the test scheduling is done as per the plan. A history of all test runs is maintained and audit trail, to trace the history of tests and test runs, is also maintained.

During this phase, Test Sets are created. A test set is a set of test cases. For example, a login test set is the set of test cases to test the login process. In addition, execution logic is also set. The logic specifies what to do when a test fails in a series of tests. Consider the sequence of tests—login to a database, update a record and logout. Suppose during testing, the login test itself fails. One alternative is to stop the testing completely; the other alternative is to go ahead with the testing, but report that the login test has failed.

9.2.4 Test Results Analysis

In this phase, the test results are analyzed—which tests passed and which tests failed. For the tests that failed, an analysis has to be carried out as to why they failed. Also, each bug is classified based on its severity. A simple way of classification is

- Critical
- Major
- Minor

  A more detailed way of classification is

- Cosmetic or GUI-related
- Inconsistent performance of the application
- Loss of functionality
- System crash
- Loss of data
- Security violation

  When a bug is reported to the developer, it is not enough if you inform that there is a bug. You need to give additional information such as what is the problem, what is the system configuration on which the test was run, what is the version of the software (e.g., version of the browser and whether Internet Explorer or Netscape Navigator was used when the problem was encountered), which testing tool was used, what is the step-by-step procedure to reproduce the problem etc.

The bug report is stored in a database. The privileges to read, write, and update the database need to be decided by the QA manager. For example, the test engineer will update the database to indicate the new bug and give the status as "new". The developer may remove the bug and update the status as "cleared". The QA manager may change the status to "approved" or "to be fixed". It is also possible to assign priorities to the bugs, critical bugs have high priority as compared to cosmetic bugs.

Based on the bug tracking and analysis tools, the QA manager and the project manager can take the decision whether the software can be released to the customer or still more testing is required.

9.3 Managing the Testing Process Using Testdirector

In this section, we will study how to use TestDirector to manage the entire testing process through a case study. We will discuss how to manage and control various phases of the software testing process. We will study how to prepare the test plans, analyze the test results and identify the defects in the application. We will discuss the details of the three phases:

- Planning the tests
- Running the tests
- Tracking the defects

Planning the tests: In this phase, we specify the testing goals, define what has to be tested, define the tests and define the detailed step-by-step procedure for each test.

Running the tests: In this phase, we will run or execute the tests as planned in the earlier phase.

Tracking the defects: In this phase, we analyze the test results, identify the defects and study the cause of the defects.

Let us now consider the "EmpDB" application to create the test plan and analyze the results. This application is given in the CDROM that accompanies the book. The procedure for installing this application on your system is given in Appendix E. The GUI for this application is shown in Fig. 9.1.

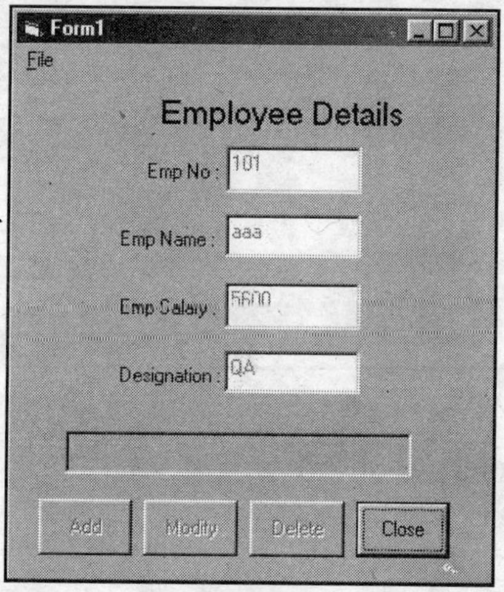

Fig.9.1

9.3.1 Creating a New Project

You need to first create a new project using the "Project Administrator" utility for retrieving and storing the information related to your tests. To create a new project, follow the steps given below:

Step 1: Open the "Project Administrator" utility.

Start → Programs → TestDirector → Project Administrator

This displays the dialog as shown in Fig. 9.2.

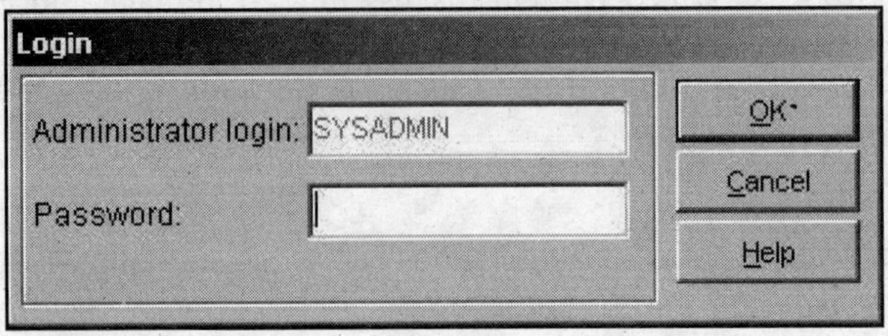

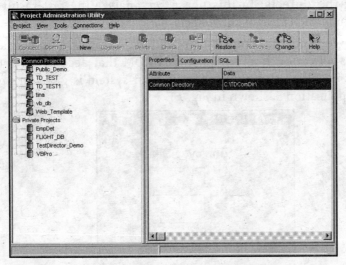

Fig. 9.2

If you login as "SYSADMIN" then you need not enter password. Click the "OK" button to login.

Step 2: When you click on the "OK" button, the dialog shown in Fig. 9.3 is displayed.

Fig. 9.3

Step 3: Create the new project as shown in Fig. 9.4

Project → New Project

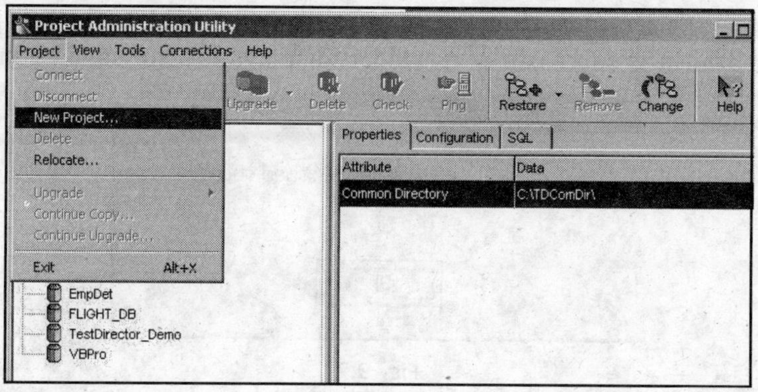

Fig. 9.4

Step 4: On selecting the "New Project" option, the dialog shown in Fig. 9.5 is displayed which prompts you to enter the name of the project.

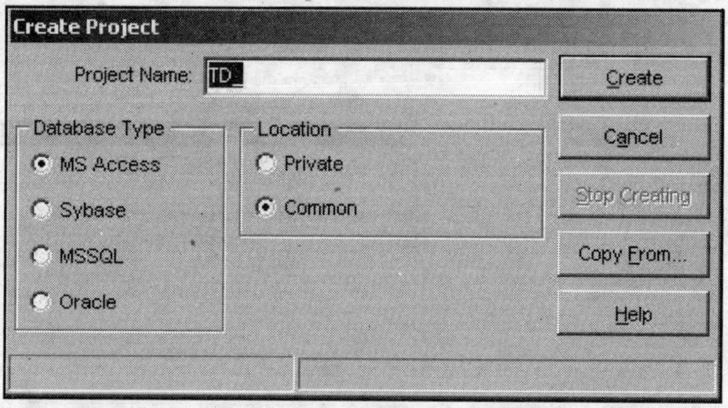

Fig. 9.5

Enter the Project Name as "EmpDetails", select the Location as "Private" and select the Database Type as "MS Access" as the database of our application is a ".mdb" file as shown in Fig. 9.6.

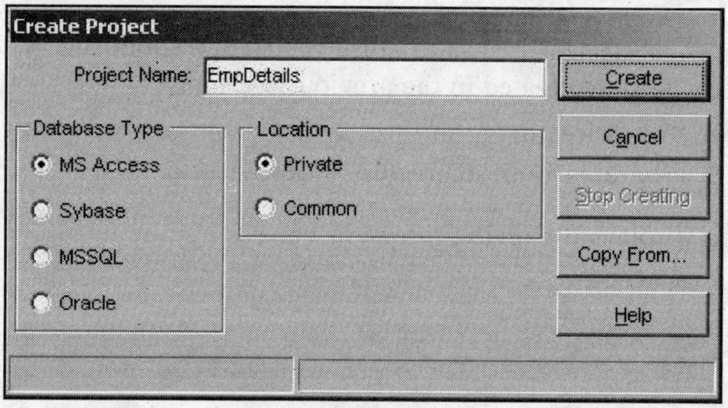

Fig. 9.6

Click the "Create" button to create the new project with the specified details. Once the project is successfully created, it displays the message as shown in Fig. 9.7.

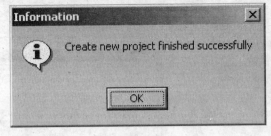

Fig. 9.7

Click the "OK" button. The project "EmpDetails" just created would be added to the "Private Projects" section of the Projects tree structure as shown in Fig. 9.8.

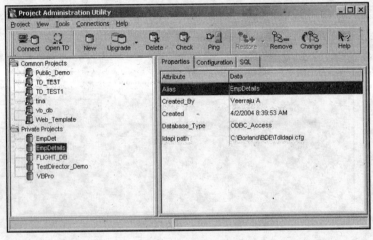

Fig. 9.8

9.3.2 Creating the Test Plan

We will now create test plan and store their corresponding results in the project "EmpDetails" that we created in the previous section.

Step 1: Open "Test Director"

     Start → Programs → TestDirector → TestDirector

Step 2: This displays the dialog shown in Fig. 9.9.

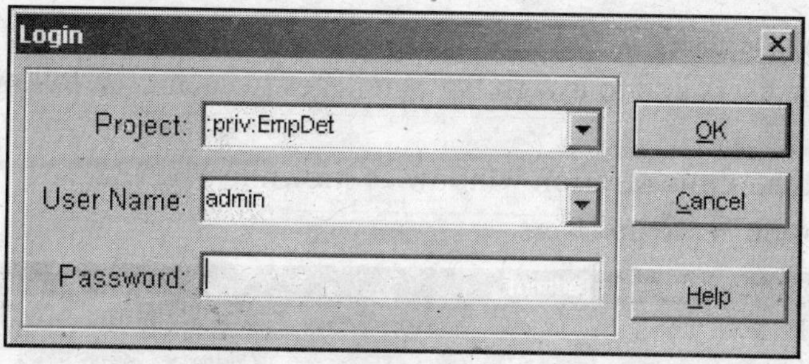

Fig. 9.9

Select the required project from the Project combo box. Select "EmpDetails" from the list, enter the User Name as "admin" as shown in Fig. 9.10. If you login in as "admin", there is no need to enter the password.

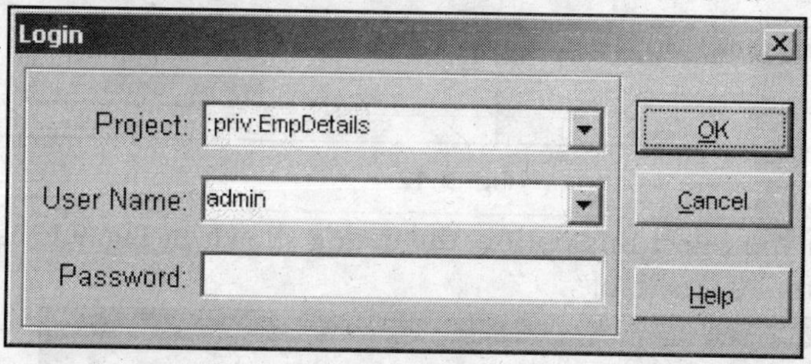

Fig. 9.10

Click the "OK" button to login.

Step 3: When you click the "OK" button, the initial screen of TestDirector as shown in Fig. 9.11 is displayed. Select the "Plan Tests" tab.

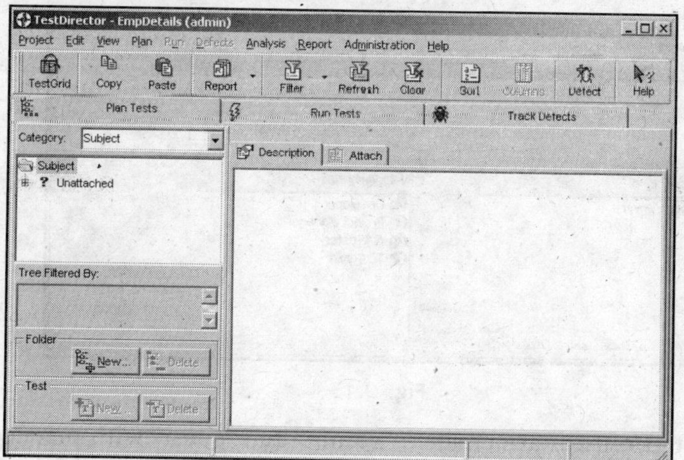

Fig. 9.11

Step 4: Creating the users

To create the users and to assign the privileges to each user, follow the steps given below:

Step 4.1: Open the Administration window as shown in Fig. 9.12.

Administration → Setup Users.

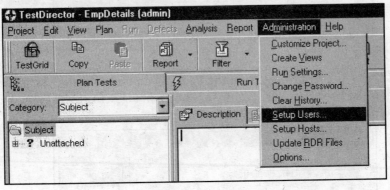

Fig. 9.12

Step 4.2: When you select this option, the dialog shown in Fig. 9.13 is displayed. Select the "Users" tab.

Fig. 9.13

By default, two users are created: "admin" and "guest" with privileges "TDAdmin" and "Viewer" respectively. To create new users click the "New" button.

Step 4.2: When you click the "New" button, it displays the dialog as shown in Fig. 9.14 prompting you to enter the "Login" (Username), "Full Name" and the "Password".

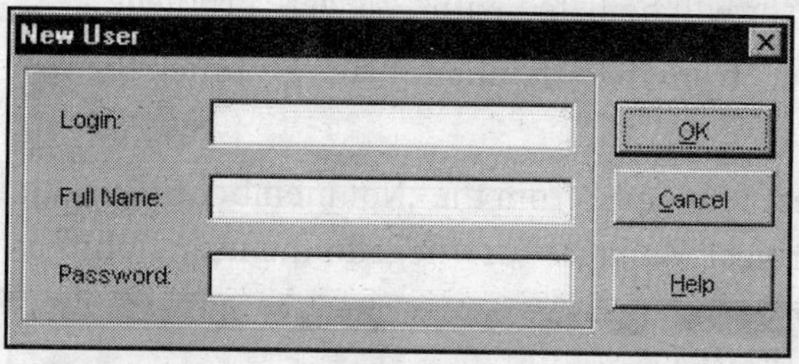

Fig. 9.14

Step 4.3: Enter the "Login", "Full Name" and "Password" as shown in Fig. 9.15.

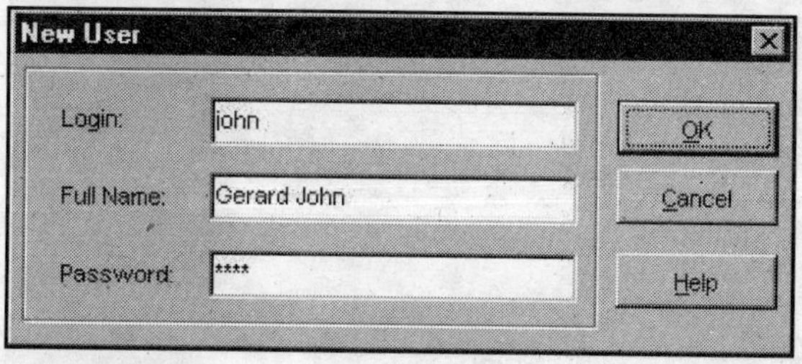

Fig. 9.15

Click the "OK" button to add the new user to the "Users list" in the "Setup Users" dialog as shown in Fig. 9.16.

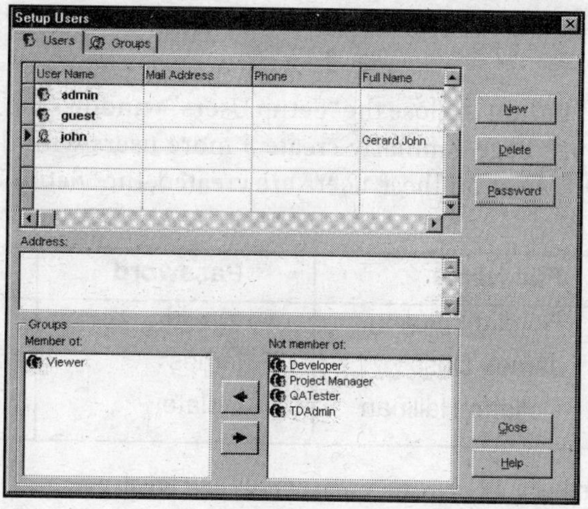

Fig. 9.16

Step 4.4: To assign privileges to the user "john":

- From the user table, select the user "john".
- By default, the user will be listed with "Viewer" privilege.
- Select the "Viewer" from the "Member of" list and click the ➡ button to remove the default privilege.
- Select the "Project Manager" from the "Not member of" list and click the ⬅ button to assign the "Project Manager" privilege to the user "john" as shown in Fig. 9.17.

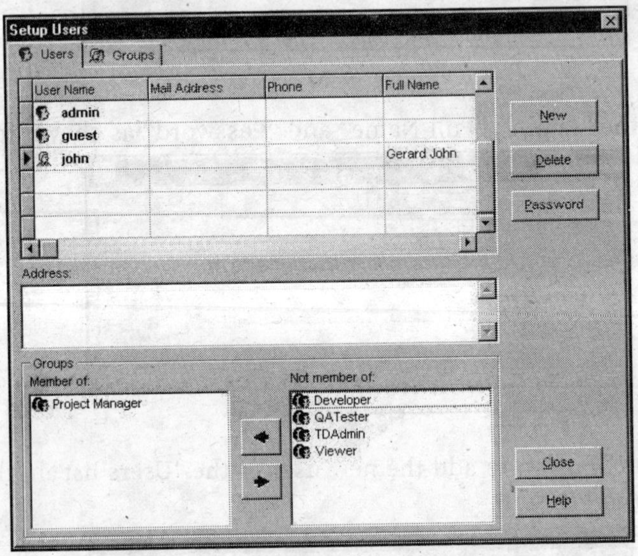

Fig. 9.17

Click the "Close" button to close the "Setup Users" window. The user is now assigned "Project Manager" privilege. Similarly create 3 more users with details and privileges as shown in Table 9.1. After all these users are created, the "Setup Users" screen will be as shown in Fig. 9.18.

Login	Full Name	Password	Privilege
Ronald	Ronald Fleming	ronald	Viewer
James	James Doss	james	Developer
Collate	Collatte Hallinan	collate	Tester

Table 9.1 Usernames, passwords and Privileges

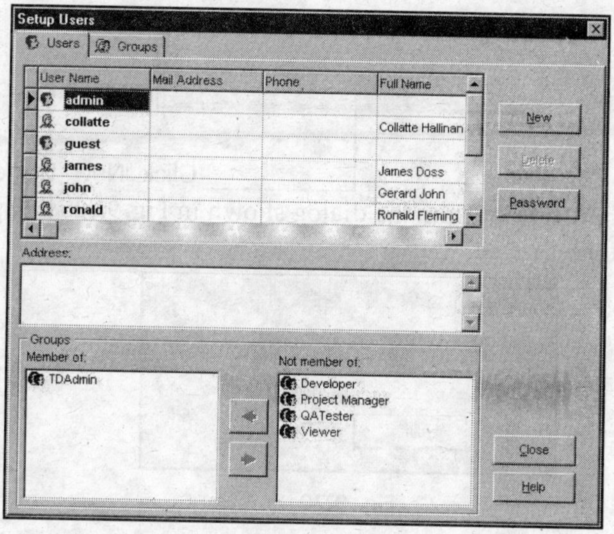

Fig. 9.18

To assign the required privileges, select the "Groups" tab as shown in Fig. 9.19.

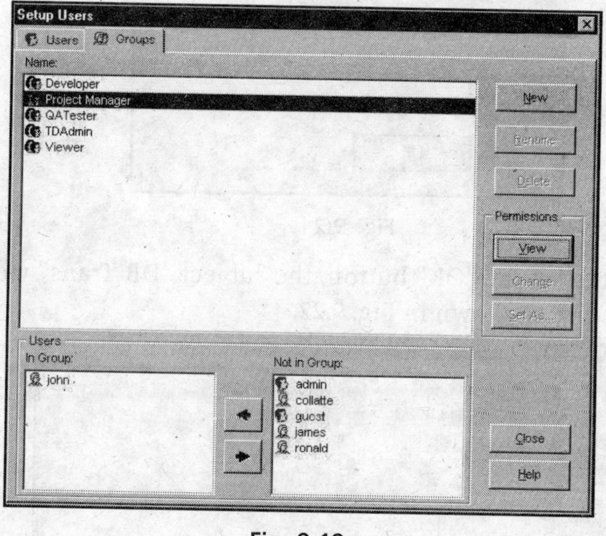

Fig. 9.19

Select the user group for which you want to assign new privileges and click the "New" button and check the required properties for the user group.

Step 5: Creating the test plan

■ Select the "Plan Tests" tab from the "TestDirector" window.

■ Add the Subject folders to the tree.

To create a folder, click the "New" button in the "Folder" group box of the TestDirector window.

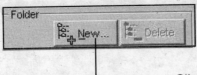

Click "New" to create a new folder.

On clicking the "New" button, the dialog shown in Fig. 9.20 is displayed prompting you to enter the folder name.

Fig. 9.20

Enter the name of the folder as "DB Trans" and click the "OK" button as shown in Fig. 9.21.

Fig. 9.21

Step 6: When you click the "OK" button, the subject "DB Trans" will be added to the tree structure as shown in Fig. 9.22.

Fig. 9.22

Step 7: Create the test plan for the subject "DB Trans" defined in the tree structure.

- Select the "Plan Tests" tab.
- Select the "DB Trans" subject from the tree.
- Click the "New" button from the "Test" group box to create the new test.

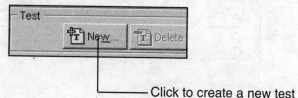

Click to create a new test

Step 8: When you click on the "New" button, the "Create New Test" dialog appears as shown in Fig. 9.23.

Fig. 9.23

Select the "Test Type" as "WR-AUTOMATED" and enter the "Test Name" as "AddEmp" as shown in Fig. 9.24.

Fig. 9.24

Click the "OK" button to add the test to the tree hierarchy as shown in Fig. 9.25.

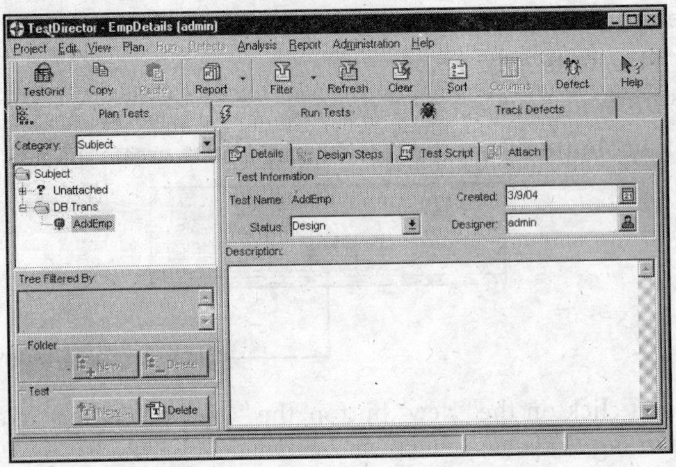

Fig. 9.25

Step 9: Select the "Details" tab and enter the "Description" of the test case as shown in Fig. 9.26.

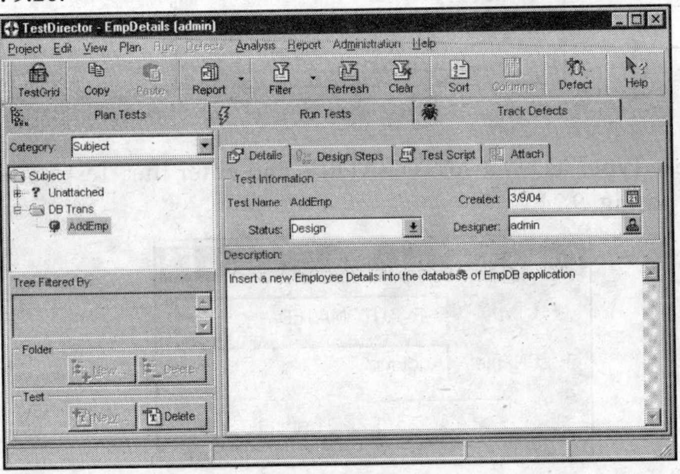

Fig. 9.26

Step 10: Select the "Design Steps" tab to define the steps of the test case. Click the "New" button. It opens a "Design Step Editor" window. In our database example, provide the steps to insert a new record into the database in the "AddEmp" test case. Enter the Description and the expected result of step1 as shown in Fig. 9.27.

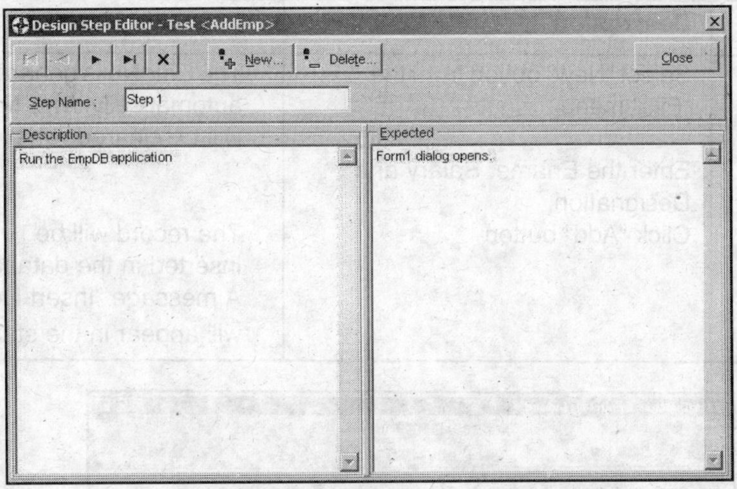

Fig. 9.27

Click the "Close" button. It inserts the Step1 into the dialog as shown in Fig. 9.28.

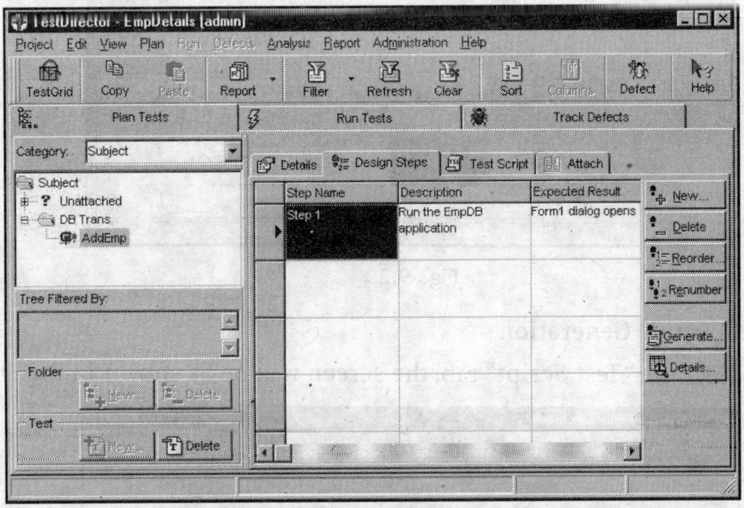

Fig. 9.28

Step 11: Insert all the steps required to insert a record into the "EmpDB" application as per the following table and as shown in Fig. 9.29.

Step Name	Description	Expected Result
Step2	Select "New" option from the "File" menu	The EmpNo is generated automatically. The fields will be cleared.
Step3	Enter the Ename, Salary and Designation.	
Step4	Click "Add" button	The record will be inserted in the database. A message "Insert Done" will appear in the status bar.

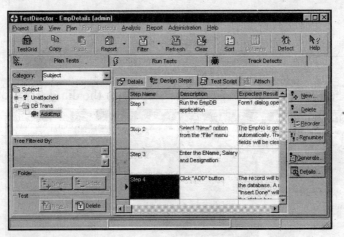

Fig. 9.29

Step 12: Test Script Generation.

Step 12.1: Select the "Test Script" tab, the screen will be as shown in Fig. 9.30.

Fig. 9.30

Step 12.2: Click the "Launch" button to open WinRunner. The dialog as shown in Fig. 9.31 is displayed.

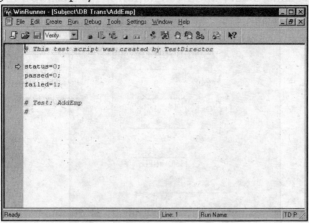

Fig. 9.31

■ Open the "EmpDB" application. The dialog shown in Fig. 9.32 is displayed.

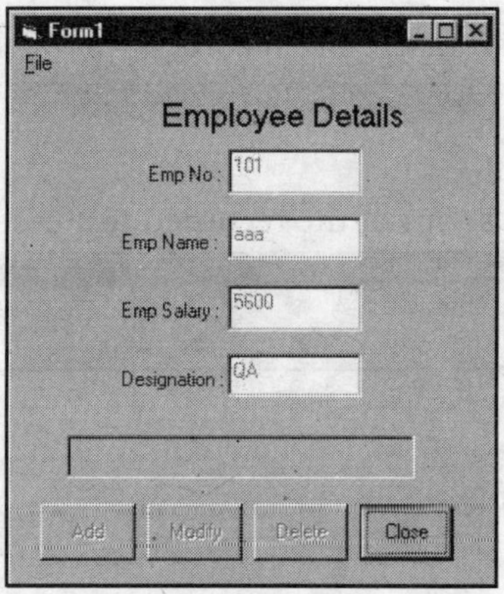

Fig. 9.32

Step 12.3: Start recording

■ Select the "Record – Context Sensitive" mode from the "Create" menu as shown in Fig. 9.33.

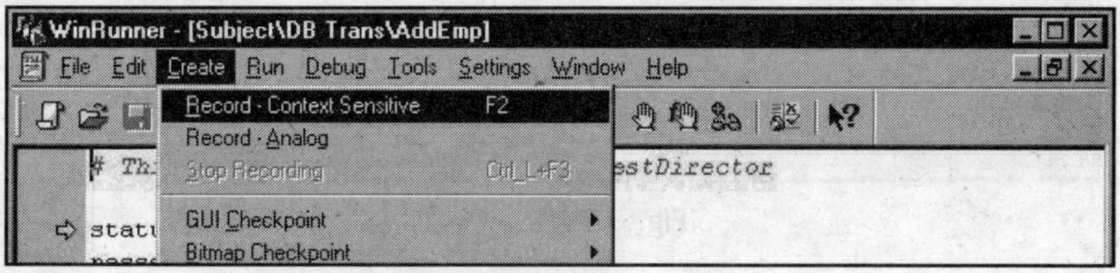

Fig. 9.33

- Select "New" from "File" menu to insert a new record into the database.
- Enter the EmpName, Salary and Designation fields as shown in Fig 9.34.

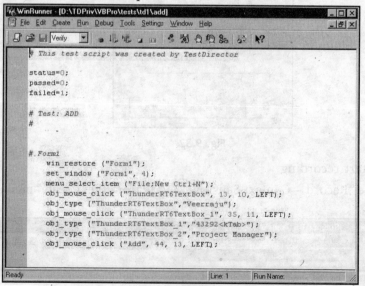

Fig. 9.34

- Click the "Add" button to insert the record.
- Stop the Recording.

  Create → Stop Recording.

The Fig. 9.35 shows the test script of the recorded test case.

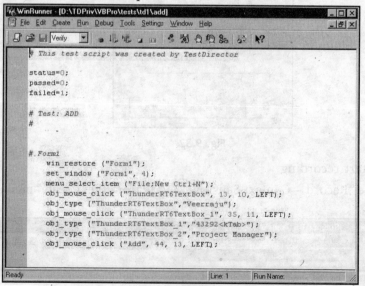

Fig. 9.35

■ Save the test script file and close the Test Script window.

File → Close.

Step 12.4: Click the "Refresh" button in the "TestDirector" window as shown in Fig. 9.36.

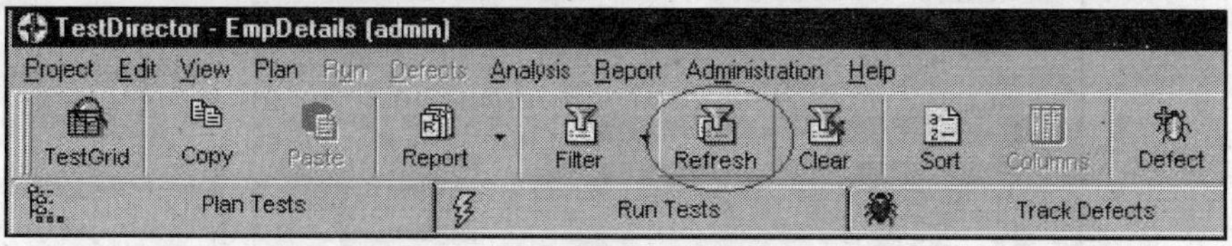

Fig. 9.36

Step 12.5: The test script file, just created/recorded in WinRunner will be loaded into the view window as shown in Fig. 9.37.

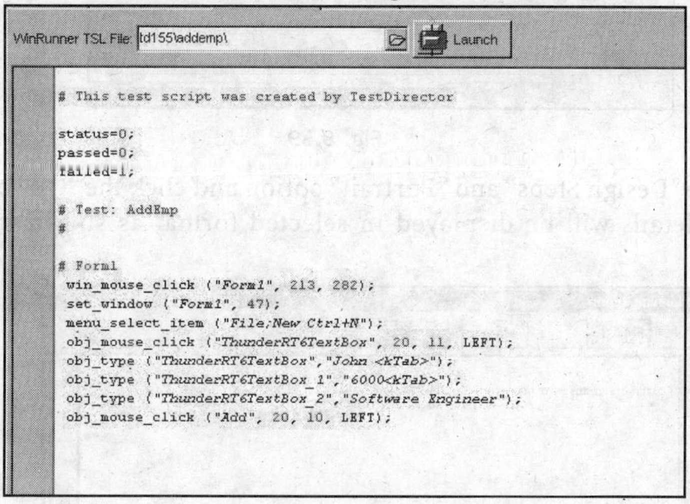

```
WinRunner TSL File: td155\addemp\          Launch

        # This test script was created by TestDirector

        status=0;
        passed=0;
        failed=1;

        # Test: AddEmp
        #

        # Form1
        win_mouse_click ("Form1", 213, 282);
        set_window ("Form1", 47);
        menu_select_item ("File;New Ctrl+N");
        obj_mouse_click ("ThunderRT6TextBox", 20, 11, LEFT);
        obj_type ("ThunderRT6TextBox","John <kTab>");
        obj_type ("ThunderRT6TextBox_1","6000<kTab>");
        obj_type ("ThunderRT6TextBox_2","Software Engineer");
        obj_mouse_click ("Add", 20, 10, LEFT);
```

Fig. 9.37

Step 13: Analyze the test plan by generating a report as shown in Fig. 9.38.

Report → Standard

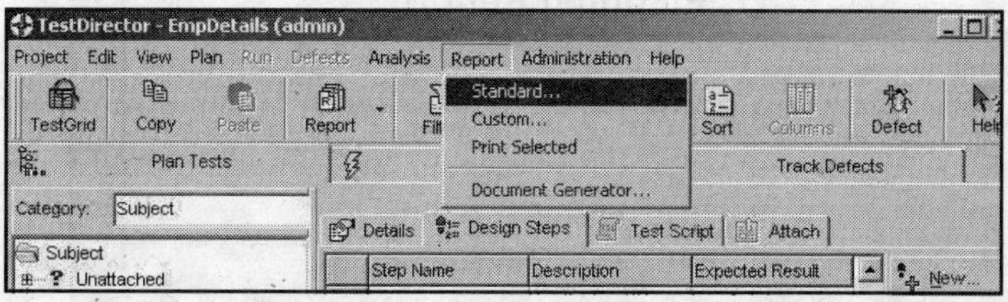

Fig. 9.38

Step 14: On selecting the "Standard" option, the dialog shown in Fig. 9.39 is displayed.

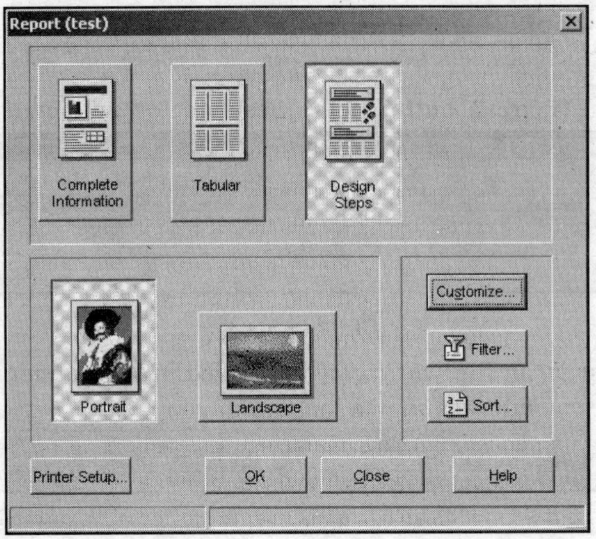

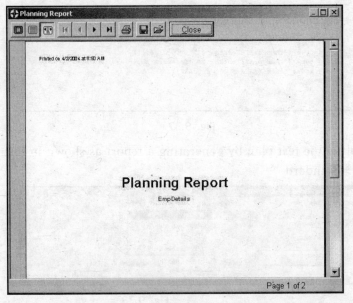

Fig. 9.39

Select the "Design Steps" and "Portrait" option and click the "OK" button. A report of selected details will be displayed in selected format as shown in Fig. 9.40 and Fig. 9.41.

Fig. 9.40

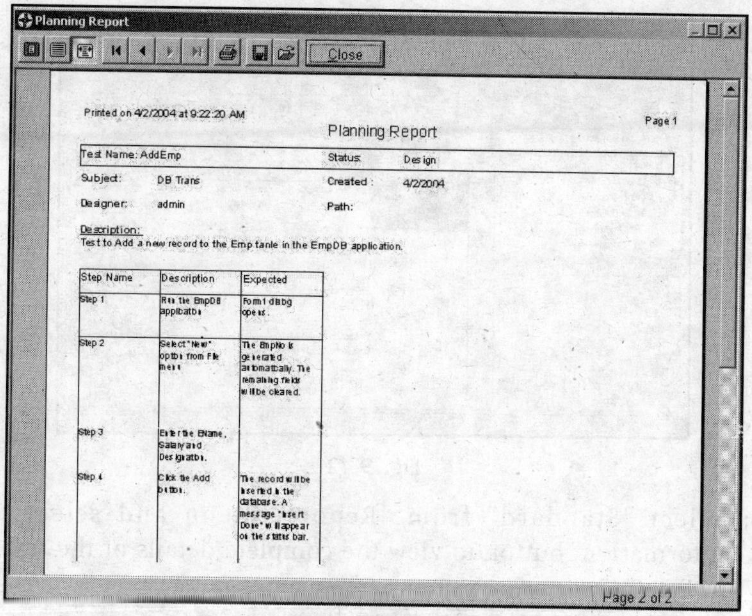

Fig. 9.41

Step 15: Create the test plans for "Update" and "Delete" operations in the "DB Trans" subject.

Steps for Updating a record:

- Run the EmpDB application
- Open the existing record by clicking the "Open" option in File menu.
- Select the "By Emp No" option
- Enter the Emp No
- Click "OK" to display the retrieved record.
- Make the required changes
- Click the "Modify" button to update the changes

Steps for Deleting a record:

- Run the EmpDB application
- Open the existing record by clicking the "Open" option in File menu
- Select the "By Emp No" option
- Enter the Emp No
- Click "OK" to display the retrieved record
- Click "Delete" button to delete the record
- A confirmation message is displayed
- Click "Yes" to delete the record

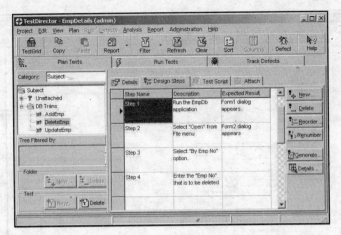

Fig. 9.42

Step 16: Select "Standard" from "Report" menu and select the "Complete Information" button to view the complete details of the test plans as shown in Fig. 9.43.

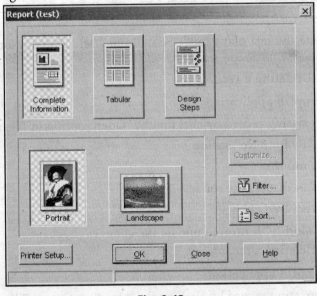

Fig. 9.43

Click the "OK" button to see the results that are displayed in Fig. 9.44.

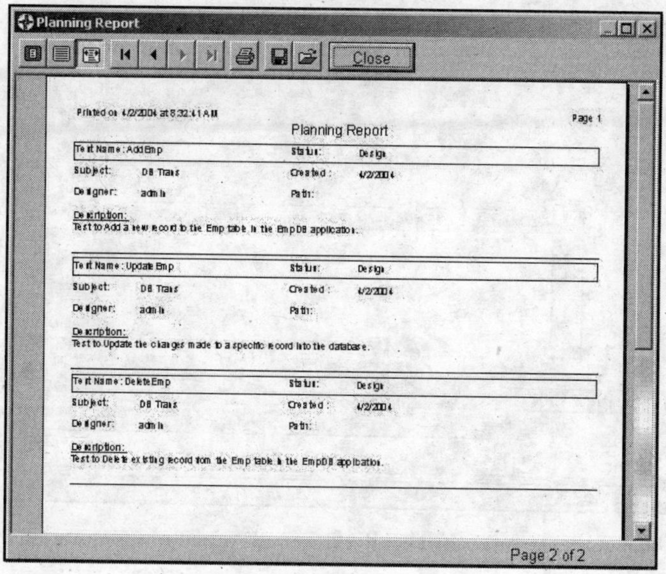

Fig. 9.44

9.3.3 Running the Automated Test

When you run the test script of "AddEmp" test case in WinRunner, it displays the result as shown in Fig. 9.45.

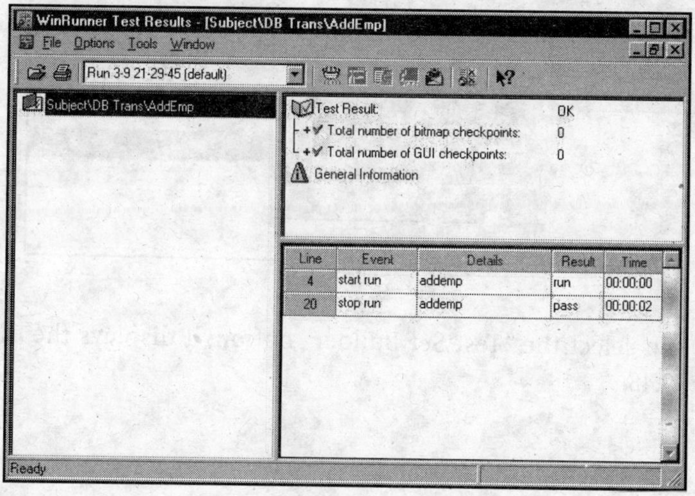

Fig. 9.45

To run an automated test plan, follow the steps given below:

Step 1: Select the "Run Tests" tab from the "TestDirector" window as shown in Fig. 9.46.

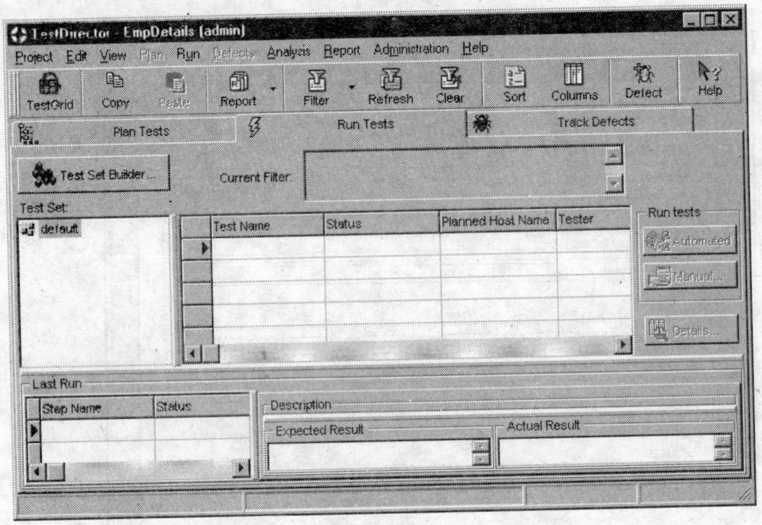

Fig. 9.46

Step 2: Select "Test Set Builder" from the "Run" menu as shown in Fig. 9.47.

Run → Test Set Builder

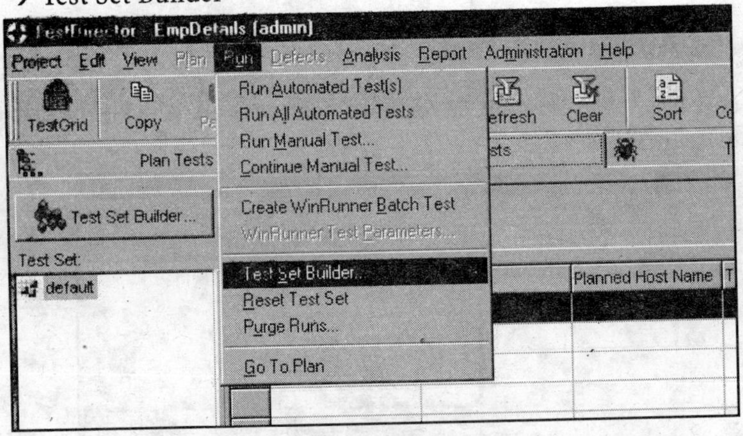

Fig. 9.47

Step 3: When you select the "Test Set Builder" option, it displays the dialog as shown in Fig. 9.48.

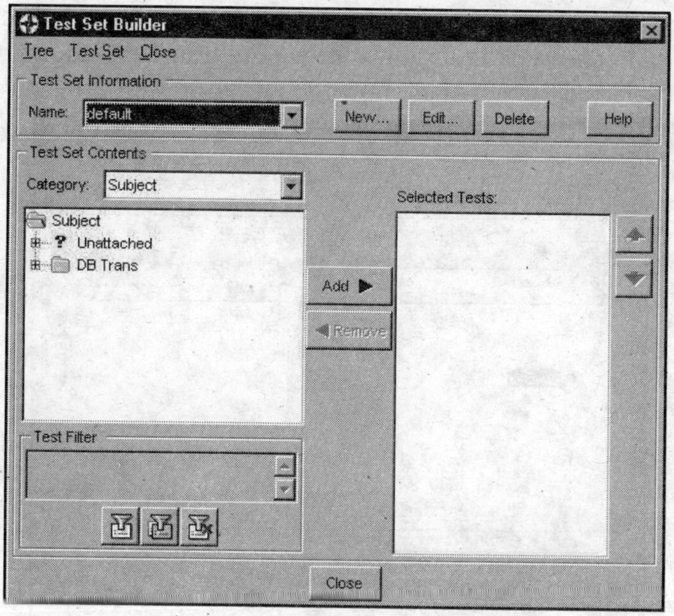

Fig. 9.48

By default, the "Test Set Information" is set to "default". If not, select the "default" from the combo box and select the "Category" as "Subject".

Step 4: Select the "DB Trans" folder and explore it. It will display all the test plans that are created under that category as shown in Fig. 9.49.

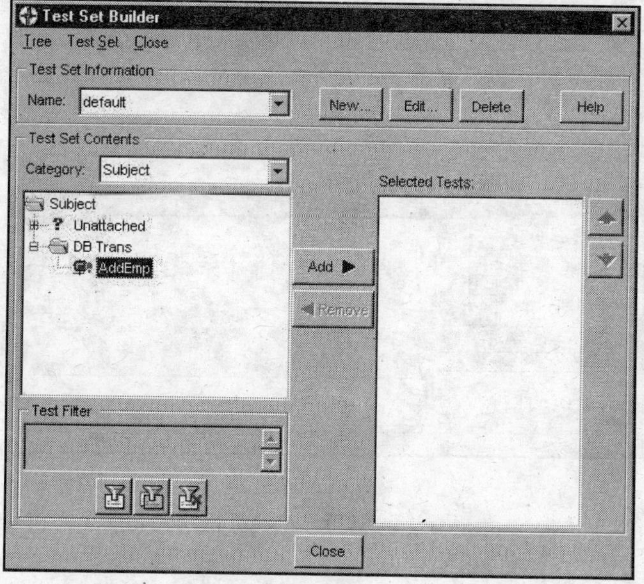

Fig. 9.49

Step 5: Select the test plan that is to be executed. In our example, select the "AddEmp" test plan and click the "Add" button. The test plan "AddEmp" will be added to the "Selected Tests" list as shown in Fig. 9.50.

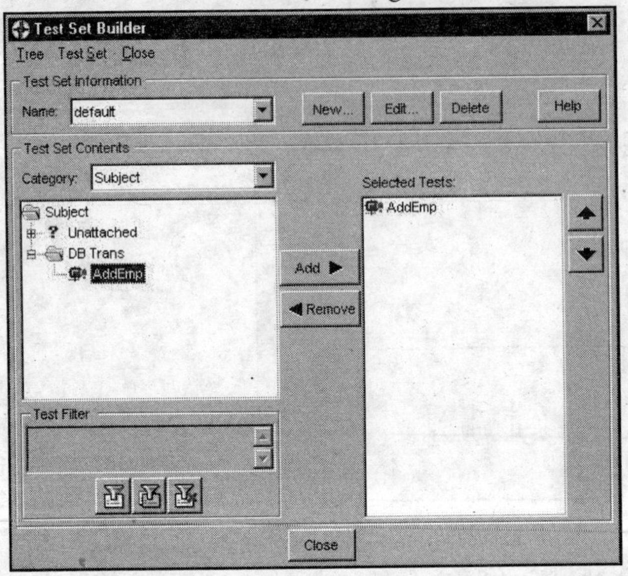

Fig. 9.50

Step 6: Click the "Close" button to close the "Test Set Builder".

Step 7: The name of the selected test in the "Test Set Builder" dialog will be displayed in "TestDirector" window as shown in Fig. 9.51.

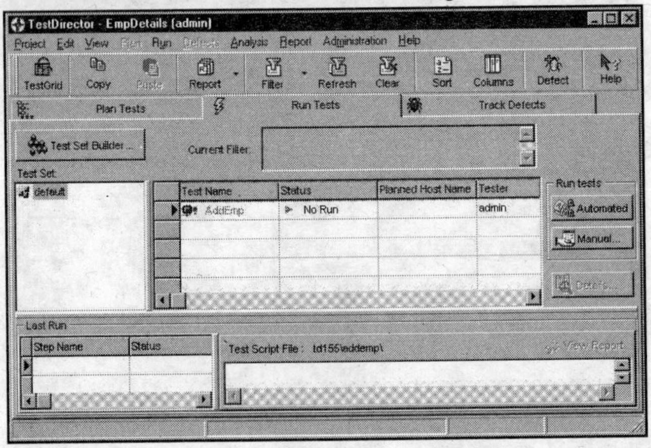

Fig. 9.51

Step 8: Select the "AddEmp" test and click the "Automated" button from the "Run Tests" Group. It displays the "Test Run Scheduler" dialog as shown in Fig. 9.52.

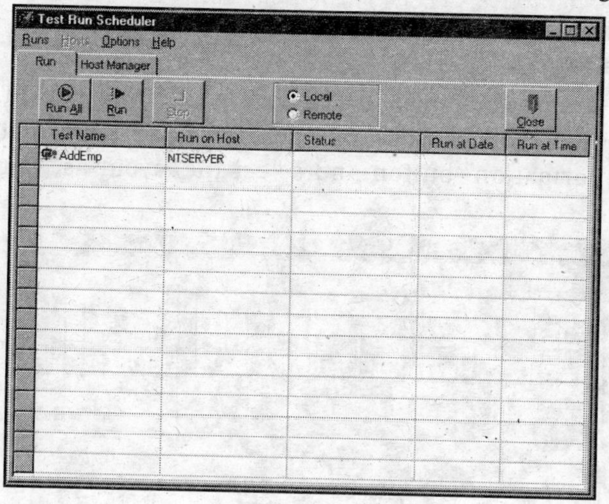

Fig. 9.52

By default, it is in "Remote" mode. Set it to "Local" mode.

Step 9: Select the "AddEmp" test and click the button to run the selected test.

Step 10: Once the execution of the test plan is completed, TestDirector displays the result as shown in Fig. 9.53.

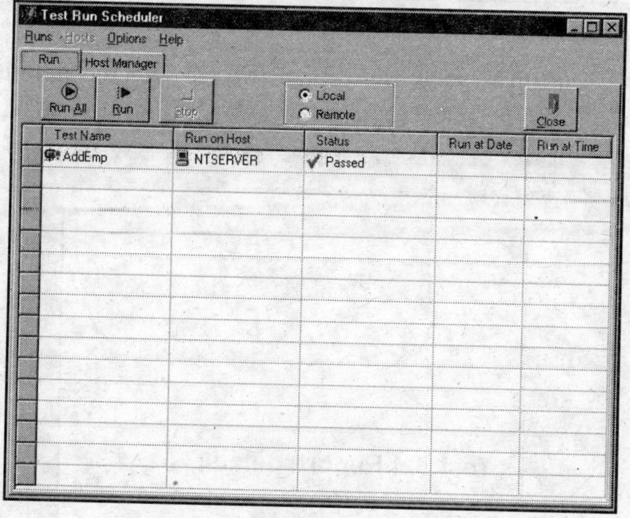

Fig. 9.53

If the test is successful, then "Passed" is displayed in green color in the "Status" column as shown in Fig. 9.53. If the test fails, then "Failed" is displayed in red color in the status column. Click the "Close" button to close the "Test Run Scheduler" dialog.

Step 11: Generating test run reports:

- Select the "Run Tests" tab.
- Select the "Standard" option from the "Report" menu.

Report → Standard

It displays a dialog as shown in Fig. 9.54 prompting you to select the type of information for which the report has to be generated and the format of the report. Click the "Complete Information" button and select the layout as "Portrait" as shown in Fig. 9.54.

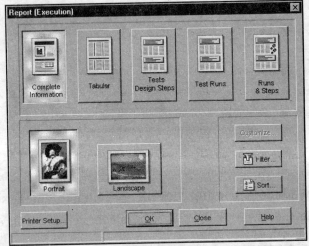

Fig. 9.54

Click the "OK" button to view the report for the selected details.

Step 12: The report is displayed as shown in Fig. 9.55 and Fig. 9.56.

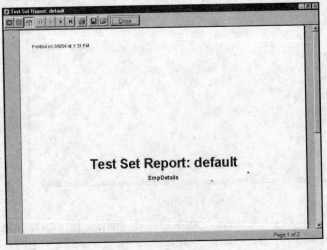

Fig. 9.55

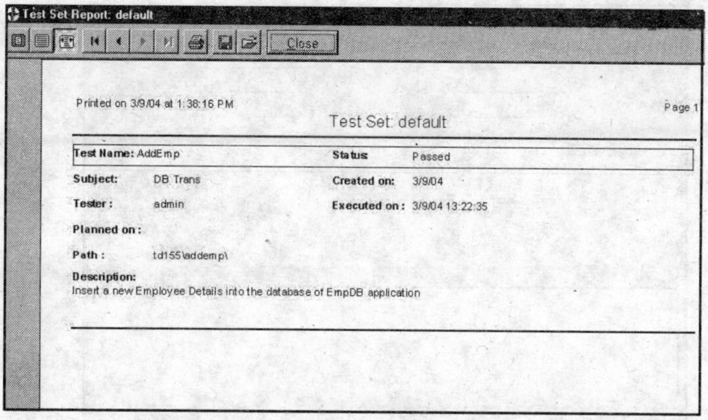

Fig. 9.56

9.3.4 Tracking Defects

It is very important to track the defects in the application so that they can be rectified to make the application more effective. You need to first identify the defects, identify the effect of the defect on the application and report the details of the defect to the developer so that he can rectify it as soon as possible.

To identify the defects in the application, follow the steps given below:

Step 1: Select the "Test Defects" tab in the application as shown in Fig.9.57.

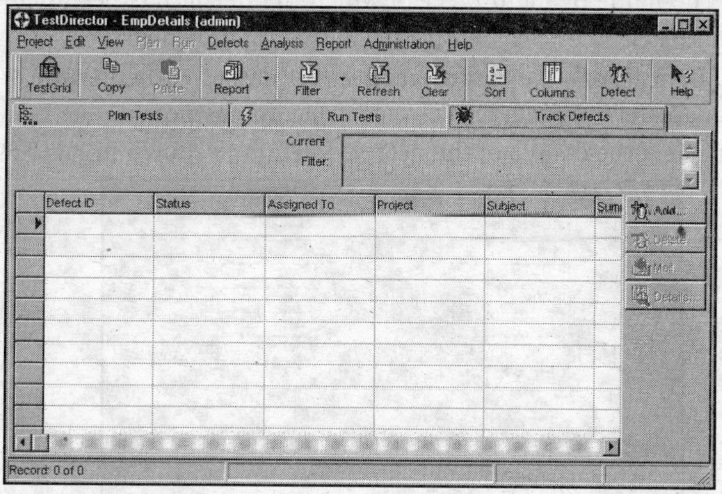

Fig. 9.57

Step 2: Click the Defect button or the Add... button to add a new defect.

Step 3: The "New Defect" dialog appears prompting you to enter the details of the detected defect as shown in Fig. 9.58.

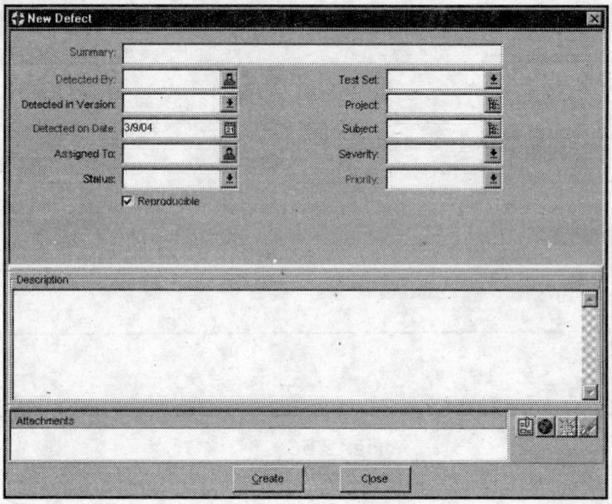

Fig. 9.58

Enter the following details:

Summary: Brief description of the defect.

Detected By: The name of the user who detected the defect.

Detected On Date: The date on which the defect was detected.

Assigned To: The name of the person to whom the job has been assigned.

Status: The status of the defect.

Project: The name of the project in which the defect has been detected.

Severity: The degree to which it affects the application.

Priority: Indicator of the 'importance' of the defect—whether the defect has to be repaired immediately, or whether the repair can be postponed.

Enter or select the details of the detected defect as shown in Fig. 9.59.

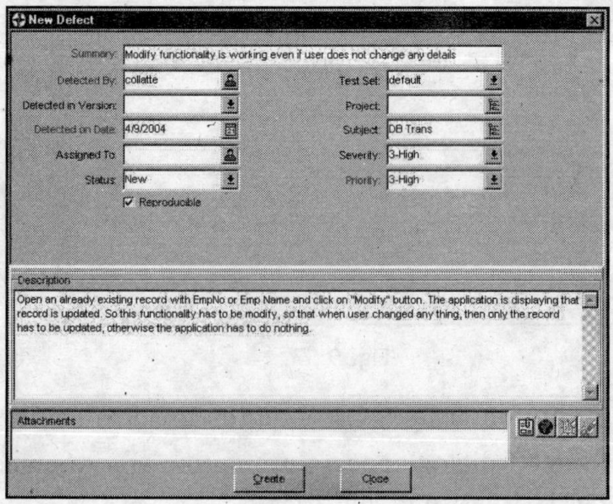

Fig. 9.59

Click the "Create" button to create the defect. Once the defect is created successfully, it displays the message as shown in Fig. 9.60.

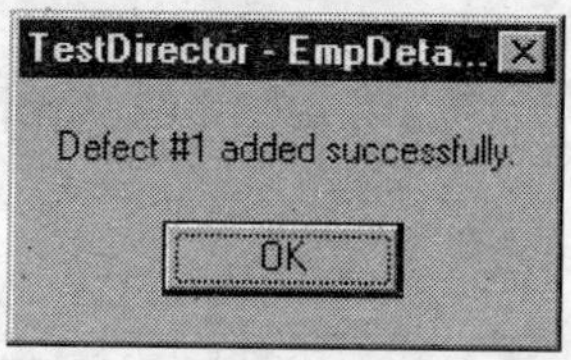

TestDirector - EmpDeta... ✕

Defect #1 added successfully.

[OK]

Fig. 9.60

Click the "OK" button.

Step 4: When you click the "OK" button, it adds the newly created defect to the "Defect List" in the "TestDirector" dialog as shown in Fig. 9.61

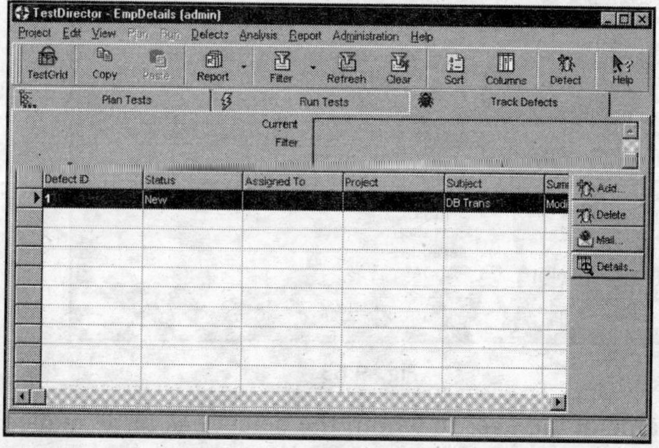

Fig. 9.61

Step 5: To View/Modify the details of the defect, select the defect and click the  button. The "Defect Details" dialog is displayed as shown in Fig. 9.62.

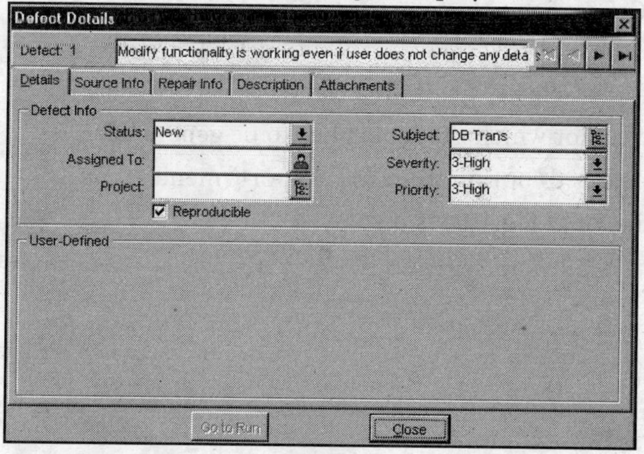

Fig. 9.62

Change the required properties of the defect. In our example, assign the defect to the "Project Manager" by selecting the user name "john" from the "Assigned To" list box and click the "Close" button to update the changes.

Step 6: Mail the defect to a project team member (project users).

- Select the defect
- Click the "Mail" button
- The "Compose" dialog shown in Fig. 9.63 is displayed.

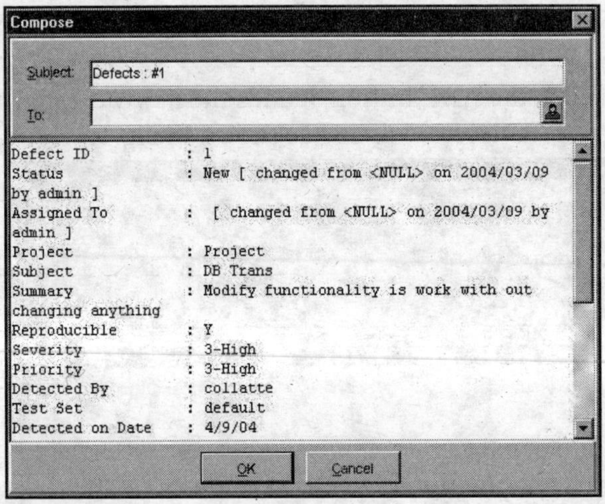

Fig. 9.63

Select the name of the user to whom the defect has to be mailed (for example, by selecting john, user can send the mail to Project Manager) by clicking the ▣ button. The mail will be sent to the selected user if the internal mail server is configured. Click the "OK" button to send the mail.

Step 7: Report Generation

To generate the report:

- Select the "Track Defects" tab if not selected.
- Select the defect for which the report has to be generated.
- Select the "Standard" option from the "Report" menu.
- The dialog shown in Fig. 9.64 is displayed.

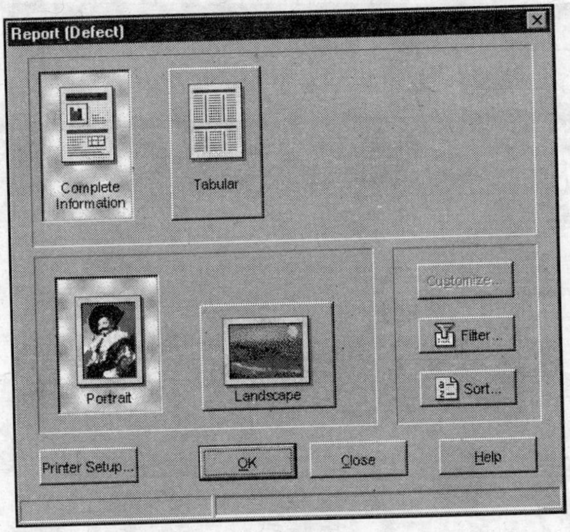

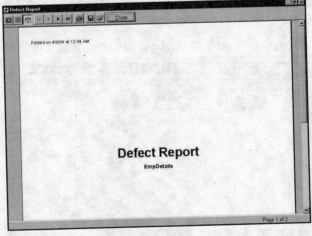

Fig. 9.64

- Click the "Complete Information" button and select the layout as "Portrait".
- Click the "Filter" button to select the defects based on particular condition. For example, if you want to select all the defects whose priority is ">" high (i.e. all those whose priority is either "Very High" or "Urgent") then select the "Priority" filter and give the required condition. Then report will be generated only on those defects, which will satisfy this condition.
- Click the "OK" button to see the generated report as shown in Fig. 9.65 and Fig. 9.66.

Fig. 9.65

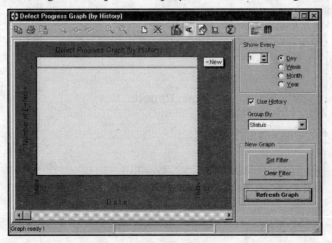

Fig. 9.66

Step 8: Defect tracking with the help of Progress Graphs

- Select the defect.
- Select the "Defect Progress Graphs" from the "Analysis" menu as shown in Fig. 9.67.

Analysis → Defect Progress Graphs

Fig. 9.67

- The "Defect Progress Graph" is displayed as shown in Fig. 9.68.

Fig. 9.68

This graph displays the progress of the graph from the day it was created till today. To select the defects based on a condition, click the "Set Filter" button.

Step 9: Defect tracking with the help of Summary Graph

- Select the defect.
- Select "Defect Summary Graphs" from the "Analysis" menu as shown in Fig. 9.69.

  Analysis → Defect Summary Graphs

Fig. 9.69

- The graph shown in Fig. 9.70 is displayed.

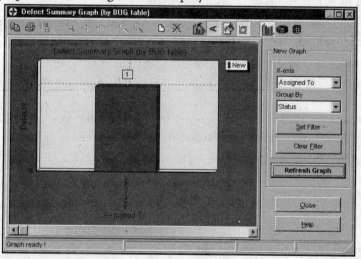

Fig. 9.70

The X-Axis represents the person to whom the defect has been assigned. (User can change the X-Axis by selecting from the drop-down list box). The Y-Axis represents the number of defects.

The productivity of the entire SQA group and testing group will increase many fold if a testing management tool is used. The workflow automation feature of these tools will lead to a very systematic and disciplined testing process. If you are already using other tools such as MS Excel, MS Project etc., you can integrate them with TestDirector. You can also use any standard RDBMS (such as MS SQL, Oracle) for storing the defects database.

Summary

This chapter presented the details of Mercury Interactive's TestDirector testing management tool. The important points to be remembered are:

- Using TestDirector, a process-oriented testing management can be done efficiently.

- Testing management involves arriving at the testing requirements, test planning, designing the test cases and test sequence, carrying out the testing and analyzing the defects and taking the follow-up action.

- As the software has to be tested against the requirements, the requirements need to be linked to the test cases.

- TestDirector facilitates generation of a test plan and execution of the tests as per this plan.

- You can integrate TestDirector with WinRunner and LoadRunner to generate test scripts and integrate them with your test plan.

- You can create users with different privileges so that only authorized persons can view or modify the defects database.

- The defect tracking system facilitates assigning defects to a person for rectification, assigning priorities to the defects and carrying out analysis of the defects using filters.

- You can generate a variety of test reports based on which you can take a decision as to when the software can be released to the customer.

10 ■ Source Code Testing Utilities in Unix/Linux Environment

In this chapter

- Learn about the various utilities available in Unix/Linux environment for source code testing and maintenance
- Understand how to find out the time taken for execution of portions of a program and how to optimize the code
- Learn about productivity tools
- Know how to check whether C programs are portable or not
- Learn how to use configuration management tools: SCCS and RCS
- Know the coding guidelines to be followed for C and Java programming languages.

10.1 GNU Tools

Under GNU GPL, a number of development tools are available. These tools can be obtained free of cost and can also be distributed. In this chapter, we will use these tools for testing the programs. You need to become familiar with the following tools:

GCC	C compiler
G++	C++ compiler
GDB	source code level debugger
GNU make	make utility

If you have a C file with the filename hello.c, to invoke the GCC compiler in Linux environment, give the following command:

$gcc hello.c

The executable file with the name a.out is created. You can execute the file by giving the command:

$./a.out

Alternatively, you can create an executable file with the name hello, using the command:

$gcc –ohello hello.c

You can now execute the file, by giving the command:

$./hello

If your program uses mathematical library, give the command:

$gcc hello.c –lm

Gcc provides a number of options which can be obtained from the online manual.

The "$" symbol is the default system prompt and you need not type this symbol.

10.2 Timing of Programs

When you are testing your software, you may find that the program is taking too much time for execution. Before optimizing the code, you need to study how much time each segment of the program is taking. To measure the time taken to execute a portion of a program is important for many applications such as embedded software development, communication protocol development etc. This is useful while carrying out simulation studies of algorithms to be implemented on the embedded system. In addition, the timing analysis gives valuable information as to which portions of the code are taking longer time, so that the code can be optimized, or a more efficient algorithm can be chosen to improve the speed.

In C language, the functions time() and clock() are used to measure the time taken by the program segments. We will illustrate the use of these functions through two examples. Listing 10.1 shows the use of time() function.

Listing 10.1 ttiming.c 7

```
#include <stdio.h>
#include <stdlib.h>
#include <time.h>
#include <math.h>
int main()
{
    int i;
    double j,l;
    time_t t0,t1;
    t0=time(NULL);
    printf("Time at Start %ld \n",t0);
```

```
printf("Calculations.......\n");
for(i=0;i<100000000;i++){
j=sqrt(2.0*i);
l=1.0/j;
l=l+j;
}
t1=time(NULL);
printf("Time at the End %ld \n",t1);
printf("Elapsed time %ld\n",(t1-t0));
return 0;
}
```

Here are the important aspects of this program:

- You need to include the file time.h

- Time_t is a structure which stores the time in number of seconds that elapsed since 00:00:00 hours of GMT on 1st January 1970. The significance of this time and date is that Unix was born at that time.

- Just before doing some heavy computation, you need to call the time() function which returns the time in seconds since the birth of Unix.

- Then do some computation—here we did square root calculation and taking the inverse of it in a loop.

- After the computation, again call the time function, it returns the seconds elapsed since the birth of Unix.

- Now calculate the difference in the times, that is the time taken for the computation. You can compile the program using the command:

$gcc –ottiming ttiming.c –lm

You can execute the program using the command:

$time ./ttiming

The output will be as shown below:

Time at Start 1061968846

Calculations.....

Time at the End 1061968898

Elapsed time 52

real 0m52.3565

user 0m52.3505

sys 0m0.005

You can compare the CPU time obtained through the time function and the time command of the shell. They will be approximately same.

The following program, given in Listing 10.2 illustrates the clock() function call. Note that clock does not give the time in seconds, but in clock ticks. The number of ticks in a second is obtained using the parameter CLOCKS_PER_SEC.

Listing 10.2 ctiming.c

```c
#include <stdio.h>
#include <stdlib.h>
#include <time.h>
#include <math.h>
int main()
{
    int i;
    double j,l;
    clock_t t0,t1;
    t0=clock();
    printf("Time at Start %ld \n",t0);
    printf("Calculations.......\n");
    for(i=0;i<100000000;i++){
        j=sqrt(2.0*i);
        l=1.0/j;
        l=l+j;
    }
    t1=clock();
    printf("Time at the End %ld \n",t1);
    printf("No of clocks %ld\n",(t1 - t0));
    printf("Elapsed time %ld\n",(t1-t0)/CLOCKS_PER_SEC);
    return 0;
}
```

This program is similar to the preceding program in which we used the time function. Here are the differences:

- The clock_t returns the value in integer, not long int.
- Call the clock() function just before the computation
- Call the clock() function after the computation
- Calculate the difference in the return values and then divide by CLOCKS_PER_SEC to obtain the number of seconds for doing the computation.

You can compile the program using the command:

$gcc –octiming ctiming.c –lm

And then, execute the program using the command:

$time ./ctiming

The output will be as follows:

Time at Start 0

Calculations.....

Time at the End 64880000

No. of clocks 64880000

Elapsed time 64

real 1m4.8855

user 1m4.8805

sys 0m0.0005

The timings obtained from the clock function and the shell command time will be approximately the same.

While doing performance testing of software, you may realize that the execution time for the total program is very high. You need to find out which portions of the program are taking long time. For this, the timing functions are of immense use.

10.3 Profiler

While developing embedded software on the host system, you need to check how much time it takes to execute some of the functions/modules. This information is required to find out the time-consuming functions so that either you can optimize the code or you can write computationally intensive portions of the code in assembly language for faster execution.

The command "gprof" gives the timing of different functions. To obtain the timings, you need to compile the program with profiling option as below:

$gcc –pg –oprogram program.c

Now you can run the program using the command:

$./program

A file with the name gmon.out is created.

The output will display the time taken by various functions. You can analyze the timings to find out which portions of the code are taking longer time.

In embedded/real-time software development, if proper timing analysis is not done during the design stage, only during testing time the performance limitations will be evident. The profilers are of immense use during module testing to do the timing analysis.

10.4 Code Optimization

In software development with strict performance requirements, the two important considerations are speed of execution and memory requirements. Writing the code in assembly language increases speed of execution and also results in optimal code. However, maintaining the code written in assembly language is difficult. Hence, the code is generally written in a high level language such as C or C++ and then some portions of the code, which take lot of execution time, are written in assembly. Even while writing the code in a high-level language, code optimization can be done to make the execution faster. Some important code optimization guidelines are given below:

- **Eliminate dead code:** Dead code is that portion of the code that will not be executed at all. Novice programmers include such code, declaration and initialization of variable that will not be used at all, use of functions that will not be called at all etc. Profilers help in elimination of dead code.

- **Remove unnecessary debugging code:** A lot of code is written during development time for debugging purposes. Unnecessary debugging code needs to be removed. However, note that some debugging code may need to be left out in the final software that helps in debugging the system in the field.

- **Avoid recursion:** Recursive functions require a large stack resulting in higher memory requirement. For example, instead of using recursion for calculating a factorial of a number, a better approach is to use a lookup table that will pick up the factorial.

- **Avoid floating-point operations:** If necessary, floating-point operations can be converted into fixed-point operations.

- **Use unsigned integers:** Use unsigned integer variables wherever possible.

- **Avoid large library routines:** To the extent possible, large library routines need to be avoided.

- **Remove loop-invariant code:** The code that has no effect on the loop counter is called the loop-invariant code. Consider the example:

```
for (i=0; i < 10; ++i)
{
  x= 1.0/b;
y = x + i;
}
```

In this code, the statement x=1.0/b; is loop-invariant because the value of x is not dependent on the value of i. Hence, this statement can appear above the beginning of the for loop. Otherwise, the value of x is calculated every time resulting in unnecessary execution of a statement.

- **Use the correct optimization level of the compiler:** The compiler has an in-built optimizer. Generally, the compilers provide different optimization levels, level 0 to level 3. Level 3 offers the highest optimization. Based on the need, the optimization level can be set.

 Elimination of dead code, avoiding recursion, avoiding floating-point operations to the possible extent, avoiding large library routines and removal of loop-invariant statements are some of the important guidelines for code optimization.

10.5 Productivity Tools

Unix/Linux provides a number of tools that increase your productivity. These tools are very important for developing software systematically. In this section, we will discuss the most important tools.

10.5.1 Makefile

When a number of people are working on a project, each person will work on a module and then ultimately all the modules are combined into a single software package. Even if you are working alone on a project, you may like to write the code by splitting into different files. Makefile is an excellent utility to combine different project files and create the executable file. We will illustrate the use of makefile through an example. To start with, create a number of files as given below:

Listing 10.3 makefile

```
helloworld: main.o hello.o world.o
    gcc -o helloworld main.o hello.o world.o

main.o: main.c
    gcc -c main.c

hello.o: hello.c hello.h
    gcc -c hello.c

world.o: world.c world.h
    gcc -c world.c
```

Listing 10.4 hello.h

```
char str1[] = { 'H','e','l','l','o','\0'};
```

Listing 10.5 hello.c

```
#include"hello.h"
char* fun1()
{
    return &str1[0];
}
/*int main()
{
    printf("%s",fun1());
    return 0;
}*/
```

Listing 10.6 world.h

```
char str2[] = { 'w','o','r','l','d','\0'};
```

Listing 10.7 world.c

```
#include "world.h"
char* fun2()
{
    return &str2[0];
}

char str2[] = { 'w','o','r','l','d','\0'};
/*char* fun2()
{
    return &str2[0];
}*/
```

Listing 10.8 main.c

```
extern char* fun1();
extern char* fun2();
int main()
{
    printf("%s %s",fun1(),fun2());
    return 0;
}
```

There is one file containing the main() function, two files containing two functions fun1() and fun2() and two header files. The makefile is a file that describes the rules for creating the object files and the interdependencies of these files. You can execute the makefile by giving the command:

$make

The system will display the following lines:

gcc –c main.c

gcc –c hello.c

gcc –c world.c

gcc –o helloworld main.o hello.o world.o

If you modify a file, say main.c, you can give the command:

$touch hello.h

Next time when you invoke the make command, the compilation will be done using the latest main.c.

If you create a file with a name different from 'makefile', you need to give the command:

$make –f filename

makefile has a large number of options which can be obtained from the online manual pages.

The make utility is very useful while doing integration testing and system testing. The latest version of the developed files need to be compiled and linked. Manually doing the integration of the latest versions is very cumbersome and make utility can be used effectively.

10.5.2 Debugger

The utility "gdb" is the most widely used debugger for system software development. You need to write a program which has some bugs and then you can try to debug using the gdb (How difficult it is to write a program which has bugs!). To use the debugger, you need to give the compilation command with the following options:

$gcc –g –o lousyprog lousyprog.c

You can invoke gdb using the command

$gdb lousyprog

The prompt (gdb) will be displayed. You can give a number of debugger commands as listed below:

(gdb) help	(to obtain help)
(gdb) run	(to run the program)
(gdb) print i	(to print contents of variable i)
(gdb)list	(to see program listing)
(gdb) break 20	(to set breakpoint at line 20)
(gdb) cont	(to continue)

gdb is used extensively in embedded systems. You can connect the target system to the host system using an RS232 link. If the RS232 port on the host system is specified by /dev/tty01, the command for debugging a program "myprogram" is

$gdbserver /dev/tty01 /usr/prasad/myporgram

(gdb) target remote /dev/tty001

10.5.3 Indenting

When you write lengthy programs, indenting the code increases the readability. The shell command "indent" provides the automatic indenting feature:

To indent a C program, say hello.c, the shell command is

$indent hello.c

The following options are available:

-bad	blank lines after indentation
-bap	blank line after each function/procedure body
-bbb	blank line before boxed comments
-sob	remove unnecessary blank lines in the source code
-bl	braces after if line
-bli	brace indent
-bls	braces after structure declaration line
-br	braces on if line
-nbbo	break after Boolean operator
-bbo	break before Boolean operator
-clin	case indentation
-cn	comment indentation
-nsc	do not star comments

In some Unix systems, the equivalent command is C beautifier (cb). The command format is:

$cb hello.c

The SQA team has to make sure that the source code written by the development engineers is maintainable. One important feature of maintainable code is readability. If the source code has proper indentation, readability will be more.

10.6 Portability Testing Tool

To test the portability of C programs is important when the software has to be ported from one platform to another for example, from Unix system running on a Pentium platform to a Solaris system running on SUN SPARC platform. The "lint" utility available on the Unix/Solaris system can be used to check the portability of the code.

In addition to portability problems, lint also gives messages regarding "bad programming style". The various messages given by lint are:

- Unused variables and functions
- Assigning a 'long' variable to an 'int'
- Variables which are used first and set later
- Unreachable break statements
- Function that returns a value which is never used
- Type casting problems
- Non-potable character use [for example, if c is a character variable, the code "if((c = getchar() < 0) is not portable]
- Unusual constructs [for example, *p++; does nothing]
- Control statements that never succeed [if x is an unsigned integer, if(x < 0) is never a success]

The command format of lint is as follows:

$ lint hello.c

The output will display the potential portability problems. We will show the lint output for very simple files. You can pass your C programs through the lint utility and study the output messages to see what kind of good (or bad?) code you write.

Here is a small C program with an include directive and the main function in which a variable is declared and printf function is called.

```
#include <stdio.h>
void main(void)
{
    int i;
    printf("Hello\n");
}
```

Let us pass this program through lint utility by giving the command:

```
# lint -n test.c
```

The output of link will be as follows:

```
test.c (as included in test.c)
==================
(4) warning: variable unused in function: i in main

name declared but never used or defined
    _iob                         stdio.h(170)

  value type declared inconsistently
        _lastbuf                 llib-lucb:stdio.h(172) struct __FILE * ::
stdio.h(172) struct __FILE *
        fopen                    llib-lucb:stdio.h(207) struct __FILE *() ::
stdio.h(274) struct __FILE *()
        fdopen                   llib-lucb:stdio.h(257) struct __FILE *() ::
stdio.h(274) struct __FILE *()
        freopen                  llib-lucb:stdio.h(208) struct __FILE *() ::
stdio.h(274) struct __FILE *()
        popen                    llib-lucb:stdio.h(258) struct __FILE *() ::
stdio.h(274) struct __FILE *()
        fread                    llib-lucb:stdio.h(239) unsigned long () ::
stdio.h(280) int ()
        fwrite                   llib-lucb:stdio.h(240) unsigned long () ::
stdio.h(280) int ()
        fopen64                  llib-lucb:stdio.h(323) struct __FILE *() ::
stdio.h(326) struct __FILE *()
        freopen64                llib-lucb:stdio.h(324) struct __FILE *() ::
stdio.h(326) struct __FILE *()

  function returns value which is always ignored
        printf
```

You can easily make out the problems associated with the above program by studying the lint output.

Now let us slightly change the program, and run the lint utility again:

```
void main(void)
{
    int i;
    printf("Hello\n");
}

# lint -n test.c
```

The output of lint is as follows:

```
test.c (as included in test.c)
==================
(3) warning: variable unused in function: i in main
(4) warning: implicitly declared to return int: printf

function returns value which is always ignored
    printf
```

Now, let us revise the program again slightly and run the lint utility:

```
void main(void)
{
    printf("Hello\n");
}

# lint -n test.c

test.c (as included in test.c)
==================
(3) warning: implicitly declared to return int: printf

function returns value which is always ignored
    printf
```

If the SRS document specifies that portability is a requirement, then the test engineers can use the lint utility to check the portability related issues. If the programming language used is C, it is always a good practice to use the lint utility because it analyzes the code and shows if the programming style is bad.

10.7 Configuration Management Tools

Software engineers develop different versions of a program. Every time a program is revised, it is a good practice to record what changes have been made. Also, when several persons are working on a project, only one person should be able to modify the file at a time. To control the revisions to the source files (they can be C/C++ programs are text documents), Source Code Control System (SCCS) and Revision Control System (RCS) are used extensively in Unix/Linux. We will illustrate the use of RCS and SCCS using simple examples.

10.7.1 Revision Control System

Suppose you created a text file called "schedule" with the following lines:

10 am	meeting
11 am	lecture
12noon	lunch
2 pm	sleep

You need to give control of this file to RCS so that whenever you make changes, the system will force you to add the necessary comments.

When you give the following command, RCS will take control over the file:

$rcs –i schedule

The following message will be displayed, giving a prompt to enter description. You can enter the description as "My schedule for the day" as shown below:

RCS file: schedule,v

Enter description, terminated with single ".' Or end of file:

NOTE: This is NOT the log message!

>My schedule for the day

>.

done

$

When you see the directory listing, you will find that a new file with,v (comma v) will be created:

$ls –l

You need to "check-in" the file to give a version number to your file, using the command (note that the message displayed by the system is also shown below):

$ci schedule

schedule,v ← schedule

initial version: 1.1

done

$

Now you can verify that the original file 'schedule' is removed by using the command

$ls –l

To change the file, we must check-out using the command:

$co –l schedule

schedule,v → schedule

revision 1.1 (locked)

done

$

The file is locked so that others cannot modify it.

Now you can see that the file "schedule" reappears by giving the command:

$ls –l

Now you can make modifications to the file 'schedule'. You replace 'sleep' by 'seminar on Linux'.

Now, you need to check-in the file using the command:

$ci schedule

The system will prompt you to add a log message. You can type "changed the schedule at 2 pm" and enter dot on the next line as shown below:

Enter log message

>>changed the schedule at 2 pm

>>.

done

$

Now, again the file disappears, as you can see by giving the command:

$ls –l

To see the summary of the changes you can give the command:

$rlog schedule

The complete log information will be displayed including the summary of changes made.

To obtain the first revision of the file back, give the command:

$co –r1.1 schedule

To specify the version number as version 2.1, while checking-in, you can give the command:

$ci –r2 schedule

You can find out the difference between two versions of the file by giving the command:

$rcsdiff –r1.1 –r1.2 schedule

RCS file: schedule,v

Retrieving version 1.1

Retrieving version 1.2

Diff –r1.1 –r1.2

4c4

< 2 pm sleep

> 2 pm Seminar on Linux

For software engineers, it is very important to keep track of the various revisions/versions of the code. Revision Control System (RCS) is an excellent tool for revision/version control of the code.

10.7.2 Source Code Control System

Source Code Control System (SCCS) is an equivalent of RCS, available on many Unix flavors such as AT&T Unix, Berkeley Unix, and Sun Solaris. We will illustrate the use of SCCS through a simple text file. You can use these concepts for maintaining your C source files.

Use your favorite editor (such as ed or vi) to create a text file with the following line and save it as "lang".

C ADA FORTRAN

You can see the contents of the file using the command:

$cat lang

Give the custody of "lang" to sccs using the command:

$admin –i lang s.lang

The system will display the message: No id keywords (cm7)

Remove "lang" file, it is no longer required. To remove the file, use the command:

$rm lang

Retrieve the file s.lang using the command:

$get s.lang

1.1

1 lines

No id keywords (cm7)

Check the directory using the command:

$ls –l

lang is also displayed, but read only.

If changes have to be made to lang, give the command:

$get –e s.lang

1.1

new delta 1.2

1 lines

Modify lang file by adding the following two more lines:

JAVA

LISP

To record the changes issued to lang, give the command: [Note that the system gives a prompt to enter the comment and you need to type the comment "Added two languages".]

$delta s.lang

Comments? Added two languages

No id keywords (cm7)

1.2

2 inserted

0 deleted

1 unchanged

To retrieve version 1.2 of the file:

$get s.lang

1.2

3 lines

No id keyword (cm7)

$get –r1 s.lang (get latest version)

1.2

3 lines

No id keywords (cm7)

$get r1.2 s.lang

1.2

3 lines

No id keywords (cm7)

When significant changes are made, change the release number, by giving the command:

$get –e r2 s.lang

1.2

new delta 2.1

3 lines

SCCS works as follows: The file created by you is given to the custody of SCCS. Whenever you make a change to the file, it is called a delta. You can store each version with a different version number. When you make a new version, SCCS will force you to add some comments. Hence the developer is forced to make other developers know the reason for making a change. As you keep changing the contents of the file, you can create a number of versions. If you want to retrieve a particular version, it is very easy, you 'get' the file by giving the version number as argument. Another interesting feature of SCCS is that in a multi-user environment, if one user is making modifications to a particular version, others will not be allowed to make changes. These features help in maintaining consistent and documented versions of the source code. Though many other sophisticated configuration management tools are available now commercially, SCCS and RCS continue to be the darlings of many Unix buffs.

10.8 Coding Guidelines and Standards

Many programmers do not follow any discipline while writing the code. This leads to many maintenance problems—nobody would like to maintain the code written by someone else. It is said that maintaining someone else's code is like using someone else's toothbrush. This attitude arises mainly because the code written by one programmer cannot be understood by anybody else. The use of cryptic names for variables, objects etc., use of some 'magic numbers', lack of any on-line documentation etc. lead to such problems. Even simple things such as giving meaningful file names are not taken care of. So, if a programmer leaves a project in the middle, the other team members will not even know where the files are located.

Every organization has to develop a set of guidelines for all the programmers to follow so that the code can be maintained easily. This aspect is discussed in this section.

The SQA team has to make sure that the development team follows the coding guidelines while writing the code. The SQA team needs to develop the coding guidelines for each programming language.

10.8.1 Programming Style

Every programmer has to follow certain guidelines while doing the coding. Some such representative guidelines are given below:

1. The layout of the code should be in such a way that it is easy to read. Proper indentation of the code is required. After the code is finalized, it can be passed through a utility (such as C beautifier for C language) which will give the necessary indentation.

2. Names: Names of files, functions and variables should not be cryptic but meaningful. Temporary variables are to be indicated.

3. Function size to be limited to 40/50 lines.

4. Module size to be limited based on cohesion and coupling.

5. Deep nesting to be avoided.

6. Robustness: exceptions/errors should be handled using the code.

7. Single entry single exit control structures should be used and 'goto' must be avoided.

8. User defined types increases readability (such as enum, typedef)

9. Internal documentation:

Each file must have a header containing the name of the programmer, date on which the code was written, and the revision history—when the code was revised.

There should be no magic numbers e.g., i = 256 //explain why 256.

The functionality of each module/function must be explained briefly.

The input and output parameters for each function/method must be explained.

Assumptions made during the coding/design to be mentioned.

If there are any known defects in the code, they should be mentioned in the header of the program.

10.8.2 C Coding Guidelines

Every software engineer has his own idiosyncrasies that are reflected in the code developed by him/her. Cryptic filenames, irrelevant variable names, lack of proper commenting etc. make the code difficult to read, understand and maintain. All the project team members need to follow some guidelines while doing the coding. Every organization should have a document called 'coding standards' for each programming language. Every engineer needs to follow these guidelines. The guidelines specify simple rules to be followed by all the engineers. Some important guidelines are given below:

- For every project, a folder should be maintained that contains all the source code files. The folder name should be the name of the project. This folder should have a readme file that gives the list of files and the contents of the file.

- The backup of the project folder should be taken everyday so that at most one day's work only is lost in case there is a major failure of the systems.

- The filenames should reflect the functionality of the source code given in that file.

- Every file should contain a header that gives the copyright information, name of the file, author of the code and revision history as shown below:

```
/* Copyright Dr. Prasad, 2004 */
/* Name of the author: Dr. Prasad */
```

```
/* This is a header file containing global constants */
/* Version 1.0 */
```

- Identifiers such as variables, structure/union members, functions and macros should have meaningful names. ANSI C supports up to 32 characters for these names and hence the identifier name should reflect the functionality. However, temporary variables such as loop counters can be given names such as i, j, k etc. Strings can have a prefix of s, character names can have a prefix of 'C' and pointers can have a prefix of p.

- On-line documentation (comments) should be relevant. A good commenting style is to have the comment in the same line as the code:

```
int max_temperature = 50; /* threshold on temperature is 50 degrees*/
```

Constants and macros should always be in upper case.

```
                   #define PI 3.14.15
```

- Proper indentation helps readability and understandability of the code. Simple rules that are followed in normal typing need to be followed while coding as well. Comma (,) and Semi-colon (;) need to be followed by a single space. There should be no space between the unary operator and the operand. For binary operators, the operator should have a space before and after. The following code snippets demonstrate these indentation guidelines.

```
-b       not -    b       (unary operator)
a = 0      not a=0 or a =0 or a= 0    (binary operator)
if (d  > 0) {
    root = sqrt(d);
}

if (d > 0 {
    root1 = -2 * a / d ;
    root2 = 2 * a/d ;
}

else {
printf("No root\n");
}

do {

statements;

} while ( x > 0);
```

You can use the gindent (GNU indent) for indentation.

- Whenever changes are made to a source file, modify the header indicating the date of modification and why the modification has been done.

/* Revision history */

/* Date: 17 July 2003 max_temperature initialization value changed to 55 as per client requirement */

- It is advisable to use the source code configuration software (SCCS or RCS, or any other equivalent software) if there are a large number of source code files to be maintained.

- During the course of development, the code written by one engineer should be given to another engineer who has to check whether the coding guidelines are being followed or not.

Peer reviews are an effective way of doing code review. The code written by one engineer should be reviewed by another engineer to check readability, understandability, and maintainability.

10.8.3 Java Coding Guidelines

This section gives the guidelines to be followed by all software engineers while doing programming in Java. These guidelines have been framed to ensure that the code can be understood easily by persons other than the original author of the software, for easier maintenance.

As the objective of coding is not to reduce coding time or effort but to reduce testing and maintenance effort and time, all engineers are advised to follow these guidelines.

Backup policy and schedules during development phase:

During the development phase, the backup activity of the unit/module level code is the responsibility of the individuals. At the end of each day, the software has to be backed up in the specified folder on the server. This ensures that at most only one day's effort is lost in case of a system failure.

Project folder

Each software developer will have a folder with the name of the project in his/her directory on his/her machine in the root directory. In this folder, a file with the name 'readme' should be present which gives a description of all the sub-folders and file names in the folder corresponding to the project. The version number of the software should be reflected as a part of the filename. For example, quest 1.0 should be the file name for the quest project version 1.0.

All the names of the directories and files should be meaningful indicating the module name or the unit name. In case of abbreviated names, the readme file should clearly explain the contents of the directory or file. A logical hierarchy should be maintained, with one folder for each module, with files corresponding to each unit/ function within the module. The readme file should be in the format:

Filename   Description   Status (tested OK, testing in
                                            progress)

File name extensions will be as per the standards required by the compiler/ programming language/OS.

Once a program module is tested and found OK, the readme file should be updated with the new status.

If older versions of the module need to be kept, they should have a different extension (e.g., v0.9) and listed in the readme file.

Java coding conventions

The header should be in javadoc format.

Use documentation comments immediately before declarations of interfaces, classes, and member functions. Documentation comments are processed by javadoc.

Example:

```
/**
Subscriber: A subscriber is a person who uses
The IVR system
@author KVKK Prasad
*/
```

The important *javadoc* tags are given below:

@author name: Used for classes and interfaces to indicate the author(s) of the code. One tag has to be used per author.

@deprecated: Used for classes and member functions to indicate that the API for the class has been deprecated and should not be used any longer.

@exception name description: Used for member functions to describe the exceptions that a member function throws. One tag per exception should be used and full class name for the exception has to be given.

@param name description: Used for member functions to describe a parameter passed to a member function, including its type/class and its usage. One tag per parameter has to be used.

@return description: Used for member functions to describe the return value, if any, of a member function. The type/class and the potential uses of the return value should be indicated.

@since: Used for classes and member functions to indicate how long the item has existed since JDK 1.1.

@see ClassName: Used for classes, interfaces, member functions and fields. It generates a hypertext link in the documentation to the specified class. You should use a fully qualified class name.

@see Classname#memberfunctionName: Used for classes, interfaces, member functions and fields. It generates a hypertext link in the documentation to the specified member function. Use a fully qualified class name.

@version text: Used for classes and interfaces to indicate the version information for the code.

Naming methods

Methods should be named using a full English description, using mixed case with the first letter of every non-initial word capitalized.

Examples:

```
openConnection()
printAddressLabel()
save()
delete()
```

This convention, though increases the typing effort of the programmer, enhances readability and hence understandability of the code as the purpose of the method is immediately known.

Naming Getters

Getters are methods that return the value of a field. Prefix the word 'get' to the name of the field. If it is a boolean field (returns true or false), use the prefix 'is' to the name of the field instead of 'get.'

Examples:

```
GetLastName()
getAccountNumber()
isPersistent()
isAtEnd()
```

Naming Setters

Setters are methods that modify the values of a field. You should prefix the word 'set' to the name of the field, regardless of the field type.

Examples:

```
setLastName(String aName)
setAccountNumber(int anAccountNumber)
setReasonableValues(Vector newValues)
setPersistent(boolean isPersistent)
setAtEnd(boolean isAtEnd)
```

Naming Constructors

Constructors are methods that perform the necessary initialization when an object is first created. Constructors are always given the same name as their class. For example, a constructor for the class Patient would be Patient().

Examples:

```
Customer()
SavingsAccount()
```

Naming Fields (Fields/Properties)

Fields that are collections, such as arrays or vectors, should be given plural names to indicate that they represent multiple values.

Examples:

```
lastName
zipCode
unitPrice
orderItems
```

Naming Components/Widgets

Components/Widgets have to be named appropriately (instead of button1, button2, raju etc.) so that it will be easy to identify their purpose and type.

Examples:

```
okButton
customerList
fileMenu
newFileMenuItem
```

Naming Constants

In Java, constants are typically implemented as *static final* fields of classes. The convention is to use full words, all in uppercase, with underscores between the words. Ensure that there are no magic numbers. When constants are initialized to specific values, indicate why you are initializing to that value in comments.

Examples:
```
MINIMUM_BALANCE
DEFAULT_START_DATE
```

Naming Local Variables

A local variable is an object or data item that is defined within the scope of a block, often a method. The scope of a local variable is the block in which it is defined. In general, local variables are named following the same conventions used for fields i.e., by using full descriptors with the first letter of any non-initial word in uppercase.

When there is a single input and/or output stream being opened, used, and then closed within a method, the common convention is to use **in** and **out** for the names of these streams, respectively. For a stream used for both input and output, use the name **inOut**. An alternative to this naming convention is to use the names **inputStream**, **outputStream,** and **ioStream** instead of **in**, **out**, and **inOut** respectively.

Naming Loop Counters

Since the scope of the loop counters is limited, use counters such as i, j, k. Counters such as counter1, counter2 are appropriate for member functions.

Naming Exception Objects

Use the letter **e** for a generic exceptions.

Naming Parameters (Arguments)

Convention to be followed for parameters is same as for local variables. Use full description of the value or object being passed, prefix the name with the letter 'p' to indicate that it is an argument.

Examples:
```
pCustomer
pInventoryItem
```

Naming Classes, interfaces and packages

Naming Classes: Use a full English descriptor starting with the first letter capitalized using mixed case for the rest of the name.

Examples:
```
Customer
```

```
Employee
Order
OrderItem
FileStream
String
```

Naming Interfaces: Use mixed case with the first letter of each word capitalized. The preferred convention for the name of an interface is to use a descriptive adjective, such as Runnable or Cloneable, although descriptive nouns, such as DataInput or DataOutput are also common.

Example. Runnable, Contactable, Prompter

Naming Packages: Use full description of the package appropriate to the main function. Put all classes that can be grouped together into their own packages. Use sub-packages for smaller components of a big project.

Examples:

```
package Forms;
package Widgets;
```

What To Document

The following guidelines are to be followed to document the various items:

Arguments/Parameters: The type of the parameter, any restrictions or preconditions, the significance of the parameters.

Fields/Property fields: Description, documentation of all applicable invariants, concurrency issues and visibility decisions.

Classes: Purpose of the class, development and maintenance history of the class, applicable invariants, concurrency strategy and known bugs.

Compilation units: Each class/interface defined in the class, including a brief description, file name and other identifying information, copyright information and name of the author.

The ratio of commented lines to non-commented lines is a coding metric that indicates the amount of documentation embedded in the source code. A ratio of 1:1 is considered good i.e., if there are 1000 lines of non-commented lines, there should be 1000 lines of comments. Many development engineers think this is crazy, but the SQA people know better and let us face the fact: the SQA team will have the final word.

Summary

In this chapter, we reviewed the important tools for source code testing and maintenance. The important points to be noted are:

- Software QA engineers need to ensure that the development engineers follow a disciplined methodology while coding. The utilities available on Unix flavor machines help in doing the QA activity efficiently.

- While doing the performance testing of the software, if the software does not meet the desired response time or if the execution is very slow, code optimization needs to be done. The timing functions can be used to find out the time taken by different portions of the code. Then, code optimization can be done by changing the algorithms or using more efficient data structures.

- Productivity tools such as make utility, indenting utility, profilers and line profilers help in increasing the productivity of development engineers and testing engineers.

- The 'lint' utility can be used to test whether the C code is portable or not. This utility also gives the information about bad programming style such as unused variables, unused functions etc.

- Configuration management is a very important activity for software developers and testing engineers. The version and release control utilities—SCCS and RCS—are used to maintain multiple versions of the source code.

- The SQA team has to ensure that the programmers follow the coding guidelines/ standards. Every organization has to develop a set of coding guidelines to be followed for each programming language. The SQA engineers need to review the code developed and check whether these guidelines are being followed.

11 QuickTest Professional (QTP)

In this chapter

- Discover the features of QuickTest Professional
- Learn the procedure for functional/regression testing of various applications
- Understand how to create data-driven tests
- Learn how to do synchronization of test cases
- Know how to test database and web applications

QuickTest Professional (QTP) is a very sophisticated testing tool for carrying out functional/regression testing of a variety of applications; and it is extremely easy to learn and use. In this chapter, we will study how to test a variety of applications using this testing tool.

11.1 Overview of QuickTest Professional

Mercury Interactive's QuickTest Professional (QTP) is a very sophisticated testing tool. If you are already familiar with WinRunner, learning QTP is just a matter of few hours. QTP is much more powerful and you can migrate to it very easily.

Like WinRunner, QTP is also a functional/regression testing tool that can be used to generate various test cases and run them automatically. Its important features are summarized below:

- It has the record/replay provision to record the user interactions with the application software. You can record your keyboard entries and mouse clicks of the application GUI. QTP automatically generates the test script. You can run the test script repeatedly for regression testing of your application.
- This testing tool has a recovery manager and in case the application halts due to an error, it will automatically recover—this is very useful for unattended testing.

- It uses VBScript as the scripting language and its syntax is very similar to Visual Basic; hence learning this scripting language is very easy. The Keyword-driven testing feature through Keyword View provides a facility to build tests without writing the scripts.

- QTP provides checkpoints option.

- It provides a facility for synchronization of test cases.

- Its 'auto-documentation' feature provides the feature of creating test documentation.

- Test report data is stored in documented XML format. This facilitates transferring the report data to another third party tool or into HTML web page.

- It supports Unicode and hence you can test applications written for any of the world languages such as Hindi, Japanese, Chinese etc.

- Using special add-in modules, you can use QTP for testing a variety of applications such as:

  - ERP/CRM packages such as SAP, Siebel, PeopleSoft, Oracle
  - .NET WebForms, WinForms, .NET Controls
  - Web service applications and protocols including XML, SOAP, WSDL, J2EE and .NET
  - Multimedia applications such as RealAudio/Video and Flash.

In this chapter, we will demonstrate how to use QTP for testing a Windows application, a database application and a web site.

11.2 Testing an Application Using QTP

After installing QuickTest Professional on your computer, invoke the QuickTest Professional application:

- Start → Programs → QuickTest Professional → QuickTest Professional

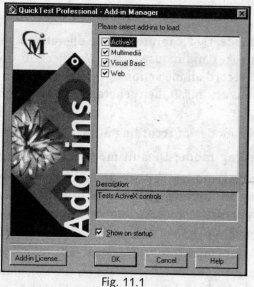

Fig. 11.1

When you click the "OK" button, QuickTest Professional's Welcome screen is displayed prompting you to select one of three options, as shown in Fig. 11.2.

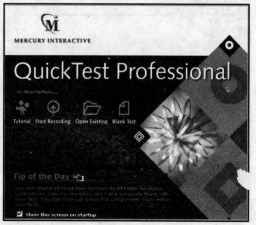

Fig. 11.2

Select the "Blank Test" option to create a new test case.

The testing process involves the following steps:

- Recording a test case
- Running the test case
- Analyzing the test results

11.2.1 Recording a Test Case

In the recording mode, QTP captures all the operations performed on the GUI (such as the keyboard strokes and mouse clicks). You need to work with the application in the usual way and record all the actions. While recording a test case, QTP captures all the images of various actions. It then generates the test script for the actions performed in VBScript language.

There are three modes of recording a test case:

- **Normal recording mode:** Default mode of recording.
- **Analog recording mode:** This mode is used when exact mouse positions or keystrokes play an important role in recording. For example, in case of bitmap validations, signature testing etc., analog recording mode is used.
- **Low level recording mode:** This mode of recording enables you to record on the objects even if QuickTest Professional fails to identify the object.

Let us now perform the testing process on the Calculator application. The GUI of the Calculator (Standard mode) is as shown in Fig. 11.3.

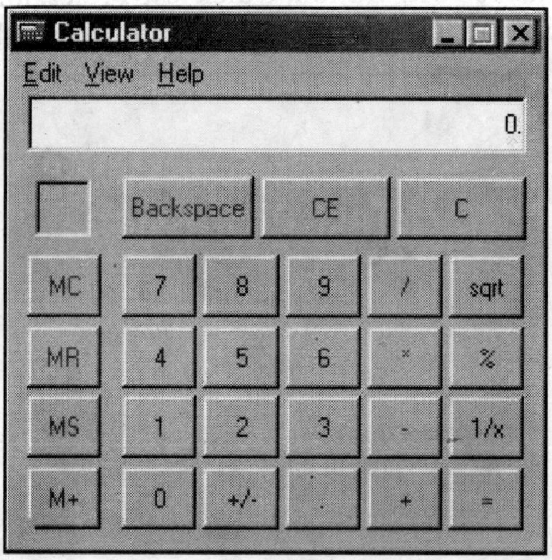

Fig. 11.3

The symbols on the buttons of Calculator application represent the following functions:

+   :   To perform addition

-   :   To perform subtraction

*   :   To perform multiplication

/   :   To perform division

. :   Decimal point

sqrt :   To find square root of a number

% :   To find percent

1/x :   To find inverse of a number

MC: To clear the memory

MR: To recall from memory

MS :   To save in the memory

M+:   To add to the memory

C :   To clear the current calculation

CE :   To clear the displayed number

Backspace: To remove leftmost digit

+/- :   To give sign of the number (positive or negative)

Table 11.1 gives the various test cases and the expected output for each test case.

Test Case	Expected Output
4 1/x	0.25
-6 sqrt	Err: "Invalid input for function"
4 C	Clears the Display
1.2 * 3	3.6
5 / 2.0	2.5
7 + 8 – 9	6
600 * 2 %	12
2, MS, C, MR	2
MC, 2, M+, 3, M+, C, MR	5

Table 11.1 Test Cases and Expected Outputs for the Calculator Application

Test Case #1: To test the Inverse operation (inverse of 4 using 1/x button)

Step 1:   Open a new document (File → New) or select "Blank Test" [icon] from the QuickTest professional's Welcome screen. The main GUI of the QuickTest Professional is as shown in Fig. 11.4.

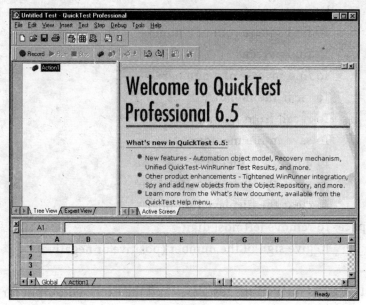

Fig. 11.4

Step 2: Click the "Record" button to start recording. The screen shown in Fig. 11.5 will be displayed.

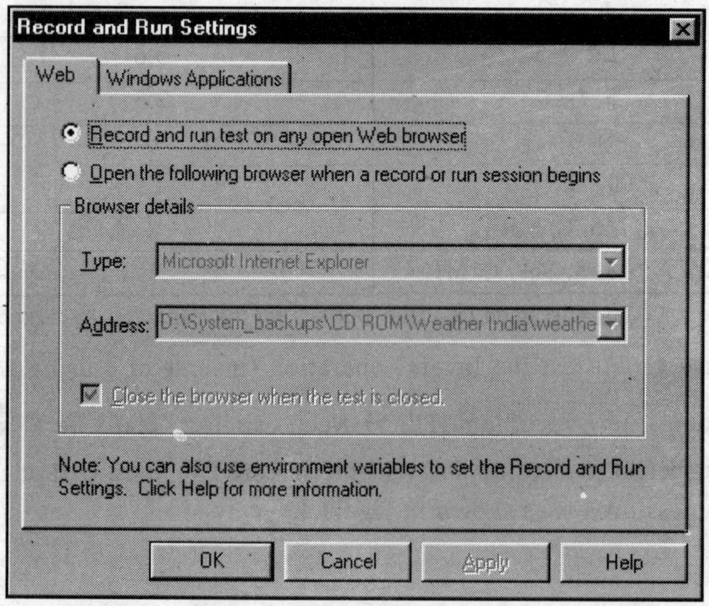

Fig. 11.5

Step 3: Select the "Windows Applications" tab. The dialog box for that tab is shown in Fig. 11.6.

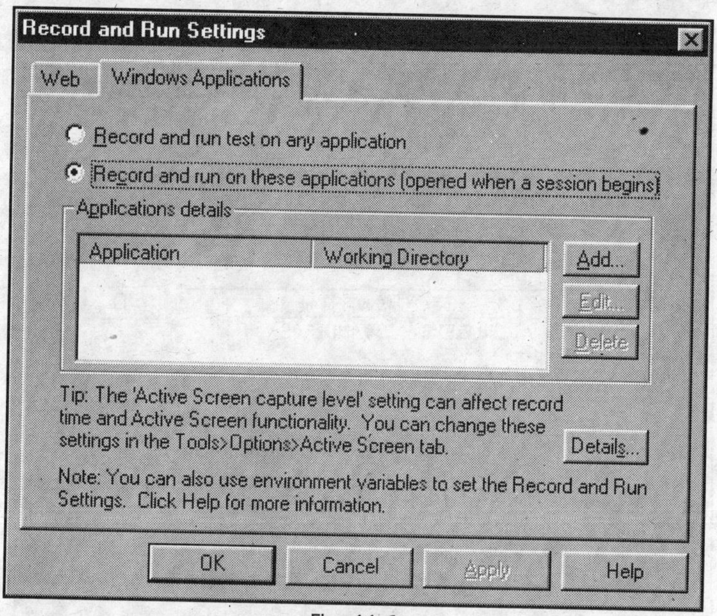

Fig. 11.6

- Select "Record and run on these applications" option.
- Click the "Add" button to select the application. The dialog, shown in Fig. 11.7, is displayed.

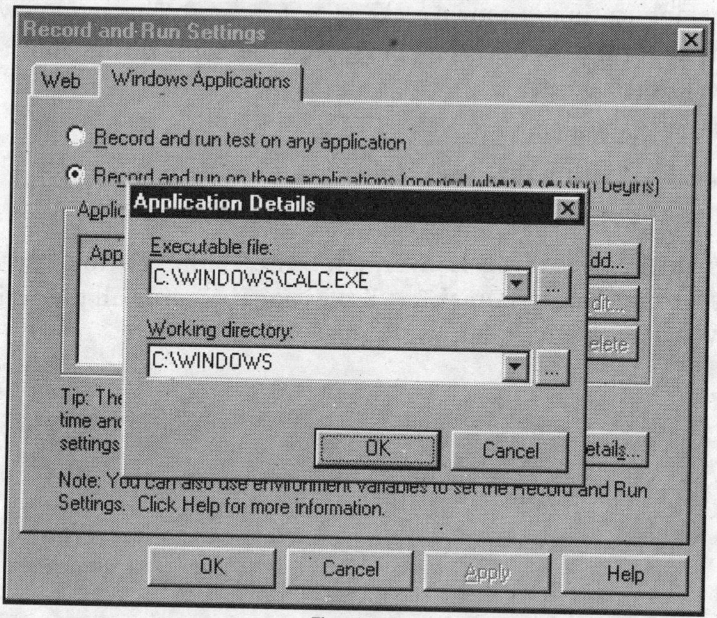

Fig. 11.7

■ Select the "Executable File" and "Working Directory" and click the "OK" button. The selected application will be added to the Application Details, as shown in Fig. 11.8.

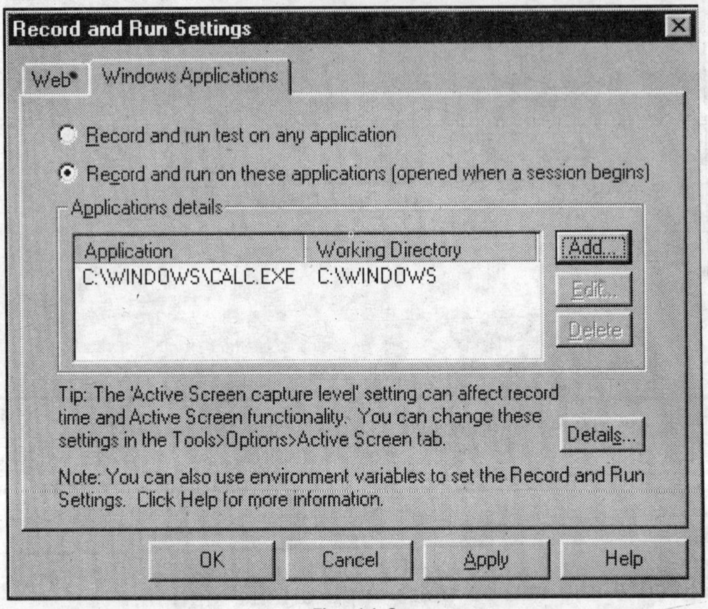

Record and Run Settings   ☒

| Web* | Windows Applications |

○ Record and run test on any application

◉ Record and run on these applications (opened when a session begins)

┌─ Applications details ─────────────────────────────

Application	Working Directory	[Add...]
C:\WINDOWS\CALC.EXE	C:\WINDOWS	[Edit...]
		[Delete]

Tip: The 'Active Screen capture level' setting can affect record time and Active Screen functionality. You can change these settings in the Tools>Options>Active Screen tab.   [Details...]

Note: You can also use environment variables to set the Record and Run Settings. Click Help for more information.

[OK]   [Cancel]   [Apply]   [Help]

Fig. 11.8

Step 4: Start recording the test case. While recording is in progress, the status of the application is shown as . The actions will be recorded in the form of a Tree View, indicating the name of the object and the action performed on it.

■ Click "4" on the Calculator.

■ Click the "1/x" button on the Calculator to find the inverse of 4.

■ The result, (0.25) will be displayed on the Calculator.

Step 5: Once the recording is over, click the "Stop" button ■ Stop to stop the recording process. QuickTest Professional records all the actions performed by you as shown in Fig. 11.9.

cal_tectCase1 - QuickTest Professional
File Edit View Insert Test Step Debug Tools Help
Record Run Stop
Action1
"Calculator"
"Button" Click
"Button_3" Click
"Button_2" Click
"Button_4" Click
Calculator
Edit View Help
Backspace CE C
MC 7 8 9 / sqrt
MR 4 5 6 * %
MS 1 2 3 - 1/x
M+ 0 +/- . + =
Tree View Expert View
Active Screen
Ready

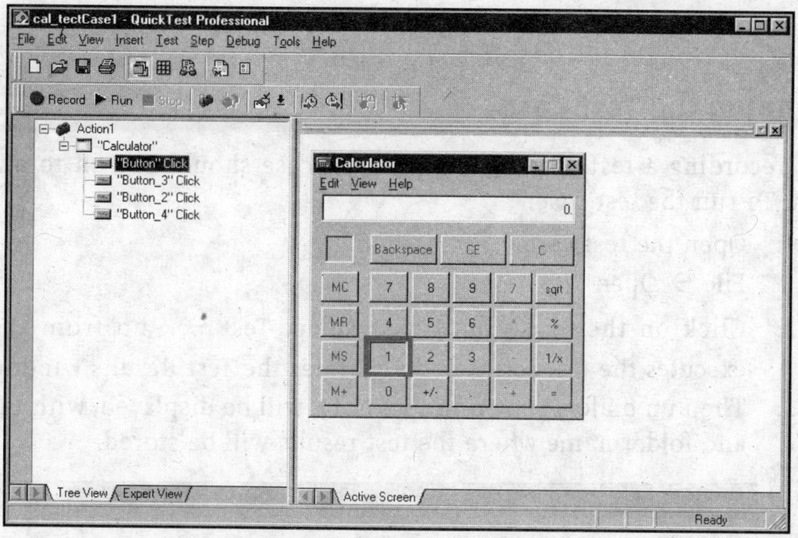

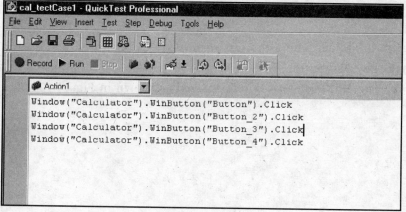

Fig. 11.9

There are two views, as shown in Fig. 11.9—Tree View and Expert View.

1. **Tree View:** This view displays the details of all the objects and the actions performed on these objects.
2. **Expert View:** This view displays the VBScript code generated for the recorded actions. If required, you can modify this code.

Once the test case is recorded, VBScript code is generated, as shown in Fig. 11.10.

cal_tectCase1 - QuickTest Professional
File Edit View Insert Test Step Debug Tools Help
Record Run Stop
Action1
Window("Calculator").WinButton("Button").Click
Window("Calculator").WinButton("Button_2").Click
Window("Calculator").WinButton("Button_3").Click
Window("Calculator").WinButton("Button_4").Click

Fig. 11.10

Step 6: Save the test case.

11.2.2 Running the Test Case

Once recording a test case is over, the test case should be run to analyze the test result. To run the test case:

Step 1: Open the test case.

File → Open

Step 2: Click on the ▶Run button or select Test → Run from the menu. This executes the test script and generates the Test Results window.

Step 3: The Run dialog, shown in Fig. 11.11, will be displayed, with the default path and folder name where the test results will be stored.

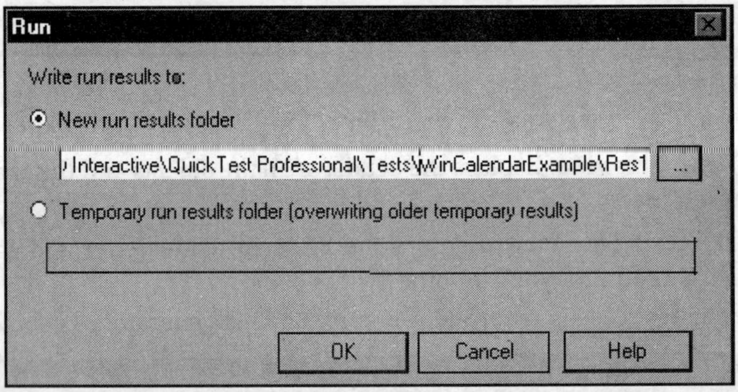

Fig. 11.11

- Select the folder where the test results are to be stored by clicking on [...] and click the "OK" button.

Step 4: The Test Results will be displayed as shown in Fig. 11.12.

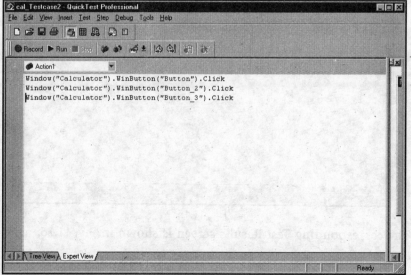

Fig. 11.12

The Test Result of the recorded test case can either be "Done", "Warning", "Passed" or "Failed". The test cases that contain checkpoints are marked either as "Passed" or "Failed". In test cases where there are no checkpoints, yet the test goes on smoothly, they are marked as "Done". When the test was not successful, but did not cause the test to stop running, they are marked as "Warning" in the test result.

Test Case #2: To test the operation square root of -6.

Fig. 11.13 shows the Expert View.

Fig. 11.13

Fig. 11.14 shows the result window when you run the test case.

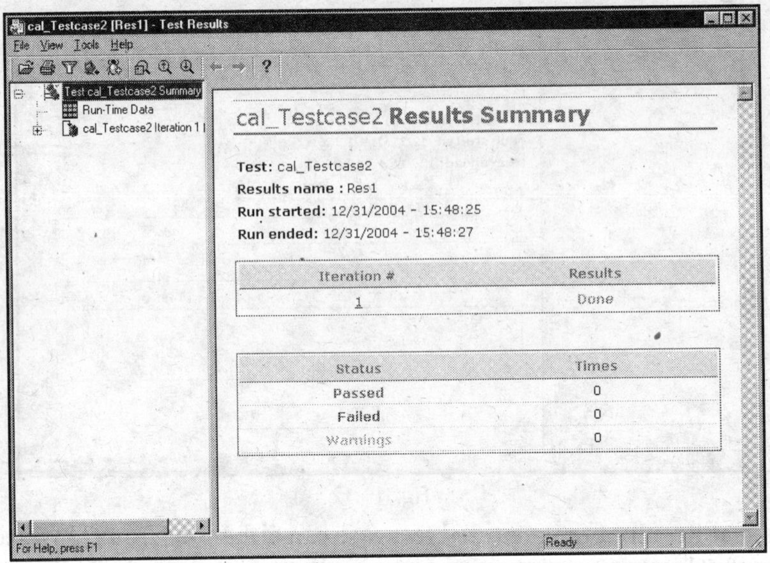

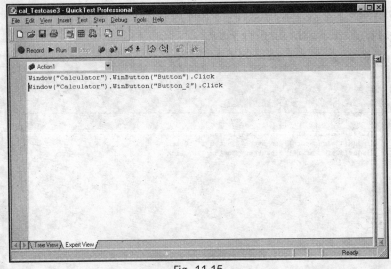

Fig. 11.14

Test Case #3: To clear the display after performing some operations.
Fig. 11.15 shows the Expert View.

Fig. 11.15

The corresponding Test Results screen is shown in Fig. 11.16.

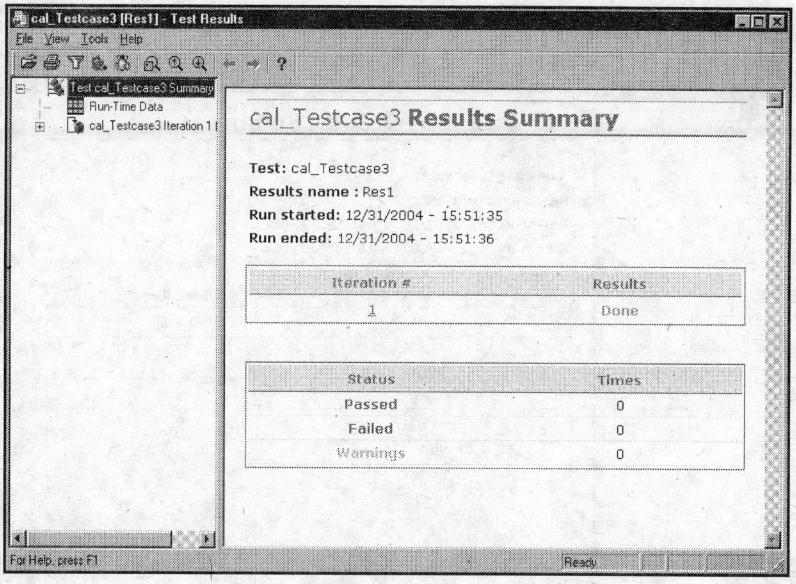

Fig. 11.16

Test Case #4: Multiplication of two numbers. (1.2 * 3).

Fig. 11.17 shows the Expert View.

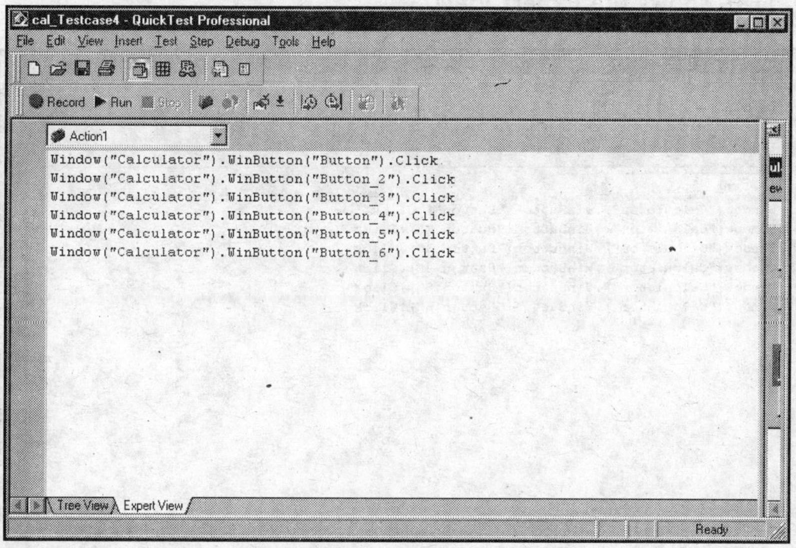

Fig. 11.17

The corresponding Test Results screen is shown in Fig. 11.18.

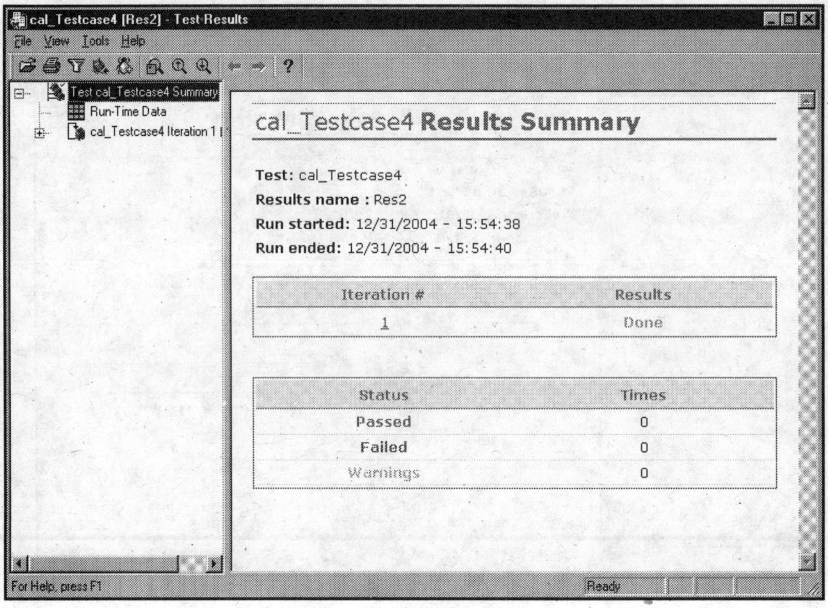

Fig. 11.18

Test Case #5: Division of two numbers. (5 / 2.0).

Fig. 11.19 shows the Expert View.

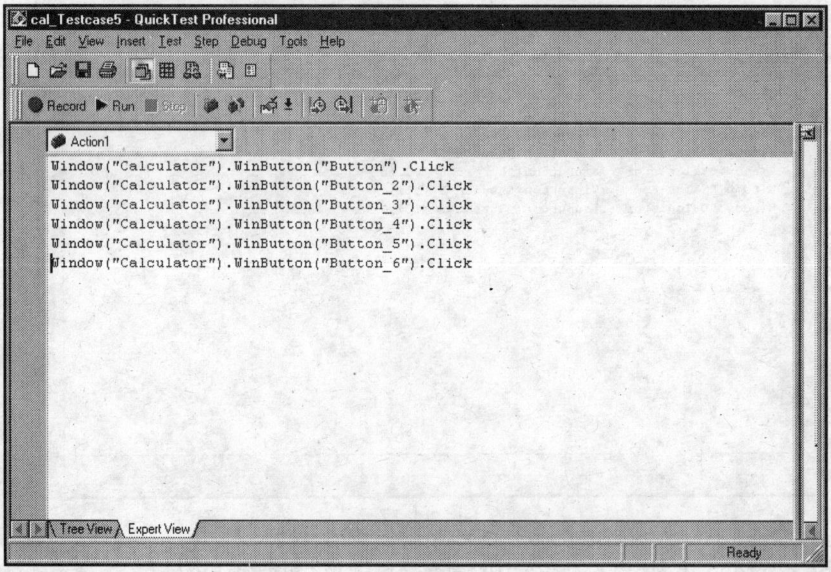

Fig. 11.19

The corresponding Test Results screen is shown in Fig. 11.20.

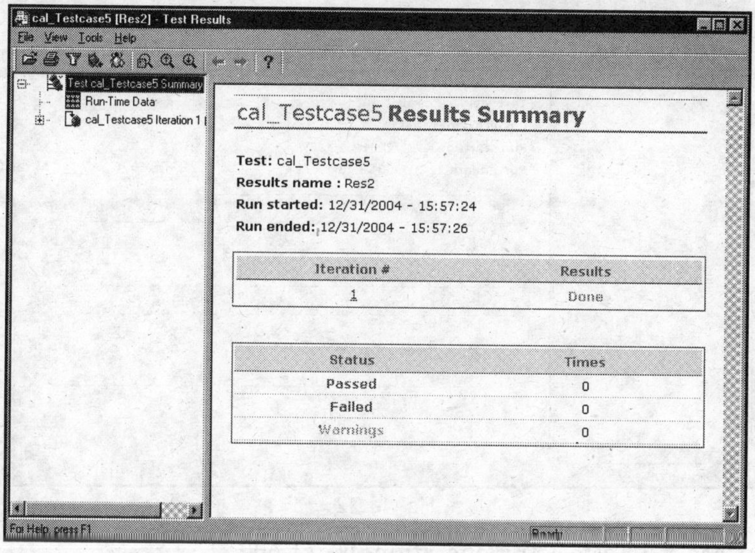

Fig. 11.20

Test Case #6: To test the operation (7 + 8 – 9).

Fig. 11.21 shows the Expert View.

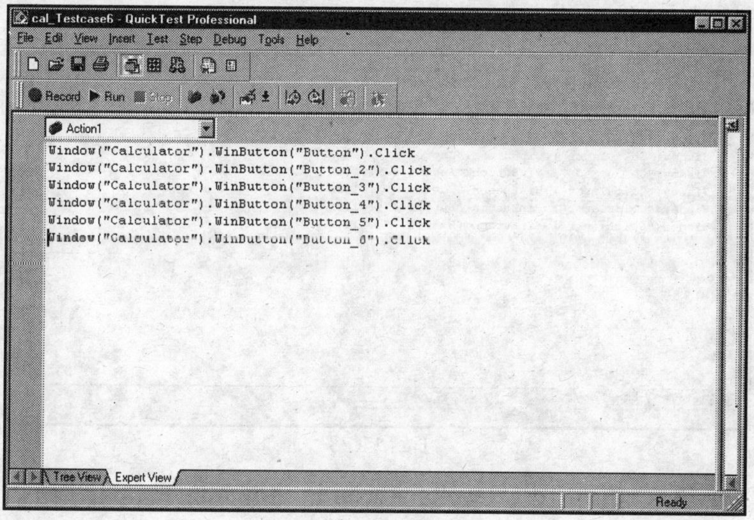

Fig. 11.21

The corresponding Test Results screen is shown in Fig. 11.22.

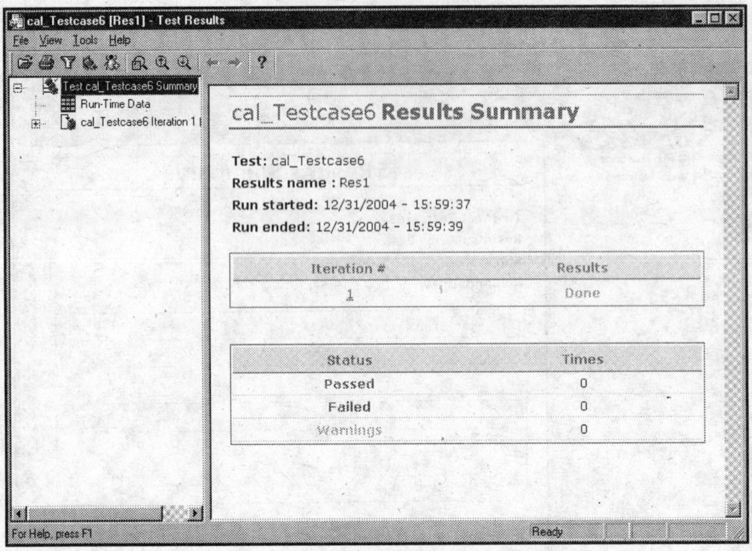

Fig. 11.22

Test Case #7: To test the operation 2% of 600.

The Expert View is shown in Fig. 11.23.

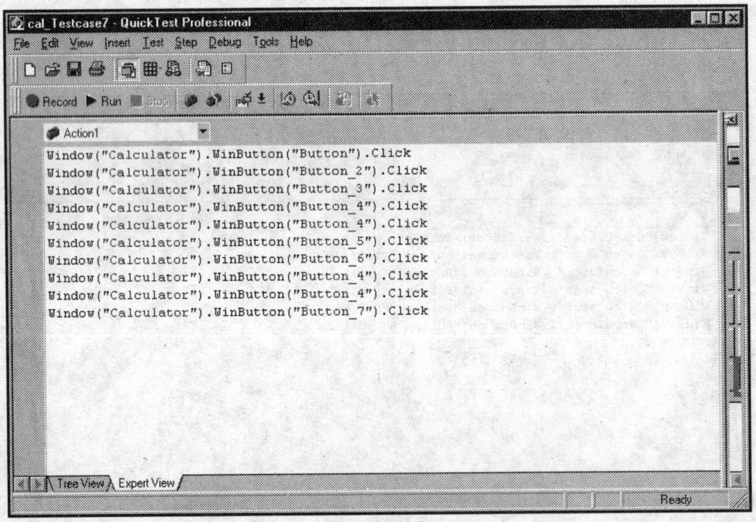

Fig. 11.23

The corresponding Test Results screen is shown in Fig. 11.24.

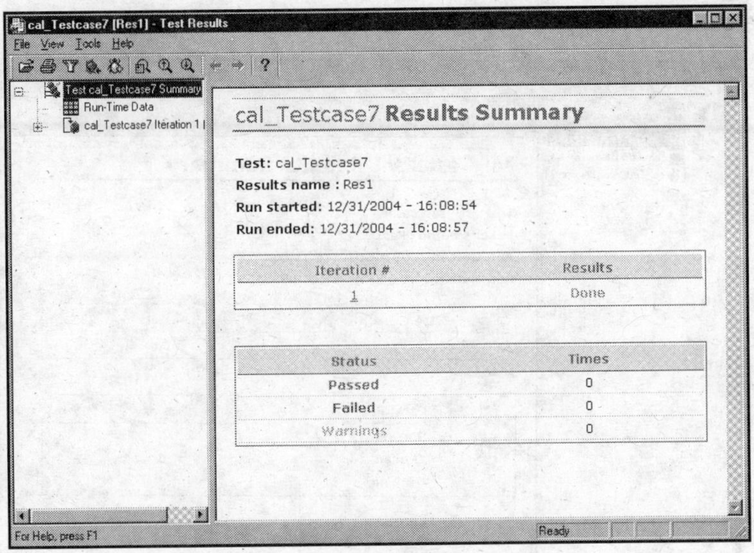

Fig. 11.24

Test Case #8: To test MS and MR buttons.

The Expert View is shown in Fig. 11.25.

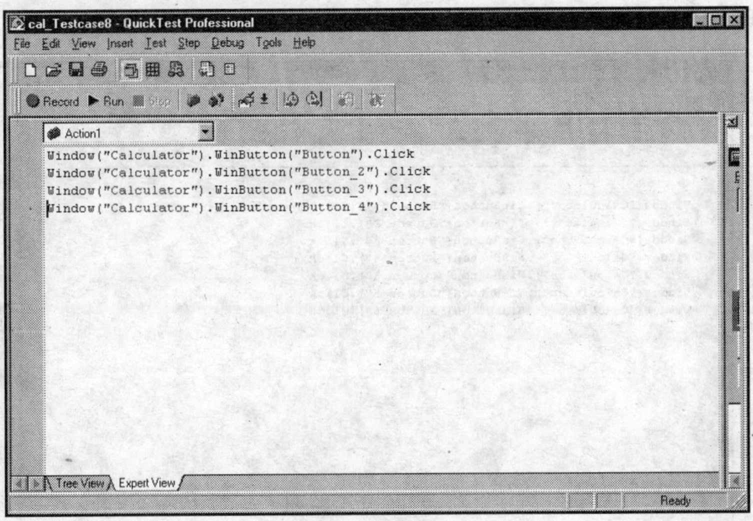

Fig. 11.25

The corresponding Test Results screen is shown in Fig. 11.26.

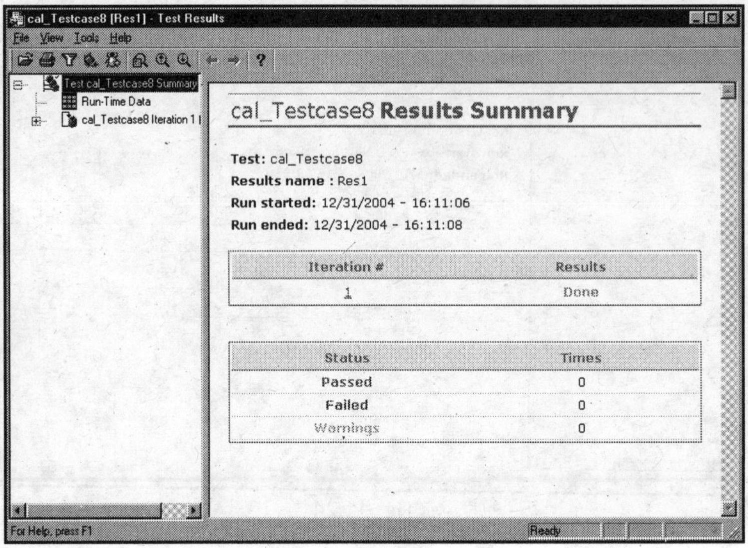

Fig. 11.26

Test Case #9: To test M+ and MR buttons.

The Expert View is shown in Fig. 11.27.

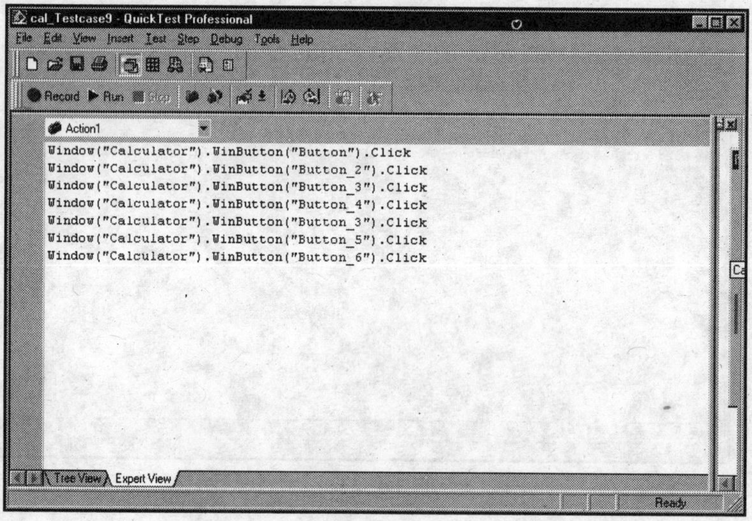

Fig. 11.27

The corresponding Test Results screen is shown in Fig. 11.28.

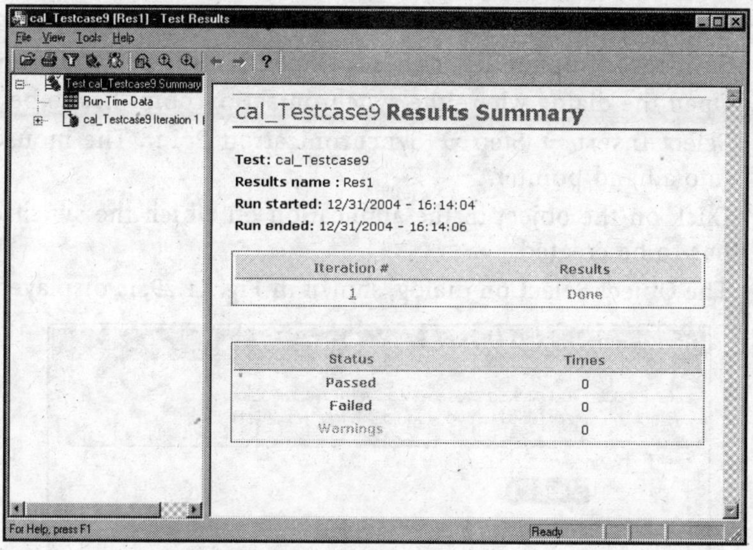

Fig. 11.28

During the software development phase, you can design the test cases and create the test scripts as discussed above. You can repeatedly execute the test cases whenever you make modifications to the source code. Here, we have tested an application that has no bugs, but during the development of software, you can repeatedly run the test cases. Then based on the test results, you can modify the source code.

You can integrate QTP with test management tool such as Test Director. This facilitates process-oriented testing and leads to defect-free software.

11.3 Synchronization of Test Cases

While testing some applications, QuickTest Professional has to wait for a specified time to accept data from the user or till the current operation is complete, before executing the next statement. This is called synchronization of test cases. For example, you need to use the synchronization point to display a progress bar and want the testing process to halt when the progress bar reaches 100%. In such cases, the synchronization point is used to make the testing process wait till the expected output occurs.

If the application is not synchronized properly, it will affect the entire flow of the application and the test case may not work as expected. So, it is very important to recognize the point where synchronization is required and then insert the synchronization point. We should also specify the maximum timeout time for which QuickTest Professional should wait for the expected result. In case the application does not receive the expected output before the timeout time, the test case fails.

Let us see the step-by-step process for creating such a synchronization point.

Step 1: Start recording the test case as specified in the previous steps.

Step 2: Open the dialog where the synchronization point has to be created.

Step 3: Select Insert → Step → Synchronization Point. The mouse pointer turns into a hand-pointer.

Step 4: Click on the object in the application on which the synchronization point has to be created.

Step 5: The Object Selection dialog, shown in Fig. 11.29, is displayed.

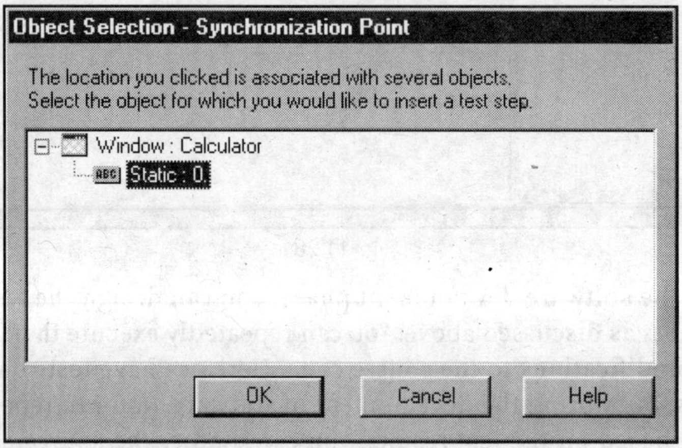

Fig. 11.29

This dialog prompts you to select the object on which the synchronization point has to be created. This is used when the object on which the user clicked is associated with more than one object. Click on the "OK" button.

Step 6: The "Add Synchronization Point" dialog, shown in Fig. 11.30, is displayed. Select the required Property name and Property value. Enter the maximum Timeout time. Click the "OK" button to proceed further.

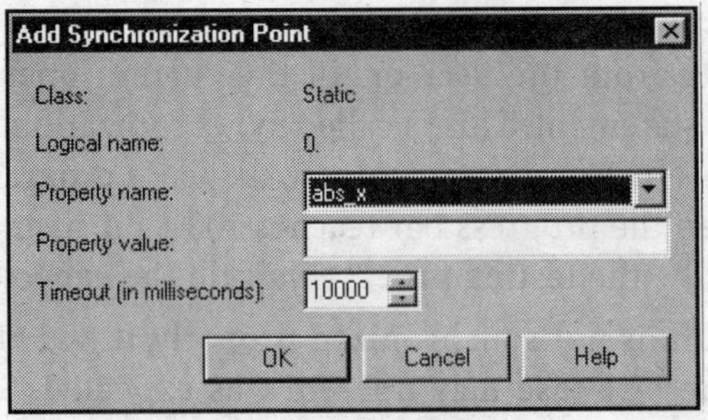

Fig. 11.30

Step 7: The "Wait Property" statement will be inserted into the Tree View as shown in Fig. 11.31. If any changes are to be made, such as changing the Timeout time, then select the "Expert View". This displays the VBScript for the recorded action and you can change the timeout time to the required value.

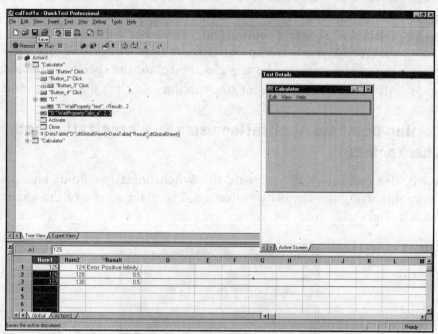

Fig. 11.31

Step 8: Now run the test case by clicking the ▶ Run button or by selecting Test → Run menu option.

11.3.1 Creating Checkpoints

QuickTest Professional enables you to add checkpoint to the test case for checking the current state of the object to the expected state of the object. If the state of the object matches with the expected state, then the result of the test case is 'passed'; otherwise the result is 'failed'. There are various kinds of checkpoints:

- Standard Checkpoint
- Image Checkpoint
- Bitmap Checkpoint
- Database Checkpoint
- Table Checkpoint etc.

Let us now see the steps for creating a Standard Checkpoint:

Step 1: Record the test case and save it.

Step 2: Right click on the statement where the checkpoint has to be created and select the "Insert Standard Checkpoint" option.

Step 3: Check the Property for which the checkpoint has to be created.

Step 4: Select the "Constant" option, enter the expected value in the edit box that is provided and set Checkpoint Timeout time. The testing tool will wait for the expected output on the specified object for the specified timeout.

Step 5: Also select "After Current step" option and click the "OK" button.

11.3.2 Testing Database Application using Synchronization and Checkpoints

We will demonstrate how to create the Synchronization Point and the Standard Checkpoint, using the EmpDB application. The main screen of the application is as shown in Fig. 11.32.

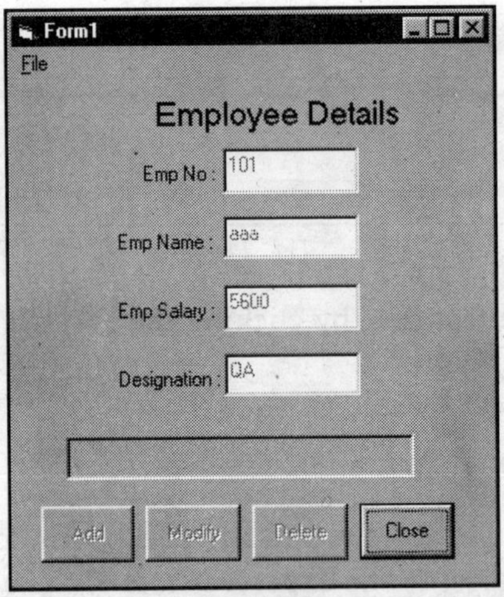

Fig. 11.32

The employee database (EmpDB) application is available on the CDROM that accompanies this book. The procedure for installing this application is given in Appendix E.

Execute the EmpDB application. Now add an employee record to the database. It takes few seconds to insert a record into the database. QTP should wait till the following conditions are satisfied:

- The Progress bar reaches 100%
- "Insert Done" string appears in the status bar.
- The "Add" button gets disabled.

To wait for the expected output, we make use of the Synchronization Point and Standard Checkpoint.

Step 1: Open QuickTest Professional and create a new test case.

Step 2: Open the EmpDB application.

Step 3: Start recording the test case.

Step 4: Create a new Employee record as shown in Fig. 11.33.

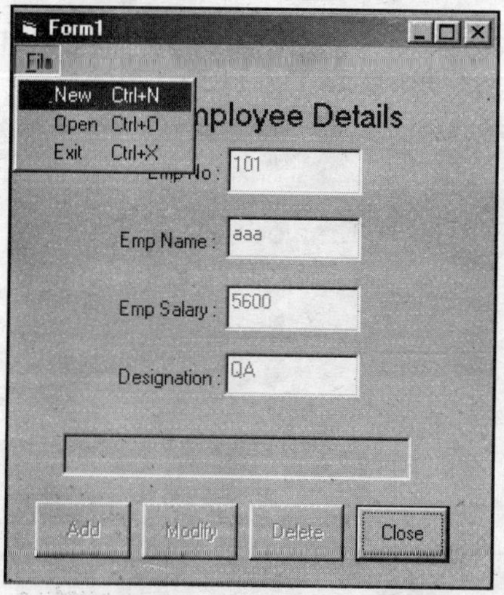

Fig. 11.33

Step 5: Once you click the "New" menu option, it displays a dialog where the Emp No. is automatically incremented and prompts you to enter the remaining details like Emp Name, Emp Salary, Designation as shown in Fig. 11.34.

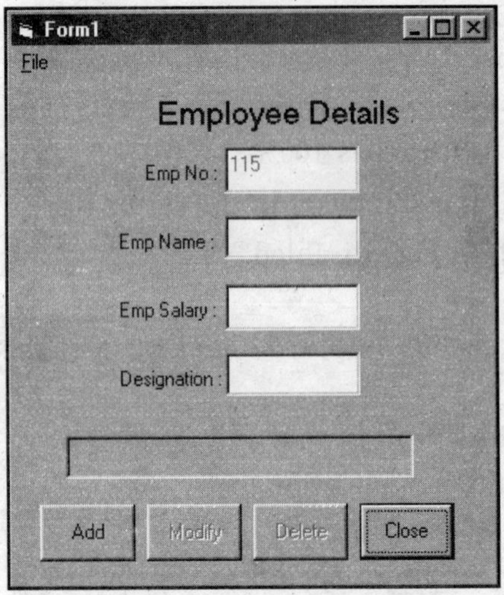
Form1
File
Employee Details
Emp No :
115
Emp Name :
Emp Salary :
Designation :
Add
Modify
Delete
Close

Fig. 11.34

Step 6: **After entering all the details, click on "Add" button to insert the record into the database as shown in Fig. 11.35.**

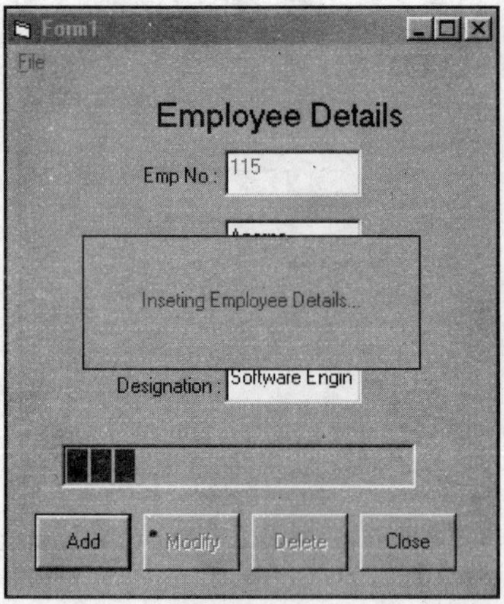
Form1
File
Employee Details
Emp No :
115
Inseting Employee Details...
Designation :
Software Engin
Add
Modify
Delete
Close

Fig. 11.35

Step 7: When the insertion is complete, "Insert Done" message appears on the status bar along with the"Add" button disabled, as shown in Fig. 11.36.

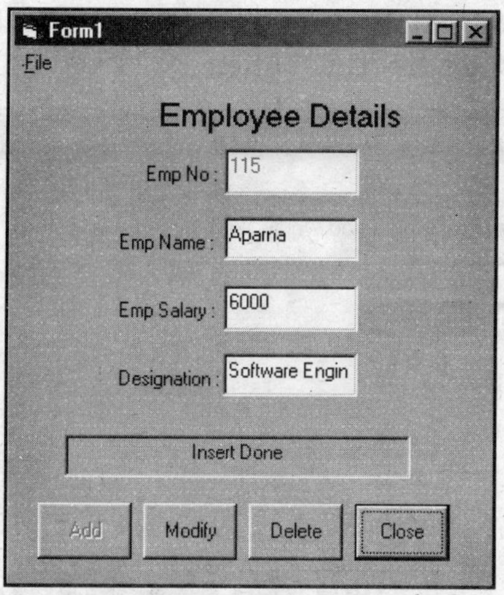

Fig. 11.36

Step 8: Select File → Exit and close the EmpDB application.

Step 9: Stop the recording process.

Step 10: Save the test script.

Step 11: Select the following line in the test script:

```
VbWindow("Forms1").VbButton("Add").Click
```

Step 12: Click the "Record" button to insert the Synchronization Point.

Step 13: Select Insert → Step → Synchronization Point as shown in Fig. 11.37.

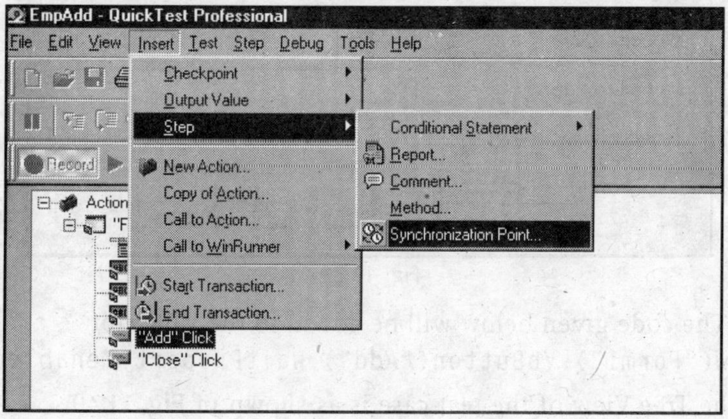

Fig. 11.37

Step 14: The Object Selection dialog is displayed as shown in Fig. 11.38. Select the object and click the "OK" button.

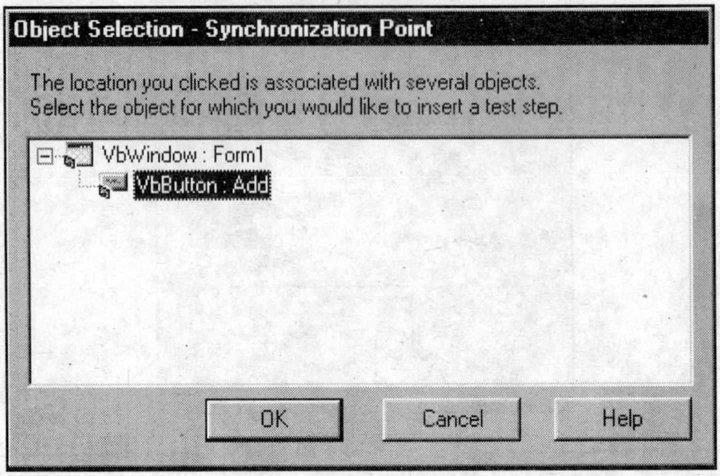

Object Selection - Synchronization Point

The location you clicked is associated with several objects.
Select the object for which you would like to insert a test step.

- VbWindow : Form1
  - VbButton : Add

OK   Cancel   Help

Fig. 11.38

Step 15: The "Add Synchronization Point" dialog appears which prompts you to enter the Property name, Property value, Timeout as shown in Fig. 11.39. Click the "OK" button.

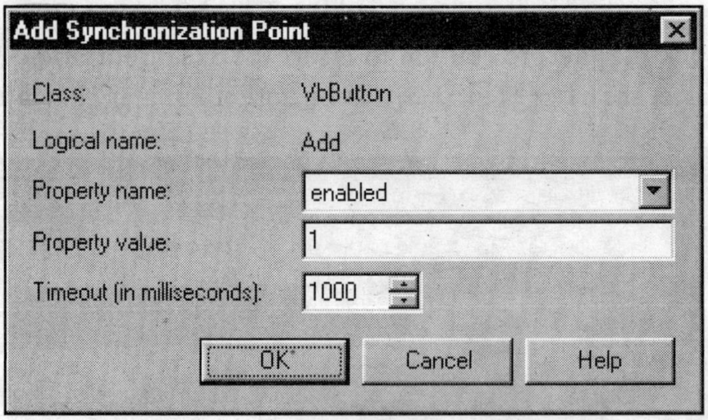

Add Synchronization Point

Class: VbButton
Logical name: Add
Property name: enabled
Property value: 1
Timeout (in milliseconds):   1000

OK   Cancel   Help

Fig. 11.39

Step 16: The code given below will be added to the VBScript.

```
VbWindow("Form1").VbButton("Add").WaitProperty"enabled", 1,  1000
```

The Tree View of the test case is as shown in Fig. 11.40.

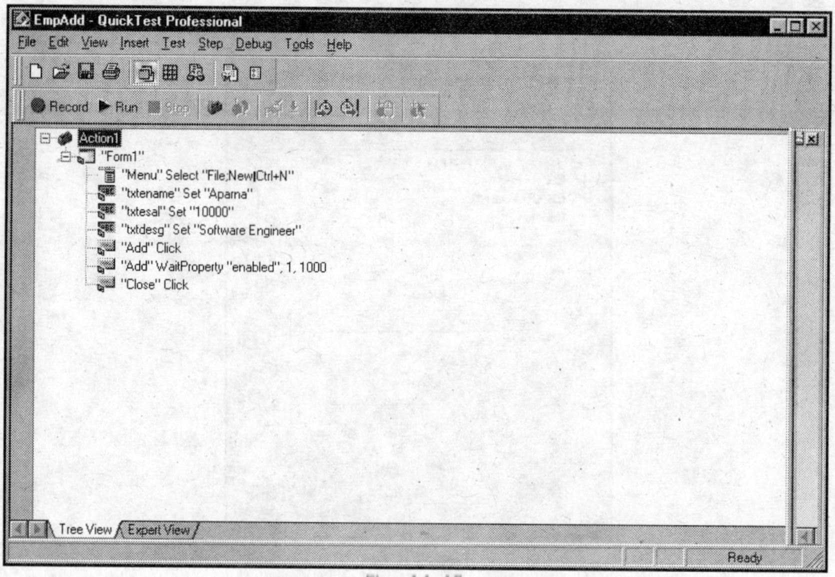

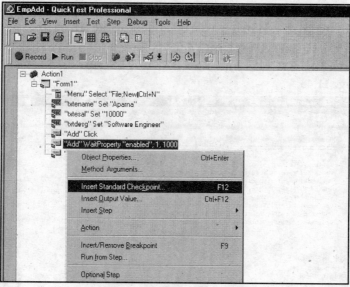

Fig. 11.40

Step 17: To create the Standard Checkpoint, right click on "Add" WaitProperty "enabled", 1, 1000 from the Tree View of the script and select "Insert Standard Checkpoint" option, as shown in Fig. 11.41.

Fig. 11.41

Step 18: The "Checkpoint Properties dialog" shown in Fig. 11.42 is displayed.

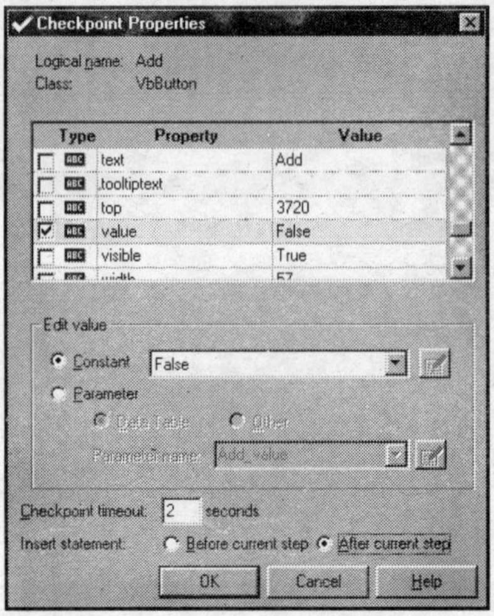

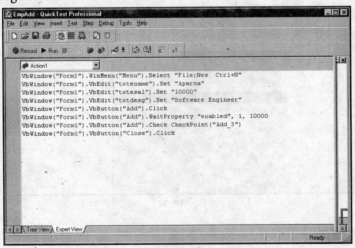

Fig. 11.42

We are creating the checkpoint on the "Add" button to check whether it is disabled after inserting a new record into the database.

- Select Property as "enabled" and the value as "false".
- Select the "Edit Value" as "Constant" and set it to "False".
- Check the "After current step" option and click on the "OK" button.

  The statement shown below will be added to the VBScript.

```
VbWindow("Form1").VbButton("Add").Check CheckPoint("Add_3")
```

Step 19: Save the test case and Run it. The VBScript of the test case is shown in Fig. 11.43.

Fig. 11.43

Step 20: The test results of the test case will be displayed in the Test Results window as shown in Fig. 11.44.

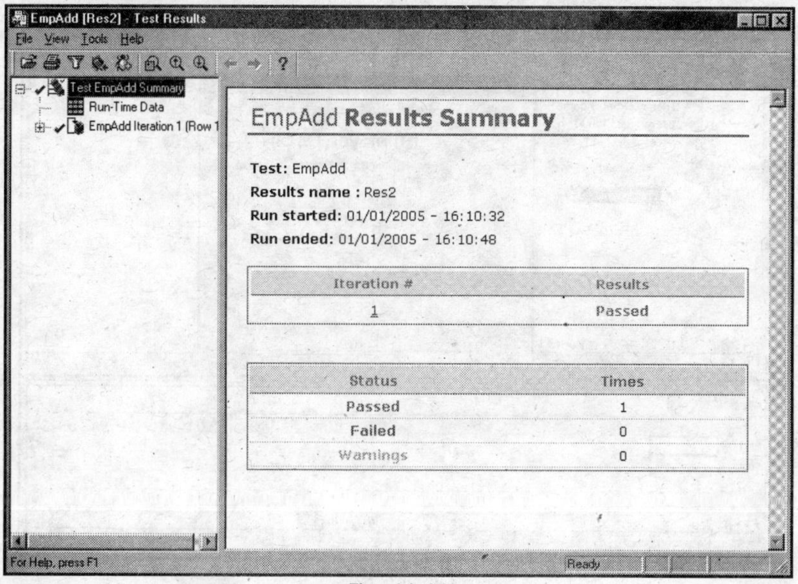

Fig. 11.44

11.4 Data Driven Testing

Once the test script is created, you may sometimes want to check how the test script behaves for multiple data. This can be done by creating that many number of test cases and by running each test case individually, which is a very tedious process. In such cases, we make use of Data-Driven Testing. This involves the following steps:

- Create the test case
- Parameterize the test case
- Provide the required data
- Run the test case

The procedure for creating a data driven test is as follows:

Step 1: Create a test case for inserting one record into the database, as explained in the previous section "Testing Database Application using Synchronization and Checkpoints", from steps 1 to 10 (Fig. 11.45).

Step 2: Stop the recording and save the test case.

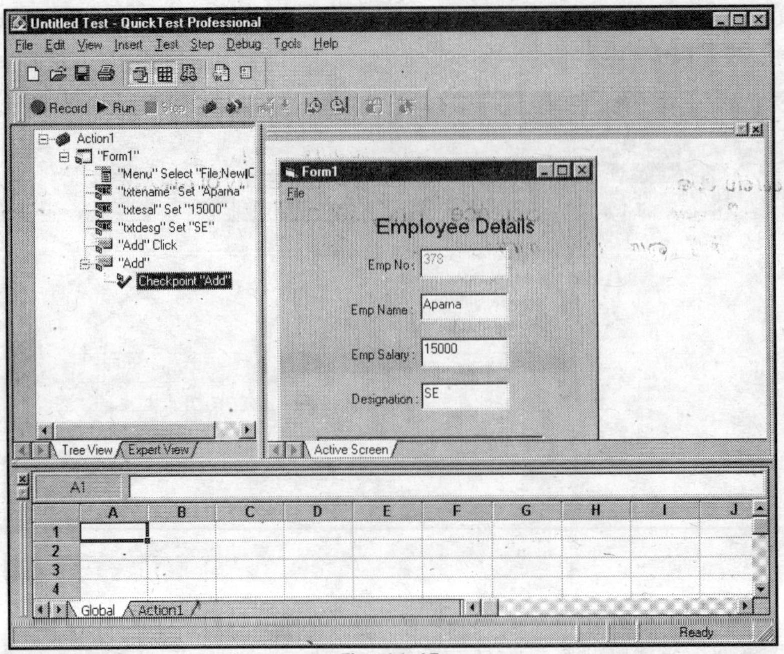

Fig. 11.45

Step 3: Change the Data Table column name that is to be used by the test case, as shown in Fig. 11.46, by double clicking on the column.

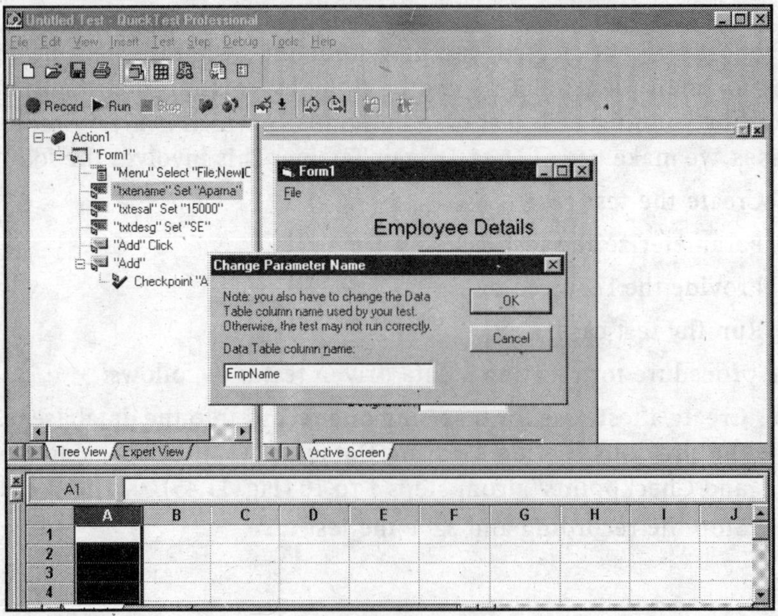

Fig. 11.46

Step 4: Specify Data table column names for all the fields by specifying the Data table column names and provide the required data, as shown in Fig. 11.47. Note that we would like to test the database application for different values of employee name, employee salary and designation.

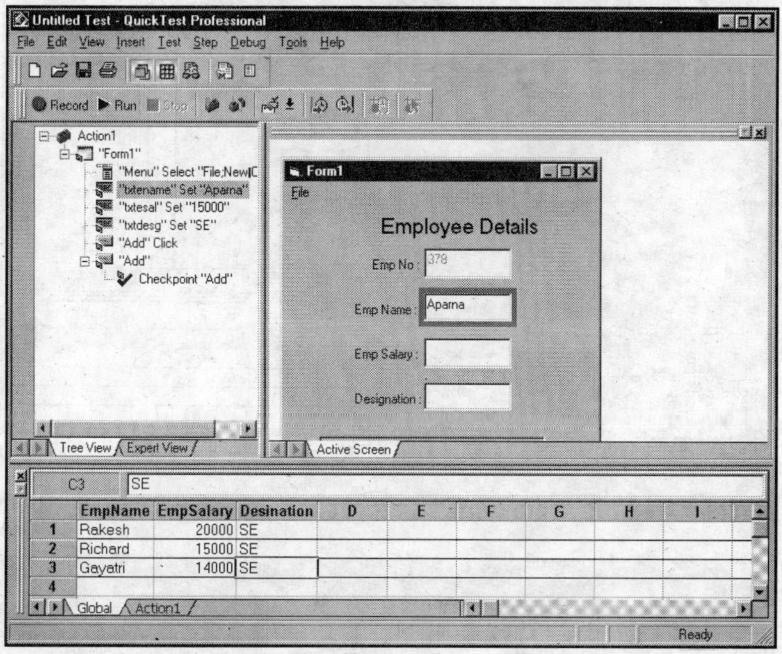

Fig. 11.47

Step 5: Parameterize the edit fields of the application to the Data table columns specified in the above step. To parameterize the fields do the following:

- Select the field in the Tree View
- Right click on it and select "Method Arguments" as shown in Fig. 11.48.

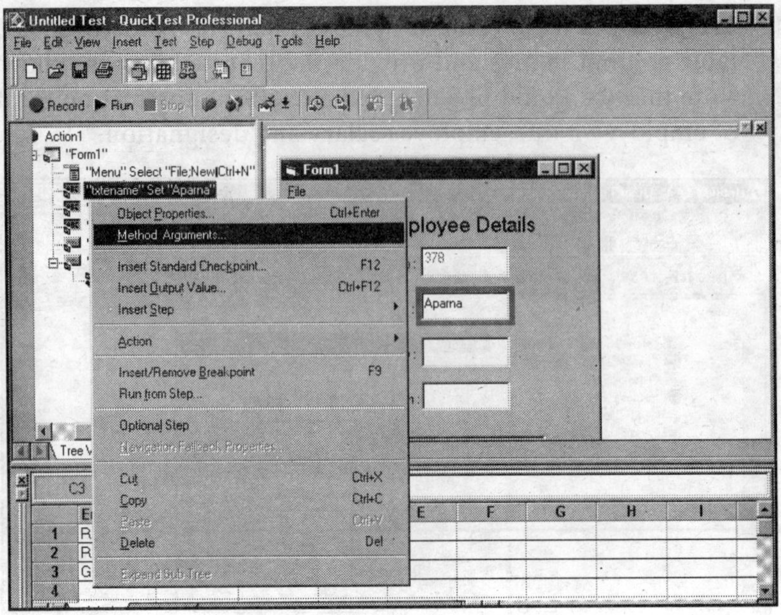

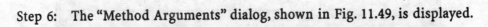

Fig. 11.48

Step 6: The "Method Arguments" dialog, shown in Fig. 11.49, is displayed.

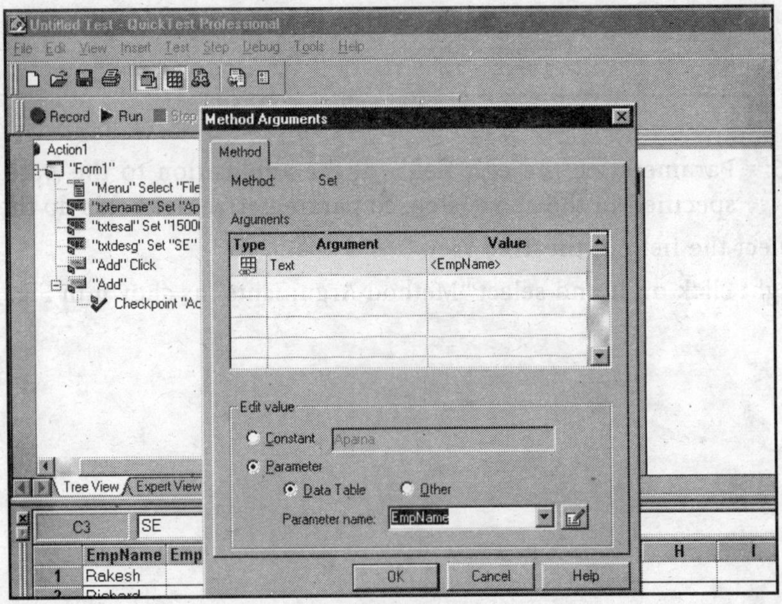

Fig. 11.49

- Select the "Edit value" as "Parameter" and "Data Table" for "Parameter". Since the first field in the Data Table is EmpName, select "EmpName" from the "Parameter name" list and click the "OK" button. Similarly parameterize all the fields in the application to the Data Table column names.

- Once all the fields are parameterized, the Tree View of the test will be, as shown in Fig. 11.50.

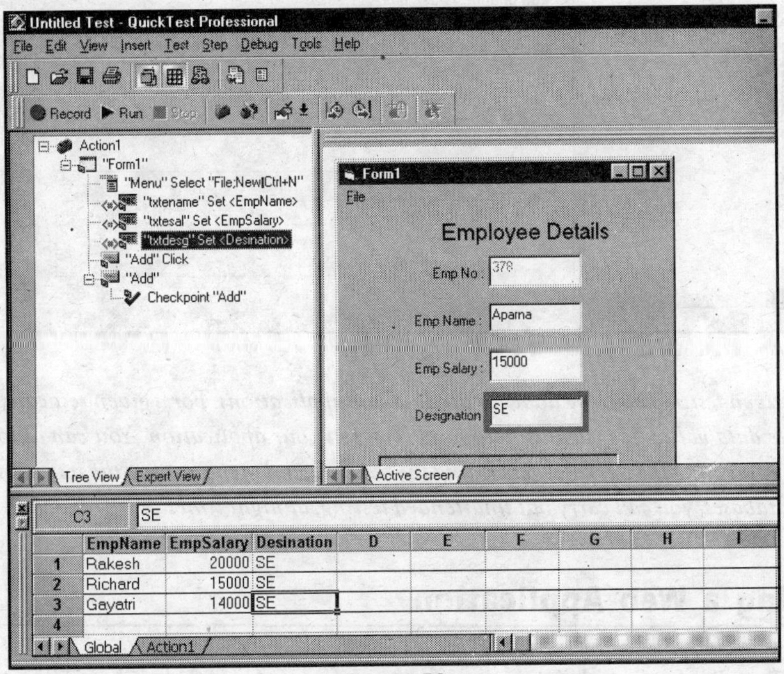

Fig. 11.50

Now the test case will take one row at a time from the data table and execute the test script. Finally it displays the test results for all the data driver records, as shown in Fig. 11.51.

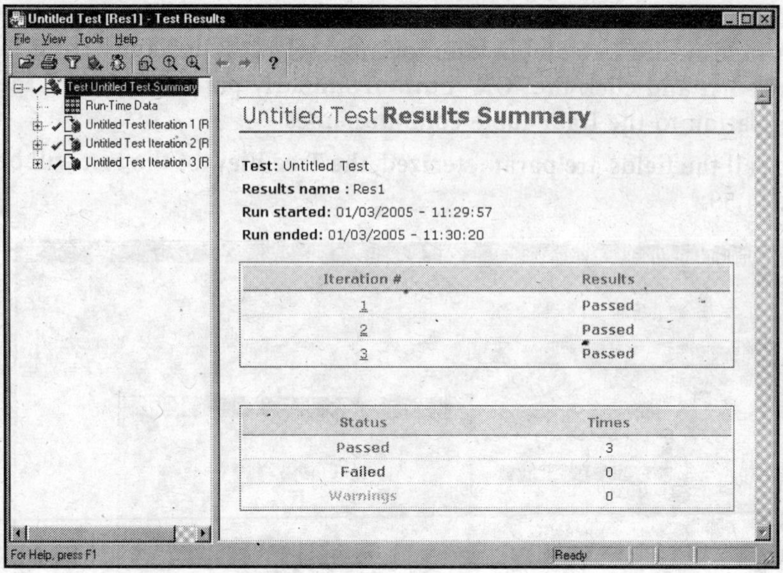

Fig. 11.51

Data-driven testing has to be done for all database applications. For a given test case, you need to give multiple data values for various fields and then test your application. You can automate the testing process by creating the test case, generating the test data and then running the test cases. For testing very large databases, you can carry out unattended testing, at night times

11.5 Testing a Web Application

QuickTest Professional is a powerful tool for testing the web applications. It allows you to test the number of links, number of images, load time, web buttons, web radio buttons, web tables etc. We will demonstrate how to test a web site using the Weather India web site.

Weather India web site is available on the CDROM that accompanies this book. The procedure for installing this application is given in Appendix E.

To check the number of links and the expected URLs, follow the steps given below.

Step 1: Open the Weather India application. The home page of the application is as shown in Fig. 11.52.

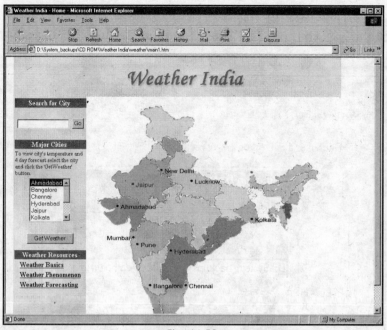

Fig. 11.52

Step 2: Open QuickTest Professional. The initial screen is as shown in Fig. 11.53.

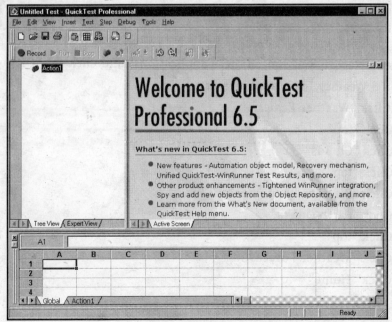

Fig. 11.53

Step 3: Start the Recording process.

- Click the button. The "Record and Run Settings" dialog, shown in Fig. 11.54, is displayed.

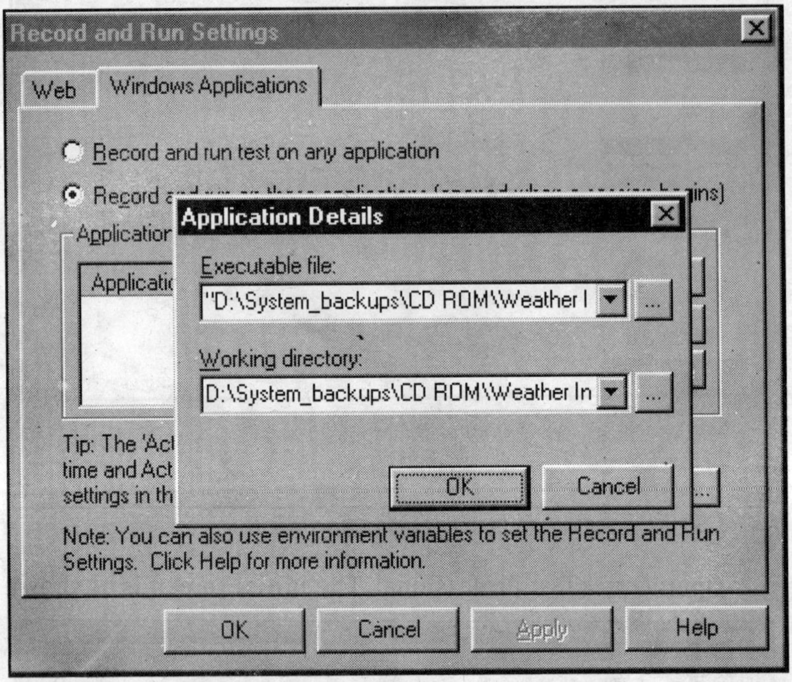

Record and Run Settings

| Web | Windows Applications |

○ Record and run test on any application

○ Record and run on these applications (opened when a session begins)

Application

Application Details

Executable file:

"D:\System_backups\CD ROM\Weather I ▼ ...

Working directory:

D:\System_backups\CD ROM\Weather In ▼ ...

OK   Cancel

Tip: The 'Act
time and Act
settings in th

Note: You can also use environment variables to set the Record and Run Settings. Click Help for more information.

OK   Cancel   Apply   Help

Fig. 11.54

- Select "Record and run on these applications" and click the "OK" button.
- In the Weather India application:
  - Click "Weather Basics"
  - Click "top"
  - Click "Clouds"
  - Click "top"
  - Click "Weather Phenomenon"
  - Click "Earth Quake"
  - Click "top"
  - Click "Weather Forecasting"
  - Click "Home"

Step 4:   Stop the recording process.

■ Stop the recording process by clicking on the ■ Stop button.

■ Save the test script.

Step 5:   **The Tree View of the test case is as shown in Fig. 11.55.**

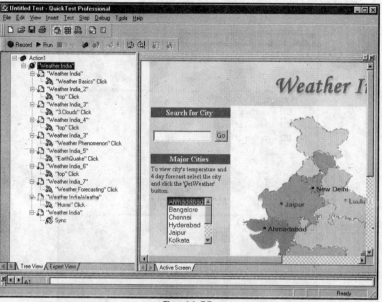

Fig. 11.55

Step 6:   To check the number of links and the expected URLs, double click on the
           ● "Weather India" image in the Tree View. It then displays the captured image
           on the right side of the window.

Step 7:   Right click on the image and select "Insert Standard Checkpoint" option. The
           "Object Selection: Checkpoint properties" dialog is displayed as seen in
           Fig. 11.56.

Fig. 11.56

Step 8:   Select the "Page: Weather India" and click the "OK" button. The "Page Checkpoint properties" dialog, as shown in Fig. 11.57, is displayed. By default all the options will be selected. Uncheck all, except the "number of links" checkbox.

It displays the number of links observed during the recording phase in the selected page.

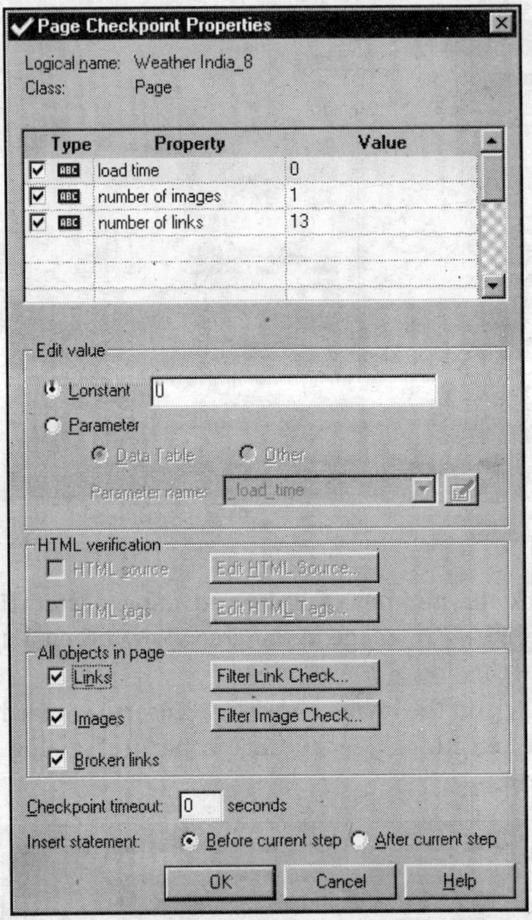

Fig. 11.57

- To change the number of links to the expected value, select the "Constant" option in "Edit value" and enter the expected number in the edit box that is provided.
- In the "All objects in the page" section, check the "Links" option and uncheck all others.
- Click on the "Filter Link Check" button. The "Filter Link Check" dialog is displayed as shown in Fig. 11.58.

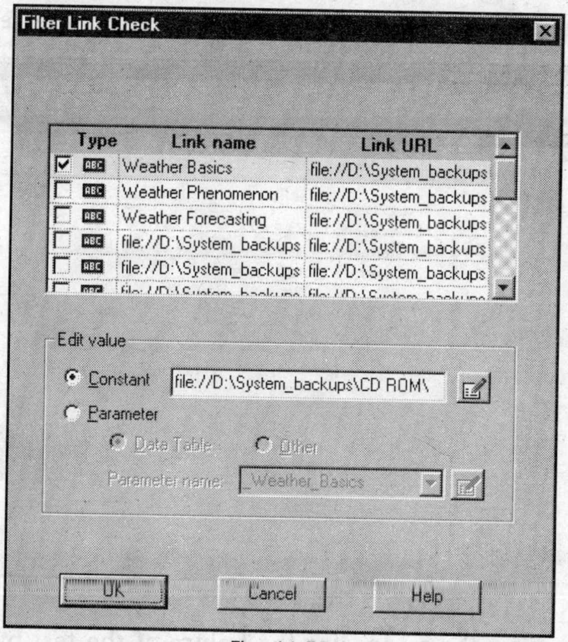

Fig. 11.58

- The Link name and the corresponding URL, recognized during the recording time, are displayed.

- Select the link, change the Link URL to the expected URL, and click the "OK" button.

- Check the required Link names. In our example, check only the "Weather Basics" link name and uncheck all others. Fig. 11.59 displays the test script generated during the recording process.

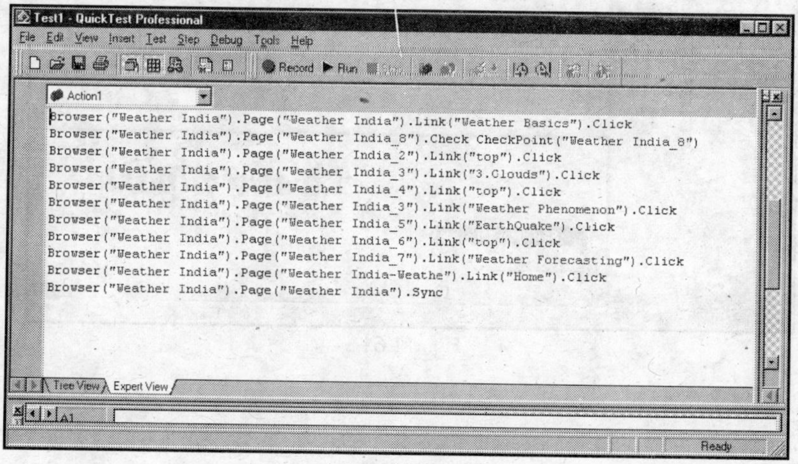

Fig. 11.59

Step 9: Save the test script and run it. Fig. 11.60 shows the Test Results window.

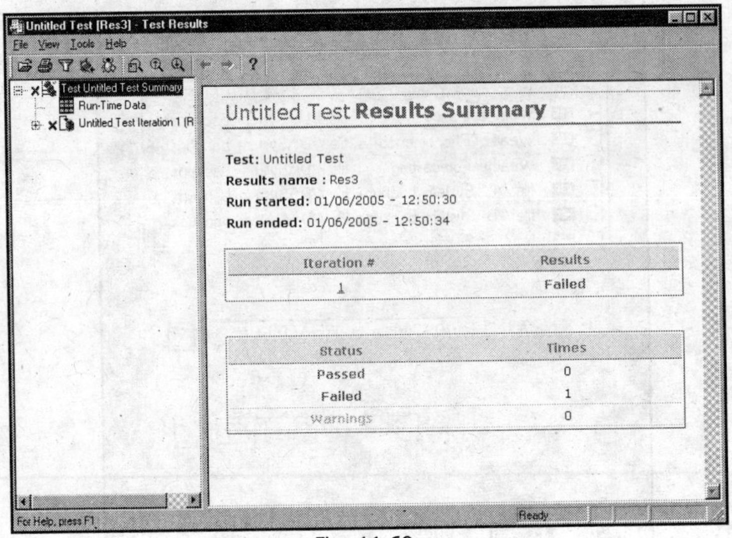

Fig. 11.60

Step 10: We can view the reason for the failure of the test by expanding the "Test1 Iteration 1" node in Tree View, as shown in Fig. 11.61. The test case failed because the expected URL is not same as the URL recognized during the recording phase.

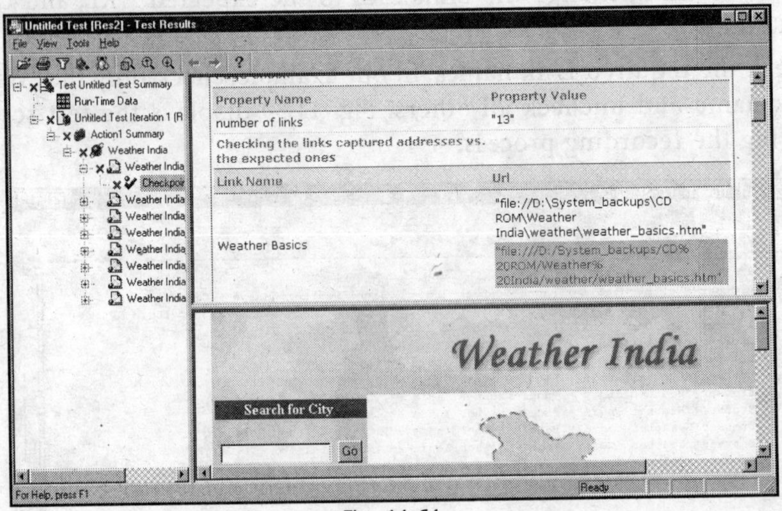

Fig. 11.61

Step 11: To edit the expected URL, right click on the checkpoint, as shown in Fig. 11.62.

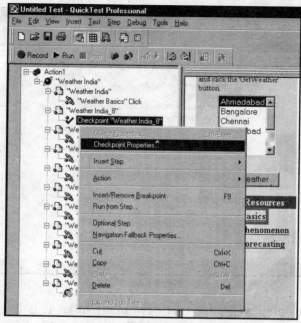

Fig. 11.62

Step 12: The "Filter Link Check" dialog, as shown in Fig. 11.63, is displayed. Uncheck all except the "Weather Basics" and edit the Link URL to the one specified below (replace the forward slashes with backward slashes).

```
file:///D:/System_backups/CD%20ROM/Weather%20India/weather/
weather_basics.htm
```

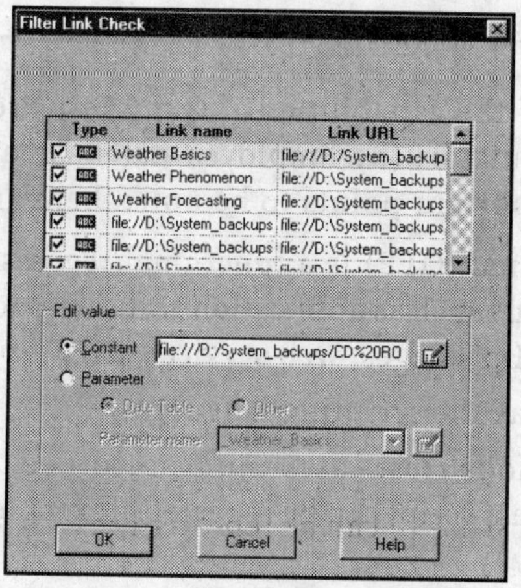

Fig. 11.63

Step 13: Save the test case and run it again. It then displays the Test Results window in which the test case is declared as 'Passed' (Fig. 11.64).

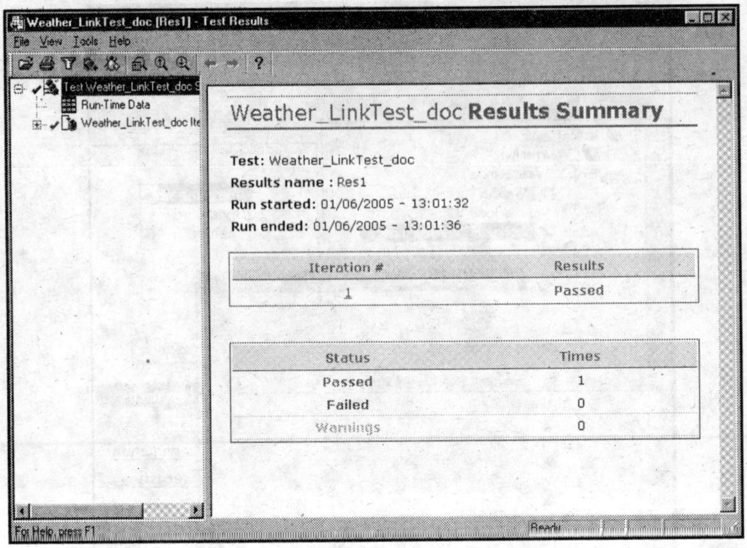

Fig. 11.64

While developing web sites that have many links, it is likely that you forget to provide all the links. Link test described here is very helpful for checking whether all the links are available.

You need to carry out load testing of the web sites also to test the performance. You can use load/ performance testing tools described in the previous chapters.

Summary

This chapter presented the capabilities of QuickTest Professional (QTP) using three case studies—(a) Calculator; (b) Employee database application and; (c) Weather India web site. The important points to be noted here are:

- QuickTest Professional (QTP) is a functional/regression testing tool for testing a variety of applications such as application software packages, database applications, web sites, ERP/CRM packages, web services, .NET applications etc.

- QTP uses VBScript as the scripting language.

- Using the 'record mode', test cases can be recorded. QTP automatically generates the test script. The test script can be repeatedly executed for carrying out regression testing.

- Using the data-driven testing feature, you can run a test case for different data values. This is very useful for testing database applications.

- The 'auto-documentation' feature of QTP facilitates automatic generation of test reports. The test report data is generated in XML format and hence the report data can be transferred to a third party tool or HTML web page can be created.

- QTP supports Unicode. So, applications written in languages such as Hindi, Japanese, Chinese etc. can also be tested.

- QTP can be integrated with testing management tools such as Test Director.

Acronyms and Abbreviations

4GL	4th Generation Language
ANSI	American National Standards Institute
ASCII	American Standard Code for Information Interchange
ATM	Any Time Money/Automatic Teller Machine
ATP	Acceptance Test Procedure (or Plan)
ATR	Acceptance Test Results
AUT	Application Under Test
BVA	Boundary Value Analysis
CASE	Computer Aided Software Engineering
CEO	Chief Executive Officer
CMM	Capability Maturity Model
CMMI	Capability Maturity Model Integration
COQ	Cost of Quality
CRM	Customer Relations Management
C/S	Client/Server
DBMS	Database Management System
DDT	Data Driven Test
DLL	Dynamic Linked Library
DoD	Department of Defense
DSN	Data Source Name
ECN	Engineering Change Note
ECR	Engineering Change Request
EIA	Electronic Industries Association

ERP	Enterprise Resource Planning
FTP	File Transfer Protocol
GNU	Gnu's is Not Unix
GNUCC	GNU Compiler Collection
GPL	GNU Public License
GUI	Graphical User Interface
HTML	Hyper Text Markup Language
HTTP	Hyper Text Transfer Protocol
IEC	International Electro-technical Commission
IPD	Integrated Product Development
IS	Interim Standard
ISO	International Organization for Standardization
IT	Information Technology
ITU-T	International Telecommunications Union-Telecommunications sector
JDBC	Java Database Connectivity
KPA	Key Process Area
LDAP	Light-weight Directory Access Protocol
MMS	Multimedia Messaging Service
MR	Management Representative
MTBF	Mean Time Between Failures
MTTF	Mean Time To Fail
MTTR	Mean Time To Repair
ODBC	Open Database Connectivity
OOA	Object Oriented Analysis
OOD	Object Oriented Design
OOP	Object Oriented Programming
OOT	Object Oriented Technology
OS	Operating System
PSP	Personal Software Process
PWS	Personal Web Server
QA	Quality Assurance

QMS	Quality Management System
RAD	Rapid Application Development
RCS	Revision Control System
RDBMS	Relational Database Management System
RTE	Remote Terminal Emulator
SCCB	Software Configuration Control Board
SCCS	Source Code Control System
SDLC	Software Development Life Cycle
SEI	Software Engineering Institute
SLO	Service Level Objectives
SMS	Short Messaging Service
SQA	Software Quality Assurance
SQL	Structured Query Language
SRS	Software Requirements Specifications
TQM	Total Quality Management
TSL	Test Script Language
UML	Unified Modeling Language
URL	Uniform Resource Locator
V & V	Verification and Validation
VB	Visual Basic
WML	Wireless Markup Language
XML	eXtensible Markup Language

Glossary of Testing and QA Terminology

Acceptance testing: Testing carried out by the client to accept the software. An acceptance test procedure is prepared by the QA team in association with the client and testing is carried out as per this procedure.

Accessibility testing: Testing carried out to ensure that the software can be used by the physically challenged persons.

Adaptive maintenance: To make changes in the software based on the client's request for modifications.

Ad hoc testing: Testing done without any defined process.

Application Programming Interface: Function calls provided by the software vendor to develop applications. For example, Java Media Framework (JMF) is a set of API calls to develop multimedia applications using Java programming language.

Application Under Test: The software package which is being tested.

Audit: To verify whether software development is being carried out as per a defined process. Auditing is done periodically (say, every three months) in software organizations. Internal auditing is done by the QA team. Auditing by external agencies periodically (every six or nine months) is compulsory for organizations having ISO 9000 or CMM certification.

Automated testing: Testing carried out with minimal manual intervention. Automated test tools discussed in this book help in carrying out tests automatically, though smart test engineers are still required to make best use of these tools.

Basic block: Portion of the software in which there are no branches.

Baseline: First version of a work product, after it has reached a mature stage. For example, the first matured version of SRS document is considered as a baseline document, though there are likely to be some changes. Any change to this baseline document has to be done through configuration management process.

Beta testing: Testing carried out on a software product at the user's site, in the absence of the development team. There were about 400,000 beta test sites for testing Windows 95 operating system.

Black box testing: Testing carried out to check the functionality of the software. The software is considered as a black box to which defined inputs are given and from which defined outputs are obtained. The implementation details are not taken into consideration while doing black box testing.

Boundary value analysis: Values that are on the boundary of equivalence classes are high yield test cases. Example: for (i=0; i <= 100; ++i) {statements}. In this code, i = 100 is a boundary value.

Bug: A colloquial term used to indicate defect in software. "Defect" is a more formal and accurate word. We use the words bug and defect interchangeably in this book.

Capability Maturity Model: A model developed by Software Engineering Institute, Carnegie Mellon University, to grade software development organizations based on their process maturity. An organization is given one of the 5 grades or levels: Level 1 to Level 5. Level 1 organizations do not follow any processes to develop software; they do everything on ad hoc basis. Level 5 organizations have very mature processes and continuously improve their processes to improve product quality. However, note that CMM levels indicate only the process quality and not product quality. A Level 1 organization may produce high quality product; Level 5 organizations may not deliver a high quality product.

Checklist: A list that is used to check whether the requirements are met. A design checklist is used to check whether the design meets all the design goals. A coding checklist is used to check whether the source code is written as per the coding guidelines, whether there are no unused variables etc. Checklists are very useful in verification of the different work products.

Classification of defects: Based on the severity of the defect, defect classification is done. Defects are classified as minor, major, and critical. For example, a minor defect is a spelling mistake in a message box, a major defect results in some portions of the software unusable and a critical defect may result in a system crash.

Co-design: The process of hardware-software partitioning. When you have to build a system that consists of both hardware and software, it is necessary to identify which portions have to be implemented in hardware and which portions in software. This is known as co-design. Co-design has to be done keeping in view the speed of execution, production cost, flexibility etc. Hardware implementation is faster, but costlier; software implementation is flexible but slower.

Code walkthrough: To review the software source code line by line by a team of developers/test engineers.

Coding metrics: Measures used to quantify the source code. Number of lines in the source code, ratio of number of source lines to number of commented lines, number of function points, number of defects found per 1000 lines of code etc. are some coding metrics.

Coding standards: Every organization will develop a set of coding standards to be followed by all development engineers. These standards specify how to name the variables, functions, methods, classes etc., how to name project files, what information has to be given at the top of each source code file such as copyright information, online documentation regarding the functionality of the module etc. Coding standards are developed for each programming language (C, C++, Java etc.) and each markup language (HTML, XML, XHTML etc.) separately.

Compatibility testing: Testing carried out to ensure the compatibility of an application or web site with different hardware platforms, different operating systems and different browsers.

Configuration management: A systematic procedure to make changes to any work product such as the SRS, design document, source code.

Conformance testing: Testing carried out to ensure that the application conforms to a standard—an international/national standard or industry standard.

Corrective maintenance: To remove the defects reported by the client.

Cost of quality: Quality does not come free—you have to put in the required effort (or cost). According to Watts Humphrey, the three principal elements of cost of quality are: failure cost, appraisal cost, and prevention cost. Failure cost is the cost of fixing the bugs. Appraisal cost is the cost of assessing the product to check if it has defects. Prevention cost is the cost of modifying the process to avoid defects.

Co-verification: The process of finding out whether the bug is in hardware or software. In many projects which involve both hardware and software development, the hardware engineers and software engineers blame each other if the system does not work. Co-verification process helps in systematically integrating the hardware and software and then carrying out the testing.

Customized software: Software developed as per the specific requirements of a customer. Contrast with generic product.

Defect: A software bug. A more formal word as compared to bug.

Defect density: Number of defects per 1000 lines of code.

Defensive programming: Defensive programming is a technique used to ensure that the software does not fail even if wrong inputs are given. Making use of exception handling features of programming languages, defensive programming can be done. However, this is a challenging task because the developer has to foresee all possible inputs likely to be given for the allowed input and write the code in such a way that for all wrong inputs, the software gives appropriate error messages but never crashes.

Design phase: In the design phase, the architecture of the software is worked out. It involves identification of various modules, algorithms, data structures etc. and documenting the design.

Development life cycle models: The models used for developing software. Depending on the type of the project, the life cycle model needs to be chosen. For commercial projects with clear SRS, waterfall model is the best choice. If the client is not IT-literate and the requirements are not clear, prototyping model is a good choice. For research projects, evolutionary development model is the right choice. For projects involving high risk, the spiral model is to be chosen. To develop innovative products in very short time, synchronize-and-stabilize model is used.

Equivalence class partitioning: A method used for selecting the test cases. To test a software product, all possible valid inputs and valid outputs are identified. The test cases are chosen from two types of classes: valid inputs and invalid inputs.

Engineering Change Request: Whenever a change has to be made to a work product (SRS, design document, source code etc.), an engineering change request is sent by the person. This request is analyzed and approved/rejected by the project manager, after discussions with all the persons concerned.

Evolutionary development model: In this model of software development, software is developed in stages. Based on the initial requirements given by the client, the software is developed and demonstrated. Then, the client gives additional requirements and the software is further upgraded. This process is continued till the client is satisfied with the software product. This is a good model for research projects; not for commercial projects.

Exhaustive testing: Testing carried out by giving all possible inputs. Exhaustive testing is very time consuming, and is impossible to do for many large software projects.

Field trial: Testing performed in the actual working environment before releasing the software to the client. The development team conducts the field trial to observe the performance of the software in real environment.

Functional testing: The testing carried out to check the functionality of the product. In functional testing, the inputs and outputs are considered without bothering about the software implementation (or coding) details.

Gantt (bar) chart: The chart used to monitor the progress of a project. This chart gives the various activities of the project and the start and end dates of each activity.

Generic product: A software package that can be sold to a number of customers. Operating Systems (Windows, Unix, Solaris etc.), database management engines (MS Access, Oracle, Sybase etc.) and anti-virus software fall under this category. Contrast it with customized software.

Gorilla testing: Gorilla testing is used to test the GUI of a software package. Assume that the software is given to a Gorilla, what does it do? It presses the keys randomly! While you are testing GUI (particularly for games software), this type of testing is very useful.

GUI objects: The various GUI objects are static objects (rectangle, oval, lines etc.), check boxes (yes/no boxes), combo boxes (pop up list with a field for entering data), current row pointers, list boxes (list of scrolling items for selection), menus and menu bars, pop up lists (list of items for selection), push buttons, radio buttons, radio button frames, scroll bars (vertical and horizontal), static text, text field for entering data, tool bars, status lines etc.

Integration testing: Testing carried out while combining different modules of a software package. Each module is tested separately and then modules are integrated and testing is carried out. This is a much better approach than trying to combine all modules in one shot and carrying out the testing, because debugging is easier by incrementally building the software.

Load testing: Load testing is a generic name for performance testing and stress testing.

Lines of code (LOC): The number of source code lines in a software package. Generally, the comments are excluded from the count. An equivalent measure is Delivered Source Instructions or Kilo Delivered Source Instructions. Note that the LOC count varies from organization to organization. The statements for (i =0; i< 100; ++i) { sum+= i} can be counted as 4 lines or 2 lines or just 1 line, depending on how you actually type the code.

Metric: Measure. Software 'metrics' are used to estimate the project complexity as well as to measure the productivity of the developers and test engineers. If you want to manage effectively, you need to use metrics.

Module testing: Module is an independent entity in the software. For example, in a DBMS package, database is one module and GUI is another module. Each module is tested separately and then integration is carried out. For example, database can be tested independently by giving SQL commands and then, it can be integrated with the GUI and testing can be done.

Non-functional requirements: The non-functional requirements of a software product are: reliability, portability, usability, efficiency, delivery time, hardware/software development environment, safety requirements, security requirements, standards to be followed etc.

Object-Oriented Technology (OOT): OOT is based on the concept that real world objects can be represented as 'objects' in a programming language. Example: In banking software, an account holder is an object with different attributes. A bank account is an object. Object-oriented analysis (OOA) and Object- oriented design (OOD) are carried out during requirements and design phases and an Object-Oriented Programming (OOP) language is used for implementation. All modern languages such as C++ and Java use OOT.

Open source software: A revolutionary concept in software development. The source code is freely distributed by the author, and it can be redistributed without any license fee. You can study the terms of GPL to understand the finer details.

Outsourcing: Sub-contracting of specialized work. Many organizations in developed countries are now outsourcing their software development and maintenance work to software companies located in developing countries. Outsourcing of testing services is now catching up very fast.

Peer review: Reviews carried out by peers or persons at the same level in the hierarchy. Peer reviews are done during design stage, coding stage, and testing stage. Peer reviews help in improving the product quality.

People Capability Maturity Model: The model developed at SEI, CMU to measure and improve the human resources development practices. Organizations are graded from Level 1 to Level 5 to measure the effectiveness of human resources development practices.

Performance testing: Testing carried out for normal, peak and exceptional load conditions. For example, a Client/Server application is checked for a number of simultaneous database operations.

Person month: If one person works for one month, the effort is one person month. A person month is equivalent to about 154 hours of effort (22 days at the rate of 7 hours per day). The effort required for execution of a project is measured in person months. Also, the testing effort is measured in person months.

Personal Software Process (PSP): PSP was developed by Watts Humphrey of SEI, CMU. PSP gives a set of guidelines to be followed by software engineers to produce quality software. The philosophy of PSP is simple: plan your work, track your work and analyze the work done so that you can continuously improve your performance and productivity.

Portability: The ease with which a software package can be transferred from one platform to another platform. For example, a software package that runs on Windows NT can be transferred to Unix machine, without changes, the software is said to be portable. Java programming language facilitates portability as Java is a platform independent language.

Postmortem analysis: Analysis carried out after completion of the project, to find out what went well and what went wrong. The postmortem analysis helps in process improvement. After all, we need to learn from history, more so from our past mistakes.

Preventive maintenance: To make changes in the software anticipating some defects in a particular environment.

Process: Step-by-step procedure to convert raw material into a finished product.

Process Area: In CMM and CMMI, an organization is graded based on the processes being followed for software development. These grades are known as Levels. At each level, a number of process areas are defined. An organization has to implement all the process areas of Level 2 and then go on to the next Levels, one level at a time.

Process quality: The quality of a process is measured using metrics such as the number of changes made to the SRS document, the number of design changes made, the number of defects found during the system testing and acceptance testing phases etc.

Product quality: The quality of a product is measured using metrics such as MTBF, number of defects found after the product is delivered to the customer etc.

Prototyping model: One of the software development life cycle models. In this model, a prototype is developed and demonstrated to the client/user. Based on the feedback, the SRS document is prepared and the actual software development is taken up. This model is used when the client is not IT-literate and has no clear idea of what the software is supposed to do.

Quality manual: The document that contains the complete description of the processes to be followed for development. The auditors carry out the audit using the quality manual as the reference.

Quality standards: Standards defined by international bodies for process improvement. ISO 9000 and CMMI are the two international quality standards widely used in software development organizations.

Regression testing: Testing carried out to ensure that modifications to one portion of software have no bad effects on other portions of the software. Whenever some changes are done to even a small portion of the software, regression testing is done. Test cases are generated for carrying out regression testing. Each new release of software also has to undergo regression testing to ensure consistent performance.

Reliability: Reliability of software is measured in terms of Mean Time Between Failures (MTBF). For example, if the MTBF value is 10,000 hours; on an average, the software should not fail for 10,000 hours of continuous operation. To measure reliability, the software has to be tested very rigorously and automated test tools come in handy.

Rendezvous points: To do performance testing of an application, the testing tool creates a situation where multiple virtual users perform an operation (such as accessing a database) simultaneously, exactly at the same time. Such points are called rendezvous points. Rendezvous means meeting or coming together, in Greek.

Requirements engineering: The first phase in software development process. During requirements engineering phase, the vague problem definition given by the user/client is converted into a software requirements specifications document. This involves studying the existing manual/semi-automatic system, interviewing the end users/client, and converting the requirements into a document and getting the document approved by the client.

Risk: An uncertain outcome. Every software project is associated with some risks such as persons leaving in the middle of the project, ever-changing user requirements, unrealistic time frames etc. But then, the first business lesson we learn is "profit is the reward for risk taking". So, if you want to make money, you got to take risks.

Risk management: Risk management involves identifying the possible risks and taking preventive/corrective action to overcome the impact of such risks. For example, people leaving in the middle of a project is a risk item. The project manager has to work out methods to overcome its effect, by taking a bond, or by keeping backup personnel on the project etc.

Scripting languages: Scripting languages are based on component framework. For example, various windows, menus, control buttons etc can be considered as components. To develop an application, the components have to be glued together. Scripting languages help in faster development of code. VBScript, JavaScript, UNIX shell script etc. are examples of scripting languages. Testing tool vendors also provide proprietary scripting languages using which test cases can be generated very easily. TSL, 4Test and SQABasic are examples of such scripting languages.

Smoke test: Testing carried out to check the major functionality of the software without concern for finer details. The phrase is borrowed from hardware testing—if the hardware is up and running, and does not catch fire, the hardware has passed the smoke test. This testing is also referred as "quick and dirty testing" and Level 1 testing.

Software engineering: Systematic development of software. As per IEEE standards, software engineering is "the application of systematic, quantitative approach to the development, operation and maintenance of software i.e., the application of engineering to software".

Software process: The step-by-step procedure to convert a problem definition into a working software product. This procedure is divided into different stages such as requirements engineering, design, coding, testing and maintenance.

Spiral model: One of the software development life cycle models. This model is used for projects that involve very high risk. The development is divided into a number of phases, and at each phase, the milestones are defined. At the end of each phase, the risk associated with further development is evaluated and a decision is taken as to continue the project or drop it.

Software Requirements Specifications: A document that captures the requirements of the proposed software. After a series of discussions with the client or end users, the development team prepares the document and then gets it validated by the client. SRS document acts as the reference for all subsequent activities in software development. The test engineers need to carry out the testing taking SRS as the reference.

Standard: British Standards Institute defines standard as "a technical specification or other document available to the public, drawn up with cooperation and consensus or general approval of all interests affected by it, based on the consolidated results of science, technology and experience, aimed at the promotion of optimum community benefits". A "standard" definition of standard.

Stress testing: Testing done at or beyond the limits of specified requirements of performance, to check where the software fails. A graceful degradation of the software is desirable. The process of performing the stress testing is same as that of performance testing, but under higher load conditions.

Structural testing: Structural testing is used to test the implementation of the program. Here, source code is looked into for testing the software. The test cases are generated in such a way that each and every line of the code is tested.

Synchronize-and-stabilize model: One of the software development life cycle models. This model is used for innovative product development. To start with, a draft requirements document is prepared and development teams work in parallel on different modules. Periodically, these modules are integrated and tested. Based on the test reports, the software is again modified and integrated. The advantage of this model is that the software will be a feature-rich product but the specifications are available only on completion of the project.

System testing: After all the modules are combined together, testing carried out on the total system (or software) is called system testing. System testing is done after integration testing and before acceptance testing. Functional testing and performance testing are done during system testing.

Test cases: A set of input parameters for which the software will be tested. Test cases are selected in such a way that the bugs can be uncovered in the software. Generation of test cases is the most challenging task for the test engineers.

Test plan: A document that gives a detailed plan for the testing process. This document covers the test setup (hardware and software tools required), test engineers and their responsibilities, types of testing to be carried out, schedule for different types of tests, test cases to be used, defect report format, defect tracking mechanism etc.

"Trust, but Verify": The famous words of Ronald Reagan after signing the ballistic missile treaty with erstwhile USSR. All test engineers have to remember these words when the developers say that their software is 'perfect'!

Unit testing: Unit is the smallest piece of source code that can be independently tested. Only when unit testing is done, the units are combined into modules and module testing is carried out.

Validation: Validation is to check whether the software meets the customer expectations. It answers the question: are we building the right product?

Valid test cases: A set of test cases is called valid if at least one test case reveals the errors.

Verification: Verification is to check whether the software conforms to the specifications.

It answers the question: are we building the product right?

Version and release control: It is likely that a software product may be released first with some features and subsequently it is enhanced with more features. Whenever, a new version is released, the source code corresponding to all the versions need to be organized properly by the development team. Configuration management tools are used to do this.

Virtual users: To test the performance of an application when multiple users access the application (database or a web site), the actions of multiple users can be simulated on a single machine. Hence, instead of real users, 'virtual' users access the application through test scripts generated by the testing tool.

Waterfall model: The most widely used software development life cycle model for commercial projects. In this model, the development is divided into five stages: requirements specifications, system design and software design, implementation and unit testing, integration and system testing, and operation and maintenance.

White box testing: Testing carried out taking into consideration the implementation details. White-box testing is done to ensure that each and every line of the code is tested.

Work product: The various documents generated during the software development. Project plan document, SRS, design document, QA plan, test plan, acceptance test procedure, test results, source code, user manual, maintenance manual are the important work products to be generated in a software development project.

Review Questions

1. "Software engineering" is applicable to (a) generic software product development only (b) customized software development only (c) both generic product development and customized software development.

2. "Because of the 30 years of research in software engineering, now software projects are managed and executed perfectly." (a) true (b) false.

3. Software engineering addresses (a) development issues of software (b) operational issues of software (c) maintenance issues of software (d) all of the above.

4. Software engineering addresses (a) technical processes (b) managerial processes (c) both technical and managerial processes.

5. Ariane 5 disaster teaches us that (a) we should not take up risky projects (b) one line of code can create a disaster (c) large projects are always mis-managed (d) all of the above.

6. Quality software can be developed only when each and every engineer and manager is committed to quality (a) true (b) false.

7. Quality of a product is reflected in its (a) operational characteristics (b) transition characteristics (c) revision characteristics (d) all of the above.

8. With reference to quality triangle, usability of software is (a) operational characteristic (b) transition characteristic (c) revision characteristic.

9. With reference to quality triangle, reliability is (a) operational characteristic (b) transition characteristic (c) revision characteristic (d) none of the above.

10. Safety of software is (a) operational characteristic (b) transition characteristic (c) revision characteristic.

11. Security of software is (a) operational characteristic (b) transition characteristic (c) revision characteristic.

12. Testability of software is (a) operational characteristic (b) transition characteristic (c) revision characteristic.

13. Scalability of software is (a) operational characteristic (b) transition characteristic (c) revision characteristic.

14. Modularity of software is (a) operational characteristic (b) transition characteristic (c) revision characteristic (d) none of the above.

15. Flexibility of software is (a) operational characteristic (b) transition characteristic (c) revision characteristic.

16. Portability of software is (a) operational characteristic (b) transition characteristic (c) revision characteristic.

17. Reusability of software is (a) operational characteristic (b) transition characteristic (c) revision characteristic.

18. Interoperability of software is (a) operational characteristic (b) transition characteristic (c) revision characteristic.

19. A project can be considered successful if (a) quality software product is delivered (b) project is completed within the timeframe (c) project is completed within the budget (d) all of the above.

20. The output of requirements engineering phase is (a) draft SRS document (b) validated SRS document (c) design document (d) none of the above.

21. Depending on the type of the project, the software development life cycle model has to be chosen (a) true (b) false.

22. For commercial projects with clear SRS, which is the best development life cycle model? (a) waterfall model (b) prototyping model (c) spiral model (d) synchronize-and-stabilize model.

23. In waterfall model, at the end of every stage, there will be a visible output. (a) true (b) false.

24. Prototyping model is used to obtain the requirements from the client, particularly when the client is not IT-literate. (a) true (b) false.

25. Spiral model is used for development if the project (a) has clear SRS (b) involves lot of risk (c) is a long-term research project (d) has no end goal.

26. Synchronize-and-stabilize model is used for developing innovative products with tight schedules. (a) true (b) false.

27. For research projects, which is the best development life cycle model: (a) waterfall model (b) evolutionary development model (c) prototyping model.

28. Lines of code is used to (a) measure the size/complexity of the project (b) estimated the effort (c) estimate the budget (d) all of the above.

29. Assuming 154 hours as the average work time in a month per person, if 2 persons work for 2 months on a project, total effort in person hours is (a) 8 hours (b) 308 hours (c) 616 hours (d) 4 hours.

30. A project can be classified as small, medium or large based on the total number of lines of code. (a) true (b) false.

31. Which of the following is a productivity metric: (a) number of hours spent in the office (b) total number of lines of code developed during the entire project period

(c) number of lines of code written per hour, on an average (d) All of the above.

32. A test engineer's productivity can be measured by the following metric: (a) number of hours spent on testing (b) number of bugs detected per hour on an average (c) total time spent in review meetings (d) all of the above.

33. Which of the following metrics reflects the quality of a product (a) Mean Time Between Failures (b) Number of defects found after the product is delivered to the client (c) number of defects per 1000 lines of code (d) all of the above.

34. Non-functional requirements are not a part of Software Requirements specifications. (a) true (b) false.

35. Reliability of a product is reflected by which metric: (a) Mean Time Between Failures (b) no. of lines of code (c) no. of comments per 1000 lines of code (d) no. of people who worked on the development.

36. SRS document should be kept under configuration management (a) true (b) false.

37. Software design involves (a) identification of algorithms (b) identification of data structures (c) designing of user interface (d) all of the above.

38. The metric "number of lines of code" can differ from organization to organization. (a) true (b) false.

39. Process quality is measured by (a) the number of changes in the SRS document (b) number of defects reported after the software is delivered (c) number of changes made to the design document (d) all of the above.

40. Validation and verification are one and the same. (a) true (b) false.

41. It is advisable to get the software tested by a team other than the development team. (a) true (b) false.

42. Which of the following tests is done by the client (a) integration testing (b) system testing (c) acceptance testing (d) regression testing.

43. Black box testing is done to test each and every line of code (a) true (b) false.

44. White box testing can be done to ensure that each and every line is tested. (a) true (b) false.

45. Regression testing is done whenever changes are made to the software (a) true (b) false.

46. When is testing complete: (a) when you run out of time (b) when you run out of budget (c) when the number of bugs is less than a threshold for a defined period of time.

47. MTBF, MTTR and MTTF are indicators of reliability (a) true (b) false.

48. Software maintenance involves (a) preventive maintenance (b) adaptive maintenance (c) corrective maintenance (d) all of the above.

49. After the software is released to the client, if the client asks for any modifications (a) only the source code needs to be modified. (b) all documents such as SRS, design document, etc need to be modified in addition to the source code.

50. Whenever a change is proposed in any of the work products, the change has to be analyzed for (a) impact on budget (b) impact on time frame (c) impact on the existing design (d) all of the above.

51. If a software project requires 4 people to work for 2 months and then 6 persons for another 6 months, the total effort in Person Months is (a) 80 (b) 44 (c) 8 (d) 10

52. ISO 9000 Quality Management System can be applied to (a) services industries (b) software development organizations (c) hardware development organizations (d) all of the above.

53. Every ISO 9000 certified organization should have a quality policy (a) true (b) false.

54. Quality policy reflects the management's commitment to quality (a) true (b) false.

55. ISO 9000 focuses on continuous process improvement (a) true (b) false.

56. Capability Maturity Model (CMM) addresses (a) hardware quality management (b) software quality management (c) both hardware and software quality management (d) none of the above.

57. Configuration management is a key process area in CMM (a) true (b) false.

58. Process quality metrics and product quality metrics are one and the same. (a) true (b) false.

59. In CMMI framework, there are two representations (i) staged representation and (ii) continuous representation. (a) true (b) false.

60. ISO 9000/CMM focus on (a) defining a process which can never be changed later on (b) defining a process which has to be continuously improved.

61. CMMI level 1 organizations have no defined processes for software development (a) true (b) false.

62. Validation and verification are Process Areas in CMMI (a) true (b) false.

63. Causal analysis and resolution is a process area in CMMI level 5. (a) true (b) false.

64. You can detect many bugs in the software if you follow the definition (a) "testing is a process to prove that the software works correctly" (b) "testing is a process to prove that the software does not work correctly".

65. Validation is to check whether the software meets the customer requirements (a) true (b) false.

66. Verification is to check whether the software conforms to the specifications (a) true (b) false.

67. Unit testing is done to test (a) source code (b) design (c) SRS (d) conformance to specifications.

68. Integration testing is done to test (a) source code (b) design (c) SRS (d) conformance to specifications.

69. System testing is done to test (a) source code (b) design (c) SRS (d) conformance to specifications.

70. Acceptance testing is done to test (a) source code (b) design (c) SRS (d) conformance to user requirements.

71. Structural testing is done to test (a) functionality of the product (b) source code (c) performance of the software (d) all of the above.

72. Structural testing is done for (a) statement coverage (b) branch coverage (c) path coverage (d) all of the above.

73. Regression testing is to re-test the software whenever changes are made to the source code (a) true (b) false.

74. Beta' testing is done at (a) developer's premises (b) user's premises (c) at a third party location to avoid conflicts.

75. While designing test cases, both valid inputs and invalid inputs need to be given (a) true (b) false.

76. While doing the testing, the bugs have to be classified as critical, major and minor bugs (a) true (b) false.

77. Automated test tools help in (a) increased productivity of people (b) less infrastructure costs (c) high quality product (d) all of the above.

78. The transaction response time for database management software is obtained using (a) functional/regression testing tools (b) load testing tools (c) source code testing tools.

79. Performance/load testing tools can do performance testing with less infrastructure costs (a) true (b) false.

80. The testing carried out by the client before accepting the software is (a) unit testing (b) integration testing (c) system testing (d) acceptance testing

81. Integration testing and system testing are one and the same (a) true (b) false.

82. Black box testing is used for (a) testing the functionality (b) testing the source code (c) testing the performance requirements (d) testing the portability requirements.

83. White box testing is used for (a) testing the functionality (b) testing the source code (c) testing the reliability requirements (d) testing the portability requirements

84. Exhaustive testing is impractical because (a) it is very time consuming (b) it requires many test engineers (c) it requires lot of infrastructure (d) all of the above.

85. Hardware prototyping is done (a) to prove the design concept (b) to obtain the user requirements.

86. Software prototyping is used for (a) obtaining the user requirements (b) proving the design.

87. Software configuration management process is important if multiple versions of the software product have to be released (a) true (b) false.

88. Which of the following is not a scripting language (a) C (b) 4Test (c) TSL (d) JavaScript.

89. Portability testing tools come under the category (a) functional testing tools (b) regression testing tools (c) source code testing tools (d) performance testing tools.

90. The scripting language used in WinRunner is (a) JavaSsript (b) TSL (c) 4Test (d) C.

91. The scripting language used in SilkTest is (a) JavaScript (b) TSL (c) 4Test (d) C

92. SilkTest Agent software is installed on the same machine as the Application Under Test (a) true (b) false.

93. The component of SilkTest that interacts with the GUI of your application is (a) SilkTest Agent (b) SilkTest Host software (c) 4Test interpreter (d) none of the above.

94. Software testing management tools help in achieving a process-oriented testing (a) true (b) false.

95. Workflow automation is an important requirement of testing management tool (a) true (b) false.

96. For carrying out unattended testing, automatic recovery of the application is a must (a) true (b) false.

97. Test engineers need to test the application against the specifications (a) true (b) false.

98. The important requirements of a testing management tool are (a) workflow automation (b) bug tracking (c) test plan creation (d) all of the above.

99. Test plan has to cover (a) resources required for testing (b) test schedules (c) test cases (d) all of the above.

100. "lint" is a utility in Unix/Linux systems to carry out (a) performance testing (b) load testing (c) portability testing (d) none of the above.

Answers

1. (c) Software engineering is applicable to both generic products and customized software development.

2. (b) Even now, most of the software projects get into trouble, unfortunately.

3. (d) Software engineering addresses development, operational and maintenance issues of software.

4. (c) Software engineering addresses both technical and managerial issues.

5. (b) Ariane 5 episode demonstrates how one line of code can lead to a disaster.

6. (a) For a quality product to be delivered, each and every person in the organization should be committed to quality.

7. (d) The operational, transition and revision characteristics determine the quality of the product.

8. (a) Usability is an operational characteristic.

9. (a) Reliability is an operational characteristic.

10. (a) Safety is an operational characteristic.

11. (a) Security is an operational characteristic.

12. (c) Testability is a revision characteristic.

13. (c) Scalability is a revision characteristic.

14. (c) Modularity is a revision characteristic.

15. (c) Flexibility is a revision characteristic.

16. (b) Portability is a transition characteristic.

17. (b) Reusability is a transition characteristic.

18. (b) Interoperability is a transition characteristic.

19. (d) A project is successful only if quality product is delivered within the time and within the budget.

20. (b) The output of the requirements engineering phase is the SRS document approved by the client or in other words, a validated SRS document.

21. (a) We cannot apply the same life cycle model to all types of projects. Depending on whether it is a commercial project, research project, risky project etc. we need to choose a life cycle model.

22. (a) For commercial projects, waterfall model is widely used.

23. (a) The main attraction of waterfall model is that at the end of every stage, there will be a visible output.

24. (a) Prototyping model is used when the user/client is not IT-literate. In such a case, the user does not know exactly what the software is supposed to do. Hence, the developer shows a prototype and then the user will get a good feel of the proposed software solution.

25. (b) Spiral model is used for projects in which high risk is involved.

26. (a) Synchronize-and-stabilize model has been used for high technology product development. Netscape and Microsoft products have been developed using this model.

27. (b) For research projects, it is difficult to formulate clear specifications. Hence, evolutionary development model is the best choice.

28. (d) The metric "lines of code" is used to measure the complexity of the project. During the planning stage, this value is estimated and based on this estimate, the budget and timeframe are also calculated.

29. (c) 154 * 2 * 2 = 616 hours

30. (a) The number of lines of code is generally used to measure the complexity of the project. For example, if the number of lines is more than 128,000 it is considered a very large project.

31. (c) Productivity of employees (on an average) is measured by the number of defects removed per hour, or number of lines of code written per hour etc. The number of hours spent in the office is not a real metric—you may be spending most of the time in the canteen!

32. (b) A test engineer's productivity is measured by the number of defects detected per hour, on an average. By generating good test cases, you can increase your productivity.

33. (d) All the metrics given in a, b and c reflect the reliability of the product.

34. (b) Software requirements consist of both functional requirements and non-functional requirements.

35. (a) MTBF is a reliability metric.

36. (a) Whenever a change is made to SRS document, a systematic procedure must be followed and hence SRS document should be kept under configuration management.

37. (d) Process quality metrics reflect the effectiveness of the process. Changes made to SRS or design document as well as the number of defects reported by the customer after the product is delivered—all these reflect the process quality.

38. (a) Every organization will have its own guidelines to measure the number of lines of code. For example, the code segment if (condition) {statement} can be counted as one line or four lines depending on how the code is written. { and } can be written in separate lines and counted as two lines!

39. (d) The metrics given in a, b and c reflect the process quality.

40. (b) Validation and verification are different.

41. (a) To avoid problems associated with the psychology of testing, it is advisable to have a separate team for testing the software.

42. (c) The client/customer accepts the software after conducting the acceptance testing.

43. (b) In black box testing, the source code details are not taken into consideration, only the functionality is checked.

44. (a) In white box testing, the objective is to ensure that each and every line of code is tested.

45. (a) Regression testing is re-testing the software whenever changes are made to the source code.

46. (c) While testing, a threshold is fixed and if the number of bugs found is less than this threshold continuously for say, three weeks, then we can declare that the testing is complete and the product is ready for release.

47. (a) All these metrics reflect the reliability of the product.

48. (d) Software maintenance covers preventive, corrective and adaptive maintenance.

49. (b) Whenever software source code is modified, all documents such as SRS, design document etc. also need to be modified.

50. (d) Whenever a change is proposed to any work product (SRS, design document etc.), you need to study its impact on the budget, time and the design aspects. You may innocently accept a change, but end up in difficulties if the change calls for a major design change—you lose time and money also.

51. (b) Effort = 4 * 2 + 6 * 6 = 44 person months.

52. (d) ISO 9000 is applicable to all types of organizations including hotels, hospitals, educational institutions, even sweet shops and barber shops.

53. (a) A quality policy signed by CEO is a must for every ISO 9000 certified organization.

54. (a) Quality policy is signed by the CEO because only when the top management is committed to quality, all the employees will be committed to quality.

55. (a) ISO 9000 gives thrust to continuous quality improvement.

56. (b) CMMI addresses only the software quality management.

57. (a) Configuration management is a key process area in at Level 2.

58. (b) Process quality metrics and product quality metrics are different. However, note that process quality improves product quality.

59. (a) In CMMI, both staged and continuous representations are available. Generally, staged representation is followed by many organizations.

60. (b) Both ISO 9000 and CMM focus on continuous improvement. All process documents need to be continuously reviewed and changed if required, to improve process quality and product quality.

61. (a) CMMI Level 1 organizations have no defined processes.

62. (a) Both validation and verification are two process areas in CMMI.

63. (a) Causal analysis and resolution is a process area in Level 5. The objective of this process is to find the root cause of the problem/defect.

64. (b) You can uncover many bugs if you try to prove that the software does not work. As the development engineers do not like this, a separate team of people, other than developers, generally does testing.

65. (a) The validation process is to check whether the customer is satisfied with the product. The customer is involved in this process.

66. (a) The verification process is to check whether the software is as per the specifications. The specifications may include characteristics such as portability, maintainability, testability etc. and the customer may not be interested in these. Verification process is to ensure that a process-oriented development is being done.

67. (a) Unit testing is done by the developers to test the source code of the individual units (smallest code segments that can be tested).

68. (b) During integration testing, the modules are integrated and tested. Hence, integration testing is to ensure that the design is OK.

69. (c) System testing is done to ensure that the software conforms to the specifications. System testing involves both functional testing and performance testing.

70. (d) Acceptance testing is carried out to ensure that the software meets all the requirements of the customer.

71. (b) Structural testing is to check the implementation details and hence it is to test the source code.

72. (d) Structural testing is done to ensure that each and every line of code is tested. Hence, it is to ensure statement coverage, path coverage and branch coverage.

73. (a) Regression testing is the testing done whenever changes are made to the source code, hence it is retesting the software to make sure that change in one portion of the code has no bad effect on other portions of the code.

74. (b) Beta testing is carried out at user/client premises, in the absence of the development team.

75. (a) You need to design the test cases in such a way that both valid inputs and invalid inputs are given and the software is tested for both types of inputs.

76. (a) Classification of bugs is important; a simple way of classification is critical, major and minor bugs. Of course, you can have a more detailed classification.

77. (d) Automated testing tools have all the advantages given in a, b and c.

78. (b) Transaction response time is a performance parameter. Hence, performance/ load testing tools are used to test this parameter.

79. (a) Performance testing tools simulate multiple users on the same machine and hence the testing can be done with less infrastructure and less manpower.

80. (d) The user/client carries out acceptance testing before the delivery of the software.

81. (b) Integration testing is done incrementally while integrating different modules. System testing is done after the integration is completed. System testing is done for checking the functionality and the performance.

82. (a) In black box testing, the source code details are not considered. Inputs are given and it is checked whether the expected outputs are coming and hence, it is only to test the functionality.

83. (b) White box testing takes into consideration the implementation details and hence source code is tested.

84. (d) Exhaustive testing consumes lot of time, requires lot of computers and manpower and hence it is impractical for most of the projects.

85. (a) Hardware prototyping is done to prove the design concept. Contrast it with software prototyping which is done to obtain user requirements.

86. (a) Software prototyping is used for obtaining the user requirements. Particularly when the user is not IT-literate, software prototyping is done.

87. (a) When multiple versions of software have to be released, to keep track of the changes made to the source code, configuration management process is a must.

88. (a) C is not a scripting language.

89. (c) Portability testing tools test whether the source code is portable from one platform to another (for example, from Unix machine to Solaris machine). They fall under the category of source code testing tools.

90. (b) TSL is the scripting language used in WinRunner.

91. (c) 4Test is the scripting language used in SilkTest.

92. (a) SilkTest Agent software must be running on the same machine as the application under test.

93. (a) The SilkTest Agent software interacts with the GUI of the application under test.

94. (a) Testing management tools help in carrying out the testing in a systematic way— these tools help in planning resources, schedules and defect analysis.

95. (a) To manage testing process effectively, the QA manager, development and testing team members need to communicate and share data/information. So, workflow automation is an important element in testing management tools.

96. (a) For unattended testing, the application software under testing has to be brought back to the initial state in case some problem is encountered during the testing process.

97. (a) For test engineers, the requirements specifications document is the reference. Each and every specification has to be tested at least once.

98. (d) All the features given in a, b and c are required in testing management tools.

99. (d) The test plan has to cover the resources, schedules as well as test cases.

100.(c) "lint" utility is used to test the portability of C programs.

Frequently Asked Questions in Job Interviews

1. What is software quality? What characteristics determine the quality of a software product?

2. What is software engineering?

3. What are the various phases in software development?

4. What is the need for different software life cycle development models? Can you name some of the models?

5. Explain waterfall model.

6. In your biodata, you have listed some projects which you have done. Can you explain how you tested the software?

7. What is a Quality Management System? What are the internationally accepted quality management systems that are applicable to the software industry?

8. Can you briefly explain the philosophy of ISO 9000?

9. What is CMMI? Can you list some of the process areas in CMMI?

10. What is the difference between system testing and acceptance testing?

11. What is the difference between verification and validation?

12. What are software metrics? Can you list some metrics which you have used?

13. What is a test case? How do you generate test cases?

14. For a project which you have done, what are the test cases using which you tested your software?

15. What is regression testing? Why regression testing has to be done?

16. What is a test plan? What aspects do you need to cover in a test plan?

17. On what basis do you decide when testing is completed?

18. Can you name some functional testing tools?

19. What is performance testing? On what types of software packages do you need to do performance testing?

20. Can you name some performance testing tools?

21. What is the difference between white box testing and black box testing?

22. What is configuration management? Are you familiar with any configuration management tools?

23. How do you test the portability of C code developed by you?

24. What coding guidelines did you follow when you wrote C programs?

25. What coding guidelines did you follow when you wrote Java programs?

26. What is data-driven testing? Explain with an example.

27. What is exhaustive testing? What are its disadvantages?

28. What are the important features of functional/regression testing tools?

29. Name some functional/regression testing tools you are familiar with.

30. Name some performance testing tools you are familiar with.

31. Suppose you are taken as a consultant to our SQA division. Which testing tools would you recommend? Why?

32. Is there a need for classifying the defects or bugs? If so, why?

33. Can you explain how the performance tools can reduce the testing infrastructure and manpower costs?

34. Explain how you can do unattended testing in WinRunner.

35. How do you test the performance of a web site or a database when multiple users access the service simultaneously? Can you name one or two tools which do this?

Appendix D # References and Internet Resources

[Bamberger 1997] J. Bamberger, Essence of the CMM, IEEE Computer, Vol. 30, No. 6, June 1997, pp. 112-114.

[Boehm 2000] B. Boehm, The Art of Expectations Management, IEEE Computer, Vol. 33, No. 1, January 2000, pp. 122-124.

[Computer 1999] Feature Articles on Software Engineering in the Small, IEEE Computer, Vol. 32, No. 10, October 1999.

[Cusumano 1995] M.A. Cusumano and R.W. Selby, Microsoft Secrets, Simon & Schuster Inc., 1995.

[Cusumano 1999] M.A. Cusumano and D.B. Yoffie, Software Development on Internet Time, IEEE Computer, Vol. 32, No. 10, October 1999, pp. 60-69.

[Fairley 1985] R. E. Fairley, Software Engineering Concepts, McGraw Hill Inc., 1985.

[Ghezzi 1991] C. Ghezzi, M. Jazayeri, D. Mandrioli, Fundamentals of Software Engineering, Prentice Hall Inc., 1991.

[Glass 1999] R.L. Glass, Computing Calamities: Lessons learned from Products, Projects and Companies That Failed, Prentice Hall Inc., 1999.

[Humphrey 1997] W.S. Humphrey, Introduction to the Personal Software Process, Addison Wesley Longman Inc., 1997.

[IEEE 1990] IEEE Standard 610.12-1990, Standard Glossary of Software Engineering Terminology (ANSI), IEEE Press 1990.

[IEEE 1994] IEEE Software Engineering Standards Collection (1994 Edition), IEEE Press, 1994.

[Jezequel 1997] Jean-Marc Jezequel and B. Meyer, Design by Contract: The Lessons of Ariane, IEEE Computer, Vol. 30, No. 1, January 1997, pp. 129-130.

[Jones 1994] C. Jones, Software Management: The Weakest Link in the Software Engineering Chain, IEEE Computer, Vol. 27, No. 5, May 1994, pp. 10-11.

[Lethbridge 2000] T.L. Lethbridge, What Knowledge is Important to a Software Professional, IEEE Computer, Vol. 33, No. 5, May 2000, pp. 44-50.

401

[Meyer 1979] G. Meyer, The Art of Software Testing, John Wiley & Sons, 1979.

[Pfleeger 1994] S.L. Pfleeger, N. Fenton and S. Page, Evaluating Software Engineering Standards, IEEE Computer, Vol. 27, No. 9, September 1994, pp. 71-79.

[Prasad 2003] K.V.K.K. Prasad, Embedded/Real-Time Systems: Concepts, Design and Programming—The Ultimate Reference, Dreamtech Press, 2003.

[Prasad 2003] K.V.K.K. Prasad, Principles of Digital Communication Systems and Computer Networks, Dreamtech Press, 2003.

[Pressman 1997] Roger S. Pressman, Software Engineering: A Practitioner's Approach, McGraw Hill Inc., 1997.

[SEI CMU 1994] The Capability Maturity Model: Guidelines for Improving the Software Process, CMU-SEI, Addison Wesley, 1994.

[SEI CMU 2002] Capability Maturity Model Integration (CMMI) Version 1.1 Staged Representation, SEI, August 2002.

[Sommerville 1996] I. Sommerville, Software Engineering (5th Edition), Addison Wesley Publishing Co., 1996.

[Wood 1996] A. Wood, Predicting software reliability, IEEE Computer, Vol. 29, No. 11, November 1996, pp. 69-77.

[Yourdon 1997] Edward Yourdon, Death March, Prentice Hall Inc., 1997.

Internet	Resources
www.autotester.com	AutoTester
www.betasoft.com	Betasoft Inc.
jakarata.apache.org	Apache Jakarta Project (for Open source testing tools)
www.compuware.com	Compuware
www.fsf.org	Free Software Foundation
www.gnu.org	The GNU Free Software Foundation
gcc.gnu.org	GNU Compiler Collection
www.mercuryinteractive.com	WinRunner/LoadRunner/TestDirector
www.qajobs.net	Site for jobs in software testing and QA
www.qaforums.com	Software testing and QA discussion site
www.rational.com	IBM Rational Suite
www.segue.com	SilkTest/SilkPerformer/SilkPlan
www.sei.cmu.edu	Software Engineering Institute, Carnegie Mellon University
www.softwaretestinginstitute.com	Software Testing Institute

CDROM Contents and Installing Sample Applications

The CDROM contains the following folders:

EmpDB	Contains the sample application "Employee Database"
Weather India	Contains the sample application "Weather India"
Chapter 10	Source code listings of Chapter 10
JMeter	Contains the open source software Apache JMeter

Employee Database (EmpDB) Application

1. What are the prerequisites to install EmpDB application?

   To run the EmpDB, copy the "EmpDB.exe" and "db1.mdb" files from the CDROM on to your system.

The two files (EmpDB.exe & db1.mdb) must be in the same folder.

NOTE

2. How to run the "EmpDB" application?

   Double click on the "EmpDB.exe" to run the application. Fig. E.1 shows the initial screen of the "EmpDB" application.

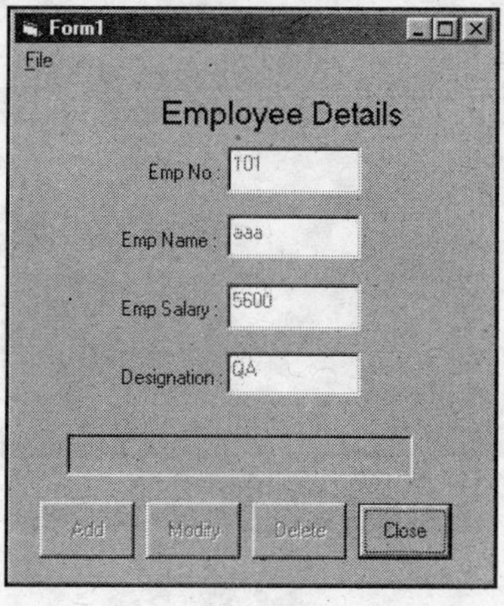

```
Form1                          _ □ ×
File
                Employee Details

      Emp No :  101

      Emp Name : aaa

      Emp Salary : 5600

      Designation : QA

      [                        ]

      [ Add ] [ Modify ] [ Delete ] [ Close ]
```

Fig. E.1

3. What is the table format?

The EmpDB application makes use of the "Emp" table from the "db1.mdb" file. The structure of the "Emp" table is as shown in the table given below:

Field Name	Data type	Description
EmpNo	Number	Employee Number
EmpName	Text	Name of the employee
EmpSal	Number	Salary of the employee
Designation	Text	Designation of the employee.

4. Is DSN creation required?

Creating a DSN (Data Source Name) is not required to run the EmpDB application.

Weather India Web Site

1. What are the prerequisites to install Weather India web site?

Personal Web Server (PWS) is required on Windows 95 or Windows 98 systems. Internet Information Server (IIS) is required on Windows NT systems.

Personal Web Server:

■ Install the Personal Web Server.

■ Open the Personal Web Server

Start → Programs → Accessories → Internet Tools → Personal Web Server → Personal Web Manager. It opens the dialog as shown in Fig. E.2.

Fig. E.2

Click the "Start" button to start the Personal Web Server as shown in Fig. E.2 or right click on the 🕐 icon in the system tray as shown in Fig. E.3.

Fig. E.3

Select the "Start Service" option to start the Personal Web Server service.

To check whether Personal Web Server is working or not:

- Invoke Internet Explorer
- Enter the URL as http://<IP address of the System>/. (For example, http://131.200.2.63, where 131.200.2.63 is the IP address of the system on which the Personal Web Server is running.) It displays the Welcome page of the Personal Web Server as shown in Fig. E.4.

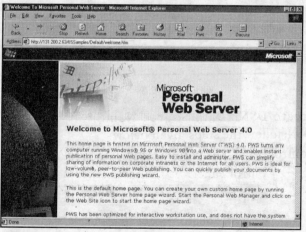

Fig. E.4

2. What is the directory structure of PWS or IIS?

The directory structure of the Personal Web Server and Internet Information Server is shown in Fig. E.5. Inetpub is the home folder of the Personal Web Server/IIS.

Fig. E.5

3. Where to copy Weather India site files?

■ Create a new folder "WeatherIndia" in "C:\Inetpub\wwwroot".

■ Copy all the files in "Weather India" folder from the CDROM.

■ Paste them in "C:\Inetpub\wwwroot\WeatherIndia" folder as shown in Fig. E.6.

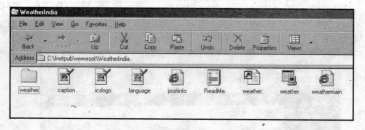
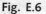

Fig. E.6

4. How to create DSN (Data Source Name)?
   To create DSN, follow the steps given below:

■ Open the Control Panel. The window shown in Fig. E.7 is displayed
Start → Settings → Control Panel

Fig. E.7

Click on the  icon to create the DSN.

■ The "ODBC Data Source Administrator" dialog is displayed as shown in Fig. E.8.

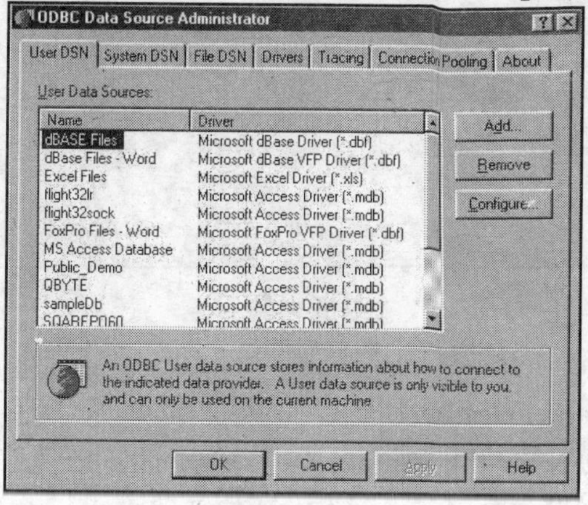

Fig. E.8

■ By default "User DSN" is selected. Select it if it is not already selected, and click the "Add" button to create a new DSN.

■ "Create New Data Source" dialog is displayed as shown in Fig. E.9.

Fig. E.9

Select the driver as "Microsoft Access Driver (*.mdb) and click the "Finish" button.

■ The "ODBC Microsoft Access Setup" dialog appears as shown in Fig. E.10.

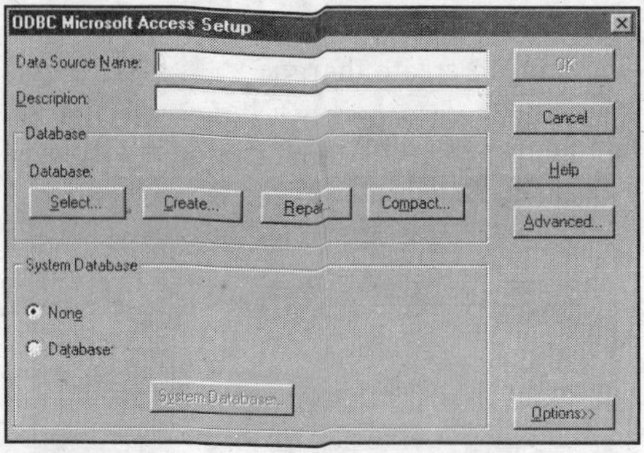

Fig. E.10

Enter the following details:

- ▪ Data Source Name: weather1
- ▪ Description: DSN for the Weather India application.
- ▪ Click the "Select" button from the "Database" group box and select the "weather.mdb" file as shown in Fig. E.11.

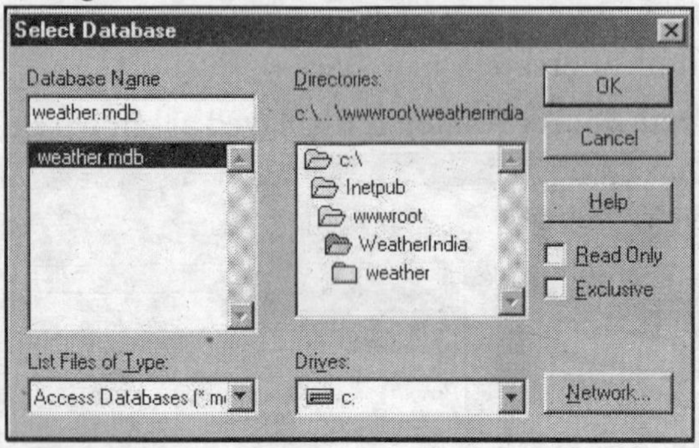

Fig. E.11

Click the "OK" button to select the "weather.mdb" as database.

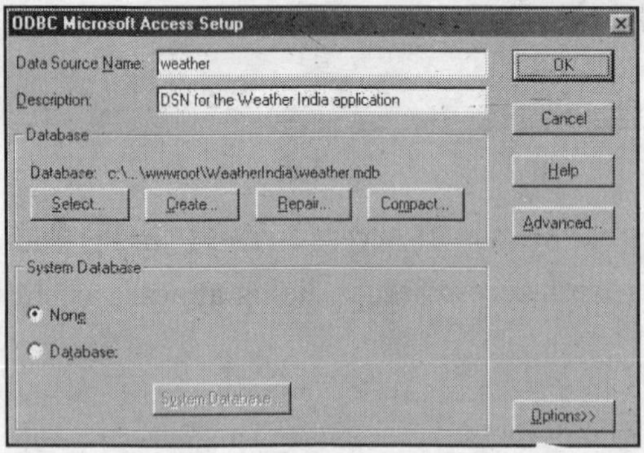

Fig. E.12

■ Click the "OK" button. The "ODBC Data Source Administrator" window is displayed. The "weather1" DSN will be added to "User DSN" list as shown in   Fig. E.13.

Fig. E.13

Click the "OK" button to close the "ODBC Data Source Administrator" window.

5. How to run the "Weather India" website?

To run "Weather India" website

■ Invoke Internet Explorer.

■ Enter the URL as http://131.200.2.63/weathermain.htm where "131.200.2.63" is the IP address of the system. Replace this IP address with your system's IP address.

The main screen of the "Weather India" application is displayed as shown in Fig.E.14.

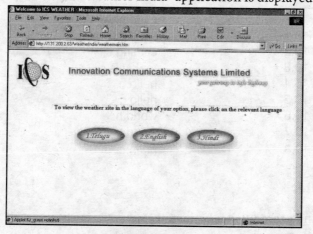

Fig. E.14

Click the "English" option. It displays the screen shown in Fig. E.15.

Fig. E.15

Chapter 10 Source Code Listings

The following table gives the filenames and the corresponding Listing numbers. You can copy these files on to your Linux system to execute them as per the procedure given in Chapter 10. You can view these files by opening them in notepad on your Windows system.

Listing	Filename
Listing 10.1	ttiming.c
Listing 10.2	ctiming.c
Listing 10.3	makefile
Listing 10.4	hello.h
Listing 10.5	hello.c
Listing 10.6	world.h
Listing 10.7	world.c
Listing 10.8	main.c

Apache JMeter

1. What are the prerequisites to install JMeter?
    To install the JMeter:

- J2SDK 1.4.1 or higher version should be installed in your system.
- WinZip software should be installed.

2. How to install JMeter?

From the CDROM, copy the "jakarta-jmeter-1.9.1"zip file into your system's hard disk. Unzip the file using the "WinZip" software by following the steps given below.

■ Right click on the "jakarta-jmeter-1.9.1"zip file as shown in Fig. E.16.

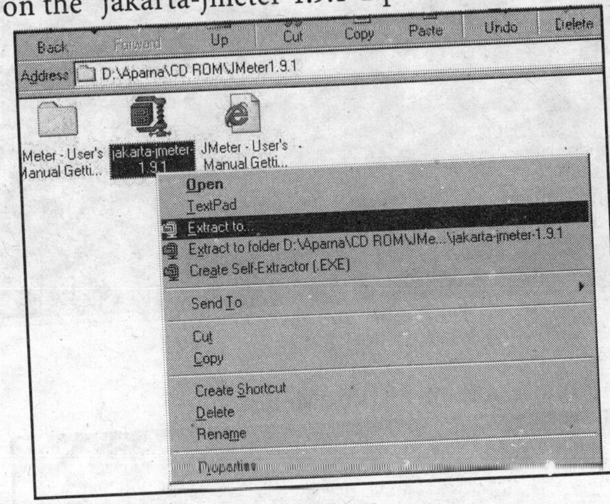

Fig. E.16

■ Select "Extract to..." option from the menu and select the location where the unzipped files have to be stored.

3. How to set the ClassPath?

Set the ClassPath as given below:

JMETER_HOME = C:\JMeter (Specify "C:\" if the JMeter is installed in drive C, otherwise specify the path where it is installed).

JAVA_HOME = C:\j2sdk1.4.1\ (Specify "C:\" if the j2sdk1.4.1 is installed in drive C, otherwise specify the path where it is installed).

CLASSPATH = %CLASSPATH%; JMETER_HOME\LIB\EXT; JMETER_HOME\LIB; JAVA_HOME\LIB

4. How to run JMeter?

At the command prompt, go to the directory (drive:\JMeter\bin) where the JMeter is installed and type "jmeter" at the command prompt to run JMeter as shown in Fig. E.17.

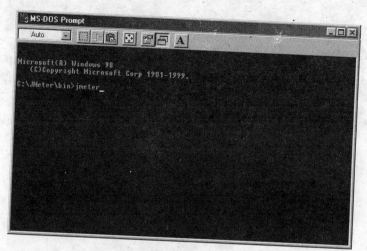

Fig. E.17

Fig. E.18 shows the main screen of the JMeter.

Fig. E.18

Note that to experiment with the sample programs given in this book, you need to install the EmpDB and Weather India applications on your system. To carry out JDBC and HTTP tests discussed in Chapter 8, you need to install JMeter and Weather India sample application. While using the testing tools, you need to run the tool as well as the application under test (e.g., EmbDB or Weather India) simultaneously. Hence, please remember the path name in which your application is installed. You may also require the IP address of the machine, and hence, if necessary, take the help of your system administrator to find out the IP address of the machine.